W9-BGC-252

Martin Walker

America Reborn

Martin Walker served as bureau chief for Britain's *The Guardian* in Washington, D.C., and other postings before retiring as the paper's assistant editor. A regular commentator on CNN, *Inside Washington*, and NPR, he is also a contributing editor of the *Los Angeles Times*. He has written for *The New York Times*, *The Washington Post*, *Newsday*, *USA Today*, and *The New Republic*, and was awarded Britain's Reporter of the Year prize. He is a senior fellow of the World Policy Institute in New York and has lectured at many American universities. Walker is the author of six books, including *The President We Deserve* and *The Cold War: A History*. He is married, has two daughters, and lives in Washington, D.C.

America Reborn

America Reborn

A Twentieth-Century Narrative in Twenty-six Lives

Martin Walker

Vintage Books
A Division of Random House, Inc.
New York

FIRST VINTAGE BOOKS EDITION, JULY 2001

The Library of Congress has cataloged the Knopf edition as follows:
Walker, Martin, [date]
America reborn : a twentieth-century narrative in twenty-six lives / Martin Walker.—1st ed.
p. cm.
Includes index.
ISBN 0-375-40316-7 (alk. paper)
1. United States—History—20th century—Biography.
2. United States—Civilization—20th century.   I. Title
E747.W18 2000
920.073—dc21
[B] 99-051491

Vintage ISBN: 0-375-70364-0

Author photograph © The Guardian
Book design by Iris Weinstein

www.vintagebooks.com

Printed in the United States of America
10 9 8 7 6 5 4 3 2

To my American friends, and all the others I have yet to meet

Contents

Contents

Introduction

I suspect that this book began unconsciously as a love letter to America from a foreigner who sees it both as a second home and as an inspiration. I first visited the United States in 1964 as a young officer cadet of the Royal Air Force, on a NATO exchange. Within five years, having sailed across the Atlantic on the SS *France* to land in time for what sounded like a promising rock festival at Woodstock, I was installed as a resident tutor at Harvard's Kirkland House on a Harkness Fellowship. Two months later, I was traveling in a bizarre road convoy that had cars and coaches from half the colleges in New England clogging I-95 and passing jokes and joints back and forth through car windows as we went to demonstrate in Washington against the Vietnam War. The oddity was made the greater by the studied courtesy of my hosts in the city, the parents of a friend whose father was a navy captain based at the Pentagon.

Each decade of my life since has been marked and enhanced by the wondrous contradictions of the American experience. In the 1970s, I was part of Senator Edmund Muskie's presidential campaign, and also evaded arrest outside the Justice Department as the antiwar demonstrations grew more heated and machine-gun posts were installed on the steps of the U.S. Capitol. In 1972, I was in Miami as a young reporter for the Democratic and Republican conventions, watching Governor George Wallace enter the convention hall in his wheelchair while the Youth for Nixon delegates in their straw hats chanted, "Four more years." I sat on the beach with Hunter Thompson the night after Senator George McGovern won his nomination, before I caught the morning plane to visit the new Disney World at Orlando.

In the 1980s, I flew in from glasnost Moscow to lecture on the Chernobyl disaster and on the new phenomenon of perestroika and watched the ecstatic Washington crowds greet Mikhail Gorbachev at that extraordinary moment of the Cold War that the *Washington Post* dubbed "Gorbasm." By the end of the decade, I was counting dead birds on the oil-drenched beach of Knight's

Island in Alaska's Prince William Sound as the *Exxon Valdez* spewed out its cargo, and sipping beer on President George Bush's speedboat as we raced to see the seals on the rocks outside Kennebunkport, Maine. In the 1990s, as the U.S. bureau chief for *The Guardian,* I renewed an old Oxford acquaintance-ship with Governor Bill Clinton in Little Rock, was sheltered from an angry mob by a shotgun-wielding Korean family in the Los Angeles riots, went to White House parties, and traveled on *Air Force One.*

There is no land on earth more enthralling, more welcoming, or more generous than America. And as I stood in Oklahoma City looking at the wreckage of a terrorist bomb, and in the smoking wreckage of a black church in Georgia, and as I plucked a bullet from the charred earth of the Branch Davidian compound at Waco, Texas, no country had seemed so bafflingly alien in its appetite for violence and extremism. America has been, through-out my life, a country that has known the best of times and the worst of times, sometimes almost simultaneously.

The paradoxes of the country are surreal. It is not easy to conceive how one country can embrace such extremes of wealth and poverty as the gilded oasis of Palm Springs, California, and the very different desert of the Oglala Sioux reservation at Pine Ridge, North Dakota. A country with over a million law graduates also has well over a million of its fellow citizens behind bars. The nation that provides much of the world with its graduate schools, with nearly 2 million people pursuing master's degrees and doctorates, depends upon a deeply flawed public school system, almost a fifth of whose products are functionally illiterate. Perhaps the American system needs the constant, threatening, and warning presence of the price of failure as a social spur to achievement and success. As Gore Vidal has suggested, "It is not enough to succeed. Others must fail."

The cult of the winner is a powerful one, in a land in which sporting con-tests are seldom permitted to end in draws, in which schoolchildren vote for their classmate "most likely to succeed," and in which college entrance is based on rigid competition. And there is no doubt that America has been the outright winner in the twentieth century's game of nations. It began the cen-tury just starting to feel its strength and to assert itself on the world stage, and ended it, as French foreign minister Hubert Vedrine put it, not as the only superpower, but as something altogether new.

America had become "the hyperpower," Vedrine suggested. It not only dominated by the usual criteria of wealth, military power, and global influ-ence but also boasted the most advanced and innovative technologies. It enjoyed the most far-reaching cultural and commercial influence, all resting upon a democratic system of free speech and free markets that had, with the end of the Cold War, become the most self-confident ideology on the planet.

Introduction

Its military supremacy was unmatched since the days of ancient Rome, and its reach was incomparably wider. For the relatively modest investment of some 3.5 percent of its annual GDP, the defense budget's lowest share of national wealth since 1940, the United States by the late 1990s could maintain with ease an unmatched military power. Even 3.5 percent of the GDP meant that the Pentagon was outspending the next nine military powers combined.

The striking paradox is that the wielder of this awesome power was famously reluctant to deploy it, or at least to put the men and women of its professional forces at risk, particularly since cruise missiles and stealth warplanes allowed and even encouraged devastatingly accurate and virtually invulnerable bombardments. The country has always been uneasy about "foreign entanglements," ever since George Washington's farewell address warned his countrymen against them. America has always been of the world, explaining in the founding document of its nationhood the need for "a decent respect for the opinions of mankind," without being overly eager to join it. The only nation that has rivaled America's hyperpower status, Britain in the nineteenth century, was less fastidious. Lord Palmerston, the British foreign secretary who coined the term *Pax Britannica* at the height of its sway, had a saying: "Trade without rule where possible, trade with rule where necessary." America found rule to be as unnecessary as it was uncongenial; the overwhelming reality of its influence was sufficient to avoid the formal trappings and entanglements of empire.

Some presidents sought to correct this national reluctance. Teddy Roosevelt built a canal and a fleet to prod his people into a global assertion, once the manifest destiny of continental expansion had been achieved. He was not even partially successful. It was Woodrow Wilson, that unwilling, almost apologetic interventionist, who finally took the nation into world war, but only with the understanding that he might then outlaw war altogether. The U.S. Senate rejected even this most noble of justifications for remaining a member of Europe's great power system, and it refused to ratify his Treaty of Versailles. Nonetheless, Roosevelt and Wilson between them set the parameters of American engagement with the world in the twentieth century. Roosevelt wanted it to become dominant as the richest and most powerful of nations; Wilson sought a moral dominance that would lead the way to a new kind of world altogether, based on international law rather than on military force. The history of the second half of the century suggests that these two goals were not entirely incompatible. John Kennedy and Ronald Reagan, two presidents who secured a particularly cherished place in the nation's heart, acted on the assumption that the country's military and moral dominance were two sides of a single coin. The country was great because it was good, and it was good because it was great. As fortunate in the crises and the opponents they faced as in their rhetorical ability, Kennedy and Reagan were broadly able to reconcile the Rooseveltian and Wilsonian traditions of military and moral leadership. Lyndon Johnson, less astute in choosing his foreign confrontation, was not. Perhaps the most politically gifted of the postwar presidents, Johnson, during his five years in office, brought Americans back to the deeply uncomfortable and divisive thought that a great power was not necessarily a good country, and that a good power might not always be inclined or even able to assert its military greatness.

The United States, against its instincts and traditions, was forced into a global role. It was bombed into war by Japan in 1941, and lured into remaining in Europe after 1947 by the blunt British warning that it alone could no longer afford to sustain the old continent against the Soviet threat. Either the United States had to assume the role or watch Stalin's empire spread into Europe's resulting vacuum of power by default. Even then, the deployment of American power in the Cold War was limited. It mounted an airlift to relieve West Berlin, rather than seeking a military confrontation on the ground, despite its brief monopoly of the atomic bomb. It stood by as East Germans, Hungarians, Czechs, and Poles successively rose against their Soviet masters.

America's power, when deployed, was repeatedly withdrawn or its punches pulled. The country accepted a bloody draw in Korea, defeat in Vietnam, and a stalemate with Cuba, in part because the conflicts were seen as limited ones, which didn't need to be fought to a finish with every available weapon, and in part because of public opinion. Behind the public doubts over America's minor wars lay a principled conviction that America was differently founded and more honorably directed than the traditional great powers of Europe with their realpolitik and empires of exploitation. This persistent American ethic required that its assumption of global power was as spasmodic as it was hesitant. It unfolded only under explicitly moralistic and usually utopian banners, from "the war to end wars" to the defense of the Free World and the expansion of the Four Freedoms and free markets.

The enduring irony of the American century is that this new country of European immigrants started its global rise in Asia with the conquest of the Philippines, and fought five wars there. And yet the United States still sees its grand strategic challenge for the twenty-first century in the economic prowess of Japan and the rising forces of China and India. Asia remains the problem, because its ancient civilizations remain more resistant to American values. By contrast, the American grand strategy in World War II and the Cold War had essentially resolved its European problem. The American century opened with three distinct threats to American equanimity: the British Royal Navy, the ambition of the German Empire, and the rising challenge of Russia. It

Introduction

closed with the European powers locked into an American-led military alliance and an American-inspired economic system, and with Russia making its own historic and strategic choice to align itself with the West. The greatest fruit of American power was to create a congenial and unthreatening Europe, a task made easier because America itself was Europe's greatest creation.

A distinctively American culture emerged from beneath its European shadow as the century began, through the exploitation of the technologies of the gramophone, radio, film, and TV. The crucial factor was the expansive appetites of the American market to nurture and then to export a homegrown American sound, an American voice, an American vision, and an American sensibility. Every city on earth is now defined by the skyscrapers pioneered by Louis Sullivan, and their suburbs are shaped by the aesthetic of Frank Lloyd Wright, the mass-production techniques of Levittown, Long Island, and the requirements of the automobile culture unleashed by Henry Ford. To a stunning degree, modern life has an American taste—working with Windows 95 on an IBM clone, eating at McDonald's, drinking Pepsi, staying in touch through CNN, relaxing to Hollywood entertainment, and paying for it all on American Express.

The key to America's twenty-first century will be, just as it was to the twentieth, the absorption of the new wave of immigrants. It is striking how few of the Americans celebrated in this book were not native-born: Albert Einstein, Emma Goldman, and Lucky Luciano. Each of them made his or her way by dissidence, an overt challenge to the rules and ethics of the new country. It would be interesting to see, in a similar book that might be written a century hence, whether the new Asian and Hispanic Americans might feature more prominently. In any event, they are redefining the planet's first multiethnic democracy, creating a global Americanism of what had been an essentially European and African mix. That hackneyed phrase "the melting pot" is precisely the wrong metaphor to capture the way in which American culture managed to preserve so many of the distinctive cultural traditions of its immigrants. The result has been more of a long-simmering stew, in which the individual components retained their distinctive shapes and textures while producing a common flavor.

A central reason for this, and for the remarkable American refusal to establish a European form of class system, has been the way in which America insisted almost from its birth on the primacy of the individual. Enshrined in its system of property ownership as well as in the Constitution, the almost endless availability of land meant that most Americans until the 1890s could realistically and easily expect to become property owners. The right to own land by homesteading remains to this day in Alaska, but for most of the

Introduction

United States, the twentieth century was a long experiment in how the cherished traditions of individualism and self-reliance, property ownership and local self-government could survive the closing of the frontier.

In some ways, they have not. The signal difference between America in 1900 and in the year 2000 is that the role of the federal government has swollen to dwarf almost every other source of power and wealth. In 1901, the federal government's revenue was $588 million, barely 3 percent of the GDP. By century's end, the government's income had grown three thousand–fold, and even in a time of peace and prosperity was routinely taking 20 percent of the national wealth. A small standing army had become a vast global force. And yet the costs of central government in the United States remained strikingly low by comparison with most other advanced countries, less than half of the usual rate in Europe. The balance of power between citizens and the nation-state had shifted heavily, but not overwhelmingly so. Local communities in different states could impose different rules on crime, the death penalty, gun ownership, alcohol consumption, local taxes, and education systems, to a degree extraordinary almost anywhere else on earth.

America has thus remained a land in which the concept of the individual retains a real as well as a symbolic force. Herbert Hoover overstated the case, but he was not altogether wrong, in a speech in 1928, when he suggested that "we were challenged [at the end of World War I] with a peace-time choice between the American system of rugged individualism and a European philosophy of diametrically opposed doctrines—doctrines of paternalism and state socialism." The cult of the individual has reinforced the American resistance both to labels of class and to ideologies, and created a two-party political system without an organized socialist movement. And while being a deeply materialist society, America has also been consistently wary of believing in those great impersonal economic and social forces that have underpinned most ideological positions, but in whose tides individuals become the pawns of history.

The one exception to this has been the belief in the great impersonal force of America itself, its mission to expand into and dominate its continent while also acting as a beacon and a model for the world. "We speak of the American Way of Life as though it involved the ground rules for the governance of heaven," John Steinbeck suggested. "We are able to believe that our government is weak, stupid, overbearing, dishonest and inefficient, and at the same time we are deeply convinced that it is the best government in the world, and we would like to impose it on everyone else." Americanism has been the one ideology to have flourished, although more as a comfortable assumption than as a cause or rallying cry. It proved particularly agreeable to the national temperament because it was so undemanding. By imposing so few constraints upon the citizen, it sustained the constitutional and legal primacy of the individual and the right laid down by the Founding Fathers to "life, liberty, and the pursuit of happiness."

That is the prime reason why this book seeks to describe and explain the American century through the lives and careers of a handful of individual Americans. It is not a country to be understood by looking simply at its economic history, its political struggles, or its diplomacy. It has never been a nation-state in the European sense, a singular actor on history's stage with an agreed-upon or imposed consensus on the national interest. The president does not even have the legal right to declare war without the authorization of Congress, which is itself designed to be at least as responsive to the views of individual voters and campaign contributors as to the disciplines of party.

If I have come to one profound conclusion about the United States, after half a lifetime studying, traveling, working, and living in it, it is that the motto on the national coinage is unusually revealing: *E Pluribus Unum,* "from the many, one." And the most agreeable aspect of this, for the historian as for the country itself, is that the Pluribus tend to be far more important, more revealing, and incomparably more interesting than the Unum. This is the story of some of them.

America Reborn

1.
Teddy Roosevelt
and the American Ambition

In 1901, the year that Theodore Roosevelt inherited the presidency after the assassination of William McKinley, America's biggest oil field was tapped at Beaumont, Texas, producing 110,000 barrels a day. Guglielmo Marconi received the first wireless transmission across the Atlantic. J. P. Morgan bought out Andrew Carnegie to form U.S. Steel, thereby controlling two-thirds of American steel production. King C. Gillette launched his safety-razor company in Boston, and the first American bowling tournament was held in Chicago. With oil, steel, and radio, consumer goods, brand names, and sports for the masses, the American century had begun.

"We stand on the threshold of a new century big with the fate of mighty nations," Roosevelt had told the Republican convention of 1900, seconding the nomination of McKinley. "Is America a weakling, to shrink from the work of the great world powers? No. The young giant of the West stands on a continent and clasps the crest of an ocean in either hand. Our nation, glorious in youth and strength, looks into the future with eager eyes and rejoices as a strong man to run a race."

When he accepted the nomination for vice president, Roosevelt was forty-one. He was the governor of New York and a certified national hero after leading the charge of his Rough Riders up San Juan Hill in the decisive battle of the Cuban campaign of the Spanish-American War. He had also played a crucial part in the most significant feature of that war. As assistant secretary of the navy, and a powerful voice for war within the administration, he had ordered Commodore George Dewey to take the Pacific Fleet to Hong Kong, and to keep his ships fully stoked in order to launch an instant attack on the Spanish fleet in the Philippines once war was declared. That telegram was sent two months before the formal declaration of war on April 25. By May 1, news had arrived of Dewey's stunning victory in Manila Bay, destroying Spain's Asiatic squadron without the loss of a single American life.

America's Pacific empire had been launched that same year, again with passionate lobbying and careful naval deployments by Roosevelt, when President McKinley formally annexed the islands of Hawaii. Now the old Spanish colony of the Philippines was falling under American sway. It was all going according to the plans Roosevelt had been devising with his partners in what became known as the "expansionist" lobby. His oldest friend, Senator Henry Cabot Lodge, was a key member, along with Charles Dana, editor of the New York *Sun;* the naval historian Alfred Thayer Mahan; and the aggressive Commodore George Dewey.

Roosevelt's appointment as assistant secretary in 1897 represented the expansionists' opportunity, and Roosevelt's address to the Naval War College on June 2 was the occasion when their grand design was first paraded on the public stage. His credentials were sound, after the publication of the second of his thirty-eight books, *The Naval War of 1812.* It remains a classic, although he was but twenty-three when he wrote it. A copy was ordered to be placed aboard every U.S. Navy ship, and Britain's proud Royal Navy paid Roosevelt the compliment of asking him to write the relevant chapter in their own official history. As well as splendid history, its preface contained a sharp warning that the U.S. Navy could not do nearly as well in a similar war in the 1880s: "It is folly for the great English-speaking Republic to rely for defense upon a navy composed partly of antiquated hulks and partly of new vessels rather more worthless than the old." The U.S. Navy, if not its elderly senior ranks, understandably saw him as a useful political friend and valuable strategic thinker, and his address to the Naval War College was eagerly anticipated. He delivered a masterful performance.

"All the great masterful races have been fighting races, and the minute that a race loses the hard fighting virtues then it has lost its proud right to stand as the equal of the best," Roosevelt declared. "No triumph of peace is quite so great as the supreme triumphs of war."

He defined the danger for America at a time when Britain, Germany, and Japan were engaged in a naval arms race—the need for a crash building program, and the development of the dockyards, seamen, and ammunition stocks that were required in an age when most wars were decided in the first ninety days. Widely published in the press, the speech caused a national sensation. It was accompanied in the Navy Department by his orders for a flurry of war planning, for possible conflict with Japan over Hawaii, with Spain over Cuba. "I do not fear England—Canada is hostage for her good behavior," he wrote to Mahan.

The fact that such a lobby had to be organized, and the apathetic nation had to be persuaded of its global destiny, is of central importance. America had been built largely by people who had turned their backs on Europe and its quarrels. Its first president had warned them against foreign entanglements, and ever since George Washington's day, Americans had been keen and venturous traders but reluctant expansionists in any region but their own ever-open frontier to the west. As a historian of that West, Roosevelt was an admirer of Frederick Jackson Turner, whose seminal 1893 address, "The Significance of the Frontier in American History," had made the point that the empty West had finally filled with settlements. "The frontier has gone, and with its going has closed the first period of American history," Turner concluded. What now would be the new horizons for "American energy . . . continually demanding a wide field for its exercise?"

Turner offered no answer to his own question, but Roosevelt did. The wide world, the great race among the Great Powers, was to be the new canvas for American visions. But Americans, still introspective, still suspicious of the merits and the costs of foreign quarrels, were not easily persuaded. The wide oceans themselves provided adequate security for the young nation, and the isolationist current remained powerful enough to deter activist foreign policy presidents until the 1940s. Roosevelt's genius was to turn isolationist sentiment to his strategic advantage. He argued that the security of isolation could be upheld only by regional expansion, by fortifying the protective moats with advance posts in Hawaii and the Philippines, and by building the Panama Canal to facilitate the swift passage of the fleets from one coast to the other. The canal itself required further protective expansion into the Caribbean, which itself required war to evict the Spanish from their colonies. Roosevelt promoted America's advance as a series of defensive measures.

Beyond these practical and strategic considerations, however, Roosevelt's speech carried a potent spiritual theme, insistent on the kind of state and people he wanted America and Americans to be: "There are higher things in this life than the soft and easy enjoyment of material comfort. It is through strife, or the readiness for strife, that a nation must win greatness. We ask for a great Navy, partly because we feel that no national life is worth having if the nation is not willing, when the need shall arise, to stake everything on the supreme arbitrament of war, and to pour out its blood, its treasure, and its tears like water, rather than submit to the loss of honor and renown."

Much of this was the general rhetoric of the day, the same bellicose calls to greatness that were being heard from the Kaiser's Germany, the same references to the future of the race that were commonplace in Britain. The concept of life as a contest to be won, a series of challenges to be met and overcome, ran through the school textbooks of the day as it did through the poetry of Roosevelt's friend Rudyard Kipling. Social Darwinism, the view that the iron laws of evolution and the survival of the fittest governed nations and races as well as species, was deployed throughout the countries of the self-proclaimed "civilized" world to justify their martial patriotism and their empires with scientific sanction.

Roosevelt was very much a product of this time, of that Victorian era that combined belief in scientific progress with a marked preference for deep sentimentality and heroism in its literature. On his first family grand tour to Europe in 1869, when he was ten, a visit to the home of the novelist Sir Walter Scott made a deep impression on the young Theodore, and his diary records that Loch Lomond stuck in his mind because it was there they had laid to rest the Lady of the Lake. His second trip across the Atlantic, to the Middle East at the age of fourteen, was memorable not only for his father's gift of a gun, with which he shot his first bird (a Nile warbler) but also for the learning of German in Dresden and the discovery of the *Song of the Nibelungen*. The legends of the old Teutonic gods, with manly feasting in Valhalla for those who died in glorious battle, were to recur repeatedly in his speeches, as they did in the speeches of the young Winston Churchill, a similar type of young patrician-turned-politician in the heroic mode. Like Roosevelt, Churchill combined books and journalism, expeditions and splendid little wars in the tropics into a stellar public career. Indeed, Churchill's famous wartime speech about "blood, toil, tears and sweat" was a direct quotation from Roosevelt's address to the Naval War College.

Wars for empire and wars against savages, brave deeds and the nobility of valor, were simply part of the customary mental furniture of a well-read European or North American youth of the late nineteenth century. For Roosevelt, they were also part of a family tradition. His mother, a southerner, recalled the family estate being burned by Gen. William Tecumseh Sherman in the Civil War, while his uncle James Bulloch held a treasured place in

Theodore's memory as the builder of the Confederate warship *Alabama.* He recalled how his mother would "talk to me as a little shaver of ships, ships, ships and the fighting of ships, till they sank into the depths of my soul."

It was a comfortable childhood, with holidays abroad and summers in the Adirondacks and private tutors, with an easy passage to Harvard. When his father died while Theodore was still in college, and having already published his first book (on the birds of the Adirondacks), he inherited an income of eight thousand dollars a year. He went to Columbia Law School, but the success of his book on the War of 1812 and the attractions of politics lured him from the law into public life. At the age of twenty-three, he was elected to the New York State Assembly and campaigned energetically against machine politics. Then election defeats sent him off to try ranching in the Dakota Territory. He loved it, became friendly with cowboys, and made several arrests as a deputy sheriff. He lost a lot of money, but he wrote a splendidly patriotic book about Thomas Hart Benton, the Missouri senator who was the apostle of what Roosevelt called America's "manifest destiny to swallow up the land of all adjoining nations who were too weak to withstand us."

Roosevelt came back into public life as a civil service commissioner in 1889. Characteristically, he made this sinecure of a job into a driving force for reform, and he wrote more books and articles to make money to support his fast-growing family. *Hero Tales from American History,* swiftly written for boys, made it clear he wanted the next generation to grow in the same heroic and patriotic mold in which he had been shaped. He became commissioner of police in the new reform administration of Mayor William L. Strong, who had been elected in New York City. Roosevelt swiftly sacked the corrupt old chief of police and astutely used his friendships with two prominent reporters, Jacob Riis and Lincoln Steffens, to trumpet his achievements. None too popular in New York for his vigorous enforcement of the laws against Sunday drinking, he was becoming a celebrity in the rest of the country. "Must be President some day—a man you can't cajole, can't frighten, can't buy," noted Bram Stoker, the author of *Dracula,* after observing him in action at the police court.

At the same time, Roosevelt was itching for a wider canvas for action. During the brief crisis in 1895 over British claims in Venezuela, he wrote to the Civil War veteran Gen. James Wilson: "If I were asked what the greatest boon I could confer upon this nation was, I should answer, an immediate war with Great Britain for the conquest of Canada." Almost any war would do. He thought of fighting Japan for Hawaii, and Spain for the sake of Cuba. "If you have the lust of battle in you, you will have a pretty good time after all," he told University of Chicago students on a speaking tour. Still in Chicago, for a Washington's Birthday address, he mourned "an unhappy tendency among certain of our cultivated people to lose the great manly virtues, the power to strive and fight and conquer."

Roosevelt was the kind of man to take these ideas of social Darwinism to their logical conclusion. In his multivolume history of the American frontier, *The Winning of the West,* the expansion into the North American continent is portrayed as "the crowning and greatest achievement" of the English-speaking peoples. In this racial epic, the original inhabitants of the West are seen as "a few scattered savage tribes, whose life was but a few degrees less meaningless, squalid and ferocious than that of the wild beasts with whom they held joint ownership."

"The most ultimately righteous of all wars is a war with savages, though it is apt to be also the most terrible and inhuman. The rude, fierce settler who drove the savage from the land lays all civilized mankind under a debt to him," he wrote. "It is of incalculable importance that America, Australia and Siberia should pass out of the hands of their red, black and yellow aboriginal owners, and become the heritage of the dominant world races."

And yet Roosevelt, a man inclined to let his gift for rhetoric run away with him, and who entered the White House with such racially authoritarian views, was signally fair in dealing with Native American rights. He vetoed a bill passed by Congress that would have allowed settlers in Oklahoma to "buy" 500,000 acres of Kiowa, Apache, and Choctaw land for $1.50 an acre, and raised the minimum price to $5 an acre. For this and other actions, the state of Oklahoma took the administration to the Supreme Court, which finally upheld Roosevelt's decisions.

Paradox was in the nature of the man. He was a sickly weakling who built his powerful frame through constant exercise and willpower; a big-game hunter who believed in conservation and using the power of government to preserve the wilderness and its wildlife. The craze of the period for teddy bears began, and the most enduringly popular of all soft toys was named after him, when he pointedly insisted on saving a bear cub when out hunting. He was famous for the phrase "Speak softly and carry a big stick," whereas he seldom spoke softly, and despite his boasts, the U.S. Navy never seriously challenged for mastery of the seas. When he demanded four new battleships from Congress, it grumpily agreed to two, although it funded only one a year, at a time when the British and German fleets were building four new *Dreadnought*-type battleships a year. Roosevelt's shipbuilding program resulted in an obsolescent fleet, with mixed twelve-inch and eight-inch guns, and limited to a speed of eighteen knots. They were no match for the twenty-one-knot *Dreadnought*-style ships, with their full battery of twelve-inch guns. Roosevelt's naval legacy was made plain in the 1914 edition of *Jane's Fighting Ships,* which listed the numbers of frontline battleships and battle cruisers available to each power: Britain, thirty-four; Germany, twenty-one; United States, eight; France, four; Japan, four.

Perhaps the greatest paradox regarding Roosevelt is that he spoke much of the glories of battle and the need for the national test of combat but was careful as president to keep the country out of war. Indeed, he became the first president to win the Nobel Peace Prize, for his efforts in brokering peace in the Russo-Japanese War. The paradox is shared, as in a mirror image, by Woodrow Wilson, that man of peace who spoke of the glories of remaining out of wars almost as much as Roosevelt spoke of the joys of fighting them, but who became the president who took the United States into the conflict that is still known as the Great War.

There are striking parallels between the presidencies of Roosevelt and Wilson. They were each simultaneously popular and scholarly writers who could earn their living by the pen, and at the same time impress the academic world and attract a far wider general audience. There was a sharp contrast in their appearance, between the stocky and bustling Roosevelt and the tall, spare, and self-controlled Wilson. The two personalities could hardly have been more different: Roosevelt was gregarious, combative, and enthusiastic; Wilson was austere, cool, and reserved. But in their joint commitment to broadly progressive reforms, and in their similar plunges into global affairs, their joint domination of the two opening decades of the new century becomes almost a single era. Indeed, Wilson might never have been elected in 1912 but for Roosevelt's quixotic decision to run as an independent candidate for the Bull Moose party, which resulted in splitting the anti-Wilson vote.

Both their presidencies faced similar challenges. As the century began, America had the fastest-growing economy on earth and, thanks to mass immigration, one of the fastest-growing populations. Its railway boom had created railway magnates and iron and steel magnates (who were naturally strong supporters of Roosevelt's naval program), and its teeming cities were giant markets for grain and meat from the prairies and for luxuries like sugar and tobacco. Businessmen began to forge conglomerates and trusts to take advantage of the new opportunities for profit. Some took the opportunity to conspire to create monopolies and raise prices, but in many cases the motive was also to rationalize making what had been a series of far-flung regional and local markets into a coherent national one. But the sugar trust and the tobacco trust became notorious, and the way the railroads fixed prices so that farmers subsidized manufacturers, and the South and West subsidized the industrial Northeast and Midwest, provoked outrage.

In turn, these developments provoked their own response. Labor unions organized against exploitation, and public interest groups lobbied against bad food and bad housing, against drink and prostitution. A new kind of journalist, the muckraker, exposed in the new mass media the evils of tumultuous growth. *McClure's* magazine was selling 350,000 copies by the time Roosevelt entered the White House. In its pages, Lincoln Steffens condemned "Pittsburgh—Hell with the Lid Lifted" and "The Shamelessness of St. Louis," which inspired other journals and journalists to expose other outrages. Upton Sinclair worked in the Chicago meat-packing industry and wrote *The Jungle,* the savage novel about its filth and degradation. Roosevelt read it and wrote to Sinclair, "The specific evils you point out will, if their existence be proved, and if I have power, be eradicated." Ida Tarbell spent five years investigating Rockefeller's Standard Oil group, and she produced devastating accounts of fraud, chicanery, bribery, and violence, which made an overwhelming case for such a gross and powerful organization to be brought under public control.

Roosevelt and Wilson were progressives, not only by virtue of their outrage and conviction and because it was politically popular to claim the title but also because the tenor of the times required it. Prosperity was creating a mass middle class, which wanted its food and its cities to be wholesome, and which had the energy and articulate skills, and, thanks to the muckrakers, the ammunition, to mount their own campaigns. In city after city, the immediate targets of these progressive reformers were the political bosses and their election-winning machines. Roosevelt and Wilson, each in his own time, made temporary truces with the machine bosses in order to get elected, then used their power as state governors and as presidents to attack them.

But it was more than specific abuses and specific targets that explain the great political restlessness of the time. There was something in the air, perhaps as vague as the coming of a new century, perhaps as ambitious as the desire, now that America was complete, her West tamed and her frontier closed, to make her worthy of the land. These moods are indefinable. But in almost every aspect of life, from art to architecture, from foreign policy to civic politics, from education to medicine and psychology, new ideas and new ambitions strode onto the stage to disparage the old.

A new generation of historians insisted on challenging the great myths of the American nation. Charles Austin Beard, in his *An Economic Interpretation of the Constitution,* investigated the Founding Fathers and concluded that the "first firm steps toward the formation of the Constitution were taken by a small and active group of men immediately interested through their personal possessions in the outcome of their labors." Thorstein Veblen used the new art of sociology to pillory the idle rich in *The Theory of the Leisure Class,* which noted, "Elegant dress serves its purpose of elegance not only in that it is expensive but also because it is the insignia of leisure . . . pointedly suggesting that its wearer cannot when so attired bear a hand in any employment that is directly and immediately of any human use." The patrician historian Henry

Adams wrote, "Politics, as a practice, whatever its professions, has always been the systematic organization of hatreds." He expected little from its practitioners, since "practical politics consists in ignoring facts." Adams expected even less from the avowed reformers: "Power is poison—its effect on Presidents has always been tragic."

Certainly there was tragedy in the fate of Wilson, who collapsed of a stroke and witnessed the frustration of his great dream of a League of Nations, and of Roosevelt, who died after condemning his Republican party to defeat and suffering Wilson's rejection of his plea to be given command of an American division in France. And yet the two presidents were able to introduce sweeping reforms of the trusts and the abuses that the muckrakers exposed, and they invented the modern presidency in the process.

"I did not usurp power, but I did greatly broaden the use of executive power," Roosevelt wrote in his autobiography. "I acted on the theory that the President could at any time in his discretion withdraw from entry any of the public lands of the United States and reserve the same for forestry, for water-power sites, for irrigation and other public purposes. Without such sanction, it would have been impossible to stop the activity of the land thieves." Before Roosevelt, some 40 million acres of public lands had been made into reserves; he added another 190 million acres, and Senator Robert La Follette, his usually admiring radical critic, concluded, "This is probably the greatest thing Roosevelt ever did."

There were other achievements. He challenged the color bar and outraged much of the white South by inviting Booker T. Washington to the White House. He became the first president to intervene directly in strikes, and he summoned the coal owners and miners to the White House to arbitrate a settlement. He revived the little-used powers of the Sherman Anti-Trust Act and brought suit against the massive Northern Securities Company, through which J. P. Morgan had brought together the Union Pacific, the Burlington, and the Northern Pacific railroads. The outraged Morgan, who had put ten thousand dollars into Roosevelt's New York gubernatorial campaign, went directly to the White House to demand a deal. "That can't be done," said Roosevelt. Then Morgan wanted to know if his other interests would come under similar attack. Not unless they had done something wrong, Roosevelt replied, and he later wrote, "Mr. Morgan could not help regarding me as a big rival operator, who either intended to ruin all his interests or else could be induced to come to an agreement to ruin none." Then Roosevelt moved against Morgan's beef trust.

These high-minded reforms, which challenged the financial base of his Republican party, were deployed by a ruthless political operator, one who deliberately delayed the statehood of Oklahoma, New Mexico, and Arizona for fear that they would vote Democratic in the 1904 election. In his first term, Congress set strict limits on his reforms, only authorizing his Bureau of Corporations, which had the power to examine the books of any business in interstate commerce, when Roosevelt promised no more regulatory measures. Once reelected, he returned to the fray, pushing into law the Hepburn Act, which gave the Interstate Commerce Commission the power to fix maximum railroad rates. This was the crucial precedent on which the state's right to intervene in business affairs—to set prices and regulate the market—was based. This required a clever ploy: to intimidate the Republicans in Congress with a threat to reform the tariff and then to drop the tariff in order to win the regulatory principle.

The constant theme of Roosevelt's reforms was to insist that there was a common interest of the nation as a whole, and that the president was the man elected to define it and protect it. "When I became president," he wrote later, "the question as to the method by which the United States government was to control the corporations was not yet important. The absolutely vital question was whether the Government had power to control them at all."

> The big reactionaries of the business world and their allies and instruments among politicians and newspaper editors . . . demanded for themselves an immunity from government control which, if granted, would have been as wicked and as foolish as immunity to the barons of the twelfth century. Many of them were evil men. Many of them were just as good men as many of these same barons, but they were as utterly unable as any medieval castle owner to understand what the public interest really was. There have been aristocracies which have played a great and beneficent part at stages in the growth of mankind, but we had come to the stage where for our people what was needed was a real democracy; and of all the forms of tyranny the least attractive and most vulgar is the tyranny of mere wealth, the tyranny of a plutocracy.

During his presidency, Roosevelt shrank from the title of Progressive, dismissing many Progressives as "rural Tories" who wanted to abolish big business rather than control it. And while some of the trusts were tamed, and Northern Securities and Standard Oil were broken up, Roosevelt did not want to dismantle the extraordinary wealth- and job-creating machine that the U.S. economy had become. He was ready to work with J. P. Morgan when required. During the panic of 1907, Morgan and John D. Rockefeller jointly stepped in with cash to shore up the market. It may not have been a direct reward, but Roosevelt's immediate approval of the merger between U.S. Steel and the Tennessee Coal and Iron Company reassured business that the Republican White House remained broadly on their side. "The action was emphatically for the general good," Roosevelt commented. "It represented the only chance for arresting the panic."

Roosevelt claimed that, as president, it was his job to be on everyone's side. "It was again and again necessary to assert the position of the President as the steward of the whole people," he recalled in his autobiography. This put him, on occasion, above party allegiance, and Roosevelt went to some pains to claim that the president had to rise above and then blend the two competing traditions that had dominated the philosophy of American politics since the birth of the republic, between the strong federal state of Alexander Hamilton and the decentralized democracy of Thomas Jefferson. "Men who understand and practice the deep underlying philosophy of the Lincoln school of American thought are necessarily Hamiltonian in their belief in a strong and efficient national Government, and Jeffersonian in their belief in the people as the ultimate authority, and in the welfare of the people as the end of government."

This was a neat debating point, but politics is about taking sides in order to make decisions. Roosevelt tried to have it all ways. His Square Deal policy sought to be evenhanded between labor and capital and to flay both the radical socialists and corrupt businessmen alike. "We seek to control law-defying wealth, in the first place to prevent its doing evil, and in the next place to avoid the vindictive and dreadful radicalism which if left uncontrolled it is certain in the end to arouse," he wrote to his attorney general, Charles Bonaparte. "We stand with equal stoutness for the rights of the man of wealth and for the rights of the wage-worker." The probably inevitable result was that he satisfied neither, and much of the task of reform still awaited the future presidency of Woodrow Wilson. More immediately, Roosevelt's attempt at evenhandedness threw his own party into a crisis, which ended, during the Taft presidency, which succeeded Roosevelt's, with a split that Roosevelt led.

By the time he left the White House in 1909, Roosevelt claimed, "the Republican party became once more the progressive, and indeed the fairly, radically progressive party of the Nation." If true, it was at the price of a severe breach between the president and his party's leaders in Congress, which he admitted in his autobiography. "We succeeded in working together, although with increasing friction, for some years, I pushing forward and they hanging back. Gradually, however, I was forced to abandon the effort to persuade them to come my way, and then I achieved results only by appealing over the heads of the Senate and House leaders to the people, who were masters of both of us." By the end, he confessed, "Relations were quite as bitter as if we had belonged to opposite political parties."

America Reborn

Roosevelt was simply too big and ambitious a political phenomenon for any conventional party structure to contain him. So in one of those intuitive leaps into the future that marked his career, he invented that crucial component of the modern presidency: the media presence that soared beyond politics directly to the people. It was indeed a bully pulpit, but only for those who knew how to use it, and Roosevelt always had an instinct for the media. When his troopship landed at Montauk upon its return from the fighting in Cuba, he strode straight to the little knot of reporters to extol the prowess of his regiment and give them a story. "This is a pistol with a history," he confided, brandishing his weapon. "It was taken from the wreck of the *Maine*. When I took it to Cuba I made a vow to kill at least one Spaniard with it, and I did."

In his own assessment of his presidency, Roosevelt claimed three great achievements: brokering the peace between Russia and Japan; sending the battleships of "the Great White Fleet" around the world to advertise the presence of a new naval power; and building the Panama Canal. Each achievement was somewhat clouded. Russia and Japan each wanted peace anyway, for their own reasons. And far from heralding a new era of American influence in the region, it was the very modesty of American naval power in the Pacific that encouraged each of them to accept Roosevelt as an almost disinterested neutral. The voyage of the Great White Fleet had made for splendid newspaper headlines, but in reality, this first display of American naval ambition was marked by appalling logistical difficulties. Its dependence on friendly ports for refueling, as well as the dire shortage of cruiser and destroyer escorts, made it a highly vulnerable parade. It was not, for established naval powers, an immediate military threat, although it laid down a portentous marker for the future. If Roosevelt's intention had been to intimidate, he did not wholly succeed. But if—as Roosevelt publicly claimed—the voyage was a gesture of goodwill, he failed; for the historian of the Japanese navy, Shigera Fukudone, it marked the moment when "the Japanese Navy made the U.S. Navy its sole imaginary enemy."

The Panama Canal was an overdue act of commercial and strategic logic for the Americas as a whole, which Roosevelt carried off in a high-handed manner that would sour U.S. relations with Latin America for decades to come. Finding Colombia too corrupt and too slow for his purposes, Roosevelt encouraged and supported a coup on the isthmus, thus carving the infant state of Panama from its Colombian trunk, and then carving, in turn, a strip of U.S. territory through Panama, the Canal Zone, through which the waterway would run. Possibly there was little alternative if the canal were to be achieved. In any event, the stupendous engineering feat was finally complete by 1914. By that time, the paternalist relationship between the United States and its southern neighbors had been made clear in Roosevelt's corollary to the original Monroe Doctrine, which asserted the right to unilateral police action throughout the region: "Brutal wrongdoing, or an impotence which results in a general loosening of the ties of civilizing society, may finally require intervention by some civilized nation, and in the Western Hemisphere the United States cannot ignore this duty."

Roosevelt, in retrospect, had through temperament and personal conviction prodded his country onto the world stage before it was fully ready to play the part. Possibly because no American president could quite so crudely affront the anticolonial tradition in which the country had been born, he was not a full-blooded imperialist. The Philippines were given decent government, education, and a promise of independence. Marines were sent to Cuba, restored order, and left again. This was arrogant and intrusive, but it was not the naked conquest of the European way. Roosevelt's actions always had limits, even if his rhetoric and ambitions raced far ahead.

The voters of the day were reluctant about foreign commitments, most visibly when faced with the ambiguous role he played in the Moroccan crisis of 1905, when for the first time American diplomats were told that supporting the Franco-British alliance against Germany was in the U.S. national interest. In fact, the American people were not much interested in foreign affairs at all. And who could blame them when the real drama of the age was unfolding on their doorsteps? It was in Roosevelt's America that the first true movie, *The Great Train Robbery,* filled theaters and Ziegfeld launched his famous Follies. And it was in Roosevelt's final year in office that Mary Pickford became the first film star. It was in America that the first black man became the heavyweight boxing champion of the world, and whatever Jack Johnson's feat represented in the popular mind, a deeper national tradition began in 1910 as W. E. B. Du Bois organized what would become the National Association for the Advancement of Colored People.

It was in Roosevelt's America that Henry Ford launched his Model T, and where the Wright brothers launched their first flight. Roosevelt himself had ensured that they got a contract to build planes for the military. Here lay the final irony: that a man who prided himself on his modernity and clear vision of a great American future should end his life so thoroughly out of tune with his times. The new kind of war that the invention of the Wright brothers heralded, and that the mass-production techniques of Henry Ford made possible, saw the Wrights' technology used to bomb civilians in their cities. The war that unfolded in Europe as Roosevelt languished out of office, with no party to lead, brought tanks and barbed wire and poison gas to obliterate those *Boys Weekly* heroics that had marked Roosevelt's life and temperament.

He may have been the last leader of any democratic nation to be able to glorify war in public speeches and to summon its young men to feats of valor and the grandeur of sacrifice. The squalid reality of the Western Front was a universe away from the grandiose racial mission of conquest and mastery to which Roosevelt always thrilled. By the time of his death, eight weeks after World War I ended, Roosevelt was a very old-fashioned man whose most enduring legacy was to take into federal protection almost 200 million acres of the American wilderness he loved. In that sense, he was still ahead of his time.

2.
Emma Goldman
and the American Dissident

Ten days after three Pinkerton security guards and ten strikers were killed in a lockout battle at the Homestead steel plant just outside of Pittsburgh, a young Russian immigrant named Emma Goldman joined the Saturday-night parade of prostitutes on Manhattan's Fourteenth Street to sell her body for the revolutionary cause. It was, Emma assumed on that humid evening of July 16, 1892, the only way she could raise fifteen dollars. She needed the money to buy a revolver to kill Henry Clay Frick, the hated industrialist with the Homestead workers' blood on his hands. Her lover and partner in a thriving ice-cream-parlor business, Alexander Berkman, had already gone to Pittsburgh to prepare for the assassination.

Emma Goldman was twenty-three, five feet tall, with light brown hair "falling loosely over her forehead, full lips, strong white teeth, a mild, pleasant voice with a fetching accent . . . a saucy, turned-up nose and very expressive

blue-gray eyes," recorded Nellie Bly of the *New York World,* who later interviewed the fiery young anarchist in the Tombs prison. Bly was sufficiently
charmed to conclude that the young immigrant charged with "incitement to
riot" and condemned by Judge Randolph Martine as "a dangerous woman"
should instead be seen as "a modern Joan of Arc."

Prostitution was not exactly Emma's strong suit, although she had borrowed money to buy some high-heeled shoes and fancy lingerie. On that
humiliating New York evening, she rejected customer after customer who
inquired after her services, dismayed by her own lack of determination.
Finally, an aging gentleman took her to a bar, bought her a drink, and suggested that she was in the wrong trade. He sent her off with ten dollars, barely
enough to pay for the shoes. She still needed money, and so she wired her sister Helena, saying that she had fallen sick and asking for fifteen dollars.
Emma sent the money she received to Berkman, who used it to buy a gun and
a new suit in order to look the part of a contractor with strikebreaking labor
to sell. He then called on Frick at the *Pittsburgh Chronicle-Telegraph* building,
carrying the gun and a dagger in his belt. Berkman shot the businessman
twice and then stabbed him twice in the legs before being overpowered by
attendants, who also removed the small capsule of fulminate of mercury that
Berkman was trying to bite to commit suicide after the deed.

Frick survived and was back at work within a month. The strike collapsed, in part because the skilled and essentially conservative men of the
Amalgamated Association of Iron and Steel Workers were appalled by the
assassination attempt carried out in their name. They did not share Berkman's conviction that "the awakening of the American worker, the long-
awaited day of his resurrection" was at hand. American workers, however
grim the recession or their pay and conditions of labor, proved highly resistant to the blandishments of Communist ideology. Unlike the superficially
similar industrialized economies of Europe, the economy of the United States
never generated a mass Socialist party capable of winning power through
elections. This was to be a cardinal example of that "American exceptional-
ism" that made the country unique. But it also created something of a vacuum on the Left, which made radical leaders like Emma, who were outside
the mainstream of American politics, all the more prominent. Almost by definition, radicals who were not connected to a powerful political base in Congress became "extremists," or at least they could be portrayed as such in the
popular press.

Emma, of course, was an extremist at this stage of her career. She had
conspired in an assassination plot. Berkman was tried and convicted of
attempted murder and sentenced to twenty-one years in prison. Had he been
given the death penalty, Emma was planning to blow up the courthouse where

his trial took place. It was as well she did not try. Before the assassination attempt, she and Berkman had tried to practice with dynamite but had failed even to make it explode.

For the next three decades, Emma was to become the best-known revolutionary in America, and probably the best-known woman radical on earth. Before being deported from the United States in 1919, in a squalid series of legal maneuvers born of antiradical hysteria, she made the career of a conservative young lawyer named J. Edgar Hoover. He used her expulsion as his springboard to a power he would wield and abuse for the next fifty years. Dispatched as part of a shipload of Red deportees to the infant Soviet Union, she was dismayed by the perversion of her revolutionary ideals that she found there. Unshakeable in her belief in free speech, she condemned Lenin to his face in his Kremlin office for the authoritarian ways of the young Bolshevik state. Hounded from country to country until she found stable exile in Britain and France, she was barred for life from entering the United States. She was given a brief ninety-day respite for a lecture tour in 1934, but after that, she returned only in death, in 1940. She was buried on the site of the Haymarket riot and bombing in Chicago, the event that had made her an American dissident.

Emma had arrived in the United States seven years before the attempted killing of Frick, drawn by the immigrant's perennial dream of freedom. She was also escaping an abusive and bullying father, who was trying to make her marry against her will. Abraham Goldman was from the Jewish Pale of Settlement, the Baltic and Polish lands that the tsars had conquered in the eighteenth century and turned into a vast and leaky ghetto where Russians ruled over German landowners and Polish peasants and all of them despised the Jews. He had lost his wife's inheritance in a failed business venture in Kaunas, Lithuania, run a small state-owned theater in the town of Popelaan, and moved back to live with his wife's family in the old German city of Königsberg, where Immanuel Kant had taught philosophy. Jews were subject to regular pogroms and once young Emma watched, appalled, as a Russian peasant was beaten bloody by an overseer. Königsberg nonetheless remained a city of learning. Emma wanted to become a doctor, an unusual career choice for a woman at the time, and she passed the tough entrance examination for the German gymnasium, or high school. But she could not go, because her religious teacher refused to give her the required certificate of good character, judging her to be insufficiently respectful of authority.

From the Pale, to which Jews were supposedly confined, the family bribed their way past Russian guards and across a frozen stream in 1881. They headed for the tsarist capital of Saint Petersburg, and Abraham borrowed money from his wife's parents to open a small grocery. It was an unruly time.

America Reborn

Tsar Alexander II had just been assassinated after a campaign of repression against a series of radical movements, one of which had included Emma's maternal uncle, who barely escaped exile to Siberia. The agitation, inspired by economic misery and tsarist rule, found its focus in a series of popular but supposedly subversive books, from Turgenev's *Fathers and Sons* to Chernyshevsky's *What Is to Be Done?* Emma read them avidly, taking as her heroine Chernyshevsky's beguiling character Vera Pavlovna, whose fictional life struck so many chords with her own. Vera rejects her mother's attempt to force her into marriage, embraces free love with a young medical student, and starts a needlework cooperative as a way to finance her own medical studies.

The right to love as she chose, to pursue a career in medicine, and to work collectively without making profits for an employer and for the propertied class that profit produced were to be constant themes of Emma Goldman's life. They were all to prove far more complicated than her young idealism assumed when she arrived in America aboard the German steamship *Elbe* at the end of 1885. The Statue of Liberty had been shipped to New York from France that year, not yet erected onto its plinth, but already promising the freedom Emma expected to find: "Ah, there she was, the symbol of hope, of freedom, of opportunity! She held her torch to light the way to the free country, the asylum for the oppressed of all lands," she recalled of that moment, as she and her sister Helena hugged each other at the sight.

Once ashore, appalled by the way the immigrants were treated by the New York authorities, the sisters went to join their sister Lena, who had settled with her husband in Rochester, New York. Emma found work in the sewing factory of Leo Garson, chairman of the United Jewish Charities. He turned out to be more businessman than philanthropist, paying a near-starvation wage of $2.50 a day. Worse, she wrote later, Garson would "exact labor in his factory for nothing, but also insisted on the pleasures the young female wage slaves could give him. He had them, or out they went."

Emma found another job, and in her loneliness, she became engaged to a fellow young Russian immigrant, Jacob Kersner. Her parents arrived from Russia, and Kersner moved into the crowded Goldman apartment as a lodger. In Emma's memoirs, she claimed to have bowed to what seemed like the inevitable, and she married Kersner. She immediately found him to be impotent, however, and divorced him within the year and left for New York. He followed her, and she relented and remarried him briefly, returning to Rochester before leaving him again, already plunging into radical politics.

She had been outraged by the hanging of four anarchist labor leaders convicted on the vaguest of evidence of the Haymarket bombing, which had taken place during her first year in America. On the day after the Chicago police had shot a striking worker, a protest rally in the city's Haymarket was dynamited, and seven policemen were killed. The person who threw the explosives was never identified, and in a mood of hysterical vengeance, August Spies and the other anarchists were convicted of conspiracy and hanged in November 1898. The evening after the execution, Emma, calling at her parents' home, heard one of the guests say the anarchists were murderers who deserved their fate, and Emma leapt upon the woman. Hauled off by other guests, she threw a jug of water at the offending woman, crying, "Out— or I will kill you."

The Haymarket executions crystallized her anger at immigrants' working conditions and the subordination of women, and her disillusion with the lack of freedom in America. She set out for New York with her sewing machine and five dollars, left her bags at the home of relatives, and went directly to the radical meeting place of Sachs's Café on Suffolk Street. That first day, she found somewhere to stay, met Alexander Berkman, and went with him to an evening rally to hear the celebrated anarchist Johann Most, whose weekly newspaper *Freiheit* she had read in Rochester. Briefly a member of the German Reichstag, Most had fled to Britain and then to America, where he had written with Spies the Pittsburgh Manifesto, a broad statement of radical and anarchist principles that proved vague enough to rally the squabbling socialist sects of America into a temporary unity. Most took Emma under his wing, encouraged her to write, and taught her public speaking.

The young Berkman, born in Vilnius, in Russian-ruled Lithuania, not far from Emma's birthplace, had, like her, gone to Saint Petersburg and been intoxicated by Chernyshevsky's novel. Tsar Alexander had been assassinated in the street outside his school, and his radicalization had come from the Nihilist and populist students of the city. He was expelled for writing an essay entitled "There Is No God" and, despairing of Russia, then emigrated to America. Slim and intense, with eyes that burned with political passion, Berkman captivated Emma. With two young anarchist friends, Fedya, an artist, and Helen, who worked in a corset factory, they established a commune together on Forty-second Street and began living the revolutionary dream of anarchy, free love and shared possessions, and political rallies each night. Emma began planning a sewing cooperative, like her fictional heroine Vera Pavlovna, but then came the Homestead strike and Berkman's attempt at assassination.

Emma was already known in radical circles, her articles and accounts of her speeches reported in the Yiddish and German immigrant press. But with Berkman's trial, the *New York World* spread her fame with a sensational front-page story headlined ANARCHY'S DEN, which portrayed Emma as the sinister and powerful mastermind of the plot. The police had already been to her home and had persuaded the landlord to evict her. Homeless, when no other landlord would rent to the infamous anarchist, she slept on streetcars until finding a room in a brothel. She had feuded with other radicals, who had condemned Berkman's deed. Her old mentor, Most, had suggested at one public meeting that the assassination attempt might have been a fake, arranged by Frick himself. Emma challenged Most to prove it. He ignored her, muttering about "hysterical women," and she took out a horse whip and beat him.

A strike of cloak workers in New York drew her back into the political fray in 1893, the year of a stock market crash that began four years of recession. She organized immigrant women and addressed a public rally of some three thousand people in Union Square. The police were waiting, and she was arrested for incitement to riot. She threw a glass of water in the face of a policeman who offered to drop charges if she became a paid informant against other radicals. At her trial, the same policeman testified that in Union Square she had said, "Nobody will give it [bread] to you. If you want it, you must take it. If you do not get it when you ask for it, upon your demands, take it by force." Emma denied these words, and although former New York mayor Oakey Hall had volunteered (for local political reasons) to act as her lawyer, the prosecution was determined to convince the jury of property owners that Emma's beliefs were an affront, if not a clear threat, to them.

"Do you believe in a Supreme Being, Miss Goldman?" asked the prosecuting district attorney.

"No, sir, I do not," she replied.

"Is there any government on earth whose laws you approve?"

"No, sir, for they are all against the people."

"Why don't you leave this country if you don't like its laws?"

"Where shall I go? Everywhere on earth the laws are against the poor, and they tell me I cannot go to heaven, nor do I want to go there."

Her celebrity continued in prison, as the New York press recounted that she ran the sewing shop, organized the nursing of the sick, and impressed her guards. Released after a year, she was hailed at a Bowery rally to welcome her home, and was taken up by New York's liberals, who had seen her arrest as a dangerous infringement on the constitutional right to free speech. For Emma, so deeply involved with the concerns and culture of immigrants, workers, and the poor, it was a revelation to comprehend that there were other, native currents of radicalism in America. There were the old abolitionist agitators, who had fought against slavery before the Civil War, and campaigners for women's suffrage. There were civic reformers who wanted to clean out the corruption of Tammany Hall, the Democratic club that ran New York's municipal politics. There were trade unionists and cerebral socialists, slum-clearance advocates, and campaigners against the demon drink, child labor, and prostitution.

Emma Goldman and the American Dissident

It was less that Emma suddenly realized that she had a particular place in a broad continuum of dissent that ran from reform to revolution and more that she discovered the potential of allies and ad hoc coalitions. Above all, she understood that there was an American politics beyond the immigrant culture, one with which connections and even alliances could be forged. She agitated and organized for a series of political, industrial, and social causes, many of which have since been achieved and are now taken for granted. She was a pioneering campaigner against war and conscription, and for birth control and women's rights. She battled for public health and the eight-hour working day, for free love without need for marriage, and for the right not to believe in God. And she took her campaigns from the semiclosed world of America's Yiddish- and German-speaking communities to the American-born workers and liberal reformers.

To her admirers, Emma embodied the fundamental freedom of the Constitution, the right to tell Americans what they did not necessarily want to hear. To her foes, she cunningly exploited the very freedoms of America in order to undermine its institutions. She was first imprisoned for a speech in New York's Union Square that was ruled "incitement to riot." She was then accused of complicity in the murder of the newly elected president, William McKinley, because of a speech that allegedly had inspired his assassin, Leon Czolgosz, an American of Polish ancestry. In fact, as Czolgosz stressed at his trial, the one speech of Emma's he ever heard had emphasized that violence was not an essential component of anarchism. It was the great irony of her life. She became notorious as "Red Emma" for having inspired an assassination in which she had no part, but she faced no charge for her direct responsibility as an accessory in the attempted murder of Frick.

The assassination of McKinley provoked an acute national reaction, leading to the passage of the 1903 Aliens Act, which declared the advocacy of "criminal anarchy" to be a felony. Its definition was taken directly from New York State's Anarchy Act of the previous year, which outlawed "the doctrine which advocates that organized government be overthrown by force or violence or the assassination of public officials or by any unlawful means." Emma argued in vain that this would have incriminated George Washington and Thomas Jefferson. The law became the judicial basis for all future expulsions and deportations. In response, she founded the Free Speech League in 1903, not simply to assert this constitutional right but also to support the militant trade unionists of the Industrial Workers of the World (IWW), whose campaigns were suppressed by local ordinances forbidding their rallies. The American Civil Liberties Union was founded at her inspiration by Roger Baldwin, who had heard her speak in St. Louis in 1908. "You always remain one of the chief inspirations of my life, for you aroused in me a sense of what freedom really means," he later wrote to Emma.

One of the consistent principles of her life in America was to insist that anarchism was no sinister alien creed, but a doctrine of self-help, education, and human empowerment that stood firmly alongside the ideals of Jeffersonian democracy. Her clearest summary of her beliefs, in the book *Anarchism and Other Essays,* captures her skill at putting dense political argument into clear and unthreatening prose: "Anarchism, then, really stands for the liberation of the human mind from the dominion of religion; the liberation of the human body from the dominion of property; liberation from the shackles and restraints of government."

But this, published in 1911, was from a different, more mature and reflective Emma, and it defined a less aggressive form of anarchism than the cause she had embraced twenty years earlier. The first political guide she embraced on arriving in New York from Rochester in 1889 had been the "fierce call to battle against the enemy" of the German revolutionary anarchist Most, who preached the need for "a revolutionary act of war against the bourgeois vermin." This was the Emma of youthful fire and fury, prepared for prostitution in order to finance political assassination. But as she read more widely, she turned instead to the profoundly humanitarian anarchism of Prince Kropotkin, a Russian idealist who believed that human society would evolve from the brutal competition of the profit motive into a system of amicable cooperation. Violence was an endemic feature of human life, and the essential catalyst of social change, Kropotkin argued. But it was the duty of the anarchist to make that violence constructive, within the context of "the broad ideas which inspire men by the grandness of the horizon which they bring to view."

For Emma, who was to support herself in later exile by lecturing on modern drama, those broad ideas included literature and the arts. Indeed, they became a part of her politics. Man Ray, an American who was to become one of the outstanding Surrealists, designed avant-garde covers for her magazine *Mother Earth* long before he produced the innovative photography that made his name. Henrik Ibsen, the dramatist whom she felt most precisely captured the flavor of her times, was taken directly into her political philosophy. His portrayal in *A Doll's House* of marriage as a property trap for women, his assault on the amoral pursuit of profit in *Pillars of Society,* and his condemnation of "the damned compact liberal majority" in *An Enemy of the People* became in her lectures so many parables for her politics. She informed the Anarchist Congress in Amsterdam in 1907 that the playwright provided the essential human counterpoint to the anarchist vision: "While Kropotkin has explained the social conditions which lead to a collective revolution, Ibsen has portrayed, in a masterly manner, the psychological effects which culminate in the revolt of a human soul—the revolt of individuality."

Emma's writings can make her sound fearfully dry. But she was a woman of passion, who lived to the full her belief in free love. Her first sexual experience, hurried and confusing, took place in a Saint Petersburg hotel room while her sister called out in search of her from the corridor outside. Thereafter, as she recorded in her autobiography, she "always felt between two fires in the presence of men. Their lure remained strong, but it was always mingled with violent revulsion. I could not bear to have them touch me."

Her one marriage was to an impotent man, and her lifelong partnership with Berkman was interrupted by his two decades in prison. She found other lovers, taking much younger or much older men as she pleased, but her great passion was her eight-year affair with Ben Reitman, "King of the Hobos." A qualified doctor who liked to travel as a hobo and use his medical skills on the tramps he met, Reitman offered her his "Hobo Hall" in 1908, when no other lecture venue would accept her. They were instantly attracted to each other, and he became the highly efficient manager of her speaking tours, as well as the most exciting lover she had ever known. "You came to me like a stroke of lightning, kindling my soul and my body with mad passion, as I have never known before," she wrote to him the year after their affair began.

This complex and passionate woman, a revolutionary intellectual of libertarian convictions and great political skills, was deliberately simplified and caricatured by the popular press. This made it all the easier for the New York and federal authorities to target and eventually to deport her as a danger to the state. In the process, she became the model for the emerging complicity between the state and the media, which demonstrated the American ability to demonize and thus marginalize its more dangerous dissidents. The judicial authorities named her as a witness, or as a suspect, or as a conspirator in various cases, and the popular press then made her into a symbol of menace to the American way of life. Once the media had made her sufficiently infamous, with her politics and her free love and her defiance of laws against promoting birth control combining into a heady stew of Red lust, further judicial action was made both easier and inevitable. She had, after all, already been convicted in the minds of many potential jurors of being licentious and un-American.

Emma thus became the template on which was drawn the fate of the dissident in a modern democracy equipped with the most inspiring of constitutional safeguards. The pattern was to be repeated throughout the twentieth century, against militant labor leaders, against Communists and their sympathizers, against civil rights activists, and against the antiwar protesters of the Vietnam era. First, the dangerous dissident is identified; then he or she is exposed in the media and sensationalized as a frightening extremist. At this point, the process does not necessarily need the further intervention of the state. Patriotic Americans can be relied upon to counterdemonstrate or to take other action, firing the targets or boycotting their businesses. If necessary, the state and its officials can take further action, from simply monitoring a dissident's behavior in order to build an intelligence file to harassing friends, family, and associates. In the gravest cases, the state can take direct action, legal or extralegal, and can put discreet pressure on public and political figures to declare the need for the democratic state to defend itself against a dissident's undemocratic attack.

The single figure who refined this process into a state strategy was J. Edgar Hoover, who started as an ambitious young employee of the Library of Congress. In his spare time, he studied law, managed to avoid conscription in 1917, and joined the Justice Department to work in the Alien Enemy Bureau. Enemy aliens, by definition, did not enjoy the constitutional protections available to citizens, and the 1903 Aliens Act could be used ruthlessly against them. Hoover worked closely with the Justice Department's Bureau of Investigation (BI), which was also investigating the antiwar movement, draft dodgers, and the IWW labor union, which challenged "the capitalist war." A name that kept cropping up in the inquiries was that of Emma Goldman.

"The America which is to be protected by a huge military force is not the America of the people, but that of the privileged class, the class which robs and exploits the masses and controls their lives from the cradle to the grave," she maintained in her essay and standard lecture, "Preparedness: The Road to Universal Slaughter," which had been the prime text of the antiwar movement since 1915. Her argument was that since the established political parties and leaders would not oppose war, an independent movement must be built to keep the United States out of such conflicts. "Like a plague, the mad spirit is sweeping the country, infesting the clearest heads and staunchest hearts with the deathly germ of militarism. . . . Roosevelt, a born bully, uses the club. Wilson, the historian, the college professor, wears the smooth, polished university mask, but underneath it he, like Roosevelt, has but one aim—to serve the big interests, to add to those who are growing phenomenally rich by the manufacture of military supplies."

On June 15, 1917, Emma was arrested at the New York offices of *Mother Earth* and charged with "conspiracy to induce persons not to register" for the draft. Her old lover Berkman, released after serving his sentence for attempting to kill Frick, was arrested with her. She had served a fifteen-day prison term the previous spring for giving an "illegal" public lecture on birth control. But this arrest was far more serious; the government was determined to crush her. Bail was set at the extraordinarily high figure of $25,000. As a band played "The Star-Spangled Banner" outside the courtroom, any spectator who did not rise was forcibly ejected. The prosecution alleged that she and the antiwar movement had taken money from secret German funds. The defense was able to prove it had come in the form of a three-thousand-dollar donation from an American supporter of Swedish origin.

Emma's closing statement in her own defense has become a classic expression of civil liberties. She began by defining her attitude to violence: "An act of political violence at the bottom is the culminating result of organized violence at the top. . . . I refuse to cast the stone at the 'political criminal.' I take his place with him, because he has been driven to revolt, because his life-breath has been choked up." Then came her peroration:

> The kind of patriotism that we represent is the kind which loves America with open eyes. Our relation to America is the same as the relation of a man who loves a woman, who is enchanted by her beauty and yet who cannot be blind to her defects. And so I wish to state here, in my own behalf and on behalf of hundreds of thousands whom you decry and state to be antipatriotic, that we love America, we love her riches, we love her mountains and her forests and above all we love the people who have produced her wealth and riches, who have created all her beauty. We love the dreamers and the philosophers and the thinkers who are giving America liberty. But that must not make us blind to the social faults of America.

Emma and Berkman were found guilty and then sentenced to two years in prison. This was not thought by the Justice Department to be enough. Hoover was ordered to investigate the details of Emma's original and brief marriage to Jacob Kersner in 1887, to establish whether he had been a properly naturalized citizen and whether, therefore, Emma could be deported as an alien. This took Hoover some time, but by 1919, he had produced the evidence required. In 1908, during an earlier attempt to remove Emma's citizenship, special U.S. attorney P. S. Chambers of Pittsburgh had established (with dubious and probably bought testimony) that Kersner had lied about his age and his date of arrival in the United States when applying for citizenship, which was thus invalid. But the government could neither find Kersner nor establish that he was alive at the time of the removal of his citizenship, which meant that they could not move against Emma. Hoover found evidence that Kersner (who had changed his name to Lewis) had died in January 1919. Emma was thus not a citizen and could be deported.

America Reborn

For a loyal servant of the state like Hoover, the political character of the enemy of the day was secondary. In the years before 1917, before communism became a threat, anarchism or unpatriotic opposition to the legally declared war were legitimate targets for the state's defenders. Thus, the Bureau of Investigation raided the IWW trade union for calling strikes against the war, and it hunted draft dodgers and opened files on those who encouraged them, like Emma. With the war's end, Hoover applied to the new attorney general, Mitchell Palmer, to be allowed to remain in office. The evidence in Hoover's files pointed to new political challenges to the state after the war. Palmer agreed to Hoover's request, and he felt his decision was vindicated when his own house was bombed in June 1919 by a young anarchist, who killed himself in the attempt. Hoover's salary was increased from eighteen hundred dollars a year to three thousand and he was placed in charge of the new General Intelligence Division of the Justice Department, with orders to identify, locate, and then deport the revolutionary aliens.

Within three months, Hoover's files contained 150,000 names. By 1921, when the purge had run its course, there were 450,000 files. Included in those investigated were labor leaders, anarchists, socialists, Bolsheviks, and antiwar activists, whether native-born or alien. Hoover focused on two new parties founded in 1919, the Communist party of America, and the rival Communist Labor party of America. Attorney General Palmer included them in the twelve "subversive" organizations, membership in which was sufficient grounds for deportation. Over two thousand radicals were arrested in New York alone in June and November of 1919, and hundreds were deported en masse. On January 2, 1920, Hoover mounted the "Palmer raids," the simultaneous crackdown on radicals in thirty-three cities, in which over ten thousand people were arrested, most of them under warrants that were signed after the arrests. As much as targeting individuals, Hoover was seeking information: membership lists, letters, party files—the raw data from which his own files could grow. The first and crucial haul came from Emma's files, and the subscription lists to *Mother Earth,* seized at the time of her arrest in 1917.

The Palmer raids proved highly controversial. The *New York Times* reported:

> Meetings open to the general public were roughly broken up. All persons present—citizens and aliens alike without discrimination—were arbitrarily taken into custody and searched as if they were burglars caught in a criminal act. Without warrants of arrest men were carried off to the police stations and other temporary prisons, subjected there to secret police-office inquisitions commonly known as the "third-degree," their statements written categorically into mimeo-

graphed blanks, and they were required to swear to them regardless of their accuracy.

The central target of this effort, of course, and the single emblematic figure who launched Hoover's career, was Emma, still in prison. More than half of Palmer's 1919 report to the Senate, "Investigation Activities of the Department of Justice," was devoted to her. Compiled by Hoover, the Goldman file contained a ruthlessly edited transcript of the McKinley assassination trial, a transparent attempt to establish her guilt as an accessory. Czolgosz's statements that he had planned the assassination before ever hearing Emma speak, and that she had specifically not said that "it would be a good thing if rulers were wiped off the face of the earth," were deleted from Hoover's version of the trial.

"Emma Goldman and Alexander Berkman are, beyond doubt, two of the most dangerous anarchists in this country, and if permitted to return to the community will result in undue harm," Hoover wrote in a special memorandum for the attorney general in August 1919. Emma was still in prison for the conspiracy charge, and Hoover was determined to rearrest her as soon as she was free. It was time to get Emma and Berkman out of the country once and for all. Hoover had the evidence to cast doubt on her citizenship, which brought her under the draconian powers of the Aliens Act. He pressed for her deportation hearing to take place in New York, rather than in St. Louis, where he feared the court would prove lenient. Berkman, who was adjudged to be an alien on the basis of his statement in court that he recognized no government and claimed to be "a citizen of the world," was kept in solitary confinement for eight months. The final hearing went against them, and on December 21, she and Berkman and 249 "anarchists" were deported on the steamship *Buford,* which had been chartered by Hoover for the task. He went to the dock to see them off, and as the ship pulled away, a patriotic congressman called out "Merry Christmas, Emma," and in Hoover's account of the scene, she thumbed her nose back.

Hoover's own internal report on the Palmer raids, entitled "The Revolution in Action," sounded an apocalyptic warning: "Civilization faces its most terrible menace of danger since the barbarian hordes overran Western Europe and opened the dark ages." He claimed that over three thousand of those arrested could be deported forthwith. A total of sixteen hundred deportation warrants were issued, but Assistant Secretary of Labor Louis L. Post canceled over eleven hundred of them. Hoover thereupon opened a file on him, and he warned that the Communist revolution in America would be launched on May 1, 1920. The army and police were put on alert, and troops were stationed in the large cities. The day passed calmly, and Attorney General Palmer's reputation suffered. But when Palmer was replaced after the Republican Warren Harding won the presidential election, Hoover was able to offer Palmer's successor, Harry Daugherty, files on a number of the new president's political enemies. Hoover stayed in office, and he was made deputy head of the Bureau of Investigation.

The Harding administration was deeply corrupt. Attorney General Daugherty was tried on fraud charges, and Hoover's immediate boss, BI director William Burns, was sentenced to prison after using his position to start his own private detective agency. The new attorney general, Harlan Fiske Stone (a critic of the Palmer raids), appointed his fellow Freemason Hoover to run the BI, on the conditions Hoover set: "The Bureau must be divorced from politics and not be a catch-all for political hacks. Appointments must be based on merit. Second, promotions will be made on proven ability and the Bureau will be responsible only to the Attorney-General." Hoover inherited a bureau with 650 employees, including 441 special agents. He fired the unqualified and corrupt, introduced performance appraisals and formal training courses, and began hiring new agents with law or accounting credentials.

The Red menace having eased with the prosperity of the 1920s, and the restrictive new immigration laws, Hoover realized that the BI's role and budget faced sharp reduction. He suggested that the federal government needed its own professional crime-fighting agency. His BI was accordingly renamed the Federal Bureau of Investigation and given a new mandate to fight interstate crime as well as subversion and espionage. When the political threat revived, as it did briefly during the Great Depression, during World War II because of Nazi sympathizers, and, above all, in the early days of the Cold War, Hoover had established a machine that could be swiftly reoriented into a form of political police.

By this time, Emma was finding herself deeply disillusioned with the authoritarian Soviet Union. In 1918, she had hailed the leaders of the Russian Revolution in her pamphlet "The Truth about the Bolsheviki," which cited their support on independence for Finland with Emma's endorsement that "they have no imperialistic designs. They have libertarian plans, and those who understand the principles of liberty do not want to annex other peoples and countries." Once installed in Russia, witnessing the military discipline imposed on factories and workers and the number of arrests, she grew appalled. "Five hundred executed at one time by a revolutionary government! A secret police that matched the old Okhrana suppression, persecution of honest revolutionaries, all the unnecessary suffering and cruelty—was it for this that the revolution had been fought?" She arranged a meeting with Lenin, who had read a book about her trial and admired her speeches. She appealed to him in the name of free speech. He mocked her. Free speech was "a bourgeois notion," he replied. "There can be no free speech in a revolutionary period," he said, and suggested she get a job to regain her revolutionary balance.

Two years after leaving New York, Emma and Berkman left Russia. The New York press besieged her with lucrative offers to describe her sense of the revolution betrayed. Instead, she wrote her accounts for the leftist press, but *The New Republic, The Nation,* and *The Freeman* all refused to publish them. As keen to get her views known as to have money to live on, she wrote seven articles for the *New York World* at three hundred dollars each. She began writing her book *My Disillusionment with Russia,* and found that while conservatives still despised her as an enemy, many of her old allies on the Left now condemned her as an apostate. In 1924, during the brief period of the first Labour government in England, she was given a temporary visa. The novelist Rebecca West organized a dinner for this most celebrated of radicals, and 250 of the leading figures of the British Left attended. After she spoke of her dismay at Russia, she sat down in total silence, broken only by the solitary applause of the philosopher Bertrand Russell. Professor Harold Laski of the London School of Economics, a future chairman of the Labour party, invited her to his home to inform her that Labour feared that attacks on the Bolsheviks were "an adventure on which [we] should not at any cost embark."

At least her English trip secured her a passport, after an old and widowed miner, James Colton, came down to London for two days, offering to go through a marriage ceremony with Emma and thus secure British citizenship for her. Until the civil war in Spain came to galvanize her into renewed effort as the overseas voice of the Spanish anarchists, political life was passing her by, even as Stalin's vicious purges were fulfilling Emma's darkest forebodings of the course of the Russian Revolution. Between writing her memoirs and giving lectures, she and Berkman tried and failed to run a holiday camp in the south of France and toyed with the idea of opening a vegetarian restaurant. When Emma was seventy, with her anarchist comrades in the streets of Barcelona being hunted down and shot by Communists acting on Stalin's orders, the anarchist leader Marino Vasquez fled to Paris and sent her a telegram hailing her as "our spiritual mother."

She died in 1940, in Canada, as her old nemesis J. Edgar Hoover was turning to new enemies of the state, Nazi sympathizers. As head of the FBI from 1924 until his death in 1972, Hoover could boast of being the most powerful man in the United States. Presidents came and went; Hoover seemed to be forever. Certified by the Gallup polling organization to be one of the ten most respected Americans of the day, he modernized the practice of law enforcement, founding the world's largest fingerprint file, its most sophisticated crime laboratory, and a training academy. He had come far since the destruction of Emma Goldman became the springboard to his career. In everything, they were opposites. She was warm, whereas he was cold; open, whereas he was secretive; and, throughout her career, committed to her vision of freedom, whereas he dedicated his life to control. She made no secret of her loves and her passions; Hoover, it now appears, sought desperately to conceal his homosexuality, although some sources suggest that both the Central Intelligence Agency and organized crime figures kept the FBI at bay with photographs of Hoover engaged in oral sex with his lifelong friend and deputy, Clyde Tolson.

Sixty years after her death, Emma remains a global symbol of feminism and of anarchism, a woman who was always honest and often right, most notably in her early and principled condemnation of the Bolshevik perversion of the Russian Revolution. Thirty years after his death, Hoover remains a deeply problematic figure of the American century. The ideas of the American dissidents whom he persecuted, from Emma to Martin Luther King, Jr., from the antiwar protesters of 1917 to their descendants of the 1960s who campaigned against an undeclared war, have triumphed, or been judged largely legitimate voices of protest. There were mortal dangers to the American state, and Nazi spies bent on sabotage in the 1940s and Communist spies bent on subversion and the theft of atomic secrets in the 1940s and 1950s evidently merited the counterespionage work of the FBI. Democracies have a right to defend themselves. But it is the cardinal duty of a secret policeman in a democracy to be utterly clear on the difference between those who seek to destroy the state and those who seek to improve it, between the spies and the critics, the subversives and the activists. In his persecution of Emma Goldman, Hoover failed that crucial test, and America was the poorer for it.

3.
"Black Jack" Pershing
and the American Army

On September 29, 1918, in the closing weeks of World War I, the French prime minister, Georges Clemenceau, drove toward the newly liberated town of Montfaucon to see for himself the glorious feat of his long-awaited allies in the American First Army. They had joined the war almost eighteen months earlier, but only now were they able to mobilize and deploy the vast armies required by the great charnel house of the Western Front, which stretched over four hundred miles, from the Swiss border to the North Sea coast, on the last morsel of Belgium not occupied by the German army. Nearly 10 million troops were deployed on the Western Front, and 4 million had died there.

The Americans' great offensive had opened the Battle of the Argonne just three days before Clemenceau's visit. With the support of 3,000 guns and 189 tanks, almost 400,000 Americans were launched into the attack on a forty-mile front, more men than had been deployed on both sides at the Battle of Gettysburg in the Civil War. Unlike most offensives of trench warfare, the American offensive began with stunning success, advancing six miles on the first day. Over twelve thousand prisoners were taken, and nearly two hundred German guns. Fit and fresh, their morale in exuberant contrast to the exhaustion of the British and French Allies after four years of war, the Americans carried a promise of the boundless reserves of manpower that their nation was sending to the Western Front at a rate of eight thousand a day. Clemenceau was naturally delighted to see and applaud their success.

But "the Tiger," as the French called their aggressive premier, arrived in the middle of disaster. He never got to the town of Montfaucon. He was blocked by the enormous traffic jam of U.S. reinforcements and supplies trying to get up to the front and by the artillery moving forward to new positions. The guns alone needed three thousand tons of shells a day, brought up by trucks and by ninety thousand mules and horses. The traffic jam lasted twelve hours before the military police could finally restore order on the shell-torn and inadequate roads.

Worse was happening ahead. Col. Charles Grant, a British liaison officer, reported that American wounded were dying of thirst where they lay, unable to be taken back to the casualty clearing stations because of the monstrous logistical tangle. He reported being told that four hundred U.S. troops died of starvation on a battlefield so dense with woods and thickets that U.S. general Hunter Liggett of I Corps described it as "a natural fortress beside which the Virginia wilderness in which Grant and Lee fought was a park."

After the triumphant six-mile advance of the first day, the Americans took another twenty-one days to advance just three more miles before their offensive sputtered to a halt. The official U.S. military history records: "The reasons for the collapse of the initial assault, other than stubborn enemy resistance, were numerous. Tank support proved ineffective, and supply broke down because of congestion and poor roads. More important was the inexperience of the divisions that were receiving their first taste of battle. Three had to be replaced by veteran outfits as soon as a lull in the battle permitted."

The man who had led them into this battle, Gen. John Pershing, might never have been given command but for a heart attack that struck down the country's best-known soldier, Gen. Frederick Funston, six weeks before the United States declared war. One of Funston's last acts had been to accuse Pershing of a disastrous blunder at the Battle of Carrizal, a small engagement in Mexico on June 21, 1916, in which ten U.S. cavalry troopers died and twenty-three were captured.

Pershing had been given command of a cavalry unit sent to hunt down the revolutionary bandit Pancho Villa, whose band had raided the New Mexican border town of Columbus in March 1916. With 6,600 men, Pershing rode over five hundred grueling miles south into Mexico in the vain hunt for the bandit. It was not a triumphant operation. Carrizal was the site of the fiercest action his men saw, a foolish uphill charge by two understrength and outnumbered cavalry troops against Mexican forces who were themselves also opposed to Pancho Villa. After that folly, Pershing's men simply remained in northern Mexico for seven months, until the politicians reached a settlement, and then the troops rode home.

It was an extraordinary change from this inglorious cavalry expedition to Pershing's new assignment in the muddy trenches of the Western Front. He was soon to command 2 million men. But any other American commander would have faced an equivalent shock. Born in Missouri on the eve of the Civil War, John Joseph Pershing embodied the transformation of the army from a small frontier force fighting against the Apache to colonial police in the Philippines, from border defense and cavalry raids against Mexico to world war. His career culminated in leading the first million-strong army the United States had ever deployed overseas, the moment when the nation established itself as a world power. In his time as an officer, the army's offensive power multiplied literally a hundredfold. In the great battle of his infancy, the Union forces fired forty thousand shells at Gettysburg; American artillery would fire 4 million in the Saint-Mihiel salient in 1918. By the time Pershing died in 1948, the atomic age had begun.

No other figure in the armed forces had undergone such a series of revolutionary changes, not only in the art of war but in the nature of American power. When Pershing graduated from West Point in 1886 at the age of twenty-five, after a brief experiment as a teacher, the American navy was outnumbered by the fleets of Sweden, Turkey, and Holland. The army numbered just 26,000 men. There were five regiments of artillery, twenty-five of infantry, and ten cavalry regiments, whose troops were stationed in the one arena where action, glory, and promotion were to be had. Pershing had been too young to know much of the Civil War, and the military life first captured his imagination at the age of fifteen, when the news came of the defeat of Gen. George Custer by the Sioux tribes and their allies at the Battle of the Little Bighorn. Pershing joined the cavalry, leaving West Point for the familiar trail to Fort Leavenworth in Kansas and the West, to spend nearly twelve years on frontier duty against the Sioux and the Apache.

Two of the cavalry units, the Ninth and Tenth regiments, recruited African-American troopers, nicknamed "buffalo soldiers." Pershing joined the Tenth, which legend says was the origin of his nickname, "Black Jack." Like the rest of the cavalry, their main task was to protect the westward expansion of the nation. Their foes, although poorly equipped and untrained in formal warfare, were magnificent horsemen and formidable guerrillas. But the Indian wars were almost over. Geronimo, the last of the war-band leaders, surrendered in the year that Pershing left West Point. Crazy Horse was killed in 1887 and Sitting Bull in 1890. Pershing saw little action, endured the grim tedium of frontier garrisons, and was seldom overworked. There was little money and less glory in the grinding and dusty duty of the West, and with an eye to changing his career, he found time to take a law degree at the University of Nebraska. This was unusual in an army that was beginning to stir with plans of reform and modernization, and he was summoned first to Washington and then posted back to West Point as an instructor in tactics.

To stay with the army was a thoughtful decision. The closing of the western frontier and the end of one kind of military life was but one of a series of decisive transitions for the country. The United States had just surpassed the traditional industrial leader, Great Britain, in the production of iron and steel. Already a great trading nation, it had become uncomfortably aware of the vulnerability of its ships and coastline to foreign naval power. "The big, fat Republic that is afraid of nothing because nothing up to the present date has happened to make her afraid, is as unprotected as a jellyfish," noted Rudyard Kipling, laureate of British imperialism, in 1891. In his annual message at the end of that year, President Benjamin Harrison noted, "It is essential to the dignity of this nation and to that peaceful influence which it should exercise on this hemisphere that its Navy should be adequate upon both the shores of the Pacific and the Atlantic."

Harrison was responding less to Kipling than to two American authors. The first was the young New York politician Theodore Roosevelt, who had published *The Naval War of 1812*. The book's popular success led the professor of naval history at the new War College, Capt. Alfred Thayer Mahan, to invite Roosevelt to give a lecture to officers. One of Mahan's own books, *The Influence of Sea Power upon History,* had been published in 1890 to international acclaim. More than a best-seller, the book was a revolution. He was lionized in Britain and awarded honorary degrees by the venerable universities of Oxford and Cambridge in the same week. The German and Japanese navies translated it for their own officers. Mahan's analysis of sea power as the guarantor of trade and wealth, in peace as well as in wartime, inspired the German Kaiser to challenge British naval supremacy with a German high-seas fleet. And it inspired Americans as well: politicians and the general public, steel magnates and their employees, who saw vast contracts in building a fleet, and the new media magnates, who saw patriotism and the navy as splendid causes.

A series of political crises in the 1890s, each of which showed the degree to which the young republic was already outgrowing its continent, illustrated the need for an American navy fit to challenge the traditional European sea powers. The sugar magnates of Hawaii, plotting successive coups to overthrow the Hawaiian tribal monarchy and annex the islands to the United States, demanded a fleet. The obscure border crisis between Venezuela and British Guiana pointed to the emptiness of American influence on its own hemisphere so long as the Royal Navy ruled the waves. The British government was baffled and alarmed by the public clamor that greeted the crisis, which it hastened to resolve. Theodore Roosevelt was one of the loudest voices for war, carelessly declaring, "Whether our seacoast cities are bombarded or not, we would take Canada." The rebellion in Cuba against the Spanish colonial masters rammed home the fact that without a major fleet, the United States would be able to do no more than watch a ramshackle and third-rate European power impose its will in the American home waters of the Caribbean.

The Spanish-American War, which came in 1898, spurred by the robust ambitions of politicians and media magnates, revealed the difficulty of a powerful navy with only a pitifully small army to deploy ashore. Sapped by years of guerrilla war, the Spanish army in Cuba was one of the few European forces of the day that could have been beaten by what was essentially an Indian-fighting army. The cavalry charge up Kettle Hill at San Juan by Teddy Roosevelt and his Rough Riders and John Pershing and his regular cavalry and the buffalo soldiers of the Tenth Regiment was a glorious affair; it should have been a disaster, had the inefficient Spanish commanders, with 200,000 troops on the island, been able to concentrate more than 1,700 troops at the battlefield of San Juan. But for every one of the 286 Americans killed in battle in Cuba, 14 died of disease. The army's logistic capabilities were pitiful. The volunteers who gathered in Florida for the invasion lacked guns, ammunition, uniforms, and medical supplies.

Before laying aside his job as assistant secretary of the navy to raise his Rough Rider regiment, Roosevelt's last official act had been to order Commodore Dewey to take the war to Spain's possessions in the Pacific, the Philippines. After the brisk victory of the Battle of Manila Bay, the army found itself with a task it was almost wholly unsuited to perform. To defeat the dispirited Spanish forces in Cuba was one thing; to occupy and police a restive native population who had been fighting for their own liberation against the Spaniards was quite another. The American republic lost a kind of virginity in the Philippines, in its first occupation of hostile overseas soil. And some of America's most eminent figures, from Mark Twain to former president Grover Cleveland, from steel magnate Andrew Carnegie to labor leader Samuel Gompers, from William James to Senator "Pitchfork Ben" Tillman, formed the Anti-Imperialist League to oppose it. Over 500,000 Americans joined them. The national flag, Twain suggested, should now have its white stripes painted black and the stars replaced by a skull and crossbones.

It was a filthy war, marked by atrocities on both sides, with American prisoners buried alive and Filipino villages burned and their inhabitants put into concentration camps. Guerrilla suspects were routinely questioned with water torture. Col. Frederick Funston was hailed as a hero in the Hearst press when he vowed to "rawhide these bullet-headed Asians until they yell for mercy, and not block the bandwagon of Anglo-Saxon progress and decency." The troops found that their Krag rifles were not powerful enough to stop a charging Moro tribesman, and they used dumdum bullets instead. And they sang, "Damn, damn, damn the Filipino/Civilize him with a Krag."

It was the kind of war that changes an army, and Pershing, with the rank of captain, was one of 75,000 in the occupation force. This was three times larger than the regular army had been before America's first imperial war. It remained something of a family affair. Pershing served under Gen. Arthur MacArthur, father of the young Douglas MacArthur, whom Pershing would decorate and promote to brigadier general on the battlefields of France. The army bureaucracy still sought to award promotions by seniority rather than for merit, fighting the reform efforts of the secretary of war, Elihu Root, a lawyer appointed to reorganize the enlarged force on rational, modern lines. He introduced a general staff and established the Army War College to train them, and he tried to establish a new enlistment system—two years in the ranks and eight in the reserves—to build a large reserve army. But the powerful political lobby behind the National Guard, composed of state militias, defeated this.

America was building her strength, but the priority was sea power and a powerful fleet that could take advantage of the new Panama Canal project to become a two-ocean navy. The army's priority was markedly lower, in part because of the maritime passions of President Roosevelt. But Roosevelt had a soft spot for his comrades in arms from the glorious charge up San Juan Hill, and Pershing was an astute officer who knew how to make the best of his political connections. A trim and stern-jawed bachelor of forty-five in 1905, known as a tough disciplinarian who would share the most rugged conditions with his troops, Pershing married the daughter of Senator Francis Warren of Wyoming. President Roosevelt attended the ceremony, and the following year he broke with military tradition to leap Pershing over eight hundred more senior officers and promote him directly from captain to brigadier general.

Pershing was not the only favored fellow veteran of Roosevelt's battle in Cuba. Leonard Wood, the army surgeon who rose to command the Rough Riders, was made military governor of Cuba and then commanding general in the Philippines. In 1910, he was appointed army chief of staff, whereupon he tried to revive Root's plan to turn the army from a small frontier and colonial police force into a body that could generate large reserves and expand quickly in time of need. Wood's problem was the new president, William Howard Taft, who blithely declared that America's defense arrangements were wholly adequate, since "there is not the slightest prospect of a war in any part of the world in which the United States could conceivably have a part." Despite Wood's efforts, when the Mexican Revolution broke out in 1910, he was only able slowly and with great difficulty to assemble a full division of regular troops to watch the Mexican border. His main legacy was to support the experiment in 1913 of a summer training camp at the Plattsburg, New York, barracks, where civilians could learn something of army life. The "Plattsburg idea" proved popular and spread across the country, with great benefit to the National Guard. As war broke out in Europe in 1914, the camps helped above all to create a constituency for American preparedness, a development that proved essential in the battle of public opinion that the war was to provoke.

The hard fact was that the army of 1914 could not really have intervened in the European war, even had the politicians wished it. It was too small, underequipped in artillery, and had too few reserves to sustain a long campaign. General Wood resigned from the army in 1914 in order to lead the campaign that would transform it, prepare America for her new status as a great power, and launch him on a political career. According to a letter to Wood from the ambitious young Capt. Douglas MacArthur, the campaign "can have but one ending—the White House." Wood stumped the country, badgered the government, put pressure on Congress, and in 1916, when Pershing was scouring Mexico for Pancho Villa, his campaign secured a kind of victory with the National Defense Act. This allowed the president, with authorization from Congress, to mobilize the National Guard under federal command for the duration of an emergency, and it stressed the principle that all able-bodied men from eighteen to forty-five were eligible for military service. It also authorized the expansion of the regular army to 288,000 men, in sixty-five infantry, twenty-five cavalry, and twenty-one artillery regiments.

These force levels were not achieved by the time the United States went to war. In April 1917, the United States opened hostilities with a regular army of 5,000 officers and 123,000 men, with another 8,500 officers and 123,000 men in the National Guard. Within eighteen months, their numbers were to increase twentyfold. Indeed, by the end of the war, U.S. forces had lost more men as casualties than they had troops when war broke out. And even when the soldiers got to France, they were dreadfully ill-prepared. They even lacked boots; young MacArthur recorded tracing the path of his troops by the blood their feet left on the snow.

America Reborn

The future chief of staff of the army, George C. Marshall, recalled:

When we embarked I discovered—and I was a member of the general staff of the division—that we had units in the division of which I had never heard. There was very little literature on the war as it was then conducted. We had one small English pamphlet, a single copy of which we studied conscientiously. Landing at St. Nazaire, I was immediately sent on a circuit of the division. I discovered that of the 200 men to a company, approximately 180 were raw recruits. I found that some of these new units not only did not have their weapons but the men themselves had never heard of them.

Under such circumstances, the surprise was that the American troops fought as well as they did. The regular troops, like the marines who stopped the German attack at Château-Thierry, were excellent. But most divisions were painfully raw, and they paid the price for their military education in blood. The stalled attacks and giant bottlenecks at Saint-Mihiel and in the Argonne came as no surprise to the Allies. The French had provided veteran English-speaking officers to teach the new arrivals something of the new arts of war in an industrial age. Modern warfare meant machine guns and barbed wire and "creeping" artillery barrages that were timed to move forward at a rate of a hundred yards every four minutes to give fire cover to the assault troops. Pershing, the U.S. commander, decided to dispense with the services of the French experts in order to make the battle into an American affair.

The British sent their finest trainer of troops, Gen. Ivor Maxse, to impart the new lessons of small-unit tactics, in which grenades and light machine guns replaced rifles and where soldiers advanced in small groups and short rushes, rather than in the parade-ground ranks in which sixty thousand British troops had been shot down on the first day of the 1916 Battle of the Somme. The Americans welcomed him politely but took little heed of a representative of an army that had repeatedly failed to break the German defenses. "Platoon commanders never took their men out to practice handling them," Maxse reported after his inspection of the Americans. "They admit their heavy losses in recent operations were due to 'bald-headed tactics' and the desire of everyone to rush through, regardless of cost. They admit that their support, reserve and front-line units were all mixed due to reinforcing every check in the line. Their Q [logistics] work was poor, with orders received late or not at all." The American brigadiers were, he said, "impossible—too old," and "the officers with few exceptions knew nothing and would learn nothing." The troops, Maxse concluded, were excellent, "keen and brave," and with the wit to make their own inquiries of the French, British, and Australian veterans on ways to fight and survive this kind of war. Finally, Maxse noted, there seemed to be a complete breakdown of the U.S. medical services and no reliable system of supplying frontline troops beyond their battalion headquarters.

Pershing, the man ultimately responsible, was baffled by the sudden reversal of his initial triumph in the Argonne offensive. On October 14, he confided to his private diary: "I hope for better results tomorrow. There is no particular reason for this hope, except that if we keep on pounding, the Germans will be obliged to give way."

That was the authentic voice of World War I generalship, the traditional military skills of command and of maneuver rendered helpless by the unique nature of the Western Front battlefield. Like Britain's Gen. Douglas Haig before him, Pershing was left with only the bloody calculus of attrition—"if we keep on pounding." Pershing was not alone in this reaction. He was treading the same awful path that the German high command had pioneered in October 1914, when they sent that year's graduation classes from German universities into untrained assaults against the skilled riflemen of the professional British army. Some dressed in gowns and mortarboards, their reserve officers on horseback, waving them on with swords, they were shot down in the thousands in what the German army called *"Der Kindermord von Ypern,"* meaning "the massacre of the innocents at Ypres." The French had learned the same dreadful lesson in the forlorn battles of the frontiers in August and September of 1914, and again at Verdun and on the Chemin des Dames. The British had to learn it at the Somme and in Flanders.

Traditional forms of warfare had been destroyed by the combination of trenches, barbed wire, and artillery. But there were new weapons, such as tanks and poison gas, and new tactics, which could achieve success through the combination of careful artillery preparation and the small-unit attacks of storm troops, in which General Maxse was training the British. General Byng's Canadian Corps had used them with stunning success to capture Vimy Ridge in 1917. Under General Hutier at the siege of Riga, the Germans developed their own version, and they had perfected them for their great attacks of March 1918. The storm troopers with their grenades, man-hauled small artillery pieces, and the fearsome new flamethrowers had almost broken the British army and pushed it back for thirty miles.

These tactics required meticulous preparation: recalibrating every gun to allow for the deterioration of the barrel and factoring in wind and barometric conditions to ensure the shells fell where they should. They required intense training of the troops and a kind of industrial revolution at home to turn out the machine guns, artillery, and ammunition in sufficient quantities. New forms of quality control had to be introduced at factories to ensure that the shells were of an exactly uniform dimension. The troops would have no faith in a creeping barrage whose shells were unpredictable.

In some ways, the Americans learned this lesson well. One of the main reasons for the British disasters at the Somme and at Passchendale was that the army was woefully underequipped in modern arms. The French deployed three times as many machine guns, as well as more than twice as many heavy guns for each infantry division. The best British troops, the Australians and Canadians, insisted their units be properly equipped. In May 1918, the Supreme War Council found that the British deployed one machine gun for every sixty-one men, while the French deployed one for every twelve soldiers and the Canadians one for every thirteen. The Americans deployed one for every twenty-seven soldiers.

Moreover, the Americans had some commanders of genius. MacArthur was made a brigadier for his efforts with his "Rainbow Division." The future general George Patton was learning the arts of armored warfare in a French-built tank. The father of U.S. military airpower, Col. William Mitchell, who had joined up as a private in the Spanish-American War, assembled an air fleet of sixteen hundred warplanes to attack the German lines and strafe their reinforcement columns. He even arranged airdrops of ammunition for the advanced American units, which had run ahead of their own supplies. Pershing had only been able to launch his Argonne offensive because his brilliant young staff colonel, George C. Marshall, had been able to organize the transfer back of some 400,000 men from the Battle of Saint-Mihiel, which had also ended in logistic confusion ten days earlier.

But the overall performance of the American armies was a disappointment. Much—indeed, almost everything—had been expected from them, in industrial production as much as in manpower, by the exhausted British and French troops. "Everyone felt that the Americans were present at the magical operation of blood transfusion. Life arrived in torrents to revive the mangled body of a France bled white by the countless wounds of four years," recorded the French writer Jean de Pierrefeu.

But without that exhausted France, the Americans could not have fought. Almost all of the artillery they deployed at the battles of Saint-Mihiel and the Argonne was French, and the rest was supplied by the British. And almost half of the artillery supporting the U.S. offensive was served by French gunners. The transport trucks were British and French, and the French also supplied 130,000 horses. The tanks were made by the British and the French. Most of the American troops had crossed the Atlantic on British ships. For all the efforts and native inventiveness in the United States, not a single American-made warplane fought on the Western Front. Billy Mitchell and

Eddie Rickenbacker, who became America's leading fighter ace after starting the war as Pershing's driver, flew French Spads.

The reason for this was simple: the shortage of space aboard ships crossing the Atlantic. German U-boats were taking such a dreadful toll that when the United States entered the war, Britain was down to less than two months' supply of food. The Americans could ship men, or they could ship equipment, but not both. As the German offensives of the spring of 1918 threatened the Allies with defeat, fresh American troops were the priority. And they came in legions, 2,086,000 of them by the end of the war, in thirty combat divisions, each of them containing 28,000 men—twice as large as the average British or German division.

This was the largest military force that the United States had ever raised, and it had done so with only a tiny standing army. West Point could not begin to churn out the leaders required, so special schools were established to train the 200,000 officers. And an army of this size, which for the first time qualified the United States to join the ranks of the traditional great powers of Europe, was deemed from the beginning to be an American instrument, under American command, and deployed on American terms.

But the first arrivals were eager to get into the fray, even though two American brigades were badly mauled when they took a brief part in the predominantly British battle fought at Passchendale. Moreover, the emergency of the German attacks of the spring and early summer of 1918, when the German advances threatened both the Channel ports and Paris, required panic measures. The newly arrived American divisions were thrust into the line wherever it threatened to break. Five divisions were sent to the British front, and fourteen were patched almost at random into the French line. Marines and the U.S. Second Division helped stop the German attack at Château-Thierry, just forty miles from Paris, and took dreadful casualties in the counterattack to take Belleau Wood.

Pershing's plan had initially called for the American army, as a coherent unit, to take over the line from the Swiss border to Saint-Mihiel, on the approaches to Verdun. Their lines of communication were to stretch back to the ports on the Bay of Biscay in order to prevent American logistics from hampering those of the British at the Channel ports. But as soon as the crisis passed, Pershing insisted that the American troops finally be gathered into a single force, under his command, to prepare America's first independent battle at Saint-Mihiel.

This led to a serious political crisis for the Allies. The supreme Allied commander, Marshal Foch, had initially agreed to Pershing's plan. But circumstances changed. On August 8, with their tanks and new tactics, the

British broke through the Hindenburg line in an attack that the German commander Erich von Ludendorff called "the black day of the German field army." Then the British and French attacked at the Somme, again with success, and from the numbers of prisoners taken and the state of their morale, Foch suspected that the German army's will to resist was finally cracking. *"Tout le monde à la bataille,"* he instructed, ordering everyone to attack at once. This included the Americans, whom he asked to defer their solitary battle at Saint-Mihiel and cooperate with the French in a bigger attack on the Argonne front. When the two men met on August 30, Pershing refused.

Pershing's memoirs describe the confrontation:

> Marshal Foch then said "do you wish to take part in the battle?" I replied "Most assuredly, but as an American army and in no other way." I was provoked to say: "Marshal Foch, you have no authority as allied commander-in-chief to call upon me to yield up my command of the American army and have it scattered among the Allied forces where it will not be an army at all."
>
> He was apparently surprised at my remark and said "I must insist upon the arrangement," to which I replied, as we both rose from the table where we sat, "Marshal Foch, you may insist all you please, but I decline absolutely to agree to your plan. While our army will fight wherever you decide, it will not fight except as an independent American army."

After what the French saw as the failure of Pershing's Argonne offensive, Clemenceau wrote to Foch, suggesting that they ask Washington to recall the stubborn American, on the grounds that "General Pershing refused to obey your orders." Foch, perhaps wiser in the ways of alliance diplomacy than his prime minister, said he would find ways of working with the Americans. And Foch knew that Pershing's orders from Washington indeed called for him to deploy his forces and lead them into action as an American army.

But Clemenceau had a point. In his view, the Americans were not pulling their weight:

> The French and British armies, without a moment's respite, have been fighting daily for the past three months battles which are consuming them at a time when it is impossible for us to reinforce them with fresh reserves of manpower. These two armies are pressing back the enemy with an ardor that excites worldwide admiration. But our worthy American allies, who thirst to get into action and are unanimously acknowledged to be great soldiers, have been marking time

ever since their forward jump on the first day. And in spite of heavy losses, they have failed to conquer the ground assigned to them as their objective. Nobody can maintain that these fine troops are unusable; they are merely unused.

It was an encounter in which all three men were right. Given their size and freshness, the American forces were not meeting Clemenceau's expectations. Foch was sensible in not pressing the matter to a political breach; alliance leaders must find ways to work with the tools they have. Pershing was indeed carrying out the orders of his government and the wishes of his people, that the Americans take part in the war as equals, rather than as an adjunct to the veteran British and French troops.

Pershing had made the point clear in a letter to Foch when first told that the Saint-Mihiel attack would be scaled back: "I can no longer agree to any plan which involves the dispersion of our units," he wrote. "Briefly, our officers and soldiers alike are, after one experience, no longer willing to be incorporated into other armies." The lessons of Passchendale and Château-Thierry had been hard-won. And Pershing knew that in raising the morale of the battered Allies, and depressing that of the equally exhausted Germans, the arrival of U.S. troops was indeed crucial. Pershing had a right to lead his men on his own, American terms.

Politically, and speaking for Americans as an ally of equal status, Pershing was evidently right. And given the less than decisive military role played by the U.S. forces, this may have been his most important historical achievement. The Americans had entered the war intent on ending it justly, in a way that would establish a new international order in which the traditional dynastic wars of Europe and the jostlings of the Great Powers would find no place. For the U.S. government, the war was a crusade as well as a clash of arms; their troops were liberators more than cannon fodder. And thus their general was more than just a military commander, more even than a highly politicized officer who could learn to play the hard diplomacy of alliance politics. He was the custodian of the American idea, the symbol of an army that was meant to be different because its nation and its war aims were different, battling in a significantly less nationalist cause. He was, in that sense, a very different kind of soldier from his peers on both sides of the Western Front. But given his background, he had to be.

The first American general since George Washington to fight alongside allies as part of a politically delicate coalition, Pershing established the crucial precedent that was to govern American military strategy for the remainder of the century: that U.S. troops could in a desperate emergency be placed under foreign command, but wherever and whenever possible, they must fight as a specifically American army. The first American since Gen. Ulysses Grant to command over a million troops in the field, Pershing was the first to take such a force overseas, pioneering the way for what was to become with World War II and the long confrontation of the Cold War an almost routine foreign assignment for the American military. He set the pattern for the way in which an essentially civilian America would develop and exercise its military potential, using the small nucleus of career officers and NCOs as cadres around which the flood of National Guard units and new recruits could be built into a mass army. In 1940, Pershing's former aide and successor as chief of staff, General Marshall, was to turn back to the Pershing memoirs (which he had ghostwritten) and to Pershing's papers to recall just how the great enterprise had been achieved, the transformation of a small professional army of fewer than 200,000 men into a nation in arms.

The lessons and traditions that Pershing bequeathed to the army endured until World War II. But there they stopped. Pershing had pleaded with the White House and Congress to slow the wholesale demobilization in 1919 of the vast army he had built and led. The reduction should be planned, he urged, to ensure that a new emergency could allow a faster and more efficient expansion to re-create the massive force he commanded at the time of the German surrender. This was a matter of equipment as much as men; never again should U.S. troops have to go to battle dependent on foreign guns, foreign transport, foreign tanks, and foreign aircraft. This was not advice that President Wilson, convinced that he fought "the war to end wars," cared to hear. The army was slashed almost immediately back to its prewar size and shrunken responsibilities, and the crisis of renewed war in Europe twenty years later was to find it slow and ill equipped to rebuild America's military strength. It was a lesson that peace-loving democracies had to learn again and again. Despite Marshall's efforts to maintain a core army capable of swift expansion after 1945, and a Congress and White House far more attuned to the new perils of the Cold War, the Korean War in 1950 found the military once more undermanned and barely equipped to respond. In that sense, the Pershing era ended when the nation accepted that America's new global responsibilities required a permanent military establishment of some 2 million troops, ten times the size of the peacetime forces Pershing had commanded.

4.
Henry Ford and the American System

Henry Ford was a maverick inventor and entrepreneur rather than a capitalist, with all the virtues and prejudices of the old and isolationist Midwest. He hated Wall Street even more than he loathed labor unions. He distrusted stocks and shares and therefore resolved to keep his company private. He refused to join associations of industrialists, suspecting that they conspired against innovation, just as the other car manufacturers of Detroit tried to use patent law to block his infant company. He was hailed as a hero in the infant Soviet Union, the first major American industrialist to invest there. And although his cars were perhaps the principal instrument in the destruction of the traditional way of life, the project dearest to his elderly heart was the building of Greenfield Village.

Today, it might be called "a heritage center," a loving reconstruction of a preindustrial village, from which cars were banned and visitors toured in horse-drawn carts. When he built it in the 1930s, from a sixteenth-century Cotswold cottage dismantled in England and carefully rebuilt outside Dearborn, Michigan, complete with a flock of Cotswold sheep and the reconstructed building where Abraham Lincoln had practiced law, it was seen as a rich man's whim. The only car allowed was kept in a barn on the outskirts of the village, the first car Ford ever built. On occasion, dripping fuel into its cylinder feed from an eyedropper, he would start the engine and watch it run. The place was also a shrine to his hero, friend, and early employer, Thomas Edison, whose Menlo Park workshop in New Jersey was lovingly rebuilt in Ford's own magic kingdom.

The man who built the quintessential machine of the modern industrial economy, which would not have been possible without the assembly-line technique he developed, was a revolutionary who found as if by instinct the way to refute Karl Marx's prediction that a mass working class would revolt against its exploitation and its misery. Quite simply, Ford realized that there was little point producing a million cars a year unless there were a million consumers. Mass production required a mass market, which meant that ordinary people, farmers and workers, had to be able to buy them. Ford, to the outrage of his fellow employers, paid his workers unheard-of sums. John Gunther, the author of the classic and best-selling compendiums *Inside Europe* and *Inside U.S.A.,* suggested that of the two seminal events of 1914, the outbreak of World War I and Ford's announcement of a five-dollar-a-day minimum wage, he suspected Ford's pay rate might in the long run be the more significant.

"Most of the babies of the period were conceived in a Model T Ford, and not a few were born in them," suggested the novelist John Steinbeck, tongue not entirely in cheek. The Model T was in itself a social revolution, the culmination and the catalyst for a series of dramatic changes that defined the twentieth century. The private car required an oil industry with a distribution and retail system that could put a gasoline pump in every small town and village across the country. Roads were needed to connect the gas stations, and dealerships to sell the cars and a far-flung army of mechanics to ensure that they kept running. The automobile transformed the face of the American countryside, making the horse redundant and forcing farmers to grow new crops to replace the hay the horses used to eat. It force-fed a financial revolution to provide the decentralized credit system that allowed customers to buy them; they did so in such numbers that the Model T itself refuted that gloomy 1906 political vision of Woodrow Wilson: "Nothing has spread socialist feeling in this country more than the automobile—they are a picture of the arrogance of wealth with all its independence and carelessness."

Ford was born one of eight children on a Michigan farm in 1863. Abraham Lincoln was president, the Civil War still raged, and fewer than one

American in five lived in a city. By the time of Ford's death, eighty-three years later, two out of three Americans lived in urban households, and most of them had a car. He went to a one-room schoolhouse for eight years and spent his summers bringing in the harvest, a classic tale of the American farm boy who makes good. Or so he chose to remember, claiming that his great career began by leaving home to walk to Detroit to look for work at the age of sixteen, just three years after his mother died in childbirth. Her death was a stunning shock, but soon afterward, already fretting at his father's assumption that he stay on the farm, he became inspired. Driving with his father in a horse-and-buggy rig one day, he saw a steam engine proceeding toward him. "I remember that day as if it were yesterday," he told a court decades later, and he even recalled the 200 rpm that its driver told him was the engine speed. Fascinated, he left home for Detroit and found work as an apprentice in the Dry Dock Engine Works.

That was the legend. In fact, it seems that he got his first job with family friends in the Flower Brothers Machine Shop. After some months, he moved to Dry Dock, pioneers of metal shipbuilding and the Bessemer steel process. He then became a jobbing repairman of farm engines for Westinghouse, gave up the city, and moved back to the farm, where he married and then ran a timber business in the hard years of falling farm prices and agricultural depression. He remained a tinkerer, fascinated by machines and watches, building a homemade "farm locomotive" powered by steam. On occasion, he traveled to Detroit on business and once to examine one of the new gasoline engines. But when the timber had all been cut, what took him back to the city was not the engines but the even more thrilling new power of electricity. He got a job running the workshop at the Edison Illuminating Company, and in his spare time, he tinkered with scraps to make a gasoline engine of his own.

On June 4, 1896, he took his quadricycle for its first run, and it broke down, eliciting hoots of derision from the drunks outside the Cadillac Hotel. It was an extraordinary vehicle, essentially two bicycles side by side, with a seat, steering bar, and an engine. Much lighter than most other experimental cars, it could go much faster, up to twenty miles per hour. He attracted prominent local backers, and in 1899, with the mayor of Detroit among the investors, the Detroit Automobile Company was launched with capital of $150,000, and Ford as mechanical superintendent. It folded the following year. Ford claimed it was because he was a perfectionist, always looking to make a better car, rather than go into production with his successful prototype. And his tinkering was inspired, producing the first spark plug and developing a way to cast an engine block in two easily assembled halves.

His backers remained faithful when Ford's workshop produced another car in 1901, which stunned the small world of automobile enthusiasts by beating the then speed champion Alexander Winton in his 40-horsepower Winton Special in a ten-mile race. They put up sixty thousand dollars to found the Henry Ford Company, but the mechanic after whom it was named lasted only four months before he was let go with a nine-hundred-dollar settlement. Again, Ford wanted to keep on designing rather than manufacturing. The firm continued under a name that became famous as the Cadillac Automobile Company, manufacturing a car designed by Ford.

Another backer emerged, a local coal merchant named Alex Malcolmson, who installed a bookkeeper and production supervisor, James Couzens, who was able to keep Ford focused on his latest design, the Model A. Much of the manufacture was subcontracted to a machine shop run by the two Dodge brothers, John and Horace, who also became shareholders in the Ford Motor Company. Their first buyer on July 15, 1903, was a Dr. E. Phennig. He paid $850, when the infant company had only $223.65 in the bank. Within three months, the company was turning out twenty-five cars a day, and by the end of 1905, it was offering a range of cars, up to the two-thousand-dollar Model B. This was how most other small car manufacturers operated, and the way Malcolmson wanted to continue. But Ford was convinced that the future lay with cheap cars costing less than five hundred dollars, which could be sold in much greater numbers.

"I will build a motor car for the great multitude," Ford vowed. "It will be large enough for the family, but small enough for the individual to run and take care of. It will be constructed of the best materials, by the best men to be hired, after the simplest designs that modern engineering can devise. But it will be so low in price that no man making a good salary will be unable to own one."

He and Couzens launched the Ford Manufacturing Company, forced Malcolmson to sell out, and developed the Model N, which in 1907 sold for six hundred dollars and became an immediate success. Within eight months, they had sold 8,243 cars and had made a profit of $1 million, which was plowed back into the next project. The focus remained on lightness and speed, as it had with the original quadricycle. The breakthrough came when Ford read of a new lightweight French alloy, vanadium steel, which was far stronger than ordinary steel. That was used to make the crankshaft. Then Ford developed the magneto as an alternative to the dry battery for delivering sparks to the cylinders; he devised a way to insulate it with heavy varnish, stewed in maple-syrup kettles. Then Ford developed his new "planetary" system for lightweight gears, installed the huge and flexible springs to handle the bumps of dirt roads, and the Model T was born. When it went on sale in 1908, it was an immediate success, advance publicity generating a thousand inquiries a day. It cost $825, almost a year's pay for a schoolteacher, and ten thousand of them were sold within the first year.

"No car under $2,000 offers more," said the publicity campaign, and for a reliable and weatherproof family-size car, this was true. But it was also a sturdy and simple car, with interchangeable parts that could be fixed or replaced by a country blacksmith, for which the still-half-rural American market with its woeful roads had been waiting. On the Western Front of World War I, a Model T took Gertrude Stein about her duties as a volunteer nurse. Within ten years, half of all the cars running in the world were Model Ts. Ten years after that, when the production of the Model T finally stopped in 1928, over 15,500,000 had been sold in the United States, another 1 million in Canada, and 500,000 in Britain.

And all the time, the price of the Model T was ground relentlessly downward as Ford took to tinkering with the production process. By 1914, the car was selling for $440, and by 1924, the price was down below $300. In the first year of production, it took over twelve hours to assemble each car from the various components. By 1914, it could be done in ninety-three minutes. By 1925, a car was rolling off the assembly line every twenty-four seconds. It was not just that the Model T was a simple design of genius but also that Ford himself had become so much more than a classic American inventor with an entrepreneurial gift. He had become something far more crucial to America's eventual dominance of the manufacturing process. He had become, like a handful of gifted Americans around him in other new fields, such as electric power and oil refining, something altogether new and distinctive, developing a skill that took the old British industrial revolution to an entirely new dimension. Ford had become a systems engineer.

This, rather than the cars or the innovative designs or the vision that a mass market was out there waiting for them, was the essence of Ford's genius and of his significance. He saw the entire process—of design, manufacture, mass market—as a single system to be planned and managed. Ford's revolutionary Highland Park, Michigan, factory, known as the "Crystal Palace" because of its plentiful windows, may not have been the first example of systems design. The eighteenth-century British Royal Navy, with its mass-produced ships and cannon, its factories for ropes and sails and barrels, its professional officers and craftsmen, and its network of communications through coded flags, was the pioneer. But Ford slowly but surely incorporated his entire manufacturing system into the single new plant at Highland Park.

The grand design was not born overnight. There were separate assembly lines for the engines, the magnetos, and the transmissions, all converging into the final assembly shop. They were coming in such numbers that these subassemblies began to pile up too fast for the final assemblers to cope. So within the year, there was another assembly line for the chassis.

"Every piece of work in the shops moves. It may move on hooks, on overhead chains, it may travel on a moving platform or it may go by gravity, but the point is there is no lifting or trucking," Ford explained. "Save ten steps a day for each of 12,000 employees and you will have saved fifty miles of wasted motion and misspent energy."

Conveyor belts carried the identical and interchangeable parts to each of the assembly lines at precisely the point when the moving lines would be ready to receive them. Railway lines snaked into the plant, bringing coal and raw materials and the subcontracted items like the tires and upholstery. To avoid having to cast metal parts, he bought the Klein Company of Buffalo for its technology in stamping. When a strike stopped production, he shipped the giant stamping machines to Highland Park, got them working within three days, and incorporated them into what became a triple system: the inputs, the manufacture and output, and distribution through the chain of dealerships.

It was all designed to be run by unskilled labor, since, as was usual at the time, labor turnover was extraordinarily high. In 1913, it was running at 360 percent, which meant hiring over nine hundred men in order to keep one hundred. At Christmas 1913, when the company decided to award a special bonus to workers with three years of service, it was found that of 15,000 employees, only 640 qualified. That was the spur to the five-dollar-a-day breakthrough, a wage that meant a Ford assembly-line worker could buy one of his own products with thirty-two weeks' pay. The five dollars was not basic pay, and almost half of it came from a profit-sharing system. Along with the cash, the simultaneous Ford innovation that stunned business America was the reduction to an eight-hour day.

"Economic blunders if not crimes," thundered the *Wall Street Journal.* But there was method to Ford's apparent madness. Previously, his factory had run two nine-hour shifts a day. With an eight-hour day, it could run three shifts, thus increasing production yet further into a market still unappeasably hungry for more Model Ts.

Even as Highland Park was revolutionizing the nature of industrial production, Ford was planning the next great leap, the design of an even bigger and better and more comprehensively planned plant at River Rouge, Michigan. This infuriated his major stockholders, the Dodge brothers, who thought the expansion reckless and complained that the endless price-cutting was reducing their dividends. Although by now manufacturing cars of their own while still holding Ford stock, they took Ford to court in 1916, and on appeal in 1919, he lost the case. But then he bought out the Dodge brothers and five other major stockholders for the extraordinary sum of $106 million, plus over

$20 million in dividends. He reorganized the Ford Motor Company under a new charter, and he and his family held all the shares. Now there were no brakes on his ambition, and River Rouge went ahead.

Ford had been infuriated by the Highland Park plant's dependency on other suppliers, particularly when World War I meant shortages and delayed deliveries. He had been forced to accumulate large inventories, which added to his costs, so the River Rouge plant was designed to be virtually self-sufficient. Ford became an integrated company, buying sixteen coal mines, 700,000 acres of forest and sawmills, glass plants in Pennsylvania, and iron mines in Minnesota, as well as building the Ford ships and railroads, which carried all the necessary materials to River Rouge.

This was the Ford system, the product of his perception of the way supply and production, workforce and markets could all be measured, planned, and combined into a giant whole that led to the concept, as much social and political as industrial, that Germany and Soviet Russia came to call "Fordismus." It had many roots. One of the strongest came from the job that had attracted Ford to Detroit, the new market for electricity spurred by Edison's lighting system. Ford's boss had been Alex Dow, who went on to establish a national reputation as a utility manager in this strange new industry, whose product could not be stored. The supply of electricity always had to match demand, even though that demand varied with the time of day and the seasons of the year. It was not simply a matter of mass-producing energy; it also involved tailoring it to a variable market. The American way of doing so required the deliberate expansion of demand, which was accomplished by hiring hordes of door-to-door salesmen to sell the mushrooming household electrical appliances that required electricity.

There were several different ways of organizing the supply of electricity. In Britain until the 1920s, small and decentralized electricity companies generated large profits from a small number of customers. In Germany, large electricity companies focused on their big industrial clients and left the household market until later. In the United States, visionaries akin to Ford, such as Samuel Insull, a British immigrant who became Edison's personal secretary, built a system that generated vast profits, accumulating in tiny amounts from a massive number of customers. Hence the need to sell vacuum cleaners and washing machines, fans and refrigerators and electric irons. Until discredited at the time of the Wall Street crash of 1929, Insull rivaled Ford as one of the giants of modern industry. By the 1920s, with Commonwealth Edison, Peoples' Gas, Northern Illinois Public Service, and Midland of Indiana, Insull controlled a utilities conglomerate worth $3 billion. It had 600,000 stockholders and 4 million customers and produced 12 percent of the electricity and gas consumed in the United States. And he still found time to design Britain's

America Reborn

National Grid in the 1920s, when Insull's homeland realized that America was organizing its electricity system in a fundamentally different but far more rational way.

The international vogue for the ideas and manufacturing systems inherent in Fordismus was reinforced by Frederick Winslow Taylor, whose book *Principles of Scientific Management* was published in 1911. Within two years, it had been translated into Russian, German, French, Italian, Japanese, Swedish, Spanish, and Dutch. "In the past, man has been first; in the future, the system must be first" was the essence of Taylor's teaching.

Taylor came from a wealthy family of Philadelphia Quakers, went to Phillips Exeter Academy, joined the Philadelphia Cricket Club, and became a national tennis champion, but forwent a college education to become a shop-floor worker and then a foreman at the Midvale Steel Company. With the support of its president, William Sellers, an innovative engineer and designer of machine tools, Taylor resolved to demonstrate that he had learned on the shop floor how to make work more efficient. In 1882, he began measuring specific items of work with a stopwatch, thereby launching into a three-year battle with his suspicious fellow workers.

"My sympathies were with the workmen, and my duties lay to the people by whom I was employed," he told a congressional committee thirty years later. Taylorism was not simply a matter of measuring work and standardizing its component parts and then planning and timing a manufacturing process that took the division of labor to its logical conclusion. It included redesigning the work space, the work flow, and the machines and improving the lighting, ventilation, and working conditions, including the provision of toilets. It meant paying higher wages for higher output, with careful supervision and training. But like Ford's standardized car parts, Taylorism also meant the end of craftsmanship. Work was no longer a complete skill that took metal from raw ingot to finished tool, but instead a set of component actions that, with the right tools and training, could be executed by semi-skilled workers who had no need of a long apprenticeship.

"So there you are, wage-workers in general, mere machines—considered industrially of course," said the labor leader Samuel Gompers. "Not only your length, breadth and thickness as a machine, but your grade of hardness, malleability, tractability and general serviceability can be ascertained, registered and then employed as desirable. Science would thus get the most out of you before you are sent to the junkpile."

The twentieth century was to be shaped to an extraordinary degree by Taylor, Insull, and Ford, because the markets, the machine tools, a new kind of education, and a new kind of skill were all falling into place around them.

One key component was added the year before Ford's birth, when in 1862 Congress passed the Morrill Act to provide funds to states that would establish colleges for agriculture and for the mechanical arts. In 1870, there were 100 engineering graduates, but by 1914 4,300 were graduating annually from 126 engineering colleges. The number of American graduate engineers rose from 45,000 in 1900 to 230,000 by 1930, and increasingly included chemical and electrical engineers, each with their own professional association. By 1924, the great corporations of Du Pont, General Motors, General Electric, and Goodyear were run by four engineers who had been classmates at the Massachusetts Institute of Technology. Taylor was elected president of the American Society of Mechanical Engineers in 1906, although perhaps more for his work on metallurgy than on the theory of organization. From this pulpit, he spread the word of social transformation through systematic organization based on sound and proven engineering principles.

"The same principles [of scientific management] can be applied with equal force to all social activities, to the management of our homes, the management of our farms, the management of the business of our tradesmen large and small, of our churches, our philanthropic institutions, our universities and our government departments," Taylor preached.

A thrill of discovery, an almost messianic sense that at last humanity had found the key to organizing its progress into a new age, runs through the writings of Ford and Taylor. It runs as well through the work of those touched by them in the arts and letters. Artists, from the Italian Futurists to the Soviet Expressionists, celebrated the wonders of industrial design as the Renaissance had celebrated the human form.

"In all the constructions of man's past, there is nothing to equal these," said the Mexican artist Diego Rivera when he first laid eyes on the vast car plants of Detroit. Rivera had been commissioned by Ford's son, Edsel, to cover the interior courtyard of the Detroit Institute of Art with murals of the industry. Rivera saw America itself as the inspiration, as opposed to the faded grandeur of Europe. "Here it is—the might, the power, the sadness, the glory, the youthfulness of our lands."

Poets hailed the electricity pylons in England and the Maginitogorsk electric plant in Russia and the Grand Coulee Dam in the United States. Architects thrilled to the potential of design systems and rational new forms now made possible by the blending of steel and concrete, with so many new commissions coming for the giant new factories and the engineers and businessmen who made fortunes from them. Financiers hurried to harness the rivers of cash that ran through the electricity supply companies and the endlessly churning factories. And politicians rode this same tide, convinced, like

America Reborn

Teddy Roosevelt and Woodrow Wilson, that rational and planned reform could deliver prosperity and decent social conditions to an ever-swelling American population.

Everything seemed new and was made possible by these innovators of the American manufacturing system and the almost godlike systems engineers. Ford wanted to title one of his own books *The Great Today and the Even Greater Tomorrow* (until he was persuaded that *Today and Tomorrow* carried more punch). But the system was morally and politically neutral. It could produce terror as well as plenty, the autocracy of production as well as the democracy of the market. And the system proved particularly well suited to world war and to the Soviet state. Even as Ford got the Model T production time down to less than two hours, his assembly lines and Taylor's principles of work organization and quality control were being applied in the vast new munitions plants of Britain, France, and Germany to churn out the shells required for the Western Front. The ingenuity that designed, as well as the systems that manufactured, tractors to cross plowed and muddy fields were swiftly applied to create the tank, and the new chemical engineers devised poison gas.

"The Soviet Republic must at all costs adopt all that is valuable in the achievements of science and technology," wrote another fan of the American manufacturing system, Vladimir Ilyich Lenin, just four months after the Bolsheviks had seized power. "The possibility of building socialism will be determined precisely by our success in combining the Soviet government and the Soviet organization of administration with modern achievements of capitalism. We must organize in Russia the study and teaching of the Taylor system, and systematically try to adapt it to our purposes."

There was a sense in which Fordism was compatible with the Soviet system. The man who had outraged Detroit's fellow employers by paying five dollars a day was unhappy with the way his workers lived. Always a spiritual man, he believed in reincarnation, and he was never afraid of a quixotic venture for a good cause, like his much-ridiculed 1915 Peace Ship to stop the slaughter of the war. This hopeful attempt to sail to the neutral countries of Europe and inspire public opinion to end the war and persuade the munitions makers to produce Ford tractors instead failed when President Woodrow Wilson declined to join the trip. After a press conference in a Norwegian hotel, Ford sailed home. Inspired by the humanitarian homilies of Ralph Waldo Emerson, Ford told his local pastor, the Reverend Samuel Marquis:

> There are thousands of men out there in the shop who are not living
> as they should. Their homes are crowded and unsanitary. Wives are
> going out to work because their husbands are unable to earn enough
> to support a family. They fill up their homes with roomers and

boarders in order to help swell the income. It's all wrong—all wrong. It's especially bad for the children. . . . Give them a decent income and they will live decently, be glad to do so. What they need is the opportunity to do better, and someone to take a personal interest in them.

Thus was born the Ford Sociological Department, a strikingly paternalistic and intrusive system of fifty inspectors who were each given a Model T to make house calls on Ford employees. They checked on the cleanliness of the home, the health of the family, the absence of boarders, and the family diet. Failure to keep the home properly could jeopardize that half of take-home pay that came from the profit-sharing bonus. The inspectors had to be provided with interpreters to translate the dozens of languages and dialects spoken by the largely immigrant workforce, so Ford established English schools at the plant. It was almost a colonial kind of capitalism, but it helped transform Detroit, with its reputation as a lawless boomtown of bars and brothels, into a solidly respectable and prosperous city of legendarily well-paid and secure workers.

Despite the sinister overtones of the inspectors as the boss's spies, there was a social conscience about Ford's employment policies. One in four of Ford's workers was handicapped, including the blind and deaf and dumb, each on full pay and assigned to a job tailored for his or her abilities, based on a work-organization survey. By arrangement with local judges, he usually had some five hundred ex-convicts in the plant, and Ford claimed that simply by hiring and trusting them, they worked better than the average hand. This was the systems theory applied to social engineering, the power of the thoughtful employer to so improve the lot of his workers that they became less a proletariat vulnerable to Marxist agitation and more a stable, prosperous, and steadily employed class of family men, encouraged to buy their own homes.

"The combination of the Russian revolutionary sweep with American efficiency is the essence of Leninism," wrote Joseph Stalin, whose own ideas of social engineering were somewhat different. If American capitalism could transform new immigrants into highly paid industrial workers and build giant factories on the fields of Michigan, then the Soviet Union could organize its own instant industrialization. Lenin even found that Taylorism could be compatible with socialism; Taylor was interested not only in increasing profits but in increasing production through making the worker more comfortable and thus more efficient. Ford may have been one of the richest men on earth, but he had become so by giving mobility to the masses.

Within three years of its writing, Ford's *My Life and Work* had been translated and had gone through four printings in Russia. "Ford means

America Reborn

America and all that America had accomplished to make her a model and an ideal for this vast and backward country," reported Walter Duranty from Moscow for the *New York Times*. By 1927, claimed Ford's publicity machine, 85 percent of the cars and tractors in Russia had been built by Ford. "The most popular word among our forward-looking peasantry is Fordson," enthused Trotsky. In 1929, Ford signed contracts with the Supreme Economic Council to build two Ford plants, one in Moscow and a second, larger factory in Nizhni Novgorod, to manufacture Model A cars and Ford AA trucks.

By this time, Ford needed the Russian contracts. Even before the Wall Street crash and the Depression, his dominance had disappeared. His insistence on retaining the Model T for so long, and then on offering only the color black, gave competitors like General Motors the chance to use his methods, catch up, and then overtake him. Ford aged; doubtful that his son, Edsel, would run the business as the old patriarch wished, he allowed his veteran security man Harry Bennett to take increasing charge of the day-to-day administration. The result was that by 1940, Ford had fallen to third in U.S. sales, behind General Motors and Chrysler, with but 19 percent of the market.

Bennett was a former sailor, a bizarre figure with close connections to the criminal world, who cooperated closely with J. Edgar Hoover's FBI to provide lists of "subversive" labor activists in Detroit and hired gangsters to keep the labor unions out of the Ford plants. He installed a target in his office so he could practice with his revolver, and he took great personal care of Henry Ford. When the old man went to a state fair and mourned the replacement of the old farm implements with machinery, Bennett had changes made. He drove his employer back the next day, where Ford found a bucolic scene of gamboling lambs, haystacks, plow horses, and contented farmhands in antique clothing surveying a fine fresh crop of waving corn. "That's nice, Harry," said the old man. But by now, the great corporation was faltering, and the five-dollar-a-day wage was cut to four dollars in the hard times of the Great Depression. And the Ford plants that had been models of enlightened employment now saw the shotgun blasts and beatings of Bennett's war on the labor unions.

It would take the giant military contracts of World War II, when Ford's Willow Run plant began turning out a B-24 bomber every hour, and a total of $5.26 billion in war-supply payments to keep the Ford Motor Company alive. And it was the war veterans, whiz kids like Robert McNamara from the Office of Statistical Control, who joined young Henry Ford II to revive the company's fortunes. They did so with the same scientific management and statistical techniques that had built the Ford empire in the first place.

5.
Woodrow Wilson
and American Idealism

On December 13, 1918, Woodrow Wilson landed at the French port of Brest and became the first American president ever to cross the Atlantic while in office, and the first to take his place among the victors in a global war. Germany's defeat the previous month had cleansed the seas of their U-boats, and he arrived symbolically aboard a lavish item of war booty, a former German ocean liner that had been impounded and then renamed the *George Washington* to carry up to five thousand American troops across the Atlantic on each crossing. Half of Brittany had gathered to greet Wilson, and women strewed flowers before his carriage. As the president's train rode through the night toward Paris, his naval doctor, Cary Grayson, was moved to see, even at 3:00 a.m., "at every village, heads bared, old men and women and children."

They were paying homage to the man who had ended the war and might

America Reborn

finally bring some of their husbands, sons, and fathers back home again after four long years in the trenches. He was also the leader of the only Allied nation that was not flirting with financial bankruptcy. By 1918, the Allied war effort depended on American finance, and Wilson had bluntly used this economic power to force into being the armistice that ended the war. Having negotiated the armistice with the Germans, Wilson sent his envoy, Col. Edward House, to inform the French and British Allies of the terms. If this peace based on the Fourteen Points was rejected, House warned, Wilson would go to Congress to ask whether America should continue the war. House faced down British objections to point two, freedom of the seas, with an explicit threat to outbuild the British fleet. "The United States had more resources, more men and more money than Great Britain, and in a contest, Great Britain would lose," he warned the prime minister, David Lloyd George. The money was the key to American diplomacy. Wilson "enjoyed a prestige and a moral influence throughout the world unequalled in history," concluded the economist John Maynard Keynes. But that prestige and moral weight was hollow without the financial strength, which, for Keynes, explained Wilson's unique situation: "Never has a philosopher held such weapons wherewith to bind the princes of this world."

Wilson embodied the nation that had foreclosed that nightmare of old Europe, perhaps at its last gasp, which had already destroyed the empires of the tsars of Russia, the Habsburgs of Austria, and the Hohenzollerns of Prussia and Germany. It had devastated the youth and treasure of the victorious but exhausted French and British. The furious and lethal ingenuity inspired by the war had brought tanks, poison gas, aerial bombing, and U-boat sinkings to a continent that had prided itself on its culture and its civilization. The result had been defined by Wilson's ambassador to Great Britain, Walter Page, as a scene from the Bible's Revelations: "monsters swallowing the universe, blood and fire and clouds and an eternal crash, rolling ruin enveloping all things—the continent has already become a bankrupt slaughterhouse full of unmarried women."

No American before or since Wilson has enjoyed a welcome so impassioned or so heartfelt in so many countries at once. In Paris and in London, in the birthplace of his mother and grandfather in Carlisle, near the Scottish border, in Rome and in Milan, the public of the European Allies thrilled to the man they saw as their rescuer as much as their peacemaker. Having stayed out of the war for almost three years, until the European powers were approaching exhaustion and tsarist Russia had collapsed, the United States offered vast resources of wealth and manpower, which seemed like a certain promise of eventual victory for the alliance against Germany, and the members of that alliance could now proudly assert that they were the democracies.

Woodrow Wilson and American Idealism

The February Revolution of 1917, which had toppled the Russian tsar, had changed the political character of the war, clearing the way for the American alliance, and it had also transformed the nature of the peace that might be achieved. Wilson, alone of all the leaders on both sides, held out the hope that the war and the sacrifices had been for a noble purpose, that an era of universal peace and justice could now be built.

"The world must be made safe for democracy. Its peace must be planted upon the tested foundations of political liberty," Wilson had told Congress on the day he asked for a declaration of war. This was the distinctive new note that America brought to what had begun as a classic contest of the old European power system. Germany had gone to war because it dared not see the humiliation in the Balkans of its ally, the Habsburg Empire of Austria-Hungary, by the Slavic alliance of the Serbs and Russians. France had gone to war because it dared not see the defeat of its ally, Russia, and because it hoped to recover the lost provinces of Alsace-Lorraine. Britain had gone to war nominally because of Germany's unprovoked invasion of neutral Belgium, but it was spurred on by a deeper fear that a Germany reigning over the Channel coast as undisputed master of the mainland would soon amass the resources to challenge Britain's command of the seas. Italy had been bribed into the war in 1915 with the promise of booty from Austrian lands.

America alone came into the war with clean and disinterested hands, albeit much enriched from the profitable trading and exporting during three years of neutrality. By the end of 1916, Britain was spending $25 million a day on the war, and $10 million of it was spent in the United States. Each and every day, Britain was raising $4 million in loans in the American markets. "If things go on as at present, I venture to say with certainty that by next June or earlier the President of the American Republic will be in a position, if he wishes, to dictate his own terms to us," Britain's chancellor of the exchequer, Reginald McKenna, told the cabinet on October 24, 1916.

The British were deeply confused by the American position. On the one hand, the Wilson administration was high-minded in its resolve to stay out of the war, and resolute for a negotiated peace. On the other hand, the administration seemed to speak with two tongues, even under the provocation of the killing of its citizens by German U-boats. The sinking of the passenger liner *Lusitania* in 1915, with the loss of 124 Americans, inspired one of Wilson's most lofty orations:

> The example of America must be a special example. The example of America must be the example not merely of peace because it will not fight, but peace because peace is the healing and elevating influence of the world, and strife is not. There is such a thing as a man being

too proud to fight; there is such a thing as a nation being so right that it does not need to convince others by force that it is right.

On the other hand, the British were aware that many influential Americans, including former president Teddy Roosevelt; Wilson's secretary of state, Robert Lansing, who changed the neutrality rules to facilitate British trade and finance; and the crucial banker who arranged the British loans, J. P. Morgan, were all firmly on the British side. In February 1916, in a burst of that secret diplomacy that Wilson's Fourteen Points were later to condemn, Wilson's adviser Edward House reached a secret understanding with the British foreign secretary, Sir Edward Grey. At a moment suitable to the British and French, Wilson would propose an international conference to end the war. If Germany rejected the invitation, or rejected terms that were deemed reasonable (which would certainly include Germany withdrawing from its conquests in northern France and Belgium), then the memorandum signed by House and Grey said that "the United States would probably enter the war against Germany."

Events then intervened. The suppression of the Easter Rising in Dublin in 1916, in which British troops used artillery to blast the Irish Republicans from the central post office that they had seized, outraged Irish-American opinion. The Germans had suspended their U-boat campaign, while the British were tightening their naval blockade and warning that any American company on a blacklist for trading with Germany would be barred from all British possessions. "I am at about the end of my patience with Great Britain and the Allies," Wilson confided to House. "He went so far as to say that if the Allies wanted war with us we would not shrink from it," House recorded in his diary. When J. P. Morgan tried to raise a new loan of $1 billion in British bonds, the Federal Reserve, after checking the wording with Wilson, announced that it did "not regard it in the interest of the country at this time that they invest in foreign Treasury bills of that character."

Within the space of less than a year, the Wilson government had plotted to go to war on the side of the Allies, considered going to war against them, promised the American public to keep out of the war, and then declared something close to economic war against the British. No wonder London was confused about American intentions. Certainly the British and French were in no mood to swallow Wilson's high-minded declarations of principled American idealism. "Humbug—a mere maneouvre of American politics," said the British prime minister, Herbert Asquith, when told of the House-Grey memorandum.

In the heated atmosphere of the 1916 election campaign, the result so close that the *New York Times* erroneously declared the Republican challenger, Charles E. Hughes, the winner the day after the election, Wilson campaigned on the promise of peace: "The certain prospect of the Republican party is that we shall be drawn, in one form or another, into the embroilment of the European war," he declared in St. Louis. The final result was a very narrow victory indeed—277 electoral votes against 254. Wilson had carried California by 3,806 votes, and New Hampshire by 56. Fewer than ten thousand votes in strategic states could have swung the result the other way.

Wilson, although a fine speaker—on occasion a magnificent one—and a tireless campaigner, never won an overwhelming mandate from the American voters. Even his election in 1912, which may have looked like a landslide, with the Democrats winning majorities in both houses of Congress, was a very odd result in a three-way race. Wilson won 435 electoral college votes, against 88 for Teddy Roosevelt and only 8 for the Republican candidate, William Howard Taft. But Wilson's total of 6,283,019 votes was significantly less than the 7,604,463 combined votes for Taft and Roosevelt. Indeed, Wilson polled fewer votes that William Jennings Bryan had in 1908.

But then, Wilson was no conventional politician. He had served just two years as governor of New Jersey before winning the White House, and he became the first southern-born president since the Civil War. His father, having persuaded himself that the Bible sanctioned slavery, served in the Confederate army until the battle of Chickamauga, then returned to his Presbyterian church and seminary in Augusta, Georgia. Wilson, four when the Civil War broke out, devoted one of his first public speeches, a college debate at the Jefferson Society of the University of Virginia's law school, to this argument: "Because I love the South, I rejoice in the failure of the Confederacy."

He arrived at law school in 1879, after four years at Princeton, having already published an essay on cabinet government in *The International Review* (edited by the same Henry Cabot Lodge who was to battle Wilson to the finish over the League of Nations forty years later), which was highly critical of the American system of government in a period of weak presidents under the powerful grip of congressional committees. "Congress is a deliberative body in which there is little real deliberation, a legislature which legislates with no real discussion of its business," he argued.

Political science was not, at the time, a conventional field of study in an America where the West was filling with agricultural and land-grant schools and the colleges of the East produced mainly lawyers, doctors, and clerics. Wilson dabbled briefly in the law but then decided to enroll in the new graduate school of Johns Hopkins, where German methods of teaching and research that relied heavily on the seminar were used. His doctoral thesis, *Congressional Government,* was published in 1885 to extraordinary acclaim, it being the first American study of the American system of politics and governance. The *Minneapolis Daily Tribune* found it "the best critical writing on the American Constitution . . . since the Federalist Papers."

By the time it was published, he had a job teaching at Bryn Mawr, a new women's college. On the surface, this may have appeared an orthodox academic career. But at the time, to give up the law for an untried and new field of research, and to pursue it at an unorthodox place like Johns Hopkins, was strikingly unconventional; to join the outspoken feminists of Bryn Mawr was almost revolutionary. These were, however, revolutionary times. The long political quiescence of the post–Civil War period was giving way to labor tumult in the mines and the new factories as America thundered her way to breakneck industrial growth.

The vast opportunities of the open West were narrowing fast as the railroads stitched the land together, and the frontier steadily closed as the prairies produced the corn and cattle that would feed the new cities. Along with this growth came new states, whose congressmen and senators were feeding into the new politics—of women, of labor, and of immigrants, with their European ideologies of anarchism and socialism. The traditional politics of American regions—of a Republican Northeast and Midwest and a Democratic South—were being blurred and reshaped as industrialization and immigration brought new allegiances of class into an American political system ill suited to contain them. America in the late nineteenth century was an extraordinary living laboratory for a political scientist like Wilson.

In 1889, he published another major book, *The State,* which brought together the latest German and European thinking and applied it to the American example. A textbook that was translated into French, German, and Japanese, and widely used into the 1920s, *The State* argued that the traditional American model of governance was becoming outdated. It was conservative in that Wilson saw society as an organic entity, with deep historical roots and powerful traditions that were not easily shaken. But it was radical in that it insisted on an active role for government. Wilson adopted the European concept of the state and used the term to describe that embodiment of the nation and its government that were permanent, rather than the changeable policies of elected governments. The state had the right and even the duty to intervene to prevent abuses like child labor, bad housing, and excessive working hours, and to foster equal opportunity for its citizens through schools. There were natural monopolies that the state should run, from railroads to water supplies, while private monopolies should be limited and controlled by the state in the public interest. This was the essence of progressivism, the cause that was to dominate American politics for the next twenty-five years.

Woodrow Wilson and American Idealism

If the term had not been created by "a radically mistaken class of thinkers, we ought all to regard ourselves and to act as socialists, believers in the wholesomeness and beneficence of the body politic," he argued. The model for this kind of interventionist state was to be found in Europe, in the Factory Acts and Housing and Education Acts of Britain, made into law by Tories like Benjamin Disraeli and Liberals like William Gladstone. An activist state that remained a parliamentary democracy was to be preferred to the authoritarian statism of the Kaiser's Germany, despite the energy with which Chancellor Bismarck was imposing old-age pensions and a form of welfare state as well as public health service on German industry for its own good—to mitigate working-class unrest.

And yet Count Otto von Bismarck exercised a curious fascination on Wilson. Wilson's first serious essay at Princeton had been devoted to the Iron Chancellor, the man who had forged the modern German state: a classic example of "men of independent conviction, full of self-trust and themselves the spirit of their countries' institutions." The key to all this, Wilson went on to argue in a seminal lecture at the University of Tennessee in 1890, was not simply politics and vision, but leadership. "He supplies the power: others supply only the materials upon which that power operates."

A full decade before Theodore Roosevelt exemplified what an activist president could achieve, Wilson stressed that the leader must understand his moment: "You must lead your own generation, not the next. Your playing must be good now, while the play is on the boards and the audience in their seats; it will not get you the repute of a great actor to have excellencies discovered in you afterwards."

The leader cannot exercise his genius in a vacuum. The time and the conditions must be right, and the issue not only must be chosen; it must itself be surging to the forefront of public life: "One of the great influences which we call a Cause arises in the midst of a nation. Men of strenuous minds and high ideals come forward as champions of a political or moral principle. . . . They are doing nothing less than defying public opinion, and shall they convert it by blows? Yes!"

Here, twenty years before he thrust himself onto the public stage before the electors, the essence of Wilson stands revealed. He had, in his analysis of the role of the state, defined the political authority and the social objectives to which a program of American constitutional reform must be directed. And in the analysis of the role of the leader, he had further identified the political instrument through which the great work might be done. The combination of the man and the hour, the energy and the ambition, the self-assurance and the "Cause," are set down plainly as the key to politics and power. The academic in his ivory tower may not yet have permitted himself to dream great dreams, but Wilson had charted the qualities and the course that his public life would take. There was ruthlessness in it, and more than a little cunning, all to be dedicated to a cause that would redeem such faults, just as his youthful essay on Bismarck had acknowledged the chancellor's greatness, despite "the occasional breach of honor."

Seldom do academics and scholars enjoy the opportunity to turn theory into practice. And Wilson's first foray into the challenges of leadership and reform were on a modest-enough scale—at his old university, Princeton. From Bryn Mawr, he had gone to Wesleyan University, and then in 1890 to Princeton, from which the University of Virginia three times tried to lure him away to be their president. In 1902, Princeton offered him its leadership, and he embarked upon a dramatic series of changes, which began with a fund-raising campaign with a target of $12.5 million, an extraordinary sum in those days. He was determined to transform the curriculum; he would require each student to start with a broad liberal education, and to benefit from the beginning from the Oxford system of the individual tutorial and the Germanic practice of the seminar. This required new teachers, and forty bright young men—preceptors—were hired at once, an extraordinary infusion of fresh academic blood.

Wilson required academic rigor and higher standards, and he demanded the opening of a graduate school. And finally, in a move that tested to the limit the loyalties of the alumni, he insisted that the traditional dominance of the elitist dining clubs should go, to be replaced by the Oxford system of the quad, specially built courtyards where scholars and students of various years would live together in communities in which hierarchies of money or elite clubs would have little place. Each reform required a battle and a carefully planned campaign, all directed to the grand design of modernizing and democratizing a proud and hidebound institution.

Such a bold overhaul of an elite university was the kind of endeavor to capture the public imagination. Wilson's work at Princeton became the talk of the academic world, a modest scandal in that grand society to which so many Princeton men belonged, and a reason that their sons thought Princeton an exciting place to attend. Princeton became news, with the *New York Times* supporting Wilson and the *Herald Tribune* opposing him. His campaigns became a topic of political interest as the Republican president, Teddy Roosevelt, seized the reformist mantle of Progressivism and Democrats pondered their political future when so many of their natural allies were turning to the Roosevelt banner. A Democratic progressive with a national name, admirable credentials, and legendary speaking skills was an intriguing prospect. First raised by Col. George Harvey, editor of *Harper's Weekly,* at a public dinner in 1906, the prospect of Wilson as a presidential contender made a brief flurry in the press. It also persuaded two of the powerful local bosses of the Democratic party in New Jersey to suggest him as a candidate for governor. Their motives were suspicious, and Wilson turned them down when he realized that they were hoping to use him to defeat a liberal candidate and become further entrenched.

But the seed of personal ambition had been sown, and the prospects of the presidency as a vehicle for real leadership had been energized for Wilson by the example of Roosevelt. The American political system had changed since he had first analyzed it. The presidency was less and less the executive job that Wilson had described in *Congressional Government,* and more and more Roosevelt's bully pulpit. Inspired, Wilson published a new book, *Constitutional Government in the United States,* which waxed lyrical on the new potential of the presidency: "Let him once win the admiration and confidence of the country, and no other single force can withstand him, no combination of forces will easily overpower him. . . . If he rightly interpret the national thought and boldly insist upon it, he is irresistible; and the country never feels the zest of action so much as when its President is of such insight and caliber."

When the call next came, in 1910, at a grim moment in the Princeton wars, Wilson was receptive, even though the offer of the gubernatorial nomination "on a silver platter" came from "Boss" Smith and the most reactionary wing of the party. But Wilson was allowed to write his own platform, and a strikingly progressive document it was, enough to convert to a lifelong devotion the tough young Irish progressive politician Joe Tumulty, who had originally feared that Wilson represented the very forces of reaction he was battling against. Tumulty became his private secretary, and he remained with him during two terms at the White House. Elected as governor in a landslide, with over two-thirds of the vote, Wilson instantly moved against the boss system that had nominated and elected him, blocking Smith's bid to become a U.S. senator. A veteran of college politics, Wilson was learning the art of election politics with uncanny speed. On the eve of his inauguration, he vowed no compromise: "These are our terms. War if you are allied with the enemy. Peace if you are on the side of justice."

His program in office had three main themes. He wanted a commission to regulate utilities in the state, and a workmen's compensation law. He also wanted to clean up politics, with a new law against corruption, and a new electoral system that required primaries for all offices, from Congress to party leaders and delegates, in order "to put the whole management alike of parties and elections in the hands of the voters themselves." In effect, this destroyed the boss system that had brought him to power. He saw all his reforms turned into law, became the hero of progressives around the country, and began to barnstorm the nation, paying particular attention to the West and South. The presidential election of 1912 was firmly in his sights. And the still-potent Smith and his allies in New York's Tammany Hall were determined to stop him.

The battleground was the extraordinary Baltimore convention of 1912, which went to forty-six ballots before Wilson finally won the day. Three factors secured his victory. The first was that he went to Baltimore with the momentum gained from winning primaries in Texas, North and South Carolina, and Wisconsin. The second was that he had made his peace with the once-reviled Populist William Jennings Bryan. The third was that the Democrats knew that they could win, after Roosevelt had stormed out of the Republican convention the previous week, vowing to start a third party, which indeed would split the opposition vote.

Wilson's campaign was a tour de force. He courted the moral leader of the progressives, the Boston lawyer Louis Brandeis, and asked him to help draft a policy to dismantle the great financial and industrial trusts. He also courted labor and promised to write into law the right to strike, as well as promising more trade, more jobs, and cheaper goods through cuts in tariffs. He faced down the challenge of the Socialist candidate Eugene Debs, who was to win almost a million votes, by stressing that the Democrats could win power. He campaigned in Nebraska with Bryan, the silver-voiced son of the prairie, and with the Irish in Boston. He had a slogan: the "New Freedom." He had a theme: the need for social justice against the power of bosses, whether on Wall Street, in factories, or in politics. He had a moral energy, a passionate conviction, and he had his cause: "I say that property as compared with humanity, as compared with the vital red blood of the American people, must take second place."

Wilson's first term saw the most sweeping series of reforms—of American industry, society, finance, and working practices—of any administration before him. Only Roosevelt's New Deal would achieve a greater transformation in the way that elected government imposed itself upon American lives. Wilson introduced the income tax and established governance over national finances with the establishment of the Federal Reserve Board. He legalized the labor unions and the right to strike. He established the Federal Trade Commission, with powers to regulate businesses and enforce competition. He gave teeth to the antitrust laws, authorized the eight-hour day for railroad workers, and established a national board to extend cheap loans to farmers.

He outlawed child labor, imposed minimum standards of employment security for seamen, and cut the tariff, as he had promised.

He brought the presidency constantly into the political and the public arena, becoming the first president since John Adams to address the joint houses of Congress, and the first to hold regular press conferences. Above all, in this blaze of reformist energy, he managed to persuade the American people that they were part of a great and noble project. He stressed constantly that America was an ideal to be lived up to, that his party allegiance was almost accidental in contrast to the great and national cause to which they all were summoned.

"This is not a day of triumph; it is a day of dedication," he declared at his inauguration. "Here muster, not the forces of party, but the forces of humanity. Men's hearts wait upon us, men's lives hang in the balance; men's hopes call upon us to say what we will do. Who shall live up to the great trust? Who dares fail to try?"

"We have squandered a great part of what we might have used," he said. "Scorning to be careful, shamefully prodigal as well as admirably efficient . . . the human cost, the cost of lives snuffed out, of energies overtaxed and broken, the fearful physical and spiritual cost to the men and women and children upon whom the dead weight and burden of it all has fallen pitilessly the years through."

American presidents have traditionally been defined by their inaugural addresses. John Kennedy is remembered for "Ask not what your country can do for you," and FDR is remembered for "The only thing we have to fear is fear itself." That same authentic jolt of rhetorical electricity, that summons to the nation to be part of something greater than itself, that touch of thrilling magic that energizes a presidency for its time and for posterity—all run vitally through Wilson's address. Teddy Roosevelt may have been the first president of the twentieth century, the first modern chief executive. But Wilson, with his call to an older virtue and a more solemn dedication, was the first who had thought through the art and practice of politics and of American government from first principles.

While giving the great surge of reforms legal force, Wilson felt early the tremors of foreign alarms. He did not wish to do so, noting privately just after his election in 1912, "It would be an irony of fate if my administration had to deal chiefly with foreign affairs." But he had inherited, if not an American empire, then at least a series of American interests. They were strategic in the Caribbean, with troops stationed in Nicaragua, Santo Domingo, Puerto Rico, and the Guantánamo base in Cuba, at the Panama Canal, and in the Philippines. There were commercial interests in China and in Latin America, in which over $1 billion was invested. In Mexico alone, Americans owned 43 percent of the invested property.

Wilson was torn by the idealist's dilemma. America believed in free institutions and free trade. How far was it prepared to impose upon free nations in areas of American interest, and how hard was it prepared to push to open doors for its merchants? He declared in 1910, "We are chosen to show the way to the nations of the world how they shall walk in the paths of liberty," and wrote to Charles Eliot at Harvard that he wanted to put "moral and public considerations ahead of the material interests of individuals." But Wilson had also made this point, in his official speech of acceptance of the Democratic nomination in 1912: "Our industries have expanded to such a point that they will burst their jackets if they cannot find a free outlet to the markets of the world."

Before the United States joined the European war in April 1917, Wilson had secured a new naval base in Nicaragua, sent the marines into Haiti, established military control over the Dominican Republic, bought the Virgin Islands from Denmark, sent troops into Cuba, and invaded Mexico—from the sea to occupy the port of Veracruz, and overland to pursue Pancho Villa's guerrillas. At the same time, under the policy of "preparedness," he was enlarging the navy and building the camps and training cadres for the army and its fast-swelling reserve.

And yet the United States remained an essentially civilian country. There was, once war was declared and the country committed itself for the first time to becoming one of the Great Powers, little of that enthusiastic rallying to the colors that had filled the European armies with volunteers in 1914. Some 40,000 job seekers flooded into Washington in the first ten weeks, rather more than the disappointingly small number of 32,000 people who volunteered for the armed forces. Indeed, recruitment was so low that Wilson was forced to introduce conscription and establish the Selective Service Administration. Even in those fields where it had earlier shown mastery, in transport, distribution, and industrial organization, the war proved too great a challenge. Massive blockages of the rail systems heading to the East Coast ports, without whose coal the ships could not sail, produced a nationwide coal shortage as the winter of 1917 began. The government had to take over the railroads to clear the mess.

The new ally was almost wholly innocent of the traditional protocols of diplomacy. The first British delegation, led by Foreign Secretary Arthur Balfour, were disconcerted at their White House banquet when Wilson forgot to toast the king. The first French delegation, led by Marshal Joffre, were even more stunned to be refused wine with their dinner. But Joffre's interpreter, Emil Hovelaque, was fascinated by Wilson, the new ally on whom the fate of

France would depend. An insightful man, Hovelaque found Wilson to be both an austere mystic and a born politician. "This lay Pope, separated from everyone by an icy solitude, is attentive to the least movements of the crowd and obedient to its wishes as he perceives them," Hovelaque concluded. "I watched his austere, wise face of a Scottish dialectician, and the Celt appeared to me in the rapid flash of a smile, in the sudden humanity of its clear eyes."

The French were both intrigued and alarmed by Wilson, the man who had saved their country by joining the war, and who then frustrated them on the eve of complete victory by imposing a curiously idealistic peace. Clemenceau, who concluded after the negotiations with Wilson, "It's easier to make war than to make peace," was uncomfortably aware that Wilson was inspiring an unprecedented fervor from his own French voters. Raymond Fosdick, who had been taught by Wilson at Princeton and had traveled to France with the president, charged with making a report on the state of post-war morale, was in the Place de la Concorde as 100,000 Parisians gathered to cheer the American president. Fosdick recorded a scene "like Armistice day at home, without quite so much rough-house and with a little more love-making. Poor Wilson—the French think that with almost a magic touch he will bring about the day of political and industrial justice. Will he? Can he?"

The grim reality that the task might be beyond him had been signaled in the congressional midterm elections, held as the armistice was being negotiated. Despite, and some commentators suggest it was because of, Wilson's appeal to the voters to stick with "my leadership and sustain me with undivided minds," they returned Republican majorities to both the House and the Senate.

The European leaders were frankly puzzled by Wilson, who had won reelection in 1916 on a promise not to enter the war, and who had then fought it with fastidious disdain for Europe's diplomacy and commercial and imperial rivalries. Wilson sounded to them sometimes like a schoolmaster, sometimes like a Presbyterian preacher, and sometimes like a hypocrite. On his sixty-second birthday, he was made a freeman of the city of London, and gave a speech that chilled his audience. "There was no glow of friendship or of gladness at meeting men who had been partners in a common enterprise," recorded British prime minister David Lloyd George. But that evening, at a private all-male dinner with Lloyd George and other British leaders, he waxed lyrical: "At last, on land and sea, English and American forces have fought so closely together, that the colors of their flags were made into one banner of the free. . . . I am one of those who believe that the greatest good that has come out of this war is the bond of deathless friendship, born in a common cause, and dipped in fraternal blood, which shall ever unite the British Empire and the American commonwealth."

America Reborn

But in his call upon King George, Wilson sounded yet another note, warning him:

> You must not speak of us who come over here as cousins, still less as brothers; we are neither. Neither must you think of us as Anglo-Saxons, for that term can no longer be rightly applied to the people of the United States. Nor must too much importance in this connection be attached to the fact that English is our common language—no, there are only two things which can establish and maintain closer relations between your country and mine; they are community of ideals and or interests.

The Italian government, alarmed that Wilson's high-minded ideals of a peace without conquests might prevent the award of their promised spoils, switched his route into Rome at the last minute to avoid the enthusiastic crowds. The French leader, Georges Clemenceau, faced a difficult debate in the National Assembly. The deputies demanded to know whether France had won the war and could impose the kind of hard peace on Germany that the Germans had imposed on France in 1871, or was France to fall in with Wilson's idealist vision of a new kind of world, a vision that former president Teddy Roosevelt had already dismissed as "a product of men who want everyone to float to heaven on a sloppy sea of universal mush." Clemenceau, when he spoke after five days of debate, paid brief tribute to Wilson's "noble candor" (a word that in French carries more than a hint of naïveté) and then threw his weight behind the traditional French and European concepts of the balance of power and fate of the defeated: "There is an old system which appears to be discredited today, but to which I am not afraid to say I remain faithful."

The great gap between Wilson and the other Allies was that he saw security in the future based upon the collective force of the League of Nations, and they saw it fundamentally as still based upon the old insurance of the nation-state. "We regard the League," Wilson told the first plenary session of the Paris Peace Conference, "as the keystone of the whole program which expressed our purpose and our ideal in this war." The French insisted on firm guarantees of military alliance and protection against a renewed German attack. Wilson offered only what Clemenceau dismissed as "abstract justice." The clash between the two men came over the Saarland, a coal-rich and strategic border province that Clemenceau demanded.

"Let us avoid acting in a manner which would risk creating sympathies for Germany," said Wilson.

"You seek to do justice to the Germans," Clemenceau retorted. "Do not believe they will ever forgive us; they only seek the opportunity for revenge."

To win French backing for the League of Nations, Wilson had to promise a formal alliance that would commit America to France's defense. But then the other compromises came thick and fast. To give the new state of Poland access to the sea, 2 million Germans were incorporated into the Polish state, and a Polish corridor divided Germany from East Prussia. Another 3 million Germans were incorporated into the new state of Czechoslovakia, and the vaunted principle of self-determination appeared to apply to everyone but the Germans. The Germans stored up grievances for the future—and, with them, inevitable new challenges for Wilson's League of Nations, whose initial purity was already being tarnished by the harsh realpolitik of old Europe.

This would make the League, and the peace treaty, all the harder to sell to a U.S. Senate now dominated by Republicans. Wilson's compromises even lost the support of some of his original staff on the Inquiry, the think tank he had assembled to consider the postwar future. Walter Lippmann was one of them. The brilliant young journalist who turned his magazine, *The New Republic,* from support for the League to bitter opposition, became a potent enemy, even briefing hostile senators on the most telling questions to pose. For Lippmann, Article X, which guaranteed the territorial integrity of the League's member states, was a disaster that would freeze temporary injustice into permanent bones of contention.

Despite all the obstacles, from Japanese and Italian greed for war booty to the Bolshevik uprisings that spread from Russia to Hungary and Germany, a treaty and the League were agreed upon. Wilson wheeled and dealed, prepared to stoop to any compromise in the cause of the greater purpose. "Wilson talks like Jesus Christ and acts like Lloyd George," House confided to his diary. The Nobel Peace Prize for 1919 was awarded to the American president. But then Wilson faced the need to win a two-thirds majority in the Senate to ratify the treaty. He might just have achieved it, but his increasingly successful whistle-stop tour of the country to drum up support was ended by a sudden stroke in Pueblo, Colorado, at the end of September. The response he was winning, reported the *New York Times,* "seemed at times akin to fanaticism"; California, its reporter concluded, was "Woodrow Wilson country now." Wilson had pulled out all the stops, invoking in the League's name "the serried ranks of those boys in khaki, not only those boys who came home but those dear ghosts that still deploy upon the fields of France."

That was Wilson's final speech before the stroke, an epitaph for his extraordinary odyssey, in which his single vision had come within a whisker of establishing a rule of law and a system of collective security upon a tumultuous world. It was an attempt to barter the loss of American virginity through its decisive military intervention for the spread of a peace that would embody a wider American virtue. "Sometimes people call me an idealist. Well, that is the way I know I am an American," he told the people of Sioux Falls, South Dakota, on that last whistle-stop tour. "America, my fellow citizens—I do not say it in disparagement of any other great people—America is the only idealistic nation in the world." So it was, but as he had identified thirty years earlier in his lecture at the University of Tennessee, that idealism could take on practical force only when the country was led by a consummate politician with an inspiring cause. When Wilson collapsed, his cause collapsed with him, and an enfeebled League of Nations stumbled lamely on without the support of the America that had first conceived the "great moral force." In his absence, America was not ready for the global role to which Wilson had summoned it, and Clemenceau's "old system" clambered back to its feet and began to march again. Instead of "the war to end wars," Wilson's legacy was the brief interval before the next one.

6.
Babe Ruth
and American Sports

It was first heard in the jungles of Guadalcanal, during one of the most furious battles of World War II. "To hell with Babe Ruth," jeered the Japanese troops at the U.S. Marines, assuming this to be the ultimate insult to Americans. It was also a testimony to the extraordinary stature of the most famous baseball player of them all, the man whose name begat the term *Ruthian* for a prodigious feat, and who almost single-handedly popularized the game in Japan. At the end of the 1934 season, when he was already far past his best, the Babe toured Japan with an all-star team that had stunning success, inspiring Japan to form its first professional league.

His career covered a brief span of twenty years, and he died in 1948, but George Herman Ruth remains a towering figure of the American game. Others have exceeded the records he set. In 1961, albeit in a longer season, Roger Maris of the New York Yankees broke the Babe's record of sixty home runs in a season, and Mark McGwire hit seventy in 1998. In two World Series with the Boston Red Sox, 1916 and 1918, the Babe set the record of which he remained most proud, pitching 29⅔ consecutive scoreless innings. Not until 1960 did Whitey Ford break that one. The Babe was the best left-handed pitcher in the American League, winning ninety-four big-league games, while losing only forty-six, before the Red Sox finally woke up to the fact that the star pitcher was also the greatest power hitter the game had ever known.

He modeled his style on Shoeless Joe Jackson, standing with his feet close together and his body turned slightly away from the pitcher, so that he stared at the mound from over his shoulder. When he unleashed, his whole body would twirl a full circle, with every last ounce of his six-foot-two-inch frame and two hundred pounds behind his heavy forty-eight-ounce bat. His swing generated 44 horsepower, 24,000 foot-pounds a second, an Ohio physicist calculated in 1920. When sufficiently inspired, the Babe could call his shot, homering deep into the section of the crowd to which he had pointed.

Such, at least, is the legend of the famous home run at Chicago in the 1932 World Series. At the age of thirty-seven, perceptibly slowing, playing in only 133 games that year, with a batting average of .341 and forty-one home runs—wonderful numbers for mere mortals—the Babe was past his best. But he retained an affection for his old Yankee teammate, shortstop Mark Koenig, who had gone to the Chicago Cubs. Koenig had helped the Cubs win a National League title, but he was awarded only a half share of the pennant and World Series money. This enraged his old friends on the Yankees, and none more than Ruth, who called the Cubs "cheapskates." The Cubs and their fans responded in kind, adding the spice of a verbal war to the tension of the World Series. The Yankees won the first two games, then traveled to Chicago for the third, where Ruth and his wife were jeered and spat on as they entered their hotel. That did it. The game was tied 4–4 as the Babe came to bat in the fifth inning. After one strike from Charley Root, Ruth shook his fist at the jeering crowd. After a second strike, he pointed his bat high at the crowd in faraway center field, as if signaling where he would hit the ball. The third pitch was a change-up, and Ruth slammed it into the bleachers, exactly where he had pointed.

"The Chicago fans are givin' me hell," Ruth later recalled to sportswriter Grantland Rice. "Root's still in there. He breezes the first two pitches, both strikes. The mob's tearin' down Wrigley Field. I shake my fist after that first strike. After the second, I point my bat at those bellowin' bleachers—right where I aim to park the ball. Root throws it and I hit the **** ball on the nose, right over the **** fence."

The tales and the records, splendid in themselves, are only a part of Ruth's unique eminence. He was, simply, the first and greatest American sports star at a time when the country was becoming ready—as a consumer market, as a national audience, and as a culture that treasured superlatives—to hail one. The ever more important sports pages of the newspapers needed not just a star but also a character who could guarantee good stories on and off the field. His appetite for drink and women in that Jazz Age decade of the 1920s, which combined Prohibition with license, was as gargantuan as his appetite for runs. The Babe's famous stomach upsets, his tumultuous private life in the eleven-room suite in New York's Ansonia Hotel that he called home, his feud with the Chicago Cubs, and his famous one-liners all became the stuff of legend.

"Hot as hell, ain't it, Prez?" he cheerily greeted President Warren G. Harding one steamy afternoon. And when told by the press that his eighty-thousand-dollar salary in 1930 was higher than that of President Hoover, he retorted, "Why not? I had a better year than he did." From a poor and near-delinquent upbringing as the son of a Baltimore barkeeper, and raised in the local equivalent of a reform school by tough Catholic priests, Ruth became a classic American success story—untamed, undisciplined, but also generous with his time for the fans. The professional collector Barry Helper estimates that Ruth signed a million baseballs during his career. Beefy and usually running to fat, Ruth was no matinee idol. He had the face of a bruiser and the build of a brawler, but he could display a touching tenderness. For a hospital-ized little boy, Johnny Sylvester, he promised to hit a home run in the next game of the 1926 World Series, and he did. Ruth was so utterly, insularly American that when introduced to France's Marshal Foch, the supreme Allied commander in 1918, he said in his friendly way, "I suppose you were in the war, huh?"

"He played by instinct, sheer instinct," recalled Rube Bressler, a contem-porary player. "He was like a damn animal. He had that instinct. Animals know when it's going to rain, things like that. Nature, that was Ruth." The gift came early. By the age of eight, Ruth was playing with the twelve-year-olds. By the age of twelve, he was on the varsity team. He pitched and played short-stop and the outfield with equal flair. And he could always hit. Before his nineteenth birthday, Jack Dunn, owner of the Baltimore Orioles, then a minor-league team, signed him up. Ruth being underage, Dunn also had to take on his legal guardianship. That was the origin of the name Babe. Before that first season of 1914 was over, Dunn had sold the young wonder to the Boston Red Sox. Dunn needed the money, and the Red Sox needed a left-handed pitcher. They found that they had bought a batting phenomenon, as well. In 1919, just twenty-four years old and earning a stunning ten thousand dollars a year (half the salary of the great Ty Cobb), the Babe led the major leagues in runs scored, runs batted in, slugging percentage, and total bases. He also hit twenty-nine homers.

America Reborn

But in 1917, the Red Sox were bought by Harrison Frazee, a theater producer who loved baseball but could never resist the lure of Broadway. He used the Red Sox as a bank, selling his finest players to Col. Jacob Ruppert of the Yankees, so that he could, in a sense, export both ballplayers and stage shows to New York. His players were better than his shows. In 1919, Frazee was in danger of losing his Longacre Theatre, unable to finance *No, No, Nanette,* and losing his mortgage on Fenway Park. The Yankees were desperate for a winning season. An eager buyer met an eager seller, and the Babe was sold for what was then the record and unheard-of sum of $100,000. In fact, the real price was even higher. Ruppert also secured Frazee's mortgage on Fenway Park.

The Babe moved to New York, but he had trouble settling in during spring training, and the fans became restive. He promised to hit fifty homers in the coming season, which was more than any team had totaled the previous year. The season started badly. He dropped a fly ball in the opening game in Philadelphia, which the Yankees lost. In his first home game, he pulled a muscle and had to leave. He did not hit a homer until May 1, but then he hardly stopped hitting them. By August, he had hit forty-four, and in the last twenty-four games of the season, he hit ten more, far surpassing his own record and making good on his promise to Yankee fans. As *No, No, Nanette* became a Broadway hit, restoring Frazee's fortunes, the Yankees were breaking all records for gate receipts. Doubling the attendance of the previous year, 1,289,422 customers paid to enter the Polo Grounds to see the young Babe, whom the papers were calling "the Sultan of Swat," "Wazir of Wham," and "Caliph of Clout." "They all flock to see him," explained Yankees manager Miller Huggins, "because the American fan likes the fellow who carries the wallop."

The success of the Yankees was unsettling to the New York Giants of the rival National League, who owned the Polo Grounds but leased it to the American League Yankees. Constantly outdrawn by the Yankee upstarts, the Giants owner John McGraw informed them that the lease would not be renewed. Ruppert then bought ten acres of swampland in the Bronx, and proceeded to build the huge Yankee Stadium, just across the Harlem River Bridge from the Polo Grounds. The new stadium even had a parking lot. The official attendance on opening day in 1923, with John Philip Sousa hired to provide the music, was 74,217, with over 10,000 more milling around outside. True to form, the Babe hit the first homer in the new stadium, a drive to the right-field bleachers with two men on. That day, the Yankees beat Ruth's old team, the Red Sox. The Yankees celebrated their new quarters by winning the American League pennant by a huge margin of sixteen games, and then beating their old landlords, the New York Giants, in six games in the World Series.

Babe Ruth and American Sports

The Yankees' first decade in their new home was stunning: five pennants, four World Series. With his 455 homers, the Babe helped the Yankees draw over a million paying customers in six of those ten years. The Babe and the new stadium that was inevitably named "the house that Ruth built" had proved to be magnificent investments for Ruppert.

The 1920s were baseball's golden decade, and all the sweeter for washing away the bitter memory of the Chicago White Sox scandal in the 1919 season. Baseball itself had failed to clear up the mess, which was left to a grand jury in Cook County, Illinois, to investigate and bring charges. The trial finally began in June 1921, by which time the local district attorney had changed and key documents had disappeared from the Cook County files. Half the gamblers disappeared, the lawyers would not let their player clients take the stand, and the conspiracy suddenly became terribly hard to prove. The jury acquitted all concerned, but baseball's new czar, the magnificently named Judge Kenesaw Mountain Landis, instantly banned the suspected culprits from the game. The sense that the game had been cleansed was an important component of the magical decade, along with the economic boom of the Roaring Twenties, which saw a radio in every third American household by the end of the decade.

By November 1, 1922, 564 broadcasting stations had been licensed across the United States. In that year, for the first time, stations in New York and Chicago combined to use a long-distance phone line to make the first simultaneous broadcast of a sports event, a football game. Baseball was quick to follow, with the chief stockholder of the Chicago Cubs, William Wrigley, the first to realize that far from letting fans enjoy the game without paying admission, live broadcasts increased the interest and local support. But not all games were broadcast live. The standard form of baseball reporting was based on the curt wire reports of Western Union's P-One service. The writer James Michener, who came to love baseball from the radio reports of St. Louis's Frank Murray, once re-created his broadcasting genius. The P-One wire had read: "Foxx flies center. Higgins singles. Chapman pops third. Cramer fans." This was Michener's version of Frank Murray's glorious embellishment:

> Jimmy Foxx, second only to Babe Ruth, hunches his mighty shoulders and swings with all his power. Gomez fools him with a low curve that misses the bat by a foot. Jimmy steps out of the batter's box, rubs resin on his immense hands, and comes back, glaring. He takes ball one. Lefty Gomez studies him and delivers another tantalizing twister and again Foxx misses by a foot. Quick delivery, ball two missing the outside corner. Now Foxx means business. He crowds the

plate, daring Gomez to throw at him. The ball comes in high, nothing on it, Foxx swings. (Here he raps the desk with his knuckles to simulate the sound of a bat on ball.) What a clout. DiMaggio goes back, back, back. He's on the track, right up against the wall. A leap! He spears it in his gloved hand. The crowd roars. (Sound of crowd roaring.) What a catch, and Gomez smiles that enigmatic smile of his as Jimmy Foxx slings his bat towards the dugout.

The 1920s was also the decade of the legendary sportswriters. In 1923, the *New York Times,* proud of its writers but also hoping to improve its reputation for literary style, asked Professor William Lyon Phelps, the star of Yale's English department, to analyze the quality of writing in the paper. He reported that much of the paper was tolerably, indeed decently written, but that one department stood out. The sports department was the home of fine writing, and John Kieran was its master. Ernest Hemingway, John O'Hara, and James Reston all started as sportswriters. They shared the pages with that other unique development of baseball, the statistical analysis of such things as runs scored, runs batted in, and batting averages, whose painstaking assembly and perusal probably made American baseball fans the most numerate and statistically agile of any group of people outside a university mathematics department.

Radio, sportswriting, and statistics combined with the elevation of Babe Ruth into the first sporting superstar to make baseball into the national game and also a national obsession. Ruth was thirteen and already playing at St. Mary's Industrial School in Baltimore when the great fable was concocted to establish baseball as the national game. The sporting-goods manufacturer Albert G. Spalding, who chafed at the assumption that baseball had evolved from the English game of rounders, persuaded a friendly senator to authorize him and some carefully chosen friends to form an investigative commission to determine the origins of the game. In 1908, the commission solemnly gave its verdict: The game had been invented by Abner Doubleday, later to become a general in the Civil War, with its modern rules, name, and field design, in 1839 in Cooperstown, New York. Doubleday based his sport, the commission maintained, on a traditional American children's game called "one old cat," with a series of bases known as one old cat, two old cat, and so on.

By the time of the supposed anniversary a hundred years later, the National Baseball Hall of Fame was up and running in Cooperstown, to the gratification of local businessmen. This had begun in 1936, when a wealthy local resident, Edward Clark, one of the heirs to the Singer sewing machine fortune, was planning to open a folk art museum. A local clerk and baseball fan, Alexander Cleland, suggested that he might be able to contribute some baseball artifacts to the museum. Clark was very interested, because he had bought at auction an antique hand-sewn baseball that had once belonged to Abner Graves, who had been the main source for the legend that Abner Doubleday had invented the game on the local field. Clark resolved to establish a national baseball museum "for the purpose of collecting and preserving pictures and relics reflecting the development of the national game from the time of its inception, through the ingenuity of Major-General Abner Doubleday, to the present."

The president of the National League, Ford Frick, suggested that the museum could do even better if it established a national hall of fame in time for the centenary of Doubleday's achievement, on June 12, 1939. The first five members were picked by a special commission, which chose Ty Cobb, Honus Wagner, Walter Johnson, Christy Mathewson, and, inevitably, Babe Ruth. On the great day, with over ten thousand cheering fans packing the small town, and to the strains of "Take Me Out to the Ball Game," the Babe made his entrance for the formal induction. Characteristically, he was the only one who chose not to wear a tie. It was a great occasion, but the Abner Doubleday theory was already being challenged for the engaging fable it was. Indeed, at the time he supposedly invented the game, the young Doubleday was at West Point as an officer cadet in the army. By the 150th anniversary of the game's supposed birth, in 1989, even Cooperstown let the date pass without festivity.

Some sort of game with a ball and stick, involving hits and runs, had been played for many years, and not always to universal approval. In 1785, Thomas Jefferson wrote to a friend, "Games played with the ball stamp no character on the mind." Two years later, the Presbyterian College of New Jersey, which was yet to be named Princeton, declared a ban on "a play at present much practiced by the small boys among the students and by the grammar scholars with balls and sticks in the rear campus." The students should learn, judged their tutors, to find activities for their leisure that would be "both more honorable and more useful."

By the 1840s, the Olympic Club of Philadelphia was playing a game with five bases on a rectangular field, and the Knickerbocker Club of New York was playing a game with four bases forty-two paces apart and shaped around a diamond, with a fixed batting order and a pitcher throwing underarm. Each batter was allowed three attempts to hit before being declared out. When three men were out, the batting and fielding teams exchanged places. There was no fixed number of innings, but the winner was the first team to score twenty-one "aces" or runs. And a runner could be ruled to be out if a thrown ball reached a base before he did. This was a recognizable form of baseball, with a strict code that exacted fines for profanity or for arguing with the umpire. Alexander Cartwright, a shipping clerk who was a founder of the Knickerbockers, left for California during the gold rush of 1849, and he founded San Francisco's first baseball club after his arrival.

If any single moment marks the birth of the modern competitive game, it would be July 20, 1858, when the best players of Brooklyn met and played the best players collected from various New York clubs (and one from Hoboken, New Jersey) at the Flushing race course. New York won, by a score of 22–18. The game was organized just four months after fourteen clubs from New York and Brooklyn had established the National Association of Base Ball Players (NABBP), which by the end of the year had drafted the rules and bylaws of the game. The bases were to be set ninety feet apart, and the Knickerbocker target of twenty-one aces was changed to the highest score after nine innings. The Knickerbockers were outraged that a batter could be declared out if a ball he hit was caught after a single bounce. It was not until 1864 that the single-bounce rule was eliminated.

Over the next decade, the Civil War was to spread the game across the country. Between moments of acute terror, soldiers had considerable leisure, and the raw equipment of ball and stick was easily available. Such games (including cricket) were encouraged by the U.S. Sanitary Commission as a way to keep the troops healthy and occupied. Northern prisoners of war played it in the camps, which helped spread the game to the South, although there were baseball clubs thriving before the war in New Orleans, Richmond, and Baltimore. Confederate POWs in the vast camp on Johnston's Island in Lake Erie were encouraged to play by the camp authorities, who provided bats and balls.

By 1867, there were over three hundred clubs in the NABBP, and star players were being paid. Companies like the Pullman Car Company and Chicago's Field stores were giving jobs to players like the gifted young Albert Spalding to strengthen their company teams. As the competition intensified, gambling entered the game, with the New York Mutuals expelling three of their players for agreeing to take bribes to lose a game in 1865. Three years later, the NABBP officially recognized two kinds of players, amateurs and professionals.

One of the best professionals was Harry Wright. Born in England, he was a professional cricketer and earned the impressive salary of twelve hundred dollars a season from the Cincinnati Union Cricket Club. This was good pay when a skilled worker made ten dollars a week. For the same pay, Wright agreed to become player-manager for the Cincinnati Base Ball Club. He started an intensive training program with drills for specific plays, and he dropped the traditional casual dress for the peaked caps, short-sleeved shirts, stockings, and short-legged trousers that became the standard uniform. Wright was backed by an enthusiastic member of the club, Aaron Champion, who saw in the baseball team a way to advertise and boost the city itself. He raised funds for Wright to travel back east and hire more professionals. Wright came back with four, including his brother George, star player of the Washington Nationals, for the record salary of fourteen hundred dollars. In 1869, the Cincinnati Red Stockings became the first team to declare itself all professional and embarked on a national tour of fifty-six unbeaten games. The game against the New York Mutuals was watched by seven thousand spectators, while another two thousand gathered at a Cincinnati hotel for an inning-by-inning report over the telegraph. The team was received by President Ulysses S. Grant in the White House, and it took the new railroad and steamboat route to San Francisco on a tour that recorded a net profit of $1.25, after travel expenses and a payroll of $9,300.

The essential features of the national game were established. The clubs would be professional, trained and drilled and well paid, and particular players would be stars, better paid than the rest, and hired away from rival clubs. Teams would be run by professional managers as companies that were expected to show a profit. They would be linked firmly to their home cities, as a source of local pride and support, able to turn to wealthy local businessmen to hire new talent that would promote team and city alike. The new transportation network enabled teams to travel around the country, and what had been a game based on local leagues would spread to a national arena. The results of the games would be conveyed, thanks to the new communications of the telegraph and increasingly by the press, far beyond the few thousand who could witness a game and pay for the privilege of doing so, while generating new trade for local vendors of food and drink. When the Western League (which became the American League in 1901) was founded in 1882, the main backers of four of the franchise teams were breweries. Their owners ensured that the old ban on selling beer at games would not apply to the new league, which also played on Sundays.

The Red Stockings, Spalding later concluded, "demonstrated once and for all time the superiority of an organization of ball players, chosen and trained and paid for the work they were engaged to do, over any and all organizations brought together as amateurs." Other teams quickly learned the Red Stockings' secret, and in 1870 their still-unbeaten record of eighty-three straight victories was broken by the Brooklyn Atlantics. The Wright brothers left for Boston, taking the name Red Stockings with them, and, in another innovation that would come to characterize the game, they opened a sporting-goods store in New York. In Boston, the Wright brothers won the national championship four years in a row. But the game's popularity began to spawn rival leagues as the surging population growth of the late nineteenth century, seen in the booming new cities of the Midwest and the settling of the West, created new teams and new markets.

"Baseball is the very symbol, the outward and visible expression of the drive and push and rush and struggle of the rearing, tearing, booming nineteenth century," Mark Twain told a banquet at Delmonico's when Spalding brought his team sailing back into New York Harbor from a seven-month world tour. Baseball was clearly a sport for all Americans, in that golf and tennis were still amusements of the rich in their private clubs, and football was a sport of college boys. While basketball had been invented in 1891, it was still largely confined to the YMCA. Baseball was a sport of the streets and the sandlots, of the new immigrants but also of the settled old elite. Douglas MacArthur was so proud of the *A* (for Army) letter he won on the West Point team in 1901 that he wore it on his bathrobe the night before the Inchon landing in the Korean War fifty years later.

It is Ruth's heirs, the new sporting superstars like Michael Jordan, whose salary reached over $100 million, who now hold pride of place in national regard. And whereas Babe Ruth's old boss Colonel Ruppert reckoned the Yankees did "great business" by earning $3.5 million in the course of the 1920s, in 1997, Rupert Murdoch's News Corp. and the Disney group paid more than $1 billion between them to share the rights to broadcast major-league baseball for five years. But by contrast, the National Football League exacted $13.4 billion from two television giants for an eight-year contract, reflecting baseball's diminished role in the overall economics of sport. Even the mighty Yankees could win only a $40 million television contract for two years with Murdoch's New York station, WNYW.

The extraordinary season of 1998, when two players beat the home-run records of Ruth and of Maris, saw the contracts of baseball players approach the giddy financial heights of basketball stars. But it was no longer the preeminent game, no longer the most lucrative, nor even the game of all Americans. Strikingly, for a game that had consumed America with controversy when Jackie Robinson broke the color bar with the Brooklyn Dodgers in 1947, it was less and less a game that attracted African-Americans. Perhaps the slow and grudging way the game was integrated had left a scar. Perhaps black fans remembered the arrogant way in which the contractual rights of the black leagues were ignored as once-all-white teams began hunting the new talent. Perhaps the memory lingered of the racial abuse that Robinson suffered, the pitches aimed at his head and the base runners who stormed at him spikes-first.

Babe Ruth and American Sports

At the time, the careful strategy of Branch Rickey to pick a black player who was pale, educated, and had been commissioned as an officer in the army, and to start him off with the Montreal Royals in more liberal Canada before exposing him to the major leagues, had seemed prudent. In retrospect, the humiliation of it all looks offensive. Perhaps the most decent single act from the game's spokesmen was that of Senator Albert "Happy" Chandler, the new commissioner of baseball, who said, "If a black boy can make it on Okinawa and Guadalcanal, hell, he can make it in baseball." But if any single event sealed baseball's claim to be the American game, it was that belated and surly but, in the end, honorable act of integrating the sport, just slightly ahead of President Harry Truman's decision to integrate the army. Robinson had the final word. In his first season, he batted .297, was second in the National League in runs scored, and stole twenty-nine bases, the best in the league. *The Sporting News,* no friend to integrating the major leagues, swallowed its prejudices and named him Rookie of the Year.

Baseball has long since outgrown America, although it takes some cultural arrogance for Americans to call the national finals of their interleague baseball championship the World Series. At least they now welcome Canadian teams like the Toronto Blue Jays, although most of its players are as American as apple pie. Baseball is played in Japan, and so intensively throughout Central America that by 1990 nearly a quarter of the major-league players were Latinos. Baseball-crazy Cuba fields a superb team (the Havana Heroes has a pleasant ring). Fidel Castro even wanted to be a professional player.

The World Series remains a stubbornly American event, as particular to the culture as October revolutions in Russia or English county cricket. It is the precious home of America's most intimate nostalgia, which helps explain why no political commentator or heavyweight journalist feels properly established before bringing forth some ponderous tome on the national game. Take the following: "Human beings seem to take morose pleasure from believing that once there was a Golden Age, some lost Eden or Camelot or superior ancient civilization, peopled by heroes and demigods, an age of greatness long lost or irrecoverable. Piffle. Things are better than ever, at least in baseball, which is what matters most." These are the words of George F. Will, house laureate of the Reagan age, the thinking conservative's conservative. The liberals could field David Halberstam, the former *New York Times* reporter, whose trenchant reports from Saigon helped turn the American Establishment against the Vietnam War, but who wants to be remembered as well for his book about the golden baseball season of 1947.

Or take the poet of the game, *The New Yorker*'s legendary Roger Angell, trying to explain how he was suddenly overwhelmed during a cab ride by the national sense of loss during the baseball strike of 1981:

America Reborn

Now it came to me, unsurprisingly at first but then with a terrible jolt of unhappiness and mourning, that this radio news was altered for there was no baseball in it. It might even be better for me to do without baseball for a while, although I could not imagine why. All this brave nonsense was knocked out of me in an instant, there in the cab, and suddenly the loss of that murmurous little ribbon of baseball-by-radio, the ordinary news of the game, seemed to explain a lot of things about the much larger loss we fans are all experiencing because of the strike. The refrain of late-night baseball scores, the sounds of the televised game from the next room . . . the mid-game mid-event from some car or cab that pulls up beside us for a few seconds in traffic before the light changes . . . the scary sounds of the crowds that suddenly wake us up, in bed or in the study armchair, where we have fallen asleep with the set and the game still on—all these streams and continuities, it seems to me, are part of the greater, riverlike flow of baseball. No other sport, I think, conveys anything like this sense of cool depth and fluvial steadiness.

Marvelous stuff from the invented heartland of America, from that field of dreams where the deepest currents of the national myth flow serenely alongside the athletic grace and sporting prowess of the game. But to be prosaic, baseball can be played by anyone, including men who are shockingly unathletic in appearance. Buttocks never sagged more loosely than from the high-cholesterol haunches of the Phillies, the magnificently scruffy half of the 1993 World Series. Formally known as the Philadelphia Eagles, the Phillies looked like the roadies at the tail end of a particularly rugged Bruce Springsteen concert tour. Their style was urban redneck. They smoked more cigarettes with fewer wimpish filters, chewed more tobacco, spat farther and with more volume and disdain, scratched themselves, and broke more proud and audible wind than any other team on the planet. They were foul and mean, and in 1992, they had ended up at the bottom of their division.

But they had great hearts. They had a pitcher nicknamed "Wild Thing," who liked to train in a headband with F-E-A-R stenciled across it. When he ran out of chewing tobacco, he ate unfiltered Camels, and played with a tumor-sized bulge in his cheek, like some delinquent squirrel stocking up for a hard winter. "You gotta have a strong stomach," Wild Thing said of the challenge his personal habits posed to his managers. They had seen worse, like the regular spit-for-distance contest in the Phillies dugout to see who would pay for the beer. Or the moment when the cancer-ridden guy with half a jaw came into the bunker to warn them of the dangers of chewing tobacco, and they all stopped and spat out their chaw until the floor was awash. When he left, they all plugged fresh tobacco back in. Legend has it that Wild Thing picked someone else's soggy plug from the morass.

The Phillies were the Dirty Dozen with beer bellies, the Wild Bunch on speed, something raw and primal from the carrion-breath fantasies of a Sam Peckinpah. Their opponents in the 1993 World Series, the Toronto Blue Jays, were, by contrast, something classic from a John Ford movie. They were neat and tidy, with short hair and clean uniforms, played an elegant and disciplined game, and went to bed early. In Toronto, they played in a smoothly modern stadium that could be air-conditioned or heated or even have the roof slide open. The Phillies played in the grim old Veterans Stadium in the heart of the city that inspired the boxer Sonny Liston to observe that he'd rather be a lamppost in Denver than mayor of Philadelphia.

Their World Series was a kind of class war, a gladiatorial contest between two kinds of America and two approaches to sport and two facets of society so utterly different that only as rich a womb of metaphor as baseball could have embraced and cherished them both. It was, perhaps, the nearest America could get in the 1990s to a public confrontation of cultures, and so, naturally, baseball provided the arena.

"Just because our guys are pretty much clean-shaven, don't take that as a weakness. They're tough," insisted Blue Jays manager Cito Gaston. "Our guys might get haircuts more often than the Phillies, but that's not a problem for me. I don't care how you look as long as you play hard." The Blue Jays boasted the best hitting lineup in the game, and they also had Dave Stewart, past his prime at thirty-six, but still one of the great pitchers. There are sixty feet six inches between the pitcher's mound and the tiny seventeen-inch wide plate his ball must cross for it to be a strike. Stewart could make his ball dance and dart all the way. And he was Mr. Clean. Every Thanksgiving, he ran a personal charity to cook food for the hungry. Whenever there was an earthquake or a famine, Stewart went around the team clubhouse with a collection jar.

All baseball players wear helmets when they bat. Dick Allen, one of the great Phillies, began the tradition of wearing a helmet in the field, too, because Phillies fans had the habit of throwing sharpened coins at him whenever he made an error. "Play for the Phillies, and the name of the game is survival," Allen explained. Phillies fans became legendary for their merciless ways with their team; they claimed the loudest and most lethal boos in the game. "When the games are played out, these fans go out to the airport to boo bad landings," suggested Phillies veteran Jay Johnstone. "They boo unwed mothers on Mother's Day," added television commentator Bob Uecker. "The cops picked me up at 3 a.m. and fined me $500 for being drunk. And $100 for being with the Phillies."

America Reborn

There was wit in Philadelphia. Bruce Benedict, a catcher for the Atlanta Braves, was trying to understand why every time he played the Phillies, raw eggs would be pelted at him until his clothes were wet with yolks and whites and the shells littered the sand around him. A kindly Phillies batter scratched, spat, picked a piece of shell from Bruce's hair, and explained, "They're turning you into Eggs Benedict."

To reach the World Series the Phillies, to the delight of all true populists, trounced in the league championships the ultimate Yuppie team, the Atlanta Braves, owned by CNN mogul Ted Turner and boasting Jane Fonda as top cheerleader. Put together at great expense, and with pride of place on Turner's television networks, the Atlanta Braves threatened at one point to become the megateam. The Phillies stopped that. A marvelous group of Neanderthal rejects from other teams, who slumped down to the bottom of the baseball pack, festered and hatched out into the Phillies, creamed the glossy Braves, and became America's team in the last battle against the Blue Jays.

And it was the last battle. A chunk of baseball history ended that year, the last of the true World Series, the end of a ninety-year run. The major leagues of the big-city teams had long been divided into the National League and the American League. They, in turn, were divided into Eastern and Western divisions, and at the end of the 162-game season, which lasted all summer, came the playoffs, a special round of games between the best team of the Eastern and Western divisions to decide the championship of each league. This was the race for the pennant. The two pennant winners then met for the World Series, and the victor was the first to win four games. But from 1994, this purity of the championship between pennant holders was sullied by modernity. Instead of the traditional clarity of the pennant race between the champions of the two divisions came a third division, and the playoffs to determine the World Series contestants included second-place teams, too. This meant more late-season championship games and thus more money from television advertising, which helped the team owners vote for this revolution by a margin of 27–1.

The hope of the sport was that by breaking the old East and West and National versus American League gridlock, the result would be a more national game, able to produce national superstars of the magnitude of basketball's Michael Jordan or football's Joe Montana. And yet baseball was the game that had invented the sporting megastar. Baseball had made Babe Ruth and Micky Mantle and Joe DiMaggio into American icons—and global names. And yet they are the names of another era, before television's hegemony, that somewhat dated period when Jacques Barzun could write, "Whoever wants to know the heart and mind of America had better learn baseball."

Babe Ruth and American Sports

Those days are gone. Whatever its grip on the national psyche, as seen by Hollywood in *Field of Dreams* or by the heavyweight political commentators, baseball has in recent years looked to be a faltering game, overtaken in television and live audiences by football and basketball alike. And yet, in its irrepressible way, it keeps bouncing back, with McGwire's epic achievement in 1998 riveting not only America but a global television audience, which understood, however dimly, that a wondrous kind of history was being made. But baseball has already surrendered its sun-drenched afternoons and slowly gathering twilights to the demands of prime-time television and the fat media markets of California. Games on the East Coast can start at 8:00 p.m. and go on until well after midnight. The old myth of American fathers taking the subway after lunch to the ball game to raise patriotic sons in the mysteries of the field of dreams is fading. The subways aren't safe. The games start near a child's bedtime. Even the new, low-sodium hot dogs and lite beer ain't what they used to be. Maybe it was always this way.

"It makes me weep to think of the men of the old days who played the game, and the boys of today. It's positively a shame, and they are getting big money for it too," lamented the editor of the *Spalding Base Ball Guide.* He wrote it for the edition of 1916, and one of the boys who depressed him was the southpaw pitcher of the Boston Red Sox, Babe Ruth.

7.
William Boeing
and the American Airplane

From the tinkering of the Wright brothers in their bicycle workshop in Ohio to Charles Lindbergh's lone crossing of the Atlantic twenty-four years later, the American aviation industry has cherished the myth of its origins among bold visionaries and amateurs. In reality, the industry was to be a product of world wars, the Cold War, and government contracts to develop the aircraft and the manufacturing expertise and reliability that could eventually give birth to mass civil aviation. Along the way, as the aerospace plants grew along the West Coast, and in Kansas and Georgia, they would transform the industrial geography of America. Decades of muddle, fraud, and bankruptcy were to unfold as the various players juggled the competing demands of finance, the military, and design genius. But there was a moment of early innocence, at Dominquez Field, just outside Los Angeles, in January

William Boeing and the American Airplane

1910, when America's key aviation pioneers gathered for the country's first air show, promoted by Harry Chandler, the publisher of the *Los Angeles Times.*

William Boeing, seven years out of Yale and too busy building a prosperous timber business in Seattle to have taken his first flying lesson yet, traveled down out of curiosity. But after the tedious weeklong journey, he both hoped and suspected that aviation would dominate the new century. Glenn Martin, twenty-four, the owner of a small garage and a license to sell Ford and Maxwell cars, arrived there already fascinated by aviation. The previous year, he had built a rough copy of Glen Curtiss's "June Bug" biplane, attached an engine from a Model N Ford, and claimed to have made a long-enough hop across a field of an Irvine ranch to become the first man to fly in California. Charles Day, a graduate of Rensselaer Polytechnic Institute, had just built his own plane. He and Martin met at the show as they pored over the Curtiss biplane and the plane of the famed French aviator Louis Paulhan. On the spot, Day agreed to become chief engineer in the company Martin proposed to start. The mechanic who proudly showed off the French plane, Didier Masson, was to become the first pilot in the western hemisphere to drop bombs in anger, from a plane to be built by Martin.

They had all come to see Curtiss, the bicycle mechanic who had built his own motorbike and had created a world speed record of 137 mph in 1905. Three years later, in his June Bug, Curtiss won the *Scientific American* prize for the first public kilometer-long flight in the Americas. The Wright brothers could have taken the prize at any time during the previous five years, but the prize required an aircraft to take off on its own wheels, and the Wrights insisted on their rail system. The Wrights brought a furious lawsuit over patent rights, which crippled the industry for years. But at Dominquez Field, the attention was on the duel between Curtiss and Paulhan. The Frenchman carried off the nineteen-thousand-dollar prize, but Curtiss then did something of far greater importance. He took some sandbags and an officer from the Army Signal Corps to test a new bombsight, aiming from 250 feet at a circular target on the ground. All the sandbags missed, but the future military role of the airplane as fighting machine had been demonstrated on American soil.

Two years later, after the Italians had first used airplanes as bombers to drop hand grenades against Turkish troops in Libya, Martin outdid Curtiss with another air show in Los Angeles, this time bombing a specially built "fort" at night from a plane equipped with a small searchlight. The Los Angeles press was duly enthusiastic, and the bombing routine became a feature of Martin's regular air shows. His mechanic, Lawrence Bell, who went on to found Bell Aviation, later revealed that the "bombs" were small explosives planted on the ground, which he triggered by electric wires. Martin had really dropped oranges.

America Reborn

"The show and others like it accomplished its purpose—it attracted the attention of the War Department," Martin recalled many years later. And it helped Martin win his first export sale, to the Mexican revolutionary warlord Alvaro Obregón. Obregón bought a Martin biplane, with a fifty-foot wingspan and a 75-horsepower engine, for five thousand dollars. He hired as a pilot another veteran of that 1910 Dominquez Field air show, the French mechanic Masson, who dropped terrifying, if ultimately harmless, bombs on the Mexican gunboat *Guerrera* in 1913.

The Mexican sale was a rare success for Martin, who depended on carnival flights, prize money at air shows, and the occasional flight for the embryonic Hollywood film industry to keep going. In August 1912, he founded the Glenn L. Martin Company with $100,000 from Los Angeles investors, whereupon he opened a flying school and workshop on the site of what is now Los Angeles International Airport. His breakthrough, when the Wright "pusher" airplane had killed six army officers, was to devise the far more stable "tractor," with the engine and propeller ahead of the pilot. In 1914, the army bought seventeen of Martin's tractors for $8,500 each. That year, World War I launched the infant industry into explosive growth and made Martin rich.

"The aeroplane will practically decide the war in Europe," he wrote in the *Los Angeles Evening Herald* on August 7, three days after Britain declared war on Germany. "Veritable flying death will smash armies, wreck mammoth battleships and bring the whole world to a vivid realization of the awful possibilities of a few men and a few swift winging aerial demons." It was an article of stunning foresight, correctly predicting that war in the air would require three different types of plane. He proposed a two-seater reconnaissance plane equipped with a radio; a "flying death machine" carrying between six hundred and eight hundred pounds of bombs; and a small, fast fighter equipped only with machine guns and fuel, whose duty was "the most dangerous of all—they must protect the scout planes against the enemy's aeroplanes."

Martin was not the only young enthusiast who saw the business possibilities of war. In 1915, Boeing took flying lessons from Martin. Meanwhile, in Seattle, Boeing's partner, navy lieutenant Conrad Westervelt, who had taken some of the first courses in the new field of aeronautics at the Massachusetts Institute of Technology, began designing a twin-float seaplane with Boeing's financial backing.

William Edward Boeing was born in Detroit in 1881, the son of a wealthy timber merchant, and was educated privately in Switzerland before going to the Sheffield School of Science at Yale. Expecting to inherit the family business, and knowing that the furious pace of economic growth had cleared much of the traditional timber of the Midwest, he set off for the almost-virgin lands of the Pacific Northwest. Basing himself at Grays Harbor, Washington, he did not cut much wood, but he began building a personal fortune by trading in forestland and timber rights. In 1908, he moved to Seattle and joined the University Club, where he met Westervelt. They began a friendship based on long evenings of talk about flight, the exploits of Curtiss and Martin, and the first crossing of the English Channel by Louis Blériot. By 1915, both convinced that the war in Europe would spur military aviation, the friendship had turned into a partnership, and Boeing began learning to fly.

Both he and Westervelt had done most of their early flying in a crude and dangerous Curtiss plane, in which the pilot sat on the wing. One of the main hurdles to the expansion of aviation was the lack of any aircraft specifically designed to train the beginner. The extreme difficulty and danger of learning to fly suggested an opportunity to the new partners. America was likely to join the war, and it would need to train a lot of pilots very fast. A sturdy, reliable, and forgiving aircraft would surely find a military market, and in the process, as Boeing noted, create a market for his plywood. The test pilot for the aircraft Westervelt designed was late for the maiden flight in June 1916, so the impatient Boeing took it up himself. It was named the B&W, after Boeing and Westervelt, and they built two for sale to the navy, which turned them down. Boeing finally sold them to the New Zealand Flying School, and he resolved that his timber business was healthy enough to finance a new company, the Pacific Aero Products Company.

With war orders from France and Britain, and a construction boom in the United States, the timber business was making record profits. Investing almost forty thousand dollars a year, Boeing hired twenty-four people, including Tsu Wong, one of the only qualified aeronautical engineers in the country, and two young engineers about to graduate from the University of Washington, Phil Johnson and Claire Egtvedt. Johnson was supposed to go into the family laundry business, but he preferred flying, and he ran the workshop as production chief. Egtvedt was chief engineer, experimenting with glues and plywoods to get the best combination of strength and lightness. There were seamstresses who were paid fourteen cents an hour, sewing together the fabric that would cover the wooden frame of the wings, and a test pilot who could make ten dollars a day with bonus pay for each flight.

Tsu Wong designed a new seaplane, the Model C, and just before the United States entered the war in April 1917, the navy announced that it would hold trials of new aircraft at Pensacola, Florida. Boeing seized the opportunity, and he had the Model C dismantled to be shipped across the country by train. Wong reassembled the Model C on the spot. It started immediately, flew reliably, and impressed the judges. The navy bought two for testing, then ordered another fifty. When Boeing secured another navy order to build fifty Curtiss-designed seaplanes, he renamed his firm the Boeing Aircraft Company. By the time the war ended, Boeing was employing 337 people.

All the men whose names were to dominate the future of American aviation were gathering on the Pacific Coast. Two young brothers, Malcolm and Allan Loughead, started on a turbulent career—that would lead eventually to the Lockheed Corporation—with a floatplane launched in San Francisco Bay in 1913, but they quickly went broke and turned to gold prospecting. Malcolm even worked briefly for Obregón's Mexican air force, repairing the battered Martin plane. By 1916, the brothers had raised enough money on the hope of war contracts to start again, and they hired Jack Northrop, a young engineer who walked into their workshop looking for a job. And by then, Martin had decided his business was growing so fast that he needed a qualified engineer, someone who could design aircraft on paper, rather than by feel and experiment. From the Massachusetts Institute of Technology, where the navy had sponsored the first course in aeronautical engineering, he hired Donald Douglas for fifty dollars a week in gold. Martin picked him up at the train station and drove him to a stretch of water called Nigger Slough, where Martin did his testing. A spindly biplane rested on wooden blocks. Martin climbed in and bounced around. Douglas asked him what he was doing. "I was testing it, to see if it was strong enough," Martin replied. "But this didn't represent any load that the plane bore in flight," Douglas recalled. "Nobody there had the foggiest idea about that. That's how crude it was."

Martin and Douglas in Los Angeles, Lockheed and Northrop in Santa Barbara, and Boeing in Seattle: The brand names that were still to dominate American aviation eighty years later were assembled. But the play was about to be stolen from them by the established financiers of Wall Street and the automobile industry, their eyes fixed on the rich pickings of military contracts. America had come late to airpower. Had it not been for President Teddy Roosevelt's personal interest in aviation, and his demand that the army set up an Aeronautical Division (of one officer and two enlisted men) in 1907, which expanded to a squadron by 1913, there would have been even less. Between 1907 and 1913, the War Department spent $250,000 on aviation. (The French military aviation budget in 1913 was $7.4 million.) Then it set a budget of $300,000 a year, and in the summer of 1916, as part of the "preparedness" policy, another $500,000 was authorized. These funds were just sufficient to keep the infant companies of Martin, Boeing, and Curtiss alive.

Curtiss tried to export his planes to Britain and France, and his shipping of three seaplanes to the Royal Navy on the passenger liner *Lusitania* provoked a formal German complaint, which was then used to justify the liner's subsequent sinking by a U-boat. The British and French were not much interested in the obsolete American planes, when their own industries were rising to the challenge and learning lessons of the Western Front with far more advanced warplanes.

By the end of 1916, a year when the total American aircraft production was not quite four hundred, Britain's Royal Flying Corps fielded almost ten thousand aircraft. The U.S. government began to wake up. On August 19, 1916, an appropriations bill was passed that gave the navy $3.5 million for aviation, and the army $13,281,666 for "the purchase, manufacture, maintenance, operation and repair of airships and other aerial machines." The floodgates of public spending had opened and the businessmen moved in. In that same month, Martin was bought out by the Wright Corporation of Dayton, Ohio, in which the inventor Orville Wright was a figurehead. The company was run by the mining millionaire William Thompson and financiers from Chase and Guaranty Trust banks.

The first order of business was to resolve the long lawsuit over the original patents of Wright and Curtiss. Faced with a legal blockage on production, the government acquiesced in an expensive deal. The Manufacturers Aircraft Association was established, which would be paid two hundred dollars for every aircraft built in the United States. The money would be divided, $135 to the new Wright-Martin company, $40 to Curtiss, and the remaining $25 would defray the association's running costs until Wright-Martin and then Curtiss had each received $2 million for their patents. Since the patent fee was simply added to the sale price, the government in effect agreed to pay an extra two hundred dollars per plane. But by clearing away the legal hurdle, the deal meant that when the United States declared war on April 6, 1917, it could plausibly announce a crash program to build 22,000 aircraft and 45,000 engines, financed by a special appropriations bill of $640 million.

The American industrial strength and expertise that had brought the world the mass-produced automobile was now to be geared to war in the air. Such was the theory and the promise. The reality, amid fraud, sweetheart contracts, and industrial chaos as production was shifted from the proven aircraft factories to the giant plants that had so far produced only cars, was to prove appalling. The Wright-Martin plants in Dayton and Los Angeles, which were producing a warplane a day, were ordered to close by the Aircraft Production Board because they could not promise to produce at least three a day within six months. The big plants of the East, which promised everything, delivered worse than nothing.

"No American-designed combat plane flew in France or Italy during the entire war," concluded Gen. Hap Arnold, the future chief of staff for the U.S. Army Air Forces. "The foreign planes built in this country failed to arrive in Europe either on schedule or in the promised numbers, until what had started out as a triumphant exhibition of American know-how turned into a humiliating series of Congressional and other investigations."

There were three major disasters. Unable until too late to come up with an American design that was advanced enough to survive on the Western Front, the American industry agreed to manufacture British and French planes. The British DH-4 was selected, although it was already obsolete when chosen in 1917. A wholly new company, Dayton-Wright, agreed to build four thousand of them at a new plant built on land partly owned by Edward Deeds, president of National Cash Register. Deeds was also appointed to be head of procurement for the government's Aircraft Production Board. He was made a colonel in the Army Signal Corps, to run its Equipment Division. While all this was highly lucrative for Deeds, it was a disaster for the war effort. It took a year, until May 1918, for the first American-built DH-4 to reach France. It proved unflyable. Not until the last three months of the war did the American DH-4s start to fly over German-held positions, only to become known as the "flying coffin."

Dayton-Wright also contracted to build four hundred J-1 trainers designed by Charles Day, Glenn Martin's first mechanic, by the end of 1917. No plane was delivered until March 1918, and it proved to be a fire hazard. In June 1918, sixteen hundred of them were condemned and destroyed. The third disastrous plane was to be a British-designed Bristol fighter. Nineteen million dollars were to be paid for two thousand planes, powered with something the Americans knew they could produce, a "Liberty" engine. The project was canceled in July 1918 when every aircraft that was flight-tested crashed. "Not a suitable motor for air work," concluded Gen. Billy Mitchell, who had led the American expeditionary air force in France but had to use French, British, and Italian machines. His air fleet consisted of 1,285 foreign planes and 196 of the American-built flying coffins.

Developed from a Packard racing car engine, the Liberty proved too heavy for aviation use. Donald Douglas, by now working as an engineer with the Signal Corps, had warned that it would be dangerous inside the Bristol airframe, but he was ignored. Another problem of the Liberty engine was its ignition system, supplied by the Delco Company, owned by United Motors, of which the ubiquitous Deeds was a director and major shareholder. By the end of the war, the Aircraft Production Board boasted, 150 Liberty engines were rolling off the assembly line every day. Generating 400 horsepower, and their reliability improving as the engineers solved the ignition problem, they eventually became a sound engine, powering the innovative four-engine Curtiss seaplane. But for the war, they were a wasteful disaster.

The government had spent close to a billion dollars on aviation during the war, and it received in return on the battlefront a total of 196 defective and obsolete DH-4 reconnaissance planes. The industry claimed that by war's end it had geared up to produce twenty thousand aircraft a year. But this was too late for the fighting, and most of the planes were scrapped and the factories closed as the war ended. Still, from this vast and wasted outpouring of public money, some crumbs had gone to the more deserving.

Glenn Martin, freed from the grip of Wright-Martin, set up a new Martin company and designed a new aircraft. This was the MD-1, a three-man bomber that could carry one thousand pounds to over ten thousand feet. The army had ordered fifty, but none reached France in time for the war. Although the full order was canceled with the armistice, Martin's company survived after the war by producing a total of twenty-six in small quantities for the army, navy, marines, and airmail. This kept him going for two years, when he won a million-dollar order for twenty MB-2 bombers, thanks to Billy Mitchell's passionate advocacy for strategic bombing.

These were the planes that Mitchell used for his famous demonstration in 1921. Three years after the battleship *Ostfriesland* was captured when the German navy surrendered, the vessel was condemned to be the target for what became Mitchell's triumphant proof of his belief in airpower. But the peace-time military establishment was not much inclined to learn the lesson. The navy, horrified at the implicit threat to their own ships from bombing, complained that the sinking was "a fluke." Mitchell accused them of endangering American security, and he was court-martialed for insubordination and forced out of the service. The future leaders of the air force, young officers like Hap Arnold, Ira Eaker, and Carl "Tooey" Spaatz, risked their own careers in standing by Mitchell.

The Loughead brothers had won wartime orders for two seaplanes, and, despite suspecting that another of their designs had been poached to develop the Curtiss seaplane, went bankrupt soon after the war. Malcolm changed industries, to build what became the Lockheed hydraulic brake. Allan went into real estate, until the boom of the mid-1920s brought new investors, and Jack Northrop's genius helped him to build the futuristic Lockheed Vega monoplane.

Donald Douglas went back to California, convinced that the war had proved the technology and that the time was ripe for a civilian market. He was wrong, but, like Martin, he was saved by the military. His first design, the Cloudster, was designed because his wealthy partner, David Davis, wanted to fly a plane across the country. The Cloudster swiftly set an altitude record, and the army's Hap Arnold asked to fly it. The navy ordered three fitted as seaplanes to test as possible torpedo bombers, but Davis suddenly pulled out of the company, leaving Douglas with a $120,000 navy contract but no way to fulfill it.

America Reborn

Douglas turned to Harry Chandler, the newspaper publisher, who arranged a loan guarantee, and Douglas went on to turn a forty-thousand-dollar profit on the contract. His company never looked back. After the Cloudster, he developed a new reconnaissance plane for the army to replace the ill-fated DH-4, and over the next decade, 879 would be produced—108 for foreign buyers—so many that Douglas had to license other manufacturers to build them. Some of these were indeed sold to the civilian market, but, like the Martin Company, Douglas Aircraft became dependent on the military. Of the 375 planes built there until 1929, the army and navy bought 314.

In postwar Seattle, William Boeing thought he had found a way to survive in the civilian market. With a Model C seaplane, he made the first international postal flight, a short hop across the Canadian border to Vancouver. He developed his first civilian design, the B-1 flying boat, but found no buyers. The B-1 prototype finally made its development money back in eight reliable years on the Vancouver mail run, completing 350,000 miles, which the company suspects may have been a record for any plane of the day. In 1919, Boeing lost $90,000, and in 1920, he lost $300,000; only his deep pockets and a quick transition to making cheap furniture, including the counters and cupboards for a corsetry shop, and flat-bottomed boats called "sea sleds" kept the company afloat.

Boeing's engineering staff had shrunk to Egtvedt and one other mechanic. But with a factory and machines, Boeing decided to bid for subcontract work. With some local political help, he secured a contract to rebuild some of the dreadful DH-4s, which the army donated to the postal service. In 1921 came the deal that saved Boeing, a contract to manufacture what eventually became two hundred of an army design, the new MB-3 pursuit plane, as fighters were then called. Egtvedt then started designing his own fighter, the Model 15, using welded tubes rather than spruce. The first version was underpowered, but, upgraded to a 425-horsepower engine, it was accepted by both the army and Marine Corps. They bought a total of 157, and the plane remained in service until 1928.

Douglas and Martin had accepted the fact that military contracts were essential and feared that the civilian market might never take off. Boeing felt differently. But it was not until 1927 that he found an opening, when the U.S. Post Office Department declared that all transcontinental routes would be opened to private mail carriers. Boeing had the single-engine P-40 light transport, an economical plane that could carry four passengers and one thousand pounds of mail, ready to fly, and he won the San Francisco–Chicago leg. His wife, Bertha Boeing, christened the new aircraft in that Prohibition era with a mixture of orange juice and soda water, and she declared to the press that "it made a satisfactory fizz." Boeing's first passenger, *Chicago Herald Examiner* reporter Jane Eads, wrapped in a large feather boa to help warm her through the twenty-two hours of flight, took care of the publicity. By contrast, as she noted in her reports, the time-hungry businessman would lose three days going the same distance by train.

This was the moment that William Boeing's unique contribution to American aviation, beyond the aircraft he produced, came into play. Convinced that the industry had to grow beyond its dependence on military orders, Boeing saw the airmail service as the springboard that could launch a new civilian market with almost limitless potential. Just as he had realized in 1915 that a training aircraft would be needed, he realized in 1927 that an airmail delivery aircraft could be big enough to take regular passengers on scheduled flights. The P-40 became the first aircraft to fly scheduled passenger routes at night and over long distances. It also became the first to offer two-way radiophones, with weather and airfield reports coming from Boeing's own dispatchers.

"We are embarked as pioneers upon a new science and industry in which our problems are so new and unusual that it behooves no one to dismiss any novel idea with the statement 'It can't be done,' " he told his staff. For Boeing's aircraft manufacturing to prosper, the civilian market had to be nurtured. Airmail was a good start, but the vast distances to be traveled in America meant to Boeing that passenger flight would be the inevitable next step.

Boeing swiftly formed a new company, Boeing Air Transport, and bought another company to secure the Seattle–Los Angeles postal route. By the start of 1928, he was flying a quarter of America's airmail, as well as generating extra profits from passengers. At this point, as one of the largest aircraft manufacturers in the country and employing eight hundred people, Boeing decided to take his company public. Lindbergh's epic solo flight across the Atlantic, and the 4 million people who turned out to give him a ticker-tape parade on his return to New York, combined with the booming stock market to launch a dramatic change in aviation. For the first time since the war, banks and industry began to think there was real money to be made. By going public, Boeing made a fortune, but as the shares changed hands, he began to lose control.

The infamous Deeds of the World War I procurement scandals had put together a consortium of the auto industry and National City Bank to buy controlling shares in a series of companies and combine them into the giant United Aircraft. It bought the smaller aircraft companies of Chance-Vought, Stearman, and Sikorsky, the Pratt & Whitney engine manufacturing company, and Hamilton and Standard, the two main propeller manufacturers. The biggest catch of all was Boeing's double empire, the aircraft plants and the airline. This became an enormous agglomeration, and over the next four years, it commanded 48 percent of sales to the navy, 29 percent of sales to the army, and 48 percent of the civilian market.

At the same time, Boeing Air Transport was merged with National Air and Varney Airlines to create United Airlines, which now dominated airmail services, with only TWA as a serious rival. And Boeing had just the plane for United Airlines, the Model 80, carrying up to eighteen passengers in leather seats and having hot and cold running water and a registered nurse to act as stewardess.

Boeing was made chairman of the United group, which then bought Jack Northrop's tiny company, Avion, mainly for its innovative technique of replacing the fabric skins of aircraft with thin sheet metal. By 1930, Boeing had launched the Monomail, using the flexible strength of an all-metal plane to abandon the biplane structure. Its engine hidden under a streamlined cowling, the Monomail had a retractable undercarriage; it was, in effect, Boeing's prototype for a new generation of aircraft. The first priority was the military market. The Monomail was followed almost immediately by a military version, the B-9 bomber, which was faster than the army's latest pursuit planes, and thus created a market for high-performance monoplane fighters. Boeing soon had a further development of the Monomail, the P-26 "Peashooter" fighter, as maneuverable as a biplane, but faster and much quicker in the climb. The army ordered 136 of them, and United sold more to China, Spain, and the Philippines, where in 1941 a Peashooter became one of the first Allied fighters to shoot down a Japanese bomber. The final development of the Monomail was the 247 model, a passenger transport for United Airlines. Flying at an unheard-of 190 miles per hour, it cut the usual twenty-eight-hour flight time from Los Angeles to New York by seven hours.

This was the benefit of industrial integration, the Boeing genius, in which the postal plane begat the military planes, which begat the passenger planes, which served the airline company that dominated the airmail market that required the postal plane in the first place. The first peacetime attempt by American private enterprise to create an integrated aviation industry, it was less a trust than a cartel aimed at dominance. And had it not been for the countercartel of North American Aviation, whose chairman, Harold Talbott, was also a director of TWA, the United group might have swept the field. But North American held 86,000 shares in Douglas Aircraft, and Talbott leaned heavily on Douglas to produce a rival commercial transport.

Douglas, who in the depth of the Great Depression had prospered, thanks to his reliable military contracts, did not want to return to the uncertainties of the civilian market. But Talbott was persuasive. He offered $125,000 for the first prototype plane, the DC-1, and Curtiss-Wright engines, which were controlled by North American. And he offered an order for sixty of the improved version, the DC-2. Douglas agreed, and the airliner that inspired the Shirley Temple song "The Good Ship Lollipop" was born. Within two years, it was to be followed by the legendary DC-3, of which over ten thousand were to be built. Douglas was always eager to export, and his DC-3 was built under license in Japan by Showa, to become the backbone of the Imperial Navy's wartime transport service. By 1934, over a third of American production was being exported, at higher prices, which meant exports delivered half of the industry's profits.

Douglas stayed out of the cartel system. The New Deal government of Franklin Roosevelt was no friend to such arrangements, and in 1934, it deployed antitrust legislation to break up the giant United Aircraft and Transport Corporation. The congressional hearings that preceded the legislation were a painful and infuriating experience for Boeing, who as chairman found himself accused of greedily distorting the development of the industry that he had helped build against heavy odds. Predicting the ruin of his beloved aviation now that the government had intervened, he retired to devote his time to raising thoroughbred horses. Congress also passed a law to prevent any aircraft manufacturer from owning an airline that had airmail contracts. United was broken up into three large groups, which still exist and flourish. United Airlines continues to fly the friendly skies. The Boeing Airplane Company took the manufacturing assets in the western half of the country, including the plant at Wichita, Kansas. Those assets in the eastern half were grouped under the new company United Technologies. It was for Boeing, the founder of the twin giants, Boeing Aircraft and United Airlines, almost the end of a pivotal career, but at least the component parts of the aviation empire he had built were sturdy enough to prosper.

Claire Egtvedt took over the leadership at Boeing and focused the company on very big aircraft and a hugely profitable small one that harkened back to the company's roots in 1915. This was the Stearman Kaydet trainer, a sturdy and stable biplane on which most World War II pilots learned to fly. Over 8,500 were made at the Wichita plant. The big planes were the B-17 "Flying Fortress" bomber, and the Stratoliner, which shared a pedigree in Boeing's model 299 prototype, along with its four engines. Egtvedt liked big planes—he could envisage the military contracts for bombers subsidizing the civilian version for passengers—and erected a huge billboard outside Seattle that proclaimed Boeing Field the "World Center of Four-Engine Airplane Development." The B-17 was the plane that mattered. The army had asked for a bomber with a 2,000-mile range and a speed of 200 miles per hour; the first B-17 flew 2,100 miles nonstop from Seattle to Wright Field in Ohio, at 232 miles per hour. Before one flight test, the mechanics forget to remove the locks that kept the elevators from flapping when the plane was on the ground.

America Reborn

The plane crashed, killing the test pilot. "Don't blame the plane," said the badly injured Lt. Donald Putt, who survived and went on to be U.S. Army Air Forces project engineer for the B-29 "Superfortress."

Despite the crash, the army bought the B-17, which was to shoulder the bulk of the Army Air Forces' bombing offensive against Germany in World War II. A strong and sturdy plane, the B-17 was supposed to inaugurate a new era of strategic bombing with its long range, its ability to fly at twenty thousand feet, and its five machine-gun posts to battle its way through enemy fighters. By 1942, after the lessons learned from an experimental squadron that flew with the RAF, the B-17s that arrived in Britain with the U.S. Eighth Air Force had been transformed. They were longer and taller, with bigger engines, a bigger tail with its own gun turret, and more guns. Only the wingspan was the same. It was a formidable plane, and over twelve thousand of them were to be built. By March 1944, they were rolling off the assembly lines at a rate of ten each day.

The problem with the B-17 was its small bomb load, barely two tons on missions from the British airfields to Berlin, less than the British twin-engine Mosquito bomber. As early as 1939, Boeing was working on an improvement, and as the German armies poured into Holland in 1940, Gen. Oliver Echols unfolded the new Boeing design for a sleek giant, with a range of over five thousand miles and three times the bomb load of the B-17. Echols instantly dubbed it a "Superfortress." As the Battle of Britain opened in the skies over England, Boeing was paid $3.6 million to make two prototypes of what would become the B-29, and he came out of retirement as a consultant on the breakneck pace of factory expansion. Almost four thousand B-29s were to be made by a giant Boeing company swollen to 78,000 workers by 1945, almost half of them women. Labor was in such short supply that 12 percent of the workforce had criminal records. "We hired anybody who had a warm body and could walk inside the gate," Boeing explained. Most of the B-29s were assembled at the new Renton, Washington, plant, outside Seattle, but the only part of the plane manufactured there was the giant aluminum wing spars. The bomb bays came from Vancouver, the wingtips from Cleveland, the landing gear from Milwaukee, the engine nacelles from the Fisher works in Detroit, and the 2,200-horsepower Wright Cyclone engines from Chicago.

The promise of mass production had finally been fulfilled. In 1939, aviation had been the country's forty-first industry in terms of dollar output. By 1945, it was in first place. American factories had turned out over 300,000 aircraft and over 800,000 engines. They employed over a million people. But when the war ended, the military contracts once again suddenly crashed to a halt. Boeing slashed its workforce by almost 90 percent, to fewer than nine thousand. But by the time a B-29 dropped the first atom bomb on Hiroshima,

Boeing had already designed a cargo version, the Stratofreighter, and the civilian version of the plane, the Stratocruiser. It was intended to launch the postwar civilian market by flying from Seattle to Washington, D.C., in just six hours.

Despite the postwar contraction, Boeing, like Douglas and Martin, had accumulated sufficient reserves from the war to keep making civilian planes. Again, the military helped, ensuring design skills that could take workers the next step into the jet age. Both the Lockheed Constellation and the Douglas DC-6 were supported by military-development work, and Northrop received Pentagon funds to develop the futuristic "flying wing," until the Cold War and the Korean War boom reopened the floodgates of public spending. Civilian and military development went hand in hand. The Boeing 707 airliner had as its military variant the KC-135 refueling tanker. And when the first passenger jet rolled out, Boeing came back to Renton, and his wife again performed the christening ceremony, this time with real champagne.

The lessons of the 1920s having been learned, the structure of the industry became settled after 1945. The Pentagon and the big aircraft producers settled into a mutually profitable symbiosis. Between 1947 and 1956, aerospace stocks rose in value three times the stock market average. The Cold War guaranteed the continued military contracts, and the fast-changing technology guaranteed continued development funds, for jets, antiaircraft missiles, and space rockets. The companies were big enough and rich enough to command the votes and campaign funds that guaranteed support in Congress; Boeing was so important to the regional economy of Seattle that the hawkish Washington senator Henry "Scoop" Jackson was known as "the Senator from Boeing."

The Cold War was shifting the new manufacturing base of the United States to the Sunbelt. The southern and western states had right-to-work laws, which weakened the role of trade unions. The South also enjoyed stable state politics, which meant that sheer longevity had won southerners the chairmanships of the key congressional committees, where the Pentagon's spending decisions were authorized. Lyndon Johnson of Texas was the Senate majority leader, and Georgia's Richard Russell and Carl Vinson ran the Senate and House Armed Services committees, respectively. The resulting symbiosis brought the Houston space center to Texas, where Bell helicopters and the Vought division of LTV Industries also boomed. Georgia's boom came with military bases, and the Lockheed plants at Marietta.

Since World War II, the aerospace industry had been building new industrial bases away from the traditional industrial heartland of the Northeast and the Great Lakes. The long military spending boom and the McDonnell Douglas, North American, and Hughes Aircraft plants helped explode the

America Reborn

California population sixfold in the five decades after 1940, while Boeing expanded in the Northwest. General Dynamics and McDonnell Douglas helped create another regional military-industrial complex in St. Louis. And in the name of national security, and justified in terms of the need to evacuate the cities in the event of a nuclear alert, all of these new industrial centers were linked into a continent-wide grid through the interstate highway network.

The defense budget assumed an awesome and permanent weight in the American economy. In 1960, nominally a time of peace, defense expenditure accounted for 52.2 percent of federal spending, or just over 10 percent of the GDP. It had been even higher, peaking at 12.7 percent of the GDP in 1954, until the Eisenhower administration devised the doctrine of "massive retaliation" with nuclear weapons as a slightly cheaper way of deterring the Communists. Budgets of that magnitude created powerful political and institutional constituencies. They were to be found in trade unions, among real estate developers around the booming new defense plants of Texas, Georgia, and California, and among the politicians whose electors worked through them. They all sought to ensure that the money continued to flow. Sums of this size—the U.S. defense budget was for the first two decades of the Cold War about half the size of the entire British economy—generated their own constituencies. Moreover, the ability to control and direct a defense budget worth 10 percent of the GDP also gave government a powerful lever to stimulate the rest of the economy.

As John Kennedy came into office in January 1961, the outgoing president, Dwight D. Eisenhower, delivered a farewell address that was uncharacteristically thoughtful, and sobering. He warned that the Cold War had produced something "new in American experience . . . the conjunction of an immense military establishment and a large arms industry. . . . [Its] influence is felt in every city, every statehouse, every office in the federal government. . . . In the councils of government, we must guard against the acquisition of unwarranted influence, whether sought or unsought, by the military-industrial complex."

Eisenhower had barely stopped speaking when his successor promised to "pay any price, bear any burden, meet any hardship, support any friend, oppose any foe to ensure the survival and success of liberty." Kennedy was to inaugurate the biggest peacetime increase in military spending in American history, and then intensify it with the pledge to put a man on the moon by the end of the decade. Overnight, the aviation industry became the aerospace industry, structured on the proven wartime principle of public funds, Pentagon procurement, and big corporations that could build their civilian growth on the research and development costs and profits of military contracts. They were cartels, much like the one Boeing had built with the United group of the early 1930s, but with the crucial addition of the Pentagon and government as the financial guarantors.

The company that failed to make this system work was Douglas, which was forced to generate internally the $200 million development costs of its DC-8 passenger jet. This almost broke the company, sending it into a slow decline that saw it bought out by James McDonnell, another engineer who had graduated from the Glenn Martin stable, to become McDonnell Douglas. Douglas himself, ever since 1921 a believer in the eventual promise of the civilian market, thought that the jet age would finally vindicate his vision. And, indeed, Boeing was to make the shift in the 1970s to greater dependence on the airlines than on the Pentagon. But the cost of developing a new airliner was so high that it became a mortal choice. Companies that failed to recoup their investments in the civil market died or were swallowed up. It happened to Douglas, and it was to happen to Lockheed, and even Boeing said it had bet the company's survival on the decision to develop the jumbo jet.

The end of the Cold War meant that the Pentagon's budget for weapons procurement, close to $100 billion a year at the 1988 peak, shrank to $40 billion by 1997. Employment in the defense industry dropped from almost 4 million in 1987 to 2.6 million ten years later. All this was prefigured in the famous "Last Supper" in 1993, when the then defense secretary, William Perry, called in the industry leaders to say the Pentagon wanted an intense reorganization of a sprawling industry that could no longer prosper on Cold War defense contracts. He urged a swift restructuring that would leave America best placed to dominate world export sales. The result was a spate of mergers and consolidations that left the country with two aerospace giants.

Lockheed, a leading manufacturer of military aircraft like the F-117 stealth warplane, the F-16 fighter, and the Hercules cargo workhorse, began the flurry of mergers by buying Martin Marietta for $10 billion in 1995. The new company, renamed Lockheed-Martin, bought Northrop, which made the B-2 stealth bomber, reuniting those famous names that had first gathered in California at the industry's birth on the eve of World War I. Then Boeing merged with McDonnell Douglas, a signal that a fresh battle was joined between Boeing and Lockheed to produce the new JSF (joint-strike fighter) for the U.S. Air Force and Navy and for Britain's Royal Navy. A contract worth some $300 billion over the next twenty years, it will define the future of the industry. It already has; McDonnell Douglas agreed to merge with Boeing when it was knocked out of the competition to build the JSF. Such was McDonnell Douglas's reliance on the Pentagon that in failing to win that one crucial contract for the JSF, its independence was lost. The new pecking order put Lockheed-Martin-Northrop on top, with annual sales of $38 billion, closely followed by Boeing–McDonnell Douglas, with sales of $35 billion (of which just over half came from commercial aviation).

There is more than sentiment in the survival of those old names of Boeing, Northrop, Douglas, Lockheed, and Martin, although there was abundant sentiment when the aged Douglas and Boeing acted as pallbearers at Glenn Martin's funeral in 1955. Tribute should be paid to the bold entrepreneurs, their brilliance of design, and their sheer stubbornness to stick with the business of flying, which they all loved. But their contraction into two huge conglomerates, facing the assembled prowess of the British, French, and German aerospace industries in their Airbus consortium, emphasized the price paid by individual genius to the relentless logic of Wall Street and the Pentagon.

8.
Duke Ellington
and the American Sound

On July 2, 1929, all the stars and talents of all the new musical forms
that America had unleashed on the twentieth century came together
in a single, extraordinary moment at New York's Ziegfeld Theatre. It
was the opening night of *Show Girl,* written by George Gershwin and featuring a ballet version of his unique fusion of jazz and classical music, *An American in Paris.* The show starred Jimmy Durante and Ruby Keeler, who had
married Al Jolson the previous year, and her big number was "Liza," played
not by the pit orchestra but by the hot new band from Harlem's Cotton Club,
led by Duke Ellington. As Ellington's ten-piece band launched into the opening chords and Keeler advanced to sing, a figure in evening dress rose in the
audience and ran down the aisle singing the same song—Jolson had launched
into an impromptu duet with his wife.

"It was probably foolish of me, after spending so much money on a large

America Reborn

orchestra, to include a complete band in addition," Florenz Ziegfeld recalled. "But the Cotton Club orchestra, under the direction of Duke Ellington, is the finest exponent of syncopated music in existence. Irving Berlin went mad about them."

Show Girl brought together the distinctive traditions that made American music so universally popular. There was jazz and there was syncopation, the sprightly lyrics and dancing of a Broadway musical, and the new and approachable kind of classical music that Gershwin had pioneered. They were all blended into the fast-paced and high-energy vaudeville and showbiz that was quintessentially American, in part because American audiences and performers have been so adventurous and open in their enthusiasm and their tastes.

Perhaps the first breakthrough came in 1923, when the Canadian soprano Eva Gauthier, trained at the Paris Conservatory, gave a concert at New York's prestigious Aeolian Hall, a program forbiddingly titled "Recital of Ancient and Modern Music for Voice." She sang music composed by Henry Purcell and Béla Bartók, William Byrd and Arnold Schoenberg, and then swung into modern American song. She delivered Irving Berlin's "Alexander's Ragtime Band," Jerome Kern's "The Siren's Song," and Gershwin's "I'll Build a Stairway to Paradise" and "Swanee." The *New York World*'s music critic, Deems Taylor, noted that Gershwin "stood up amazingly well, not only as entertainment, but as music."

The roots of the distinctive American sound are in black music, repeatedly adapted for white audiences. At age twenty-one, Gershwin, the son of Russian immigrants, had his first hit with "Swanee" for Al Jolson, who performed in blackface. By chance, Jolson heard Gershwin play it at a party in 1919, incorporated it into his show *Sinbad,* and, in January 1920, recorded it, to enormous success. In the same year, Gershwin composed a blues theme adapted for a string quartet. It was a precursor of his great orchestral pieces, *Rhapsody in Blue* and *An American in Paris.* Superb American fusions of jazz and the classical tradition, they were introduced to the new mass market for popular music with gramophones and new radio stations, just as classical music itself was becoming less accessible to popular taste. The combination was almost perfectly tailored for that new American art form, the Broadway musical, which was itself almost as easily adapted for film. From *Lady Be Good!* (1924) to *Porgy and Bess* (1935), Gershwin was pioneer and master of the form.

At the same time, Gershwin helped swell a global market that later saw Elvis Presley and the Beatles in turn adapt African-American musical forms to the majority white and popular taste. This commercial inspiration, the urge to make entertainment and money rather than aspire to art, has been a consistent current of the American sound. Eclectic and deliberately not pompous, it was an all-purpose music, to dance to, slow or fast, or to enjoy in a concert hall or over the radio at home, on a bar jukebox or in a local club. It was music that repaid attention but did not require it. It was as casual or as formal as the audience chose.

It was music, moreover, whose array of styles owed little to the grand traditions of Europe. It was not a Germanic symphony, an Italian opera, a French orchestral suite, or an English folk song or music hall ditty. There were Americans composing in this tradition, such as Aaron Copland and Charles Ives, with great skill and invention, and giving a specifically American flavor to their work. Ives's *Concord* Sonata, which he wrote and rewrote over thirty years, tried to convey in music the American writers of New England—the spirit of Ralph Waldo Emerson, the domesticities of Louisa May Alcott's family, the dark dreams of Nathaniel Hawthorne, and the sublime simplicity of Henry Thoreau's love of nature. But the homage in Ives's work looks back to Beethoven, with the echo of his Fifth Symphony being played in the homely piano of the Alcott parlor.

Copland, though born in Brooklyn, and filling his *Piano Variations* with the blues notes of Negro jazz and harmonic leaps of synagogue cantors, had been trained in Paris by Nadia Boulanger, and she conveyed her reverence for Stravinsky. Even in Copland's most deliberately American music, the ballets *Billy the Kid* and *Appalachian Spring,* or his film scores for *Our Town* and *Of Mice and Men,* Stravinsky looms over the composer's shoulder, reminding him how to incorporate a folk tune into a sonorous theme.

The classical training of Paris was far removed from the Poodle Dog Café on Georgia Avenue in Washington, D.C., where the fourteen-year-old Ellington took a job as a soda jerk in the summer of 1913. When the piano player got too drunk to perform, Ellington recalled, "the boss would throw him out, take my place behind the soda fountain and have me play piano. The only way I could learn how to compose a tune was to compose it myself and work it up, and the first one was 'Soda Fountain Rag'—putting some music to the rhythm that I used in jerking ice-cream sodas."

The second was called "What You Gonna Do When the Bed Breaks Down?" which young Ellington claimed was "a pretty good hug and rubbin' crawl." The lyrics went:

> Tried it on the sofa, tried it on the chair,
> Tried it on the table, didn't get nowhere,
> What you gonna do when the bed breaks down?

America Reborn

You've got to work out on the floor.
If you can't be good be careful.
And if you can't be careful, name it after me.

In the years before World War I, Washington was the center of black culture in America, the city where the most serious attempts had been made to give some meaning to Abraham Lincoln's emancipation of the slaves during the Civil War. Washington boasted the first public high school for blacks, a black hospital to train doctors and nurses, a teacher training college, and, the prime exhibit of black culture, Howard University. But in 1896, three years before Ellington was born, the Supreme Court had ruled that the racial segregation of public facilities was acceptable under the Constitution. It was a grim time, even for a young man like Ellington, who was born into a relatively prosperous home that boasted two pianos. His father worked as a driver and butler for a white doctor, and he sometimes did extra catering work at the embassies and even on occasion at the White House.

Ellington played the piano by ear, listening to the local professionals in the ever-growing number of Washington dance halls and filling in whenever he could. A local bandleader, Doc Perry, took a liking to him and his talent and taught him to read music. Nicknamed "Duke" because of his stylish clothes, he left school at seventeen and became an apprentice sign painter by day and an itinerant musician by night, in a city where ragtime dances were becoming the rage. He played at the British embassy, getting into trouble because he had no evening clothes and arrived in a loudly checked suit. During the war, he took a job as a messenger at the Navy Department, which kept him out of the army and in Washington, available to work. Hired one night to play at a Virginia country club, he had to surrender 90 percent of his fee to the booking manager, whereupon he resolved to set up in business for himself. His ad in the 1918 telephone directory offered "Irresistible Jass furnish to our select patrons. The Duke's Serenaders. Colored Syncopators. E. K. Ellington, manager."

Within the year, he was earning enough to buy his own house and car and marry his childhood sweetheart. Within nine months he was a father, and the jobs continued to flow in. Serious about his music, Ellington took lessons in formal harmony from the music teacher at the local black high school, and he took part in "battles of the bands" with other orchestras. He even took on James P. Johnson, who had written and recorded the fiendishly fast and difficult "Carolina Shout." Impressed by the young pianist, Johnson went out with him one evening to some of the bars and speakeasies of southwest Washington, where brawls and gunfire were commonplace; they stayed up talking until 10:00 a.m. "What I absorbed on that occasion might, I think, have constituted a whole semester in a conservatory," Ellington noted.

He was doing well, but Washington was no longer the big time. In March 1923, he went to the new center of black culture, Harlem, in New York. Southern blacks, West Indians, and Africans were flocking to the area, and the Urban League and Marcus Garvey's "Back to Africa" movement and W. E. B. Du Bois's National Association for the Advancement of Colored People had launched a dynamic black political culture. Harlem, two miles long and little more than half a mile wide, claimed 73,000 black residents in 1920, and more than 200,000 by 1930. Black writers like Langston Hughes and Rose McClendon, and musicians in the new all-black revues like *Shuffle Along* and *Running Wild* (which launched the new dance called the Charleston), all combined into the era of the Harlem Renaissance. And with 786 licensed dance halls in New York City, house parties every weekend, and a new market for "race records" after Mamie Smith recorded "Memphis Blues" in 1920, there was usually work for musicians. But there were so many musicians. Ellington struggled for a few months until getting a regular gig with Elmer Snowden and his Black Sox Orchestra at a basement dive called the Hollywood Club, near the corner of Forty-ninth Street and Broadway. Ellington loved the life and the hours, saying, "Nightlife is cut out of a very luxurious royal-blue bolt of velvet." He cut his first record that year, although it was never released, made his first radio broadcast on station WDT, and began writing songs for publishers.

The band decided on a new name, the Washingtonians, and began winning a reputation for torrid, "gutbucket" sounds, anchored on the New Orleans style of trumpeter Bubber Miley and the blues trombone of Charlie Ervis. They got a new contract when the old Hollywood Club was redecorated and reopened as the Kentucky Club. The legendary Sidney Bechet joined them in 1924, and the most popular bandleader of the day, Paul Whiteman, started coming to hear them. So did an aggressive young music publisher, Irving Mills, who had already signed up Hoagy Carmichael and Dorothy Fields. In Ellington, they saw a natural bandleader. Ellington had infused the Washingtonians with a loose discipline that became his hallmark. He wrote a series of arrangements that provided a framework in which each player would have his own set number of bars to improvise within a common theme. There was an overall sound, and solo opportunities within it. And the pace of work was intense, with a radio broadcast every afternoon, a revue to play in the early evening (if they could find the work), then the Kentucky Club until long after midnight, and then jamming and rehearsing for the next day.

Ellington was becoming known as a quick and professional composer,

America Reborn

once turning out four numbers overnight for a Charleston revue called *Chocolate Kiddies.* He was paid five hundred dollars. Then he signed with Mills, who promised to arrange a recording session with the Brunswick label, and his career began to take off. The two men started a company in which each held 45 percent and Irving's lawyer held the rest. Ellington would write and record the music and Mills would publish and promote it. Since Ellington was already handling the money and writing the arrangements for the band, it started being known as Duke Ellington and the Kentucky Club Orchestra, and they held their first session to record four of Ellington's compositions. The first success was "East St. Louis Toodle-O," and in the following year, 1927, Ellington made thirty-two recordings, including "Black and Tan Fantasy" and "Creole Love Call."

The combination of the black composer and the Jewish publisher proved fertile in a New York where blacks and Jews were still on the margins of American society, able to succeed most easily in entertainment and in sports like boxing. Still outsiders, the two minorities with a history of persecution shared a common political cause that endured into the civil rights era of the 1960s. There were common artistic alliances to be made. The American Negro Ballet was founded in 1934 by Eugene van Grona, after he had seen the plight of his Jewish father back in Germany. The Ellington-Mills relationship showed how fruitful a business partnership could be, as the two men realized that recordings were not simply a way to promote the band but were to become the profitable future of the music business. Ellington was quick to take Mills's point that by composing, recording, and publishing their own songs, the two could collect three sets of record royalties instead of just one. Ellington brought something else to the partnership, as well as his musical gifts. He was a recording perfectionist, experimenting with the placing of each instrument in the studio to get the most balanced sound.

In the era of Prohibition, New York boasted an estimated 100,000 illegal drinking establishments. The most successful featured music and dancing as well as the liquor smuggled in from Canada or by boat, or concocted in bathtubs by the mushrooming gangs. One of the most legendary nightspots was the Cotton Club on Harlem's 142nd Street, which looked like a log cabin on the outside and a jungle clearing inside. It was run by the British-born gangster Owney Madden, who brewed his own scotch and gin on the Lower West Side, and it was the favored after-theater spot in Harlem for rich Manhattan whites to go slumming, drinking, and dancing. "The aristocrat of Harlem," Lady Mountbatten called it. Hours were from 10:00 p.m. to 3:00 a.m., and there were two shows each night, one at midnight, the other at 2:00 a.m. "50 Most Beautiful Creoles" read the ads; the chorus girls had to be light-skinned, at least five eleven, able to sing, and no older than twenty-one.

Duke Ellington and the American Sound

In late 1927, Ellington's orchestra was hired—probably with help from Mills, who also represented Cotton Club performers—to be the house band. There was one problem, a touring contract that required them to be in Philadelphia at the same time. The club sent a persuasive representative named Yankee Schwarz to see if the contract could be renegotiated. "Be big, or be dead" were his words. The Philadelphia contract was canceled. At first, the gangsters were not sure they liked the "weird" music that Ellington composed—tunes like "The Mooche," "Hottentot," and "Jungle Night in Harlem." But the customers loved it, particularly when *Variety* gave a rave review to Ellington's radio broadcasts: "One of the hottest bands on the air is Duke Ellington's from the Cotton Club Monday midnight. One torrid trumpet brays and blares in low-down style that defies passiveness on hearing it." Calling one tune "dirty—a real wicked ditty," *Variety* gave the music a reputation for explicit sexuality, which was precisely what many of the customers came to Harlem for. Harlem's local paper, the *Amsterdam News,* wondered whether it was healthy for their community to be known as "a raging hell after dark."

"That part was degrading and humiliating," Ellington recalled years later. "But there was another part of it that was wonderful. That was the part out of which came so much of the only true American art—jazz music." But Ellington was already starting to break into that other true American art, the movies, which had become talkies with Jolson's 1927 breakthrough *The Jazz Singer.* In 1929, Ellington's band made their first film at RKO's Long Island studio, a nineteen-minute short, *Black and Tan,* directed by Dudley Murphy, who in the same year directed Bessie Smith in *St. Louis Blues. Black and Tan* was no breakthrough, but it featured two Ellington numbers, "Black Beauty" and "Black and Tan Fantasy." And it paved the way for Ellington's invitation, as the preeminent black bandleader, to join Gershwin at the Ziegfeld Theatre for that magical opening night when all the streams of American popular music suddenly flowed together for *Show Girl.*

It was the end of an era. *Show Girl* played for 111 performances, and then the stock market crashed and Ziegfeld lost most of his money. Gershwin sued him for nonpayment of royalties. The music business began to collapse as the Depression tightened. In 1929, 75 million records had been sold in America. By 1933, sales were down to 6 million. Even the national success of Ellington's classic "Mood Indigo" in 1931 could not sell as many records as lesser tunes had sold in the boom years. It remains compelling and almost revolutionary music, reversing the usual instrumental roles, with Tricky Sam Nanton on trombone taking the higher notes and Barney Bigard on clarinet taking the low ones, producing unique and haunting harmonies and the piece for which Ellington is perhaps most remembered.

America Reborn

But it was expensive to keep a ten-piece orchestra paid and fed, and the Cotton Club was feeling the pinch. The response of Mills and Ellington was to cash in on the national reputation his radio broadcasts and records had won and take the band on tour. Hiring his first vocalist, Ivie Anderson, Ellington found he could command up to five thousand dollars a week, when the Cotton Club had been paying fifteen hundred. Touring the South was difficult, in an era of segregation, when few big-city hotels would admit black guests. Ellington solved the problem by hiring his own train cars, in which the band could sleep as well as travel. "We commanded respect. We parked those cars in each railway station and we lived in them. We had our own water, food, electricity and sanitary facilities. The natives would come by and say 'What on earth is that?' and we'd say 'That's the way the President travels.' That was in the thirties. You do the best you can with what you've got."

Sadly, when Ellington's band crossed the Atlantic, breaking all box-office records at the London Palladium, they found it difficult to find hotels to take them; the band moved into a series of boardinghouses and small hotels. The BBC was ready to pay them the highest fee the corporation had ever paid for a broadcast. Ellington was stunned by the fans' knowledge of his music in Britain and in France, and by the way the band members were automatically treated as serious musicians performing concerts, rather than as a dance band, with a twenty-four-page program and respect from the audience even when the reviews were critical. "Where oh where are the renowned British qualities of aloofness, coldness, unemotionalism, self-restraint?" asked the *London Era* as "girls wept and young chaps sank to their knees."

Back home, Ellington broke all records in Chicago, playing to a total of 400,000 people, and running into some trouble from the organized criminal gangs of the city. He called Madden in New York for help, and Madden rang Al Capone. "When the kidnapping party arrived at the club, three of Al's men stepped out from behind pillars with drawn guns," said Barney Bigard, describing the scene later.

" 'Where you fellas going?' 'To see our friend.' 'What friend?' 'The Duke.' 'Since when has he been a friend of yours? Get the hell out of here!' That was the end of the threats," Bigard added.

The Duke's reputation had now spread far beyond Harlem, Broadway, and Chicago, and beyond popular music. Percy Grainger, chairman of the music department at New York University, invited the orchestra to play for his music class in 1932. Ellington, Grainger told his class, had a natural genius for melody that reminded him of Bach and Delius. "I'll have to find out about this Delius," Duke said.

He had to find out about more than Delius. Like Gershwin, Ellington had a remarkable facility in adapting to changing musical tastes and styles.

Duke Ellington and the American Sound

When Benny Goodman thrived in the swing era of the 1930s, Ellington's relentless rehearsing and his strict orchestral discipline, along with his sharp commercial sense, allowed him to remain among the top attractions. "Jazz is music, swing is business," he said. "I'm commercial because I've got to be. The support of the ordinary masses for the music from me, which they like, alone enables me to cater for the minority of jazz cognoscenti, who certainly on their own couldn't enable me to keep my big and expensive organization going."

He recorded "In a Jam" and "Uptown Downbeat" for the crucial jukebox market. Jukeboxes had grown in number from 25,000 to 300,000 in the course of the 1930s. But at the same time, Ellington's own musical horizons were stretching. He began to experiment with a jazz form of chamber music, with small six-piece groups, and hired the hugely gifted Billy Strayhorn to be his lyricist. Strayhorn, who went on to write "Take the A Train," became a joint composer of many of Ellington's more ambitious pieces like *Such Sweet Thunder* and *Far East Suite* when they began to exploit the potential of long-playing records. Strayhorn also helped arrange the annual Carnegie Hall concerts, which took Ellington far beyond the attentions of the jazz cognoscenti.

"In the exploitation of tonal coloring, Ellington has proceeded further than any composer—popular or serious—of today. His command of color contrast and blend approaches at times an art of polytimbres," wrote the Harvard-trained musician and music critic R. D. Darrell in *Disques.* "Ellington's finest tunes spring into rhapsodic being as simply, as naturally as those of Mozart or Schubert. . . . To me the most daring experiments of the modernists rarely approach the imaginative originality, mated to pure musicianship, of a dozen arresting moments in Ellington's works."

The praise was pleasant, coming from such unusual quarters, a discerning intellectual flattery that was to start a tradition. Three decades later, when the Beatles began to attract a similar respectful attention from serious musicians, the music critic of the *Times* of London also compared their songwriting to that of Schubert and Mozart. But then, Mozart and Schubert had been the popular composers of their day. Mozart, bored by the refined tastes and demands of the imperial court of Vienna and its insistence that opera be written in Italian, relished the coarser response of the eighteenth-century equivalent of the music hall for the low comedy and magical effects of *The Magic Flute,* performed in German. In the same way, Puccini insisted on rejecting the usual grand cast of aristocrats in palaces and using real and ordinary people, like the humble seamstress Mimi and her impoverished poet lover in their garret for *La Bohème,* which was the great hit of its day. Gershwin's *Porgy and Bess,* in which impoverished black characters sang opera, and Leonard Bernstein's *West Side Story,* which adapted Shakespeare's *Romeo and Juliet* for the lower-class ethnic groups of 1950s New York, were following a proud and proven tradition. Some works may be disdained initially, but the tastes of the broader market usually impose themselves in the long run upon the classicists and upon the elite. American composers instinctively understood this from the beginning.

Ellington was not so sure about *Porgy and Bess,* grumbling that it was about time "to debunk Gershwin's lampblack Negro-isms." To Ellington's ears, the music rang slightly false, and he felt that Gershwin's attempt to marry high operatic art with the demotic rhythms of black life had "borrowed from everyone from Liszt to Dickie Wells's kazoo—the music does not hitch with the mood and spirit of the story."

Ellington was never intimidated by classical music or by classical themes. His own Shakespearean suite, *Such Sweet Thunder,* draws on *Othello.* First, there is the grandly heroic Moor, bewitching Desdemona with marvelous tales, but then, in "Sonnet in Search of a Moor," comes the sadness of Othello's essential loneliness, as a proud black man in a white world, whose very embrace of his white wife symbolizes his own vulnerability. His piece on Henry V, "Sonnet to Hank Cinq," is opéra buffe by comparison, a swaggering jazz tune set to a boogie beat. And perhaps to show that Bernstein could not have the whole field to himself, Ellington's own treatment of *Romeo and Juliet,* "Star-Crossed Lovers," is a gently sad masterpiece of a pop song, piano tinkling out tragedy amid tones of doomed grandeur within the structure of a ballad.

And yet, in the end and to the end, Ellington was a jazz musician. In the estimated twenty thousand performances that he gave in a musical career that stretched for sixty years, the most dramatic and the most satisfying took place in July 1956 at the Newport Jazz Festival. Jazz had moved on and perhaps away from Ellington, with the explosive riffs of Charlie Parker and the arcane intellectual seriousness of the Modern Jazz Quartet. The new boom market for white teenagers was rock 'n' roll, which may have had its origins in black rhythm and blues, but the artists of the 1950s were white and the black roots were kept firmly underground. Ellington's music, whether the immaculate orchestrations of his band performances or the more adventurous suites, seemed dated. He had been around a very long time, and, with his performances for European royalty and at the White House, he had become a part of the musical establishment. He composed and recorded a piece for Britain's Queen Elizabeth II, *The Queen's Suite,* but he pressed only a single copy, which he gave to her, and refused to allow it to be published again until after his death.

Duke Ellington and the American Sound

At the same time, as if to demonstrate that he was still at the cutting edge, he was recording with the King of Bebop, Dizzy Gillespie, and with modern performers like John Coltrane. All of this made Newport important, as if Ellington felt he needed a comeback. He had composed *Newport Festival Suite,* which the band played, and then went into two 1930s masterpieces, "Diminuendo" and "Crescendo in Blue." Paul Gonsalves took twenty-seven choruses, and the crowd almost rioted in their adulation, forcing encore after encore until after 1:00 a.m. *Time* wrote a cover story, and *Ellington at Newport* became his biggest-selling album. "I was born in 1956 at the Newport festival," Ellington joked, delighted, after his popularity had waned, to be back at the top.

Although black activists had criticized him in the past for refusing to take a stand on race, he began to use his status as a national treasure for the civil rights movement. In Baltimore, he made a point of going to restaurants where blacks had been refused admission, and he refused to play a 1961 concert in Little Rock, Arkansas, because the audience would be segregated. Insisting he would only appear before mixed audiences, he forced the auditoriums in Dallas and Houston to drop their color bar.

In 1963, his orchestral suite *My People,* based on Ellington's statement "The foundation of the United States rests on the sweat of my people," had its premiere in Chicago. Borrowing heavily from his earlier suite *Black, Brown and Beige,* it was a stylized homage to the black experience, running through gospel, jazz, tap dance, and blues and ending with the stirring "King fit the battle of Alabam" on the confrontation between the civil rights marchers and the police at Birmingham, and a final coda, "What Color Is Virtue, What Color Is Love?" Neither a critical nor a commercial success, it sounded more than a little forced. But Ellington then reworked it in 1965 into his last masterpiece, *Concert of Sacred Music,* a stately jazz mass commissioned for the consecration ceremony of San Francisco's new Grace Cathedral.

All this amounted to an extraordinary and perhaps unprecedented musical range, from ragtime and "The Mooche" to religion and the mass, Shakespearean suites to the slapstick of "What You Gonna Do When the Bed Breaks Down?" from *Show Girl,* to the jazz classics of "Mood Indigo" and "Sophisticated Lady." And while he was arranging *Concert of Sacred Music* and composing his *Second Sacred Concert* for its premiere at the Cathedral of St. John the Divine in New York City, he was also in charge of the arrangement and recording for the jazz list of Frank Sinatra's new Reprise record company. In a final flourish, as if to assert that no brand of music was beyond him, he even tried his hand at rock. "Acht O'Clock Rock," which he played as part of a new suite, *Afro-Eurasian Eclipse,* at the 1970 Monterey Jazz Festival, was a sad pastiche, with but a fraction of the energy of "Rockin' in Rhythm," which he had written and recorded nearly forty years earlier. Ellington died of lung cancer in 1974, having managed to survive most of that core of band members who had stayed with him for over thirty years. "A genius has passed," said Ella Fitzgerald. The Moscow Conservatory hung out black crepe, and in London's Westminster Abbey, where he had recently recorded *Concert of Sacred Music,* a requiem service was held for America's greatest composer.

9.
Winston Churchill
and the American Diaspora

W hen Congress voted American citizenship to Winston Churchill at the end of World War II, he suggested that only "an accident of birth" had prevented him from sitting among them. His mother had been an American, Jennie Jerome, daughter of a tycoon known as the King of Wall Street. Her father, Leonard Jerome, was related by marriage to the Roosevelts, which meant that the wartime alliance of Churchill and Franklin Roosevelt was a family affair. The British prime minister and the American president were distant cousins. Churchill's mother had met and fallen instantly in love with Lord Randolph Churchill at a ball at the Cowes sailing regatta, given by the Prince of Wales for his guest, the heir to the tsarist throne of Russia. Winston was the result of the union, and without doubt he was the most eminent of the children born of the fashion for marriages between American wealth and British nobility.

America Reborn

The Illustrated London News ran several series of articles on such marriages, under the title "America and the Peerage," in the generation before 1914, page after page graced by the portraits of the Duchess of Manchester, the Countess of Essex, Viscountess Deerhurst, and Lady Abinger. The Astors, the Harrimans, and the Mellons were all to join this admixture of the New World's wealth and the Old World's titles. There were over a hundred such alliances, including the wives of the eighth, ninth, and tenth Dukes of Marlborough. In 1895, the ninth duke married Consuelo Vanderbilt, who recalled that "in a small room in the church itself, the bridegroom and the bride's father signed an agreement giving Marlborough a dowry of $1.6 million in cash and the income from $2 million in gilt-edged stocks." The eventual price tag for the marriage, with subsequent gifts, pensions, and subsidies for the rebuilding of Blenheim Palace, was estimated at $20 million.

"It is a very curious fact that, with all our boasted free and equal superiority over the communities of the Old World, our people have the most enormous appetites for Old World titles of distinction," noted Oliver Wendell Holmes. And as the agricultural depression gripped the landed estates of England in the late nineteenth century, a depression deepened by the availability of cheap corn and beef from the American prairies, the British aristocracy developed an equal appetite for American money. At the age of eighty, Lord Donegall was blunt enough to put the terms in writing in a newspaper advertisement—his hand and his peerage for £25,000.

Not all the marriages involved the nobility. There were political dynasties, as well. Joseph Chamberlain, leader of Britain's Liberal Unionist party and, some said, the best prime minister Britain never had, married Mary Endicott, the daughter of President Grover Cleveland's secretary of war. Their son Neville was to prove one of Britain's worst prime ministers, his umbrella an enduring symbol of the appeasement of Hitler in the 1930s. The daughter of Dr. Tarleton Halles of Indiana was to give Britain yet another Anglo-American prime minister in Harold Macmillan. Consuelo Vanderbilt, whose expensive marriage to the Duke of Marlborough ended in separation and divorce after fourteen years, and who remained in Britain to become a leading campaigner for women's rights, was eventually elected as a Liberal to the London County Council. And in the House of Commons, Churchill, Chamberlain, and Macmillan shared the green benches with Nancy Astor, the first woman member of Parliament.

She took the seat of her husband, Waldorf, who was furious that he could not surrender the title he had inherited on his father's death and had to go to the House of Lords. The peerage had cost William Waldorf Astor over a million dollars in donations to charities—which was the subtle British way of arranging these matters—by the time he was finally ennobled in 1916. The family fortune—from the fur trade and then from hotels—could easily support it. But by then, the political power of the House of Lords had been dramatically reduced after the constitutional crisis of "the Peers versus the People" in 1911. It was no longer conceivable that a prime minister could sit in the House of Lords. For Astor's son, inheriting the title in 1919 effectively meant the end of a promising political career; he had been private secretary to Prime Minister David Lloyd George. But the family retained extraordinary influence; Waldorf owned the preeminent Sunday newspaper, *The Observer,* and his brother John Jacob owned *The Times.*

The coincidence is striking. Americans were buying into the British upper classes just as their political influence was being sharply reduced by the Liberal government that had swept into power in 1906. One of the leading members of this government, which fought and won a major constitutional battle to curb the powers of the House of Lords, was the young Winston Churchill. As home secretary, a job that included the functions of minister for justice and what mainland Europeans would call minister of the interior, Churchill, along with the humbly born Welsh lawyer Lloyd George, was one of the government's young stars. He was also, in the eyes of some members of the House of Lords, including his own family, a traitor to his class. But then as the son of a younger son of a duke, he had little hope of succeeding to the family title, the Dukedom of Marlborough, granted along with the great palace of Blenheim to his valiant military ancestor for repeated victories over the armies of France's "Sun King," Louis XIV.

These twin themes of political treachery and the accidents of noble birth were to run through Churchill's career. First elected to Parliament in 1900 as a Conservative, he soared to prominence as a Liberal, and abandoned this party after World War I to rejoin the Conservatives, rising to become chancellor of the exchequer and thus in charge of the national economy. Then in the 1930s, he became a rebel within his party. He fought Prime Minister Stanley Baldwin over his attempts to bring home rule to India, jewel of the British Empire, and over Baldwin's determination that King Edward VIII should abdicate rather than be allowed to marry the American divorcée Wallis Simpson. Churchill sought to establish and lead a king's party, but after some characteristic dithering, the king refused to cooperate. Churchill's greatest rebellion against his fellow Conservatives was to lead the opposition to the policy of Baldwin and his successor, Neville Chamberlain, of appeasing Hitler, buying him off and buying time by acquiescing to his seizure of Germany's neighbors. Finally, in May 1940, as Nazi Germany conquered Norway and prepared the great blitzkrieg invasion that would lead to the fall of France and the evacuation of some 300,000 men of the British army from Dunkirk, Churchill's long rebellion bore fruit. Chamberlain was voted out in a parliamentary coup and Churchill became prime minister and war leader. Had it not been for the political difficulty of having a prime minister in the House of Lords, Chamberlain and King George VI were both maneuvering to block Churchill by nominating the foreign secretary (and apostle of appeasement), Lord Halifax, for the job. Halifax was sent off instead to Churchill's mother's homeland, as ambassador to Washington.

Not that Churchill needed an ambassador in Washington. His prime concern was to build a personal and political relationship with President Franklin Roosevelt that would bring the United States into the war and thus maintain the Anglo-American alliance throughout the war and thereafter. The flavor of the relationship, at least in Churchill's perception, is best caught by that moment when Roosevelt mistakenly entered the bathroom while Churchill was toweling himself dry, whereupon Churchill said, "His Majesty's prime minister has nothing to hide from the President of the United States." Roosevelt, despite his natural cordiality, his affection for Churchill, and his belief in the Allied war effort, was not to be so easily seduced. Roosevelt was aware that Britain was an overstretched and declining power, and he took his relations with Stalin more seriously. Indeed, Churchill was constantly nervous that the "Big Two" might meet without him, and when they arranged to do so, during a brief interlude at the 1943 Tehran summit, he was dismayed, waspishly telling Averell Harriman that he was "glad to obey orders."

With the benefit of hindsight, perhaps the most lasting impact of Churchill's political career was his arranging the tidy transfer of global power from an exhausted Britain to an ebullient America. By insisting throughout the late 1930s that Britain must prepare to fight Hitler, and after 1940 that it must be prepared to fight on alone, Churchill was condemning Britain to a battle that it could hardly win without losing its global primacy in naval and commercial affairs to the Americans. And very swiftly after its naval and commercial power was outmatched, the British Empire was slowly but inevitably abandoned. Too poor to hang on, too proud to let go, Britain clung for another twenty years to an imperial status it could no longer sustain, comforted only by the illusory compensation—which Churchill had embraced during the war—of a lasting and binding special relationship with the American successor.

Churchill had hoped for far more. In May 1943, in a private memorandum to Roosevelt, he proposed "some common form of citizenship" between Britain and the United States, so that they would be "able to come and settle and trade with freedom and equal rights in the territories of the other. There might even be a common passport." The idea was discussed politely, although not embraced, at a White House lunch. Four months later, back in the United States to receive an honorary degree from Harvard, Churchill raised the idea of "common citizenship" in public, this time with an emotional appeal to the common heritage and destiny of "the English-speaking peoples," a theme that had engrossed him since he had begun a historical series of that title in the 1930s. Indeed, the speech for which Churchill is now best remembered, his warning at Fulton, Missouri, in 1946 of an iron curtain descending across Europe, was far more concerned with his proposal that the way to counter the Soviet threat was to establish "a special relationship between the British Commonwealth and Empire and the United States. . . . It should carry with it the continuance of the present facilities for mutual security by the joint use of all naval and air force bases in the possession of either country all over the world."

"We have become conscious of our common duty to the human race. Language, law, and the processes by which we have come into being, already afforded a unique foundation for drawing together and portraying a concerted task," he argued, returning to the theme in political retirement, in the 1956 preface to his *History of the English-Speaking Peoples.* It was, of course, a chimera, and it explains why President Truman and the other leading American politicians in the audience were at the time unmoved by a speech that has gone down in legend as the Sibylline prophecy of the Cold War. Whatever Churchill's rhetoric, a proud republic that had battled for its independence against the British crown at the summit of its powers was hardly likely to welcome merger with an enfeebled monarchy whose imperial pretensions and class system embodied all that America was not. Churchill had begun his series on the English-speaking peoples in the aftermath of the 1936 crisis over the abdication of King Edward VIII. At the 1937 coronation of his replacement, the younger brother who was crowned as George VI, the traditional text of the ceremony, unchanged for four centuries, prayed that the new sovereign should be blessed with "a loyal nobility, a dutiful gentry, and an honest, peaceable and obedient commonality." It would not be easy to draft anything less likely to attract to a common citizenship Americans born and raised within the structure of a Constitution that began with the sovereign words "We, the people . . ."

Churchill loved America, but he did not understand it. On his first visit in 1900, on a lecture tour to promote his book about his capture and escape from the Boers during the South African War, he was stunned by the hostility to this imperial venture by Americans engaged in their own first taste of colonial warfare after the United States had expelled Spain from Cuba and the Philippines. He was delighted and honored that his first lecture in New York was "chaired by no less a personage than Mark Twain himself," apparently unaware that Twain was passionately involved in the Anti-Imperialist League. "Of course we argued about the war," Churchill recalled. "After some exchanges, I found myself beaten back to the citadel, 'My country right or wrong.' 'Ah,' said the old gentleman. 'When the poor country is fighting for its life, I agree. But this was not your case.' "

Churchill might have expected a very different reception from Theodore Roosevelt when he traveled up to Albany to lunch with the governor of New York. But the two men did not get on. Churchill thought it was because they argued over whether some Boer War incident had taken place at Bloemfontein, as Churchill maintained, or Magersfontein, as Roosevelt insisted. Roosevelt was right, and Churchill later apologized. But he never realized that the real reason for Roosevelt's frostiness was an affront to his sense of good manners; Churchill had failed to stand when the ladies entered the room. Churchill never understood this. He claimed, over a lunch in 1940 with Roosevelt's grandson Kermit (who had just volunteered to join the British army), that it was all a misunderstanding: Roosevelt had been appalled by a false story that Churchill had risked the health of his native bearers by going into tsetse fly country on an African safari.

If Franklin Roosevelt was the American president on whom Churchill depended, Teddy Roosevelt was the American politician Churchill most resembled. Indeed, the inspiration for Churchill's own historical series probably came from his reading of Teddy Roosevelt's *The Winning of the West,* which begins: "During the past three centuries, the spread of the English-speaking peoples over the world's waste spaces has been not only the most striking feature in the world's history, but also the event of all others most far-reaching in its importance."

The parallels in their careers are striking. Both men were authors and historians, radicals at home but imperialists aboard, and devout believers in sea power. Neither man cared much for party loyalty, although each was to prove a devoted husband. Whether Roosevelt was New York reformer, Republican, or Bull Mooser, and whether Churchill was Liberal or Conservative, each man clambered aboard whatever political vehicle seemed most convenient, and most likely to bring personal advancement.

More than that, each was to bring the other's qualities into his own native politics. Teddy Roosevelt imposed that deeply British sense of national destiny and racial pride upon the America of his day. Churchill brought the dash of the maverick and of the lone adventurer to the class and party rigidities of Britain. Each might have had glittering and probably similar careers in the other's country, and even their Anglo-American sentiments were at times almost interchangeable. As Roosevelt wrote in 1918 to his old friend Rudyard Kipling: "I am stronger than ever for a working agreement between the British Empire and the United States; indeed I am now content to call it an Alliance."

But in 1918, Britain still appeared to be at the peak of its powers, and any such arrangement would have been an alliance of near equals. Churchill's appeals during and after World War II carried more than a whiff of supplication. There was little doubt of the respective pecking order during his first wartime meeting with FDR in August 1941, with Pearl Harbor still five months in the future. Sir John Colville, Churchill's secretary, confided in his diary that "he is as excited as a schoolboy on the last day of term." And Harry Hopkins, who accompanied Roosevelt to the meeting aboard the British battleship *Prince of Wales* in Placentia Bay off Newfoundland, noted, "You'd have thought Winston was being carried up to the heavens to meet God!" Churchill had prepared the theater of the occasion with care, and he took a personal interest in the hymns that the British and American sailors would sing during a Sunday-morning church service on board, under the muzzles of the fourteen-inch guns. The symbolism of the shipboard summit took on a more somber note the following year, when the *Prince of Wales* was sunk by Japanese bombers during the campaign that saw the capture of Singapore, Britain's main naval base in the East.

Churchill, who visited the United States repeatedly and made much of his living in the 1930s from freelance writing for American magazines (money he needed after his losses in the Wall Street crash), had understood the essence of the matter. What he was first to call "the special relationship" did not come automatically from a common language, law, and culture, or even from the dynastic and political marriages and alliances of the kind he embodied. The extraordinary intimacy that developed between the two governments was a direct result of the war, and the enforced proximity of alliance politics. In 1939, there had been nineteen British diplomats in the Washington embassy; by 1944, there were over nine thousand. It was, noted army chief of staff Gen. George Marshall, "the most complete unification of military effort ever achieved by two allied nations." This partnership continued during the Cold War, and until the Minuteman intercontinental ballistic missiles began to deploy in the 1960s, the American nuclear deterrent depended on British bases to reach their Soviet targets. It was not just a wry joke that inspired George Orwell to dub Britain "Airstrip One" in his novel *1984*.

British and American military units shared bases, equipment, and training facilities. The British used U.S. Polaris and Trident submarines; the U.S. Marine Corps flew British Harrier jets. The intelligence services of the two countries were even closer, locked together by tradition, treaty, and habit, and by the shared SIGINT data from the signals intelligence listening posts that the geographic spread of the old British Empire was so usefully able to furnish, from Hong Kong to Cyprus. Their diplomats worked together (usually) at the United Nations Security Council, the most famous of the international institutions the Anglo-American alliance built after 1945. Their economists worked together at the World Bank and the International Monetary Fund, as their military men served together at NATO, and their spies jointly built and manned the famous underground tunnel to tap the military telephone lines in the Soviet sector of Berlin. Whole generations of British and American officers, experts, and officials grew up with and passed on this unprecedented tradition of governmental partnership.

It was helped by the common language, which also helps to explain the equally striking pattern of America's writers and artists, as well as its heiresses, military officers, and businessmen, making their way across the Atlantic to put down abiding roots. On June 29, 1915, as the war gripped the Western Front, Henry James wrote a letter in characteristic prose to the British prime minister, Herbert Asquith. It read:

> I am venturing to trouble you with the mention of my personal situation, but I shall do so as briefly and considerately as possible. I desire to offer myself for naturalization in this country, that is, to change my status from that of an American citizen to that of a British subject. I wish to testify at this crisis to the force of my attachment and devotion to England and to the cause for which she is fighting. I can only testify by laying at her feet my explicit, my material and spiritual allegiance, and throwing into the scale of her fortune my all but imponderable moral weight—a poor thing but my own! hence this respectful appeal.

James became the squire of the quintessentially medieval hilltop English town of Rye, whose principal tavern, the Mermaid, proudly boasted that it had been "Restored in 1488," some years before Columbus had landed in the New World. Thomas Stearns Eliot did not go quite so native, but this seminal modern poet stayed in England to work as a teacher, then as a bank employee, and subsequently as an English publisher. The company of the Vorticists, one of those artistic movements so fashionable at the time, which included another eminent American poet, Ezra Pound, and the British poet and artist Wyndham Lewis (whose father was American), helped draw him in. It was a well-trodden path, adopted by two outstanding American artists, James McNeill Whistler and John Singer Sargent, and by the American theatrical impresario Colonel Bateman, who launched Henry Irving's stage career.

The process of the American diaspora may have begun and been more intense and enduring with Britain, but England was not the only lure. Some 2 million Americans went to Europe to fight in World War I, and many of them stayed on or returned, for the art, for the women, for the relaxed sexual code, for the adventure, or to enjoy the favorable exchange rate. From Gertrude Stein to Ernest Hemingway, Scott Fitzgerald to Henry Miller, they gravitated almost naturally to France, which for most Americans was the first foreign land they had seen. "If you are lucky enough to have lived in Paris as a young man, then wherever you go for the rest of your life, it stays with you, for Paris is a moveable feast," wrote Hemingway thirty years later. And in Paris, they found more Americans, so many that their presence is now a part of the city's own legend, and their cafés, like the Dôme, now trade on the ancient custom.

After World War II, Americans stayed on first as occupation forces of the defeated enemy and then as allies guarding countries that had been democratized under Anglo-American guidance. In Germany, the British, and to a lesser extent the French, took part in de-Nazification, and in the establishment of a free press, free trade unions, and political institutions. John McCloy, former assistant secretary of war, became as U.S. high commissioner almost a viceroy of West Germany, and the midwife of its industrial reconstruction and recovery. Having come to Germany from his last post as head of the infant World Bank, McCloy had the magic wand of Marshall Plan aid at his disposal, and he urged the big American industrial groups like Ford and General Motors to invest and start manufacturing in what McCloy saw would be Europe's biggest single market.

The intensification of the Cold War was a crucial factor in the way McCloy was able to transform military occupation into friendly alliance. The week before the invasion of South Korea in 1950, McCloy rejected the appeal of German chancellor Konrad Adenauer for a national police force of 25,000 men. Immediately after the invasion, however, McCloy quickly authorized the force. In the mood of intense panic that gripped Germany, so fearful of a Soviet invasion that Adenauer's office begged McCloy for two hundred pistols to defend its inhabitants against fifth columnists, McCloy cabled to Washington a dramatic appeal for German rearmament: "If no means are held out for Germany to fight in an emergency, my view is that we should probably lose Germany politically as well as militarily, without hope of regain. We should also lose, incidentally, a reserve of manpower which may become of great value in event of a real war."

In Japan, an even greater role was played by Gen. Douglas MacArthur, who rewrote the Japanese constitution to ensure that in the future Japan would have only self-defense forces, redefined the role of the emperor as a constitutional monarch, and insisted on education for women. Backed with a brain trust of young Americans, mainly social democrats thrilled by the opportunity to reshape an entire nation, MacArthur had begun by trying to dismantle the *zaibatsu,* the interlocking industrial and financial conglomerates that had dominated the prewar economy.

The outbreak of the Korean War, which overnight transformed Japan into an advanced industrial base for the Cold War and a potentially crucial ally, reversed American policy, and huge industrial trusts were encouraged as locomotives of future growth. The two greatest beneficiaries were the Mitsui group (including Toyota, Toshiba, and the Mitsukoshi department stores) and Mitsubishi (which includes Nikon, Kirin beer, Meiji life insurance, and NYK shipping). The Pentagon's special procurement budget, which allowed them to buy military supplies locally, pumped over $3.5 billion into the Japanese economy between 1950 and 1955. These funds, the equivalent of the American investment in West Germany through the Marshall Plan, financed the new shipyards, the railroads, and even the first Toyota truck assembly line, all to feed the embattled armies in Korea.

America's global role was the great force that drew its people overseas from the opportunities and energies of their own country. In terms of numbers, the overwhelming cause of their travels, both after 1917 and after 1941, was war or military service. France was the great attraction for the first generation, although Hemingway had served in the ambulance corps on the Italian front. Some went to the Spanish Civil War of the 1930s as volunteers in the socialist cause. And then some 4 million passed through Britain during World War II, on their way to the fronts, where they fought their way to the German heartland from Italy, from Normandy, and from southern France, or through the air in their Flying Fortresses. And then with the coming of the Cold War, the GIs returned again, some 300,000 of them as a permanent garrison standing watch on the Rhine for forty years. By the time the Berlin Wall fell in 1989, both the American and British garrisons in West Berlin boasted soldiers whose fathers and grandfathers had stood guard in the same isolated enclave. With their wives and families and the U.S. Navy crews of the Sixth Fleet, there were never fewer than half a million Americans stationed in Europe from the end of the 1940s until the early 1990s. As Senator Daniel Patrick Moynihan noted, "This is the stuff of Roman legions."

Moynihan himself, who had served in the navy in World War II, used the GI bill to study in England, and tens of thousands of veterans followed his example, at Oxford, Cambridge, and the London School of Economics; others studied at the Sorbonne in Paris, or in Heidelberg, Germany. The chance to live and study abroad was eagerly seized, and not just through the GI bill. The young Henry Luce, before founding *Time* magazine, used his fifteen-hundred-dollar share of the profits of the *Yale Daily News* in 1920 to buy himself a year at Christ Church College, Oxford. Luce spent his Christmas vacation under the wing of Thornton Wilder, then studying at the American Academy in Rome, and there met his first wife, Lila Ross Holz, of Chicago, who was spending a year at Miss Risser's celebrated finishing school for young Americans.

The classic route for Americans to study in Europe was through the Cecil Rhodes scholarships to Oxford, established by a British tycoon who made his fortune in Africa and dreamed of bringing back the lost American colonies into an Anglo-American empire. Rhodes believed that English-speaking elites around the world had something in common that could be captured by the shared experience of two years' immersion at Oxford, and then refined and reinforced by a lifetime of networking thereafter. There were two flaws in the Rhodes concept from the beginning. The first was Oxford, which gave the early scholars a cold shoulder. The Oxford Union voted heavily against having them at all. Half of the two thousand American applicants until 1919 were rejected because they could not meet Oxford's requirements in Greek and Latin. The second was Rhodes himself, who embodied a concept of authority and of empire that was more Roman or even Teutonic than British. He fancied himself a kind of reincarnation of the emperor Hadrian, commissioned endless Roman busts of himself, and arranged his funeral in the Roman style. The will that established the Rhodes Trust called for any funds left over to be devoted to the cause of establishing a new political force, the Imperial party.

Oswald Spengler, the prophet of Nazism, concluded, "Rhodes is to be regarded as the first precursor of a western type of Caesar. He stands midway between Napoleon and the force-men of the coming centuries." Spengler, sympathetic to Rhodes's view that the British and Americans as Anglo-Saxons were part of a Teutonic master race, saw Rhodes as an honorary German: "In our Germanic world the spirits of Alaric and Theodoric will come again—there is a first hint of them in Cecil Rhodes." Adolf Hitler agreed. At dinner in April 1942, musing on Britain's decline since the Victorian heights, Hitler noted that only Rhodes had understood the way in which British supremacy might be maintained, but the feeble British had ignored him.

This is not how Britain, or Oxford, or the grandees of the Rhodes concept choose to remember Rhodes now. In 1983, Oxford chancellor Harold Macmillan hosted the Rhodes reunion and declared, "From the monks of the abbeys of 1112 A.D. we have moved from the Age of Faith to the Age of Credulity. In that period, the most imaginative concept or grand design was that of Cecil Rhodes."

The most important contribution of the Rhodes scholarships was, at the dawn of the twentieth century, the creation of the first institution that allowed people from one country to study in another. Rhodes's vision was swiftly copied. The Fulbright scholarships, the German Marshall Fund scholarships, and the Harkness and Churchill fellowships far outnumber the Rhodes in the opportunities they offer. The Japanese crown prince and his princess went to Oxford, but they did not do so as Rhodes scholars. Nor is the Rhodes scholarship a guarantee of success. One who tried and failed to make the grade went on to become president: Jimmy Carter. Nor were the Rhodes scholarships quite the means that their founder envisaged of cementing an Anglo-American elite. In their prime before World War II, the Rhodes scholarships produced more American missionaries to China than they did U.S. government officials, elected congressmen, or lawyers. In the postwar period, the fruition of the Rhodes dream of force-breeding an Anglo-American official elite has also seen the slow erosion of the broader U.S.-British relationship.

Even Rhodes could hardly have dreamed of the kind of political success his legacy was to have in the 1990s, with the Clinton administration. Never has any foreign country been run so completely by such a narrowly defined and foreign-educated elite. Clinton himself was a Rhodes scholar, and he was surrounded by others, from domestic policy adviser Bruce Reed to communications director George Stephanopoulos to Ira Magaziner, who ran the ill-fated health-reform initiative. Another Rhodes scholar, James Woolsey, was director of the CIA, and yet another, Strobe Talbott, who had been Clinton's Oxford roommate, was deputy secretary of state. Two others were Walter Slocombe, assistant secretary of defense, and Robert Reich, secretary of labor. Rhodes scholar David Souter sat on the Supreme Court, and James Billington was Librarian of Congress. Six Rhodies served in the Senate (Paul Sarbanes of Maryland, Russell Feingold of Wisconsin, David Boren of Oklahoma, Paul Lugar of Indiana, Larry Pressler of South Dakota, and Bill Bradley of New Jersey). And yet this was an administration that presided over what looked to be a twilight of the Anglo-American special relationship. The United States ran roughshod over Britain's attempt to continue testing nuclear weapons in Nevada. President Clinton gave a visa to Gerry Adams of Sinn Fein, over the outraged complaints of Prime Minister John Major, as part of Clinton's successful bid to launch a peace process in Northern Ireland. His administration engaged in a public row with Britain over Bosnian policies, and made it clear that the richer Germans were their favored interlocutors in Europe. Many of these Rhodes scholars felt only limited affection and nostalgia for Britain as a result of their time at Oxford. Along with pellucid May mornings punting on the Isis and sunsets gilding the dreaming spires, they recalled snooty undergraduates, languid dons, cold rooms, and bad food. From the vantage point of an elite enclave, they experienced Britain as a country in palpable decline. The contradiction was acute between the snobbish complacencies of Oxford and the wider realities of shriveling British grandeur. Their memories were colored by strikes in the 1960s and 1970s and by the politics of class war in Margaret Thatcher's 1980s, all against the background of a simmering counterinsurgency campaign in Northern Ireland, and punctuated by the occasional terrorist bomb in Britain.

But by then, the real nature of the American diaspora had changed. By the end of the Gulf War of 1991, to which the bulk of the American forces came from the old NATO bases in Europe, and then returned home to bases in the United States, the Cold War garrison in Europe had shrunk from 300,000 to barely 100,000 American troops. This was still a formidable force, but it emphasized that the typical American abroad was no longer a young man in military uniform, but an executive in a business suit. The growth of world trade and the increasing American investment abroad throughout the Cold War period had been inspired by better opportunities abroad. During the 1950s, industrial productivity in Germany increased by 6 percent a year, and in France by 4 percent. American productivity, by contrast, was growing at 2.4 percent annually over the decade. This not only implied a relative decline of American economic efficiency; it also became a self-sustaining trend, as American corporations realized they could make better returns on their investment in Europe than at home and so began to export more capital overseas to take advantage of this fact. In 1950, the book value of American holdings in Europe was $1.7 billion; by 1969, it had increased more than tenfold, to $21.5 billion; and by 1997, it had reached $370 billion.

Most of the profits of these American-owned enterprises remained in Europe, to be reinvested, and to help swell the astonishing new international currency, the Eurodollar. The Eurodollar was homeless money, the American money that had left the United States and stayed in European banks, becoming a new financial instrument. By 1966, there were some $15 billion in Eurodollars being traded in the European markets, an uncontrolled currency whose size and volatility helped force the devaluations of the original dollar in the 1970s. From the traditional American point of view, this was a progression toward national impoverishment. But tradition was a poor guide to the extraordinary transformation that the Cold War was inducing in the American economy. Until 1940, when conscription was first introduced in peacetime, the United States had had a tiny standing army. In 1939, it numbered only 174,000 men, and although the navy represented a substantial investment, the defense budget took only 3.4 percent of the GDP. The Cold War changed all that. With the special demands of the Korean and Vietnam wars, the army grew, but even in nominal peacetime, it was maintained at a complement of over a million men, and the share of the overall U.S. economy devoted to defense remained between two and three times the levels of 1939.

The American economy was not only militarized to this degree by the

America Reborn

Cold War; it was also internationalized. American patterns of trade and investment were transformed, and what had been a virtually self-sufficient economy before World War II became locked ever more deeply into the global trading system that was emerging. The trend is plain. From the depth of the Great Depression in 1933, when total American exports were $1.65 billion, America's trading relationships with the rest of the world simply exploded. American exports in 1950 were $10.2 billion; in 1960, $20.4 billion; in 1970, $42.6 billion; in 1980, $216.7 billion; in 1990, $421.6 billion; in 1997, $1,167 billion.

Exports tell only part of the story. The investment by American companies in the Western European economy, and increasingly in Japan, too, intensified this trend of the deepening interdependence of the Western world. From a total of $1.7 billion in 1950, to $21.5 billion in 1969, this flood of private investment was running at the extraordinary level of $150 billion a year by 1989. By 1997, the total of foreign investments by the United States and the European Union in each other's economies was $750 billion. Three million Americans worked for European-owned companies and over 4 million Europeans worked for American employers. By 1997, almost a million American civilians lived and worked in European countries. This was the global economy with a vengeance. And these investments were not made by government strategists, bureaucrats, or statesmen as the Marshall Plan had been, but by wealth-seeking managers and entrepreneurs. Just as the Cold War had forced the United States to internationalize its military commitments and spread its bases across the globe, so trade followed the flag and internationalized the American economy, too.

The process also transformed the nature of industrial organization. If the classic managerial structure of the first phase of the industrial revolution in Britain had been the joint stock company, and the next phase of industrial expansion was led by the cartels of individual nations, the characteristic formation of the Cold War's global economy was the transnational corporation. By 1968, for example, a mere twenty U.S.-based corporations accounted for more than two-thirds of all U.S. investment in Western Europe, and some 40 percent of U.S. investments in France, Britain, and Germany were held by three multinationals—Ford, General Motors, and Standard Oil of New Jersey, better known as Exxon. And by far the biggest foreign investors in the United States were Europe's own biggest multinationals, BP (British Petroleum) and Royal-Dutch Shell.

This Americanization of the world's economic structure also reached deep into private lives. By the 1990s, middle-class people across the world could wake up to CNN, scan the *International Herald Tribune* and the *Wall Street Journal,* breakfast on Florida orange juice and Kellogg's cornflakes, drive to work in a Ford, and spend their day on an IBM computer using Microsoft software—and take their families to McDonald's or Planet Hollywood for dinner, paying the bill with an American Express credit card before returning home to watch a video of an American film while sipping a Budweiser.

Nor was this a wholly new phenomenon. In the nineteenth century, European women routinely began buying Singer sewing machines. By the 1880s, Singer had its own plant in Britain, and so did Otis (elevators), National Cash Register, Colt (revolvers), Eastman Kodak, Babcock and Wilcox, and the pharmaceutical firms of Burroughs and Wellcome. Alexander Graham Bell and Thomas Edison dropped their rivalry to bring the telephone system to London as the United Telephone Company. By the eve of World War I, Londoners were shopping at the American Gordon Selfridge's department store on Oxford Street, and buying Model T Fords manufactured on an assembly line in Manchester.

There was no stopping the outward flow of American goods and ideas, subtly accompanied by the values that underlay them. By the 1980s, the impending collapse of the Soviet Union could be measured by the Moscow black market's dependence on dollar bills, Levi's jeans, Marlboro cigarettes, and videos of *Dallas* and *Dynasty.* The students of Beijing's Tiananmen Square knew precisely the symbolism and appeal of their defiance when they wheeled in a giant model of the Statue of Liberty as the token of their stand. It all amounted to what Harvard professor (and later senior Pentagon official) Joseph Nye called America's "soft power," more seductive and in the long run more compelling than the traditional hard power of the aircraft carriers and military bases overseas.

By the end of the century, the two principles for which America had consistently stood, democracy and self-determination, had spread to most of the planet. A majority of the world's peoples lived under regimes that were broadly democratic, in that elections could dismiss and appoint governments, and the old colonial empires had almost entirely disappeared. Although many countries were poor, prosperity and opportunity were far more widespread, thanks to the growth of the global economy that American policies and investments and American business practices had helped to spread more than any other country. Nazism, Japanese militarism, and communism had all been withstood and defeated, mainly by the force of American arms and American industrial prowess. If any other single nation could begin to match that record, it was Great Britain under the leadership of that heir to the dynastic union of American wealth and British ancestry, Winston Churchill.

10.
Frank Lloyd Wright
and the American Space

I n February 1901, the *Ladies' Home Journal* published an article entitled "A Home in a Prairie Town: A Small House with Lots of Room in It," with two designs by a little-known young architect from the Midwest named Frank Lloyd Wright. These designs did not look revolutionary. The lines were clean, the roof low and stretched to provide generous shade and porches, and the building unadorned. The windows were generous but disciplined and extended to the corners of the homes, emphasizing the dominant horizontal line. Inside, the living areas were large and seemed to flow together with little regard for the conventions of enclosed living and dining rooms. The core of the home was the fireplace and the solid backbone of the chimney structure that anchored the whole house to the earth. Wright's design was cheap to build, less than four thousand dollars, thanks to mass-produced materials originally developed for commercial buildings.

Frank Lloyd Wright and the American Space

It looked like an exceedingly civilized farmhouse, stretching smoothly to the dimensions of a ranch, at ease in the tamed nature of the broad and park-like American garden. It was a building that marked simultaneously the closing of the American frontier, now that the West had been won and occupied, and the coming of the new suburb. The Prairie Style houses with which Wright made his name were built not in the wide-open spaces of the West nor even on the flat, eroded rocks and sandbars of the Driftless Area of Wisconsin where he had been raised and whence he drew such inspiration, but near towns. The most famous of them, the Robie House, which Wright, with characteristic lack of modesty, called "the corner-stone of modern architecture," is built in the heart of Chicago.

But the American landscape lay at the core of everything Wright thought and did. He believed that its unique nature required a specifically American architecture, complete with its own furniture, its own style, and even its own gardens. In the Prairie School of architects and designers that developed around Wright was a Danish immigrant and landscape gardener, Jens Jensen, who argued strongly that American gardens were too much in the thrall of an irrelevant English and European tradition, whose plants and style were suited neither to the American climate nor to the American democratic sensibility. "To import to our cities plans from monarchical countries, with their pompous displays, is a fad reflecting on American intellect," Jensen claimed. One of his followers, Leonard Johnson, whose *Foundation Planting* became a bible to generations of landscape gardeners, made the political and patriotic argument with even more force:

It is only fair to say that the home is the greatest institution in America. Everyone who is patriotic, therefore, and wants to do something for his country will promote to the utmost of his ability the development of ideal American homes. In the old country the primary planting is a hedge all along the street front. The American home is open to the street. The plantings, instead of forming a hedge on the street line, are pushed back against the foundations of the house. They are foundation plantings. This type of planting is therefore fundamental to the whole of American domestic landscape architecture. We may all accept the patriotic duty of promoting this campaign of planting.

This was to be the landscape that defined the American suburbs: the low-slung houses modeled on Wright's conception of a ranch, with their trim hedges and flowers tucked neatly around the building, and then vast and sprawling lawns that reached down to the street and across to the neighbors, as if each suburb was trying to re-create the grass oceans of the prairies. But the suburb represented something far more important to its inhabitants than any visual echo of the West. It represented success and stability, the social ascent of people who had escaped the city, with its rented apartments and crowds, and become home owners with a right to privacy on their own land. The history of the suburb, which began in the late nineteenth century and by the late twentieth became the way most Americans lived, is the history of a social revolution, America's extraordinary achievement in being the first nation to generate a mass middle class, people who owned land without having to farm it. For Wright, this process reflected a uniquely American form of democracy.

"Architectural features of true democratic ground-freedom would rise naturally from topography, which means that buildings would take on the nature and character of the ground on which in endless variety they would stand and be component part," Wright wrote, stressing the two key tenets of his architectural philosophy. Of equal importance, these were: that any building must organically fit the ground on which it takes root and that an American architecture should thus reflect the distinctive American landscape and the wider democratic culture that that landscape had nurtured. There was thus a clear political, as well as a geographical, essence of architecture: "The dynamic ideal we call democracy, gradually growing up in the human heart for 2,500 years at least, has now every opportunity to found the natural economic state in these United States of America by way of natural economic order and a natural or organic architecture."

Wright was an unlikely candidate to become the spiritual father of the American suburb. He had always wanted to be an architect, since his mother gave him as a child some Froebel blocks, a fashionable educational toy of the time. "That early kindergarten experience with the straight line," he recalled in 1932. "The flat plane, the square, the triangle, the circle! If I wanted more, the square modified by the triangle gave the hexagon. The circle modified by the straight line would give the octagon. Adding thickness, getting 'sculpture' thereby, the square becoming the cube, the triangle the tetrahedron, the circle the sphere. These primary forms and figures were the secret of whatever got into the architecture of the world."

His first real job, after studying engineering at the University of Wisconsin in Madison, was to join the studio of the father of skyscrapers, the architect Louis Sullivan. The bones of buildings, the engineering structures and rules that held a building up, had fascinated him since a wing of the university's engineering faculty had collapsed. No building should ever collapse, he concluded, not when the engineers had found so many new ways to build. "A building could grow right up out of the soil, wherever sand and gravel abound, a few steel strands dropped into the concrete for reinforcement. Steel has given new life, concrete new possibilities, finer purposes. When it was found that the coefficient of expansion was the same for concrete and steel, a new world opened to the architect."

Wright moved into the design studio on the sixteenth floor of the Chicago Auditorium, which Sullivan and his partner, Dankmar Adler, had just designed. It remains a stunningly successful building, with a seventeen-story tower rising from a ten-story hotel and office block designed in a U shape around a four-thousand-seat auditorium whose acoustics remain legendary among musicians for their purity.

Sullivan, whose words inspired that classic maxim of modern architecture, "Form follows function," was not the first to realize the potential of the steel frame to allow buildings of unprecedented height. But he was the first to appreciate what this might imply for the aesthetics of buildings. "It must be tall, every inch of it tall. The force and power of altitude must be in it, the glory and pride of exaltation must be in it," he maintained in his essay "The Tall Office Building Artistically Considered." In his Wainwright Building in St. Louis (on which Wright worked) and his Guaranty Building in Buffalo, New York, Sullivan did not drape the steel frame in camouflaging facades. Instead, he stressed the soaring verticals of the structure, much as the Gothic designers of late medieval cathedrals had used them to force the worshipers' eyes up to the heavens.

Sullivan, a prickly personality who argued and finally broke with almost all his collaborators, always wanted to stand out from the crowd by temperament as much as by conviction. But it was the conviction that American architects were making a collective mistake in accepting the conventions of classical architecture from ancient Greece and Rome for the public buildings and monuments of the new republic that inspired his rebellion at the 1893 World's Columbian Exposition in Chicago. All of the buildings were of white stone and marble, locked in the massiveness of Roman-style arches and the formal pillars of Greek temples, just as the chief designer, Daniel Burnham, had decreed. The exhibition was intended to be a seminal cultural event, to capture the raw energy of Chicago and put America's second city on the world map. The United States was already producing half the world's cotton, corn, and oil, as well as a third of its iron and steel, and the exhibition signaled the country's technological prowess when Alexander Graham Bell used its opening to launch the direct New York–Chicago telephone service. With its theme of America as Columbia, named after a spurious goddess who reflected the name of the "discoverer" Christopher Columbus, the exhibition sought to stress that the new republic of the western hemisphere was taking its global place alongside the grand old empires of Europe.

Sullivan rebelled, not against the themes of national pride and imperial ambition but against the assumption that this grand new republic should find its physical expression in the essentially European formalities of Greece and Rome. Wright, his young associate, heartily agreed. "Classicism is a mask," he wrote. "How can such a static expression allow interpretation of human life as we know it? A firehouse should not resemble a French chateau, a bank a Greek temple, and a university a Gothic cathedral."

With Wright's enthusiastic support, Sullivan refused to abide by the exhibition's classical standard, and he took Arab architecture as the model for his Transportation Building. He invaded the classical white of the rest of the exhibition with a riot of colors and blended it with technology to produce a stunning arched portal, all illuminated with hundreds of electric lightbulbs. Sullivan seemed at the time to be fighting a losing battle. The year after the exhibition, the American School of Architecture in Rome was launched, and three years later merged with the American Academy in Rome, so dominant was the force of the classical idea, and the habit of cultural deference to Europe that underpinned it.

This should not have been surprising. The country had indeed been founded with homage to the inspirations of Athenian democracy and the Roman republic, with the American Senate as a deliberate echo of its Roman predecessor. The veterans of the Revolutionary War had bonded themselves into a league, the Society of the Cincinnatis, in tribute to the Roman leader who twice reluctantly took temporary power as a dictator to steer the young republic through war and crisis, and then each time surrendered his authority and returned to his plow. The problem, as defined by Lewis Mumford, that perceptive critic of both architecture and society and the relationship between them, was that the rude democracy of the Roman republic had given way to the authoritarian Roman Empire. In his essay "The Imperial Facade," Mumford targeted the essential falsity of a classical architecture that put antique marble fronts onto modern steel frames. But he also warned that the symbolism of stone carried with it a reality of economic and political power, which threatened American democracy itself.

The closing of the frontier had limited the opportunities for escape from an economic structure marked by monopolies and cartels, and the robber-baron millionaires of America were assuming the style and trappings of a would-be aristocracy. And in accepting their commissions and flattering their social aspirations with classical mansions fit to house a Nero or an Augustus, American architects were betraying the realities of American history. To prove his point, Mumford cited the Lincoln Memorial in Washington, D.C. (designed in 1912), a building that houses Lincoln's statue in a giant block of blank, windowless marble, surrounded by Grecian columns. An imposing building, radiating solemn authority, it carries the classical echoes down to the arms of the chair on which Lincoln is seated; they are Roman fasces, the bound sticks and axes that were the symbol of Rome's senate. "The America that Lincoln was bred in, the homespun and humane and humorous America that Lincoln wished to preserve," Mumford concluded, could hardly have been more thoroughly traduced than by "this sedulous classical monument."

The problem for architects was that most commissions came either from rich men and rich companies or from national and local government. If they all wanted classical architecture, then that was what the architects would have to produce. Happily, American taste proved sturdier and more adventurous. Some rich families wanted something different, and after Wright fought with Sullivan and left to start his own studio in 1893, he found enough commissions for his new Prairie Style of domestic buildings to survive and prosper. This represented not only a gamble on his own talents, as the country plunged into recession that year, but also a considerable sacrifice. Burnham tried to lure away Sullivan's gifted young pupil with the offer of financing his formal training at the Ecole des Beaux-Arts in Paris. Young Wright refused; there was an American architecture to be devised and some clients bold enough to want it.

In 1904, the Larkin mail order company of Buffalo, New York, gave Wright the opportunity to explore an entirely different architectural tradition. The roots of the Larkin Building lie in ancient Egypt more than in Athens. The massive corner columns recall the temples of the Nile. But they contain ventilation shafts, because inside, all is aggressively modern in one of the first American buildings to feature filtered air and climate control and to use the new tool of reinforced concrete for the vast interior space and the great skylight. Wright's Unity Temple (1906) in Oak Park, Illinois, combines his characteristic flaring roof and great slabs of window glass with the monumental Egyptian style. It was not that Wright abandoned the classical past; far from it. He wanted to range beyond it, to Egyptian and Byzantine forms or the pre-Columbian designs of Aztec and Mayan architecture. Nothing was really foreign to him. He turned to Elizabethan England for the diamond-shaped lead panes of his windows and his fondness for minstrels' galleries, and to Japan—which he first visited in 1905—for his use of wood and ways to blur the boundaries between the inside and the outside of buildings. He loved Japanese styles, and in future years, when money was short, he would make his living by dealing in Japanese prints.

Above all, Wright wanted to design each of his buildings as a whole, in which the structure took organic shape from the landscape, and then the interior, from the lighting to the furniture, from the layout of rooms to the color of the cushions and the paint of the window frames, would come from his single controlling vision. He was an autocrat. When the curators at one of his landmark works, the spiral-shaped Guggenheim Museum in New York, complained that the walls he had designed were too small for the scale of the paintings, he grunted, "Cut the paintings in half." Having grumpily agreed to the requests of the Ennis family of Los Angeles that he use slate instead of marble, teak instead of redwood, he stormed off the project when they wanted him to change the ceiling designs. One client recalled standing to block the door of her bathroom so that Wright would not see that she had decided against his insistence on wooden fittings. More prosaic details were beneath him. Fallingwater, his extraordinary building atop and astride Bear Run in Pennsylvania, may be one of the noisiest rural retreats on earth when the spring waters run strong, and its windows leak. When another client called him about the rain leaking through the ceiling into her dining room, he grunted, "Move the chair!"

Apart from the interference of clients, what Wright could not stand was being confined to a single style. Once his Prairie School was established, he turned against it for becoming close-minded and stuck in its ways, and he wrote a critical essay, "In the Cause of Architecture." Wright was suspicious of the way other members of the Prairie School had become members of the Arts and Craft movement, which he saw as essentially backward-looking, too ready to delve into medieval mysticism about the craft guilds and too hidebound to realize the opportunities for design that were tumbling from the new materials of the mechanical and metallurgical engineers. They looked back; Wright always looked forward.

In breaking with the Prairie School, Wright was also breaking with the domestic life he had known for twenty years. He had married in 1889, then had six children, but by 1906, he and his wife had become estranged. Subsequently, Wright developed a relationship with Mamah Cheney, the wife of a client. His commissions suffered, and in 1909, the couple left for Europe, where Wright knew his work had attracted great interest. He had no regrets about leaving Chicago, "where one sells everything, and above all sells oneself," and proceeded to sell, if not himself, then his vision, hard and successfully in Europe. He took with him a laboriously gathered and redrawn portfolio of his major designs, from the Larkin Building to the Park Inn Hotel, as well as many studies for buildings not yet realized, including his own house near Spring Green, Wisconsin, Taliesin (the word means "shining brow" or "poet" in Welsh). He also took a large collection of photographs of everything he had built.

Staying at first in Fiesole, Italy, he wrote two books, one based on the designs and the other on the photographs. Each was published in German, to accompany a major exhibition of his work that was staged in Berlin in 1910. His publicist was the outstanding Dutch architect Hendrik Berlage, designer of the Amsterdam stock exchange, who helped arrange the publication of Wright's work and whose essays and lectures across Europe insisted that there was "more to America than skyscrapers and Red Indians." Wright embodied "a new architecture of a New World," Berlage claimed.

Thus marketed, Wright's ideas became hugely influential in the new architectural styles that were already developing in Europe. There was, after all, something in Wright for almost everyone. Some Europeans, like Rudolph Schindler, who in 1914 came to the United States and shortly thereafter worked with Wright, were struck by his bold use of the cantilever with reinforced concrete. Others, like Richard Neutra, who came to the United States and worked briefly with Wright in the 1920s, focused on Wright's interest in prefabrication and the use of cheap techniques of industrial design for housing. Wright's 1910 exhibition was one of the formative influences on the group of German designers who formed the Bauhaus, and they, in turn, would emigrate to the United States and then have a decisive influence on American architecture. The design for a model factory, which Walter Gropius presented at the 1914 Werkbund Exhibition in Cologne, frankly acknowledged its debt to Wright's Park Inn Hotel, which it strikingly resembled. Mies van der Rohe took Wright's Prairie Style designs as the model for his own series of house studies in 1923. Through Berlage's influence, the Dutch school of artists and architects known as De Stijl took direct inspiration from Wright's work. Robert van t' Hoff's villa at Huis ter Heide, near Utrecht, could have come directly from Wright's drawing board.

What they all saw from the 1910 Berlin exhibition and the associated books were buildings as pure design, wrenched from their real urban or suburban settings and drawn as if they stood alone on the vast and windswept prairie. The concept of the Prairie Style may have been a metaphor for Wright; for Europeans of the time attuned to Buffalo Bill Cody's traveling shows of six-guns and war-whooping Indians, and in a Germany where the most popular children's stories were the western tales of Old Shatterhand, Wright's buildings were far more than metaphor. They were an image of an imagined America, to be shaped and tamed by design, of ancient landscapes that seemed to have awaited for centuries the coming of the modern architect with his rigorous lines and his futuristic materials. For Europeans of the time, modern architecture was born to struggle, to find its place in an already-crowded environment, to overcome the general awe of the great buildings of the past that dominated so much of the urban space. Wright represented not only the new, and the legend of the Wild West, but also the uniquely infinite possibilities of American space.

Fortified by his European success, Wright and Cheney returned to the United States and Wright built Taliesen. He could not get a divorce from his first wife, and publicity about the supposed scandal of his private life, along with his own impatient temperament, meant few commissions. There was time to draw and to think. In 1912, he designed his first true skyscraper, a tall and slender slab of light concrete that gained its vertical and almost tapering lines through its own proportions, rather than from any ornamental device. Like so many of his designs, it was never built. Then he was asked to design a kind of urban theme park in Chicago, a vast complex of bars and restaurants, gardens and dance halls, called Midway Gardens. Decorated with the abstract designs, that had excited him in Europe, it was a success, although its subsequent closure during Prohibition added to his reputation as an unlucky architect.

In the midst of the Midway project, a gruesome domestic tragedy took place at Taliesin. An insane servant murdered Cheney and her children, who were visiting her, and started a fire that burned the main house almost to the ground. Devastated, trying to rebuild with little money, Wright found consolation with the sculptress Miriam Noel, and together they sailed in 1915 for Japan, where Wright had been commissioned to build that country's first Western-style hotel. The Imperial Hotel, demolished in 1968, remains famous as one of the only buildings to survive the 1923 Tokyo earthquake unscathed. Concerned about the seismic instability of Tokyo, Wright had designed the building to stand on giant cantilevered pads, which allowed it almost to float on the swampy foundations. He kept a base in Japan for six years, enchanted and mystified by turns as he wrestled with his reluctance to expose himself again to the small-minded disapproval of the Midwest and to an America where so few clients would allow him to build as he wished. Japan proved more welcoming to a foreign architect who showed a proper reverence for the country's own cultural heritage and traditions of design.

The irony of his position, designing for a civilization that he admired a hotel where foreign guests would feel comfortably at home, forced Wright to think again about the relationship between landscape and building, not simply in the shape of the land but in the cultural history and artistic forms that had developed there. There was more to a landscape than just the contours and outcrops of the earth. There was a history to be intuitively understood, just as he had paid homage to his own Welsh roots, changing his middle name from Lincoln to Lloyd and giving his home a Welsh name. When he returned to America, it was to California, to study the old Spanish missions that had endured so well in the sun and dry land, to consider the utility of adobe, and to delve into the designs of Mayan temples.

"Here I was, looking around me in Los Angeles, disgusted," he recorded in his autobiography. "They were busy with steam shovels, tearing down the hills. Nearby, tan-gold foothills rise to join slopes, spotted as a leopard-skin with grease-bush. This foreground spreads to distances so vast—human scale is utterly lost as all features recede, turn blue, recede and become bluer still. What was missing? Nothing more or less than a distinctly genuine expression of California. That was all."

While the hotel in Tokyo was being constructed, the developer Aline Barnsdall hired Wright to design and landscape an estate called Olive Hill, a complex of houses and studios that is now Hollywood's Municipal Art Gallery. He received a handful of other commissions to build individual houses, and Wright devised a new building material, a prefabricated hollow concrete block. It was a remarkably adaptable item, which could be shaped, carved, or perforated, and was designed to echo the Japanese skill of blending interior and exterior spaces. The same block seen from indoors could be a screen or a shelf, and from outdoors, it became a sheer wall, or a trellis up which plants could grow, reflecting Wright's concern that buildings should flow organically into their setting. Or as he put it in a gloomy moment, "A doctor can bury his mistakes, but an architect can only advise his clients to plant vines."

Wright seemed to have lost his way. His first wife finally divorced him; then came a second divorce, and a humiliating arrest on charges of violating the Mann Act, which was intended to stop enforced prostitution by forbidding interstate transport of women for immoral purposes. In the case of the "notorious libertine," as a county magistrate called him, Wright's offense was to drive a girlfriend across a state line. Other American architects were now the toast of the world. Norman Bel Geddes was designing the stunning "Futurama" exhibition for the 1939 New York World's Fair. Raymond Loewy and Henry Dreyfuss were redefining the concept of the modern with their aerodynamic designs. Albert Kahn, since 1903 the architect for Packard Motors, became the most celebrated industrial designer of them all. The gigantic factory space, with its saw-toothed roof with skylights, which became the industrial cliché of the age, was Kahn's design. In 1929, he was given a contract to build a $40-million tractor plant in Chelyabinsk, Siberia. And having opened an office in Moscow, he designed the Stalingrad tractor plant, which would become the centerpiece of the great battle that took place in 1942–1943; he designed a total of 521 factories for the Soviet Union. It was design by assembly line, but lucrative, so long as the Soviets paid in gold. When they ceased to do so, in 1932, Kahn closed the office, but he had already transformed the industrial face of the USSR.

Wright, by contrast, went broke. Taliesen burned down twice, and each time he rebuilt it, and with less and less money coming in, he lost his home to the bank, despite selling his Japanese print collection. Friends, devoted followers, and clients quickly rallied, establishing a company called Wright, Inc., a firm that owned his properties, his designs, and his debts, thus effectively cutting him off from the management of his own chaotic finances. With the income from his lectures and his writings, the firm stabilized his life to the degree that Taliesen became, as he had always intended, a kind of design and study center for up to sixty apprentices in design and architecture. Perhaps he had also intended the quasi-mystical sect that it threatened to become, as he expanded to build Taliesen West from a camp in Arizona.

If this was in any sense a religion, it was a religion of the earth or the landscape itself, a faith he had long held. The deserts of Arizona gave this sense of earth an austerity that attracted him. "In this stony bonework of the earth," he wrote while designing a desert compound, "the principles that shaped stone as it lies, or as it rises and remains to be sculpted by winds and tides—there sleep forms and styles enough for all the ages."

The financial rescue came just in time, before the stock market crashed and the Depression brought construction to a halt. But the designs never stopped, even though there were no clients to finance them. He pondered the implications of the automobile. He devised the bizarre St. Mark's Tower project for New York, a giant pole with studios cantilevered from a central service core that carried elevators, plumbing, and other services. (This idea was finally carried out in the Price Tower in Bartlesville, Oklahoma, in the 1950s.) In response to the Depression, he designed a low-cost system of building mass-produced and flat-roofed homes, which stood on heated pads. Since he claimed they were an American answer to an American problem, he called them—after the initials U.S.—Usonian homes. Some were built, but never in the numbers he once envisaged.

Yet, as he approached his seventieth year, his greatest work was still to come. There were to be three immortal buildings, a private home, a public museum, and an industrial building, which as a whole embody the modern movement and the main forms of a distinctive American architecture. The industrial facility was begun in 1936 in Racine, Wisconsin, for Johnson Wax, and the anchoring laboratory tower, its corners softly turned, remains one of the most perfect tall buildings in America. It fits perfectly into the flat site, echoing the curves of one of the other buildings. Inside the administration building, supporting columns of breathtaking slimness rise and slightly flare into lily-pad flatness at their peak. Because the surrounding wall is topped by a clerestory window, these columns alone seem to support the roof of a building that from within feels part cathedral, part forest. The entrance route was designed with great subtlety, passing through gates and tunnels and past balconies that make the act of going to work an event. This was the workplace made human, the office made beautiful.

Frank Lloyd Wright and the American Space

The home was Fallingwater, in the hills outside Pittsburgh, a house of rock and cantilevered concrete that embraces and soars above the stream, rocks, and waterfall that run through the structure of the house. It was built for the Kaufmanns, wealthy department-store owners. The tawny slabs of the cantilevered decks echo the broad reaches of the rocks, while the piles of gray stone that sustain them match the fall of the water, and each of the dominant horizontal and muted vertical slabs finds a resolution in the thin red portcullis lines of the metal window frames. Inside, the raw rock thrusts through the floor, to find its match in the gigantic fireplace. Glass and water, stone and rock, different forms that seem poised to take off in perpendicular explosions, are all held in perfect balance by the anchoring site.

The Guggenheim Museum in New York, designed from 1943 to 1946 and completed only in 1959, finally fulfilled a design Wright had originally made for Sugar Loaf Mountain in Maryland, a spiral viewpoint for cars that wound around a planetarium and restaurant. The spiral as a shape had attracted him for years. "There resides always a certain 'spell power' in any geometric form, which is, as we say, the soul of the thing—as for instance, the circle, infinity; the triangle, structural unity; the spire, aspiration; the spiral, organic process; the square, integrity." The organic process of the Guggenheim is to move viewers past paintings and sculptures in an endless loop, but also to exalt them with the grandeur of Wright's vast and ever-opening space. He inverted the spiral, making the top far wider than the bottom, so that light pours in. From the outside, it is pure shape, in almost magical contrast to the city's vast skyscraper canyons that surround it. From the inside, it harks back to his Unity Temple of Oak Park, Illinois, completed in 1906, with its marvelously still interior space. "The room within is the great fact about a building," he always said. "The space within becomes the reality of the building."

Wright died in 1959. He lives on, however, not only in his buildings but as an archetype of the artist, uncompromising, freethinking, driven by a conviction of his own genius and by a healthy contempt for the small-minded pieties of a society that would condemn and ruin him for "immorality." This is not only because of the defiance and tumult of his own life but also because he inspired, in the person of Howard Roark, a fictional hero in *The Fountainhead,* the best-selling novel by Ayn Rand that was later made into a film. Her architect was tall and rugged, where Wright was on the short side and more than a little vain. But Wright's passionate belief in self and in the art of design, in the dictate of the land that the building must grow organically from the site and the earth, and in the determination to live his life his own way was captured beautifully by Rand. He became an imagined hero of her faith in the individual, an American rebel who was, by that same token, an American classic.

Yet the reality was more poignant. Wright lived to see his Prairie Style echoed in vulgar and often tawdry fashion all across what was becoming a suburban country, while the inhabitants commuted to work in buildings that were so many bland and anonymous copies of the Gropius and Mies van der Rohe buildings he had inspired. By the end of the century, most Americans lived and worked in pallid echoes of Wright's visions. Some were lucky enough to know the real thing.

11.
Lucky Luciano
and the American Criminal

On September 10, 1931, four neatly dressed men in coats and hats, claiming to be detectives, arrived at the office of Salvatore Maranzano above Grand Central Station in New York. Only four months earlier, after the killing of another gangster, Giuseppe Masseria, known as "Joe the Boss," at Scarpato's restaurant in Coney Island, Maranzano had declared himself *capo de tutti capi,* "boss of all bosses," in the city. Maranzano had told his guards that he was expecting visitors, and the four men were shown into room 926. The door closed, and gunshots rang out almost immediately. Maranzano was shot dead with four bullets, and he was also stabbed in his belly six times.

The four men were not Italian. They were Jewish gangsters recruited by Meyer Lansky and Ben "Bugsy" Siegel as a favor to Lansky's boyhood friend Lucky Luciano. The visitors whom the murdered criminal boss was expecting

America Reborn

were Luciano and Vito Genovese, and Maranzano had planned to have them killed by a hired Irish hitman, Vincent "Mad Dog" Coll. Suspecting a trap, Luciano and Genovese sent the four killers instead, who ran into Coll as they made their escape, and in the curious fraternity of their trade, they warned him to disappear, as the cops would soon arrive.

"Following the death of Salvatore Maranzano, a wave of gangland slayings, known as the 'Sicilian Vespers,' swept the country," claimed the FBI's 1987 edition of *The Chronology of the Cosa Nostra*. Cosa Nostra is Italian for "this thing of ours," and the term gained public recognition in September 1963, when a former member, Joe Valachi, testified before the Senate's permanent subcommittee on investigations. The word *Mafia*, Valachi explained, was never used by the initiates. His subsequent book, *The Valachi Papers*, became a best-seller, and Valachi's recollections helped inspire the novel and later the movie *The Godfather*. Valachi was the source for the story of the Sicilian Vespers, with his claim that Luciano exploited Maranzano's assassination to become the boss of bosses, the most powerful figure in organized crime. Only a man with such power, Valachi claimed, could have launched a nationwide wave of murders, all on the same day, of "some forty Cosa Nostra leaders, slain across the country."

Despite the FBI's support of Valachi's claim, there is little evidence that this celebrated purge ever took place. In a serious academic history, *East Side, West Side: Organizing Crime in New York, 1930–1950,* Dr. Alan Block conducted a detailed survey of the press reports in eight American cities for the two weeks after Maranzano's killing, which was reported in all the papers he studied. He found only three fresh reports—two in Newark, New Jersey, and one in Pittsburgh—of what appeared to be gangland killings. The Sicilian Vespers, if they took place at all, were a most discreet affair. Whatever the nature of Luciano's ascendancy, it was neither attended nor achieved by continental slaughter.

The story of the Mafia in America has become encrusted with myth and legend, romanticized in fiction and film, and politicized by congressional investigations. The result of these embellishments has been to fix in the public mind three great exaggerations. The first is that organized crime has been essentially an Italian-American phenomenon, when in fact Irish-Americans and Jewish-Americans, who played significant parts in the supposedly seminal killing that launched the Sicilian Vespers, have had important roles. Subsequently, African-Americans and Hispanic-Americans and now the new Russian immigrants of Brighton Beach have shown that members of most minority groups have had the talent and readiness to take to a life of crime.

The second exaggeration is that the Italian Mafia has been distinguished by an ability to found a disciplined and even hierarchical national organization. A single leader supposedly had the power to order and have his henchmen enact a coast-to-coast wave of killings, and to found a nationwide structure of criminal groups steered by and paying tribute to a single overlord. Maranzano may have boasted of such power, but it did not last long. And while Luciano certainly expanded his own power by killing Maranzano, his authority was limited to the New York region, and the other families in the city had wide autonomy to run their own rackets as they chose. Doubtless, some of the criminal leaders liked to claim such powers and, like Lansky, to boast on occasion that their revenues made them "bigger than U.S. Steel." Politicians looking for issues and headlines were eager to believe them in order to build up a national menace, a secret government that only political leadership could break down. In reality, the structure of organized crime appears to have been even looser than a confederacy. It was a series of autonomous units whose leaders sometimes fought, sometimes met to discuss matters of mutual interest, and much of the time stayed carefully out of one another's way.

The third exaggeration, which again has been fueled by novels and Hollywood and the often self-serving testimony of Valachi, has to do with the importance of the Sicilian tradition and its associated code of ethics. In Valachi's Cosa Nostra, "men of honor" commanded loyalty unto death and devoted foot soldiers abided by a law of silence, in which killings were preceded by a kiss and women and children were spared—an ethnic version of a welfare state, in which Italian-American immigrants gave respect and in turn received a Godfather's justice and Christmas presents. No doubt, this sometimes happened. But the essential business of crime was profiting from illegal activity, using violence, intimidation, and murder, while seeking to suborn and corrupt the local police and political authorities. The romanticization of the Mafia can no more hide the vicious ruthlessness and greed that underpinned it than the Italian-American Civil Rights League of the 1960s could evade the fact that it was formed and promoted by a Mafia leader, Joseph Colombo, who was to be gunned down at one of his own public rallies.

Societies tend to get the kinds of crime they define, or perhaps deserve. The highly centralized and state-run Soviet system spawned its own underground economy, whose members were officially condemned as "speculators" but who, in fact, often provided the legitimate goods and services that state factories and enterprises needed. A society that chooses to outlaw or overtax some prevailing aspects of human behavior, such as the passion for gambling or prostitutes or drugs—from alcohol to opiates—will generate its own illegal suppliers to meet market demand. If a society discourages labor unions, while encouraging industrialists to defend their property rights by hiring armed thugs, it should not be surprised if the labor unions make dubious deals to acquire professional muscle of their own. If there is enough money in these illicit trades, its practitioners can become very rich, but they will tend to follow the usual unwritten rules of legal markets. They will compete for supplies, compete on price and convenience and delivery, and the most efficient at the business will prosper. Because the process is illegal and carries the risk of prison, its practitioners will take out prudent commercial insurance by corrupting local police and politicians whenever possible. And the competition can become very violent indeed.

In a fast-growing society like America of the late nineteenth century, whose population was swelling with wave after wave of immigrants from deep-rooted ethnic backgrounds, other factors came into play. The country had been settled, and its original inhabitants dispossessed, predominantly by British settlers, who had been able to monopolize the land and establish a political system that entrenched and defended their property rights. They ran the government, the banks, railroads, and shipping companies, and these commanding heights of American society had often been acquired and expanded with a ruthlessness that later criminals might envy and respect. The waves of Irish settlers who arrived with the famine of the 1840s, with their own good reasons to resent the British at home, did not find their descendants much more welcoming in their new home. "The Protestants over here don't like the Irish any better than their relatives over in England did, so don't expect much fairness from them," the grandfather of future Chicago mayor Jane Byrne was told on his arrival in 1888. Some struck out for the open spaces of the frontier, some took to crime, and others took to politics, all of them logical and even predictable ways for new arrivals to better themselves. Politics proved particularly useful, because it opened the way for successive Irish immigrants to find stable jobs in public service, from the police to the military, the fire service to municipal work.

This narrowed the options of subsequent waves of immigrants, many of whom arrived speaking little or no English and thus tended to gravitate toward their own communities, with their own churches, shops, foods, and neighborhoods. In the political system of urban America, there were advantages in ethnic communities sticking together, using the influence of their blocks of votes. They had brought their own religions, and in many cases their own priests, and much of their traditional social structure survived sturdily for a generation or even more, until the public school system began to work its miracle of social engineering by producing English-speaking young Americans.

Inevitably, this meant they also had their own patterns of crime, some of it imported directly from home. Sicilians in various cities tended to sign extortion notes with the imprint of a black hand. So when New Orleans police chief Daniel Hennessy began investigating the gang murders for control of the docks, the Black Hand was how he referred to the organization, until he was cut down by shotgun blasts outside police headquarters in 1890. When clever lawyers and intimidated witnesses secured acquittals for the Italians arrested, an angry mob of vigilantes broke into the jail and lynched two and shot nine more by firing squad. In New York, the expert on the Black Hand was a Italian-born cop, Lt. Joe Petrosino, who persuaded the police commissioners to send him to Italy in 1909 to establish a liaison system with the Italian ministry of the interior. Petrosino was assassinated—he was shot in the back four times—in Palermo, Italy.

Crime, however, was not strictly the province of Italians. In Chicago, the established Irish gangs of the Kennas and the Coughlins at first left little room for the Italians. Big Jim Colosimo began to establish a network, and when three men claiming to represent the Black Hand called on him to say they would take over, he shot two of them dead. Fearing retaliation, Colosimo persuaded Diamond Joe Esposito to bring Big Jim's nephew, Johnny Torrio, from the Five Points Gang in New York, to help out in Chicago. It was Torrio who subsequently imported to Chicago a young thug from the Five Points Gang with impressive bookkeeping skills, Al Capone. Initially employed as an enforcer to collect the extortionate interest rates in loan-sharking, Capone was then promoted to bartender in Torrio's Harvard Inn.

Every community had its weaknesses, its criminals, and its rackets. There were Jewish brothels along Allen and Forsythe streets on Manhattan's Lower East Side, and a Jewish reformatory called the Hawthorne School for underage street criminals. There were Italian lottery rackets and Irish gambling dens, and most of them were well enough established that their operators paid off the local police and had understandings with the local politicians of Tammany Hall. There was even a standard set of charges, the *New York Times* reported in 1900: $150 a month for a crap game, $1,000 a month for a big gambling house and brothel.

The communities also had their own turf to be defended against outsiders. "The Jews were locked in between Italians and Irish," Lansky recalled sixty years later, when recounting his life to an Israeli journalist. "The Irish boys would stop Jews in the street. They'd strip them to see if they had really been circumcised. They would spit on Jews and pull their beards—whenever there was a fight between Irish and Italians, or an incident involving Irish with Jews, the cops would always take the side of the Irish."

It was at such an encounter that the young schoolboy Maier Suchowljansky, who would become known as Meyer Lansky—who was born in Grodno, Belarus, in 1902 and arrived at Ellis Island in April 1911—met a gang of Italian boys on Hester Street. The gang was led by Salvatore Luciana, born in the

America Reborn

Sicilian village of Lercara Friddi, outside Palermo, in 1896. He had come through Ellis Island in 1906, and would later be known as Charlie "Lucky" Luciano. Outnumbered, and willing to take a beating rather than face humiliation, the young Jew was not about to be intimidated or robbed. "Go fuck yourself," said young Lansky. And for some extraordinary reason of human chemistry, young Luciano accepted the defiance, respected it, and warmed to the sharp-faced boy. "We both had a kind of instant understanding. It was something that never left us," Luciano later recalled. This relationship was to make Luciano unique among the mafiosi as the gang leader prepared to deal on an equal footing of respect and partnership with the other ethnic criminal groups. In the future, this was to prove lucrative, as he and Lansky entered a kind of partnership, and Lansky became Luciano's ace in the hole during the Italian feuds, providing a reserve armed force of killers whose faces were not known to Maranzano's Italian bodyguards.

They were both young toughs of the street. At age fifteen, Luciano already had a reputation as a knife fighter and had served six months in jail for dealing opium. When he came out, he joined the Five Points Gang, which ran a part of Little Italy around Mulberry Street, in the shadow of the Brooklyn Bridge. Lansky, after leaving school at fifteen and becoming an apprentice to a tool and die maker, began doing strong-arm jobs for a local labor union, beating up strikebreakers with iron bars. He had a charge of felonious assault dismissed but was fined two dollars for disorderly conduct (annoyance), on a complaint brought by two women whose addresses suggest that they were prostitutes. They were most likely fending off Lansky's attempt to become their pimp.

In each community, there was a dominant criminal figure. Around Mulberry Street, it was Joe the Boss, a squat thug who liked to devour three plates of spaghetti at a sitting. Luciano began working for him in 1920, dutifully giving him a cut of the profits from the Prohibition business and from the brothels that Luciano controlled. While Luciano rose through the system to become the chief aide to Joe the Boss, he always kept a slight distance, emphasizing that his connections with Lansky and the Jewish gangsters were his own, and too important to disrupt by any attempts to take over their business or bully them into giving Joe the Boss a cut. This was unusual. A more traditional young mafioso, Joe Bonanno, claimed that his own relation to his padrone, Maranzano, was far more feudal. He came from the same Sicilian village as Maranzano, Castellammare del Golfo, and, always keen to emphasize his sense of honor in his calling, recalled in his memoirs, "I was very much like a squire in the service of a knight," attending his padrone during the ritual loading of the shotgun shells. Luciano, Bonanno claimed, was never fully part of this mystic fraternity. "Lucky lived in two worlds. He lived among us, the men of the old tradition; but he also lived in a world apart from us, among a largely Jewish coterie whose views of life and of moneymaking were alien to ours."

In Lansky's world, the key figure was Arnold Rothstein, whose first empire was in gambling. Rothstein then used his connections to the New York politicians Big Tim Sullivan and Mayor Jimmy Walker to become a legendary figure, immortalized as the model for Meyer Wolfsheim in F. Scott Fitzgerald's novel *The Great Gatsby.* Rothstein dressed expensively, lived in considerable style on Fifth Avenue, kept an office on West Fifty-sixth Street, paid some of his taxes, dated showgirls, and owned racehorses. Neither was he discreet nor did he limit his activities to the Jewish community; his ambitions, and his friendships with politicians like Sullivan and Walker, were too grand for that. Lansky first met Rothstein at a bar mitzvah, and the playboy crook took a liking to him, invited him to dinner, and they talked for hours.

"Rothstein told me quite frankly that he had picked me because I was ambitious and 'hungry,' " Lansky remembered. Rothstein kept his eyes and ears open for other bright young men who could prove useful, and they did not have to be Jewish. Lansky introduced him to Luciano, but Rothstein also made his own Italian connections. Francesco Castiglia, before he changed his name to Frank Costello, was a member of the Rothstein stable.

Rothstein, like Joe the Boss, needed promising young lieutenants, because the enormous opportunity of Prohibition was about to expand the horizons of America's criminal world. Rothstein encouraged Lansky to open a small car- and truck-rental business in a garage on Cannon Street, premises that were highly suitable for storing and then shipping bootleg liquor. Lansky's partner was a boyhood friend from the neighborhood, Bugsy Siegel. "Rothstein taught us that mass production of cars would revolutionize many things in America," Lansky recalled. "I realized myself how important it could become in our particular kind of business." Lansky's associate, not involved in the trucking firm but ready to help with supplies, deliveries, and muscle when required, was his old friend Luciano.

Lansky, apart from his connections to Rothstein and Luciano, had two great attributes. The first was a natural skill with numbers, working out the odds at gambling, or keeping in his head the complex accounts of what was becoming a sizable business, but one in which it was never wise to write anything down. The second was an understanding that crime needed honesty. As he put it, "I listened and read about men in all kinds of endeavor. The men who mostly went to the top were men with integrity." A criminal with a reputation for being good with numbers and also honest was a rare and precious commodity. Like any other business, crime needed good bookkeepers and accountants to keep track of the costs and quantify the profits. But to grow and expand, particularly in a high-volume market like buying and selling alcohol during Prohibition, it had to develop its own kind of credit system. This, in turn, required a great deal of trust. Luciano and Lansky trusted each other. By the heyday of Prohibition, they were chartering their own ships and bringing them into ports that they controlled by bribing the police and customs officials and controlling labor unions on the docks.

Of course, trust in the crime business was often the prelude to murder. Joe the Boss was killed because he had trusted Luciano sufficiently to accept his invitation to dinner at Scarpato's restaurant. Tactical alliances followed by a double cross and murder were commonplace. Indeed, the killing of Joe the Boss had been arranged by Luciano to clear the way for Maranzano to take over. Maranzano then planned to eliminate Luciano, but, with Lansky's help, Luciano struck first.

This was the killing that changed the culture. The gangland slaughter of 1931, sometimes known as the Castellammarese war, after Maranzano's native village, has gone into legend as "the Purge of the Greasers." The old leaders, who had grown up in Sicily, largely illiterate, were replaced by the new and Americanized generation of Luciano and his allies, who were concerned far more with business and with profit than with ancient Sicilian clan rivalries or bloody power games in the streets. According to Bo Weinberg, one of the four men assigned by Lansky to kill Maranzano, "That was the time we Americanized the mobs." Luciano chose not to live in Little Italy, moving instead into a suite in the Waldorf-Astoria Towers, under the name of Charles Ross.

"Luciano mainly wanted to be left alone to run his enterprises," recalled Bonanno in his memoir, *A Man of Honor.* "He was not trying to impose himself on us, as had [Joe the Boss] Masseria. Lucky demanded nothing from us." This was a smart business decision. By 1931, Prohibition's days were clearly numbered, and the time of rich and easy pickings would soon be over. Prohibition had enriched a lot of people, including the Kennedy family in Boston; the Bronfmans in Canada, who went on to build the legitimate liquor empire of Seagram; and the Rosenstiels, who built the Schenley liquor fortune. Lou Rosenstiel, at least, kept some social ties with old criminal chums like Frank Costello. Like many other American businessmen as the Great Depression began its grip, Luciano had to devise a strategy to survive hard times. The last thing he needed were more gang wars, which were expensive, because when gunmen "went to the mattresses"—holed up in safe apartments until needed—they had to be paid and fed and provided with women. And the payoffs to police always went up after killings.

Luciano's solution was to establish a board on which other gang leaders would be represented, and that could adjudicate and conciliate business and turf problems before they got out of hand. Sometimes called the Commission or the Syndicate, Luciano's system depended on his readiness to reach out beyond the Sicilian and Italian community and work with Jewish operations like those of Lansky; Louis (Lepke) Buchalter, who ran the Garment District; and Longy Zwillman of New Jersey. The Italians, like Joe "Socks" Lanza, who ran the Fulton Fish Market as elected head of the United Seafood Workers, were naturally included. This was Luciano's particular genius, but also his deepest failure. Prohibition had generated the money, the contacts, and the opportunity for the criminals of the pre-1914 ethnic immigration to go straight. But Luciano could not or would not make that leap.

Luciano's friend Lansky tried to move into legitimate business, founding the Molaska Corporation just ten days before Prohibition ended in December 1933. Molaska would produce molasses, the raw material for legal booze. It was not entirely legitimate; Molaska was supplying distilleries that produced for the tax-evading black market. A series of raids in 1935 pushed Molaska into bankruptcy, and thrust Lansky back into the familiar world of gambling and the rackets. The end of Prohibition also forced Luciano to rely increasingly for his own income on the traditional sources of crime, the numbers games and other forms of gambling, narcotics, loan-sharking, and prostitution. Prostitution was to be his downfall. In 1936, Luciano was arrested by New York's new special prosecutor, Thomas E. Dewey, and charged with "white slavery," enforcing compulsory prostitution. He was said to have two hundred madams and over one thousand whores paying up to half their earnings through Davey Betillo, who ran the vice division of Luciano's enterprises.

Luciano liked to keep prostitutes around his hotel suite, so they would be available for him and his partners and staff, which meant they were sometimes in earshot when deals were being made. These women, therefore, found themselves learning a great deal about his operations. Betillo kept up the pressure on the girls, enforcing discipline with ruthless beatings. But that allowed Dewey to assemble his willing witnesses. Three of them testified in the Court of General Sessions, and Luciano was found guilty on sixty-two charges and sentenced to thirty to fifty years in Clinton State Prison, a maximum security facility in Dannemora, New York, known to criminals as "Siberia." Strikingly, this incarceration barely dented Luciano's reputation or his influence. "He practically ran the place," recalled one of the guards. "He used to stand there in the yard like he was the warden. Men waited in line to talk to him. Charlie Lucky would listen, say something and then wave his hand. The guy would actually back away, it was something to watch. The real mob boys when they were about to be discharged would always have a last talk with the Boss, as they all called him."

With the coming of World War II, another kind of respect came into play. Naval Intelligence, alarmed about sabotage and espionage on the docks and waterfront, decided to enlist Luciano's help. The U.S. war effort depended utterly on being able to send troops and munitions overseas to Europe and the Pacific. The New York waterfront became almost a part of the front line. The French liner *Normandie* burned and sank at her mooring in what was almost certainly an act of sabotage. The U-boats in the shipping lanes off New York were sinking ships faster than they could be built, at a rate of 272 in the first six months of 1942—more than one a day. Naval Intelligence's B-3 Division had 150 men for port security in New York, and they feared that the U-boats were receiving intelligence about ship departures. Lt. Cmdr. Charles Haffenden decided to appeal to the patriotic instincts of the mob. He got cooperation from Joe "Socks" Lanza, who declared that if Uncle Sam really needed help, the person to ask was Luciano, and the way to him was through Lansky. Through Moses Poliakoff, Lansky's lawyer, a deal was arranged.

Luciano was transferred to Sing Sing to meet Lansky and Lanza, and he agreed to help. His one condition was that his help be kept secret, since his sentence included eventual mandatory deportation back to Italy, where he feared reprisals. The B-3 teams found their work suddenly became far easier. They could get union cards to work on the docks, waterfront strikes suddenly stopped, and useful information began to flow. Eight Nazi agents, who were landed by submarine, were arrested by the FBI after B-3 teams had been informed where and when they had landed and how they were traveling to New York. In 1943, when the Germans and Italians had been evicted from North Africa and the Allies were about to invade Sicily, Luciano's cooperation provided further intelligence help. Sicilians were brought into the B-3 headquarters to provide local knowledge of Sicilian ports and beaches, and B-3 agents took part in the invasion.

A raid on the secret location of the Italian Naval Command on the island, which netted maps of minefields and all Italian and German fleet dispositions, came from intelligence supplied by those Sicilians. According to Lt. Paul Alfieri, who led the raid, the informants had been provided by Luciano. Lucky's reward was to be released after serving almost ten years of his sentence, and he was deported to Italy in 1946 aboard the ship *Laura Keene,* with a Pier 7 send-off of lobsters and wine from Frank Costello and some of the boys. Lansky, aware of the throngs of newsmen on the pier, was not among them.

Back in Italy, Luciano was welcomed as a hero in Sicily and in Naples, and after some judicious money changed hands, he was able to move to Rome and return to business. He made one brief effort to join Lansky and old New

Lucky Luciano and the American Criminal

York friends who had seen a new opportunity in Cuban gambling opportunities in the 1950s. Luciano traveled to Cuba, but the U.S. government—in the form of the Bureau of Narcotics, eventually backed by the State and Justice departments—put strong pressure on the Batista regime to deport the man who now called himself Don Salvatore. Back in Italy again, Luciano made a new fortune by organizing the export of heroin, whose manufacture "for medical purposes" was then legal in Italy. His operations were discreet. The Guardia di Finanza, Italy's treasury police, were able to pin only one offense on him—evading the currency regulations by accepting a cash payment of fifty thousand dollars. He cheerfully paid the four-thousand-dollar fine. He died of a heart attack in 1962, while on his way to meet a film producer to discuss a movie of his life.

He was given a splendid funeral as a man of honor, having returned to the Sicilian roots and ritual that he had tried to grow beyond for much of his criminal life. In the end, Luciano was a failure because he could not escape that heritage and the limited vision of the future that went with it. He died knowing it. In an interview with the *New York Herald Tribune* shortly before his death, Luciano was asked to look back and consider if he might have lived differently. "I'd do it legal," he replied. "I learned too late that you need just as good a brain to make a crooked million as an honest million. These days, you apply for a license to steal from the public. If I had my time again, I'd make sure I got that license first."

The great irony of American crime is that with the Kefauver congressional hearings of 1950–1951 and the Valachi testimony of 1963, the politicians and the public began to focus on the Mafia at a time when the most gifted criminals had already realized that there was more money and security to be made honestly. The Bronfmans and Rosenstiels had understood it back in the 1930s, when they made the relatively easy transition from the illegal to the legal liquor trade at the end of Prohibition. Lansky also understood it, risking almost his entire fortune of some $3 million in the Riviera Hotel he built in Havana in 1958, where the casino would be legal. But barely a year after it was opened, Fidel Castro's guerrillas seized power in Cuba and closed the casinos.

Lansky never went broke. An investment in the Summerfield oil well in Michigan kept him in funds. In some ways, he had replaced Luciano in the 1940s, not as *capo di tutti capi,* but as a senior diplomat and go-between of the crime world, the figure trusted by Jews and Italians alike to resolve disputes. That initial alliance forged between Luciano and Lansky on New York's Hester Street paid off through another of Lansky's boyhood friends, Bugsy Siegel, who had the vision to see that the legal gambling in Nevada could provide an alternative and legitimate future. His excesses led to his assassination in 1947, just as the investments from Lansky, Costello, and Jimmy "Blue Eyes" Alo were starting to make his casino-hotel, the Flamingo, a success. After his failure in Cuba, Lansky turned back to Las Vegas, as a finance chairman for the different interests. His most important role was to give an honest accounting of the share of the skim, that part of the gambling profit extracted before the official (and potentially taxable) accounts were made. He took a $200,000 finder's fee for the 1960 sale of the Flamingo (for over $10 million) to Sam Cohen and Morris Lansburgh (who later served prison terms for skimming), and he had interests in the Sands and the Fremont hotels. The FBI had acquired incriminating information on Lansky and others through illegal wiretaps, which led to their being questioned, but this documentation was inadmissible in court.

That was all the warning that Lansky, Alo, and the others needed. "Let's take the money and have a quiet life," said Alo. Moe Dalitz, from Cleveland, was the first to leave Las Vegas, selling the Desert Inn to Howard Hughes in 1966. The following year, Hughes bought the Sands for $14.6 million, of which Lansky's share was $1 million. Discouraged by the legal pressure, the various organizations of the Mafia gave up their grandest achievement, leaving Las Vegas to a leisure industry that would make far more money from legalized gambling than the criminals ever had. That the pressure that forced them to leave had come from the FBI, which had insisted throughout the 1950s that there was no such thing as the Mafia, was rich in irony. But in a sense, J. Edgar Hoover had been right. There were geographical understandings and connections, but there was no nationwide hierarchy. Luciano's New York organization, Santo Trafficante's Florida operation, and Moe Dalitz's Cleveland group operated independently. They were, in essence, local problems to be dealt with by local law enforcement. But by moving across state lines to Las Vegas, Lansky and the others came under federal jurisdiction, and thus became a proper target for the FBI, just as Congress was demanding that the FBI take action.

In retrospect, the withdrawal first of alcohol sales and then of gambling from the criminal arenas was the most effective crime-fighting measure ever undertaken. Prostitution continues as a fertile source of criminal income, but it has been diminished by the sexual revolution and in crucial periods by the ebb in arrivals of young and single male immigrants. Narcotics thus became the main source of criminal funds. But by the 1980s, when New York's Little Italy had become a tiny enclave surrounded by a vast Chinatown, and the generation of Lansky's and Luciano's heirs had retired, died, or been killed, the new face of American crime reflected the fresh opportunities that American laws and prejudices offered.

Lucky Luciano and the American Criminal

The remaining fascination of what might be called the Golden Age of American Crime was the degree to which it interwove itself into the mainstream of American public life. Luciano became a patriot in the war effort, working with the government against Nazi infiltration. A generation later, Trafficante and Sam Giancana, quite apart from their hopes of recovering their lost hotel investments in Havana, thought they were upholding the national interest by cooperating with the CIA in an attempt to assassinate Castro. Whether there actually was a Mafia, or simply an agglomeration of various ruthless ethnic immigrants who saw their opportunities and took them, remains open to debate. But there is little doubt that they saw themselves, in some fundamental sense, as good Americans who might be breaking the law but were making their careers in a profoundly American way. They were brutes and criminals and killers, but they built Las Vegas, they answered their country's call, they learned under Luciano to work together, and the smart ones got out while the getting was good, and put their sons through college and law school. Perhaps the classic epitaph of the old Mafia is Balzac's line on the origins of the French aristocracy and the French bourgeoisie: "Behind every great fortune there lies a great crime."

12.
Franklin D. Roosevelt and the American Solution

T he first combined operation of America's three military giants took place on July 18, 1932. Gen. Douglas MacArthur was in resolute and bellicose command. His aide Maj. Dwight D. Eisenhower was firmly against it, but he followed his orders and assembled a machine-gun detachment, the Twelfth and Thirty-fourth Infantry regiments and the Thirteenth Engineers. And Maj. George S. Patton, backed up by six tanks, led the charge of the Third Cavalry, their sabers pointing at the foe.

Their enemies were their old comrades in arms of World War I, the 25,000-man-strong Bonus Expeditionary Force (BEF), American veterans camped out with their wives and children in a makeshift shantytown that was to become a battlefield. It stretched through the formal heart of the American capital, from the Mall between the White House and Capitol to the Anacostia River and the swampy flats beyond, fetid in the steaming humidity of a Washington summer. The veterans had gathered to demand their due, war service bonus payments of one thousand dollars a head, already voted by Congress but not scheduled to be paid for another thirteen years. The sardonic social commentator Will Rogers said they held the record as "the best-behaved of any hungry men assembled anywhere in the world." Faded American flags flew over the tents, some of them drawn up in neat military-style lines, with hand-drawn unit insignia from their wartime regiments and divisions. Impoverished and with little chance of work in the Depression, the veterans had gathered in peaceful discipline, and some in their patched uniforms, to demand the money be paid early.

President Herbert Hoover, barricaded inside the White House, adamantly refused. He had said no since they had arrived with the cherry blossoms in the spring, and he continued to refuse even to meet the veterans' leaders as initial public sympathy became tinged with resentment from local shopkeepers who saw the tattered old soldiers and their families as depressingly bad for business. Finally, Hoover asked the D.C. police, who had initially set up a soup kitchen for the BEF, to clear them aside. The police went in with billy clubs. The veterans resisted with fists and bricks. The panicked police opened fire, killing two and wounding two more. Hoover then called in the army "to put an end to rioting and defiance of civil authority." The White House alleged that the veterans who had fought the police were "entirely of the Communist element."

"There is incipient revolution in the air," MacArthur declared, and ordered Patton's cavalry to charge at 4:45 p.m., just as the end of the working day was disgorging tens of thousands of Washington's clerks and bureaucrats onto the city streets. The infantry then went in with tear gas—three thousand gas grenades had been brought from the Aberdeen Proving Ground in nearby Maryland—and bayonets. The battle lasted almost until midnight, as the infantry pushed the veterans back across the Anacostia bridge, burning their shacks and tents. It ended with a final cavalry charge, two babies dead from the gas, and hundreds injured and wounded. One of the veterans was Joseph Angelino, who had won the Distinguished Service Cross in 1918 for rescuing under fire the wounded Major Patton.

"I read the papers with a feeling of horror," recorded Eleanor Roosevelt. Upstairs in the bedroom of his New York governor's mansion, her husband, Franklin Roosevelt, shook his head in disbelief and covered the newspaper photos of the battle with his hands, as if he could somehow erase them, recalled Rexford Tugwell, a member of the Brain Trust assembled for FDR's presidential campaign. In 1920, Roosevelt had trumpeted Hoover's claims to the White House. "There's nothing inside the man but jelly," Roosevelt now told Tugwell in disgust. "Maybe there never was anything else."

America Reborn

Thus began America's revolutionary moment. It was to last another nine appalling months. In Iowa, bankrupt farmers blockaded Sioux City, disarming the police who came to move their roadblocks. The farm protests spread through the heartland, to Des Moines and Omaha. In Nebraska, farmers occupied the state capitol. In Kansas, lawyers stopped foreclosing on bankrupt farms after one of their colleagues was murdered. In Iowa, vigilantes abducted a judge from his courtroom, put a rope around his neck, and threatened to lynch him unless he pledged not to authorize any more foreclosures. Nonetheless, 273,000 American families were evicted or saw their farms foreclosed that year. In the state of Mississippi, a quarter of all the land was auctioned off after foreclosures. "The biggest and finest crop of revolutions you ever saw is sprouting all over this country right now," John Simpson, president of the National Farmers Union, told the Senate in January 1933.

Beyond the devastation of the farming heartland, at a time when one American in four still lived and worked on the land, the Great Depression had shattered American finance and industry. Over five thousand banks had failed. The total value of the stocks on the New York Stock Exchange had fallen by 89 percent since the crash of 1929. American investors had lost $74 billion. World War I itself had cost the country only $25 billion. U.S. Steel was still running, barely, with over 80 percent of its productive capacity idle. In Toledo, Ohio, four out of every five workers were unemployed. Over 15 million people were unemployed. According to *Fortune* magazine in October 1932, 34 million Americans—almost a third of the population—had no income whatsoever. In Detroit, the mayor's Unemployment Commission saw "no possibility of preventing widespread hunger and slow starvation."

Not just the industrial workforce was hit. Cities could no longer pay their employees. Chicago fired one thousand teachers outright and issued paychecks to the rest only five months out of thirteen. Owed $23 million by the city, the teachers of Chicago carried on working anyhow. In Arkansas, over three hundred schools simply closed. New York City's Health Department reported that 20 percent of schoolchildren were suffering from malnutrition. Congress was told that in the coal belt of Pennsylvania, West Virginia, Ohio, and Kentucky, the malnutrition rate was over 90 percent.

The American economy shrank to less than half its precrash size. The GDP had been $104 billion in 1928, collapsing to $41 billion in 1932. Foreign trade had fallen by two-thirds, from $9 billion to $3 billion, due to the actions of America's first Mormon senator, Reed Smoot. As chairman of the finance committee, his response to the Wall Street crash was to protect American industry by raising tariffs on imported goods to 60 percent. Despite a petition signed by one thousand economists pleading for a veto against this act that would destroy world trade, President Hoover signed it into law. Within six months, thirty-three nations had imposed retaliatory tariffs of their own. American exports of food and manufactured goods collapsed. Between 1920 and 1932, total farm income plummeted by two-thirds, from $15.5 billion to $5.5 billion.

The country appeared to be trapped in a vicious spiral of decline. The fewer people working, the fewer with money to buy goods, and so fewer workers were needed. And the less food they could all afford to buy, so farm incomes shrank and so did farmers' purchases, which meant that more workers were laid off. As incomes shrank, so did federal and state tax receipts, so government at all levels had to cut its own staff and expenditures. There seemed to be no way out. In August 1932, *The Saturday Evening Post* sent a reporter to England to interview the sage of Cambridge, John Maynard Keynes. Had the world ever previously experienced anything quite like the Great Depression? "Yes," Keynes confirmed. "It was called the Dark Ages, and it lasted four hundred years."

The American disaster was but one drama of a global tragedy. Yet there were pockets, if not of prosperity, then at least of relative immunity to the spiral of decline. In Soviet Russia, the ruthless priorities of central planning by an authoritarian state seemed able to continue the drive to industrialization through forced investments. Amtorg, the Soviet trade office in New York, recorded 350 applications a day to emigrate to Russia in 1932. And in fascist Italy, Benito Mussolini boasted that his policies of state investments, military purchases, and tightly controlled foreign trade were sparing his people the worst. These remedies were deeply, even monstrously flawed. Stalin's system was ruthless enough to maintain foreign currency income by exporting food while millions were dying in the Ukraine famine. Mussolini simply falsified the unemployment statistics.

But the spurious perceptions of success under communism and fascism were plausible enough to attract the desperate. In September 1932, fifty-three of the country's prominent intellectuals and artists, including Upton Sinclair, Edmund Wilson, John Dos Passos, and Sherwood Anderson, issued a joint manifesto against "the disorder, the lunacy spawned by grabbers, advertisers, speculators, salesmen, the much-adulated, immensely stupid and irresponsible businessmen" and called for support for "the frankly revolutionary Communist Party." The American system of capitalism and democracy was seen to have failed. "If this country ever needed a Mussolini, it needs one now," declared Republican senator David Reed from one side of the American political system. From the other, Governor Floyd Olson of Minnesota announced, "Olson is taking recruits for the Minnesota National Guard, and he isn't taking anybody who doesn't carry a Red Card."

And yet when almost 40 million American voters went to the polls in

America Reborn

November 1932, they were in no mood for a revolutionary solution. Only 103,253 of them voted the Communist ticket. The Socialists won only 884,649 votes, a smaller share of the total vote than they had achieved in 1920. Voters did not want a Stalin or a Mussolini. They simply wanted a president who would do a better job of tackling the crisis than Hoover. In Franklin Delano Roosevelt, the Democratic governor of New York and former assistant secretary of the navy, they found one, and he carried forty-two out of the forty-eight states. Roosevelt himself had few illusions about the robustness of America's democratic traditions were he to fail. When a friend told him that he would go down in history as the greatest American president if he succeeded, and as the worst if he failed, Roosevelt replied, "If I fail, I shall be the last one."

There was little in his election campaign to prepare the voters for the vast sweep of reforms that he would enact. Roosevelt had promised "a new deal for the American people," without specifying what this would mean. He probably did not know himself. His campaign promises were contradictory. Sometimes he seemed to promise to protect American industry by raising the tariff, and sometimes he appeared to pledge the opposite. He promised to balance the federal budget, to restore "sound money," and on occasion spoke of America as "a mature economy" that probably could not expect to grow very much in the future. He did not propose the Keynesian device of deficit financing, spending money that the government did not have in order to get the economy moving again. Quite the reverse. He attacked Hoover as a spendthrift for having tried such heresies. At a rally in Pittsburgh's Forbes Field, he warned in sepulchral tones that because of Hoover, the federal budget deficit in the coming year could be as high as $1.6 billion, "a deficit so great that it makes us catch our breath." He went on in that same speech to promise a 25 percent cut in government spending.

"In other speeches he had committed himself to what would certainly be very costly unemployment relief. This was about as contradictory as it was possible to be," commented Tugwell, who left Columbia to join the New Deal administration. "It will seem incredible—it is still incredible to me—that the conflicting policies of those early months not only existed in the government and operated side by side, often colliding, sometimes canceling each other, but that they also existed somehow side by side in the President's mind."

Roosevelt may have been vague on specific policies, and he certainly had no prepared blueprint for recovery. But he understood the perilous mood of despair that began to swell into panic as state after state—thirty-eight out of forty-eight—closed the banks during the March weekend when he took the train to Washington for his inauguration. They had no choice but to close their doors. The panic had stripped them of their gold as those with cash lined up to demand reliable metal instead of flimsy paper. The New York Stock Exchange and the Chicago Commodity Exchange marked the day with their own signal of desperation by closing. Roosevelt also understood that the one crucial and essential act a new president could take was to use the inaugural moment to deliver a jolt of confidence.

"I have never known a man who gave one a greater sense of security," commented Eleanor, his wife of twenty-seven years. "I never heard him say there was a problem he thought it was impossible for human beings to solve." It was that security, that jaunty self-assurance, and the indefatigable cheerfulness that had survived even his crippling by polio, that Roosevelt now deployed. Locking his leg braces into place, he stalked to the podium to deliver the cure.

"So first of all, let me assert my firm belief that the only thing we have to fear is fear itself—nameless, unreasoning, unjustified terror which paralyzes needed efforts to convert retreat into advance," he declared. Having shown that he knew what the nation felt, in a way that Hoover never had, and that he was just the man to face this challenge, Roosevelt then assured the country that they had already taken the central decision of their own recovery. "The people of the United States have not failed. In their need they have registered a mandate that they want direct vigorous action. They have asked for discipline and direction under leadership. They have made me the instrument of their wishes. In the spirit of the gift I take it." Roosevelt then followed this psychological boost with a demand for extraordinary powers to turn his election into action. "I shall ask the Congress for the one remaining instrument to meet the crisis—broad Executive power to wage a war against the emergency, as great as the power that would be given to me if we were in fact invaded by a foreign foe."

The speech on that Saturday, March 4, 1933, inspired 450,000 Americans to write to the new president to pledge their relief and support. He needed all the help he could get. The next morning, rolling his wheelchair into the Oval Office, he found it utterly empty. Hoover had taken everything that could be moved except for the flag and the great seal of the presidency. There was no paper, no pen, no pencil, no phone on the vacant desk, not even a buzzer with which to summon an aide or a secretary. Alone, he confronted the immensity of the task before him and then uttered a great shout to assemble the staff and to get to work.

Roosevelt knew government. He had been assistant secretary of the navy during World War I. He had governed New York, the richest and most populous of the states, for two terms. Born in 1882 on the family country estate at Hyde Park, New York, on the Hudson River, he carried a name that echoed the presidency of his distant cousin Theodore, and his wife was Teddy Roosevelt's niece. Born rich, the son of a lawyer and railroad financier, Franklin Roosevelt was educated at the prestigious boarding school of Groton, by private tutors, and by a grand tour to Europe, where he learned to speak French and German. He graduated from Harvard in 1904, where he had rowed and played football, been elected class committee chairman, served as managing editor on the daily *Harvard Crimson,* and been an enthusiastic member of the Republican club. To his abiding frustration, he failed to be elected to the elite Porcellian Club, possibly because his secret fiancée, Eleanor, had little interest in helping him secure that aspiration, but she had helped steer his campaign for the *Crimson* and as class officer.

He went on to law school at Columbia, practiced in New York for three years, and was then elected to the state senate as a Democrat in 1910. Two years later, he campaigned for Woodrow Wilson and was immediately appointed to be deputy navy secretary in Wilson's government before he was thirty. In this gilded and brilliant career, one oddity stood out. He had in 1905 married his tall and gawky cousin Eleanor, whose mother explained that she was so shy, "such a funny child, so old-fashioned we call her Granny." She had been educated at a progressive and feminist school in England, spoke fluent French, and had scandalized her family with postcards home that related her unchaperoned explorations of Paris. Franklin's devoted mother thought Eleanor so odd and unsuitable that she spent three years trying to block the marriage.

But Eleanor was a striking girl, intelligent, thoughtful, and intensely active in the world, while other girls seemed to think mainly of balls and beaux. Above all, FDR had at last found a woman with whom he could laugh. And she had found a man who could constantly, happily, surprise her. She was to be pleasantly stunned in 1910 when her husband came out in support of women's suffrage. And she was enchanted at his readiness to be guided by her. She had volunteered for charity work with some like-minded friends on New York's Lower East Side, and she joined the Consumers' League, and then the Women's Trade Union League, which investigated and exposed working conditions in the sweatshops of the garment industry. Visiting Eleanor at the Rivington Street settlement house where she taught, he once escorted her and a sick pupil to the child's tenement home, and later told her he "could not believe people lived that way."

For the first twelve years, which produced five children, it was a strong and enviable marriage. But as World War I plunged him into endless travel and late nights at the Navy Department and her into war work at the Red Cross, strain began to show, and he embarked on what was to prove a lifelong affair with Eleanor's social secretary, Lucy Mercer. Early in 1918, unpacking his bags when he came back from a naval voyage sick with influenza, she found a package of Lucy's letters to her husband. The Roosevelts stayed together, partly repairing the breach with a long trip to Europe at the end of the war, but she could barely haul herself from deep depression for the 1920 presidential campaign, when he was the vice-presidential nominee. The next year, he was stricken with polio.

All marriages are private mysteries, and Franklin and Eleanor maintained an outwardly durable and mutually respectful union, although it sometimes looked more like a political alliance than a conventional marriage. He continued the relationship with Mercer, and he was to die in her arms in 1945. But as Eleanor forged a political career of her own in the 1920s, as a civil liberties and antiwar campaigner, as an activist for women's rights, and as a power on the Democratic National Committee, she became his buttress on the Left and his connection to the radical wing of the party. She played a key role in persuading him to accept the 1928 nomination to run for governor of New York and, just as she had first taken him to the Lower East Side tenements two decades earlier, once in the White House she became his eyes and ears and his guide to the plight of Depression America.

He needed little schooling in the severity of the crisis he faced. On his first day in office as president, Roosevelt summoned Congress to emergency session, took the dollar off the gold standard, and proclaimed a four-day national bank holiday. By the time Congress gathered on Thursday, March 9, he had a new banking bill ready for them to pass. It required private holders of gold to return it to the banks for paper money, with the penalty of jail for hoarders, and appointed public receivers to take over failing banks. It authorized the hiring of 375 new staff to start printing $2 billion in new bills, as well as ratified all actions "heretofore or hereinafter taken" by the president and his treasury secretary. This was a blank check without precedent, and Congress passed it that same day, along with the threat of imprisonment for anyone hoarding gold. The bold measures worked. By that Saturday night, $350 million in gold had been returned. Within the week, three out of every four banks in the country—over thirteen thousand of them—were open for business again. The stock exchange rose 15 percent. The Dow-Jones ticker gave credit where it was due, punching out on its wire the title of the Roosevelt campaign song, "Happy Days Are Here Again."

The day after the Emergency Bank Act was signed into law, Roosevelt presented his economy bill, cutting $400 million from veterans' benefits and $100 million from the civil service payroll. It made no economic sense to take this much money out of the economy, but this bow to the orthodoxies of thrift reassured those businessmen and bankers who were alarmed at his boldness that the president was doing something right. And right or wrong, it was action, decisive action when the country desperately needed to know that someone was at last taking charge. Ninety Democrats revolted against the bill, but it was passed within the day, with sixty-nine Republicans voting for it, a symbol of bipartisanship that Roosevelt instinctively knew was essential.

On the day of the crucial vote, he gave the first of what became an unprecedented 998 presidential press conferences, a bravura performance that ended with the reporters giving him a round of applause. Well they might. He had transformed their profession. The White House had become the dominant news beat. United Press decided to triple its Washington staff. The Associated Press reported that a quarter of all its news was coming from the capital. On March 12, Roosevelt delivered his first fireside chat over national radio. In the twelve years of his presidency, Roosevelt was to give only twenty-nine of these characteristic and homely speeches, which for many Americans would be the abiding personal memory and encounter of his era. This first chat was about banking reform.

"My friends, I want to tell you what has been done in the last few days, why it was done, and what the next steps are going to be," he began, addressing an unprecedented audience of 60 million attentive Americans, half the population; nobody in history had ever spoken to so many Americans at one time before. "First of all, let me state the simple fact that when you deposit money in a bank the bank does not put the money in a safe-deposit vault. It invests your money in many different forms of credit—bonds, mortgages. In other words, the bank puts your money to work to keep the wheels turning around."

On the next day, Monday, as the banks reopened, more Americans put money in than took it out. The same day, he urged Congress to end Prohibition by legalizing the sale of beer. The day after that came his farm bill, which authorized guaranteed prices to farmers who agreed to limit their production. It also required the slaughter of 6 million pigs and the plowing under of a quarter of the cotton crop. Prices then rose, and farm incomes began to recover. The day after that came the proposal for the Securities and Exchange Commission, the financial watchdog that would prevent any repetition of the speculative frenzy that had ended in the Wall Street crash. To run it, he appointed the Boston-based speculator Joseph Kennedy, because "he knows the tricks of the trade." The next week came the legislation for the Civilian Conservation Corps, to employ what became a total of 2.5 million young unemployed men in public work camps. They built parks, rural roads, and bridges and planted a "green belt" of 200 million trees from Texas north to the Canadian border. All this and it was still only March 21.

In April, he tackled the problem of foreclosures and evictions. The Home Owners' Loan Corporation was established to give a federal guarantee to mortgages, which were made more affordable by extending the payment term.

Franklin D. Roosevelt and the American Solution

A similar scheme was established for farm loans, and the whole financial system, which had been threatened with total seizure, was allowed to flow again by giving federal guarantees of bank accounts up to five thousand dollars—which meant the deposits of the overwhelming proportion of Americans. For home loans, farm loans, and banks, Roosevelt deployed the financial weight of the federal government to convince lenders that it was safe to lend, and savers that it was safe to entrust their money to the banks. Within eighteen months, the Farm Credit Administration had refinanced a fifth of all the farm mortgages in the country. The Home Owners' program refinanced 300,000 homes, with a combined value of just over $1 billion, and since most of these were for loans about to be called in, this saved hundreds of thousands of families from eviction.

It was not, coldly considered, a desperate gamble. The farm and home loans were secured against the value of the property. The bank-deposit guarantees were secured against the fact that two thousand weak banks had been closed, and the rest were not going to be allowed to fail. The risk that Roosevelt took was calculated on the rock-solid belief that America would endure and that the system was fundamentally sound, if only borrowers and lenders could feel confident again. He successfully pledged the faith and credit of the American government to restore that confidence.

These were not revolutionary measures, except that no American government had tried them before. They were reforms to mend the existing system, not to replace it. It had, therefore, to be seen as less a Democratic measure than an all-American structure that could rally Republicans and Democrats, employers and employees alike. Nowhere was this more clear than in the National Industrial Recovery Act (NIRA), which quietly shelved much of the existing antitrust legislation. Roosevelt unveiled the NIRA before the U.S. Chamber of Commerce in May 1933, still within the first hundred days of his administration. His plan to let businesses establish their own industry groups, with their own codes for price-fixing and noncompetition agreements (subject to government approval) and with penalties for violators, received a rapturous welcome from the Chamber of Commerce members. This meant, in effect, that they could legally charge whatever they all agreed, while being spared the threat of competition; industries were thus given an official charter to become cartels.

In return, they swallowed a system of agreed minimum wages and maximum working hours, and a guarantee of the right to collective bargaining. This was not entirely what the labor unions had wanted, because the legislation was carefully drafted to allow company unions. It was by no means a labor union charter. Like so much else of Roosevelt's program, it was a compromise designed to attract maximum support. This was the way he liked to operate, as his adviser Raymond Morley had been stunned to learn during the 1932 campaign. Roosevelt had asked him "to weave together" a speech with a strong protectionist bias, but one that also signaled a reduction of tariffs.

The boldest measure of all was to authorize $4 billion—which the government did not have—in relief for the poor and unemployed. Some of the money went directly to states and cities to support their relief measures, but the bulk went into a series of public works programs that were to endure under different names throughout the decade. Often derided as make-work and boondoggling, the $20 billion of public funds that went into the program in the eight years after it was launched gave work to over 5 million Americans. It was instrumental in the building of Hoover Dam and Fort Knox, the Lincoln Tunnel and the Triborough Bridge, the Washington Mall and the San Francisco fairgrounds and Dealey Plaza in Dallas. Harry Hopkins boasted that in his years running the Public Works Administration (PWA), he built 10 percent of all new roads, a third of all new hospitals, two-thirds of city halls and courthouses, and 70 percent of all new schools in the country. The PWA also financed the Tennessee Valley Authority.

It was all financed by debt. The federal budget deficit in 1934 was $6 billion, $4 billion the next year, $5 billion in 1936, and $2.5 billion in 1937. By 1938, the budget was almost balanced. These were piffling sums by comparison with the $30 billion annual deficits that were to finance World War II. But they were unprecedented in peacetime, and deeply worrying to orthodox bankers and Republicans who believed that the country was borrowing its way to ruin. It was not.

The money borrowed by the federal government was being recirculated into the economy, where it produced more wealth as workers were hired, food and goods were bought, and farmers and businesses found themselves with more money to spend. In 1935, 1936, and 1937, the GDP rose by 9 or 10 percent each year, which meant that the economy was growing faster than the debt, which, in turn, meant that the economy could afford to borrow from it. The year in which the budget was almost balanced, with a mere $100 million deficit in 1938, was also a year of no growth.

Strikingly, this was all achieved without calling on the extraordinary powers that Roosevelt had mentioned at his inauguration. As president, and in command of a party with firm majorities in both the House and the Senate, Roosevelt had all the power he needed, at least until the banking, financial, and industrial institutions he had saved had recovered their ebullience sufficiently to start attacking his "socialistic" measures. The one that upset them most was the increase in inheritance taxes.

During his first years in office, Roosevelt had certainly not cured the Great Depression. Unemployment had fallen from around 15 million to just under 12 million. The economic situation remained perilous, if not desperate. But he had achieved enough to receive a striking endorsement in the 1934 midterm elections. Democrats gained nineteen seats in the House and another nineteen in the Senate, giving them overwhelming majorities, the first (and until 1998 the only) such midterm gains by an incumbent party. As a result, the second phase of the New Deal proved more radical and less prepared to compromise with business than the first.

"In spite of our efforts and in spite of our talk, we have not weeded out the overprivileged, and we have not effectively lifted up the underprivileged," Roosevelt declared in his annual message for 1935. "We do not destroy ambition, nor do we seek to divide our wealth into equal shares—we do assert that the ambition of the individual to obtain for him and his a proper security, a reasonable leisure, and a decent living throughout life is an ambition to be preferred to the appetite for great wealth and great power."

Two days later, he asked Congress for $4.9 billion in new relief and public works funds—more than the entire federal revenues for the previous year—and introduced what became the Social Security Act. Granting old-age pensions, unemployment insurance, and aid to poor parents with dependent children was the most important single piece of the New Deal, the most profound in its effects, and the most politically popular. It was passed by the overwhelming margins of 372–33 in the House and 76–6 in the Senate. This was perhaps the high point of the New Deal, and almost immediately matters began to go awry. There were attacks from the Left, from Louisiana governor Huey Long and his "Share the Wealth" program, as early opinion polls were warning that an independent candidacy from Long could hold the balance of power in the 1936 elections. Attacks came from the labor unions, demanding the passage of the Wagner Act, which gave the new National Labor Relations Board wide powers to force companies to hold workplace ballots on union recognition and to end discrimination against union members. Roosevelt was dubious, but he bowed to the strength of the pro-labor Democrats in Congress. There were attacks from the Right, which was outraged by a modest tax increase that raised income taxes by only 1 percent for those with income of $50,000 a year, by 6 percent on those with incomes of $100,000, and by 16 percent for those who could best afford it, that tiny handful with incomes above $3.5 million.

But then the Supreme Court struck. On Black Monday, at the end of May 1935, the court unanimously struck down three crucial aspects of the New Deal. First, it invalidated the Frazier-Lemke Act, which gave relief to farm debtors. Second, it challenged the president's right to fire on grounds of political incompatibility a member of the Federal Trade Commission. And third, it struck down the NRA and its use of interstate commerce laws to regulate industry and to control wages and prices. This was a body blow, especially because the usually pro-Roosevelt justices Brandeis, Stone, and Cardozo had voted with the conservative majority. In fact, the NRA had done its job of controlling the crisis of 1932–1933, and it was becoming an overregulating liability. Roosevelt did not seek to revive it. But then the Court struck again three times in 1936. It challenged the right to use tax levies as incentives to farmers, which threatened the farm program. It challenged the right of the new Securities and Exchange Commission to investigate businesses. And it challenged the right of government to set a minimum wage. This time, the court's liberals opposed the majority opinion.

Roosevelt went into the 1936 reelection campaign with some obvious enemies, but also with a strong record for the voters. The national income, which had been $44 billion when he took office, had risen by 50 percent. Factory employment had risen by a third, farm prices by half, and unemployment was down to 6 million when the Democrats renominated Roosevelt that summer. Industrial production was not booming, but it was picking itself off the floor, with total output back to the level of 1925. The most striking tribute to Roosevelt's achievement was the Republican platform, which accepted the principles of Social Security, of free collective bargaining, the minimum wage, and a limit on maximum working hours for women and children.

"I should like to have it said of my first Administration that in it the forces of selfishness and of lust for power met their match," he told the pre-election rally in Madison Square Garden. "I should like to have it said of my second administration that in it these forces met their master." Despite a sweeping victory, with 61 percent of the popular vote (compared to 57 percent in 1932), the second term was no triumph. The attempt to tame the Supreme Court, by increasing the number of justices and appointing reliable Democrats, failed badly, arousing resentment and suspicions of an authoritarian regime that was prepared to tamper with the Constitution to get its way. In the event, the Supreme Court showed that it, too, could read the election returns. One conservative, Justice Van Devanter, retired to secure his full pension. Another, Justice Roberts, changed his view to approve the minimum wage. And then the Wagner Act, which secured labor union rights to collective bargaining, and the Social Security Act were both upheld by the Court. Roosevelt had lost the political battle, but he had won the legal war.

He failed, however, to conquer the Depression. A new slump loomed in the summer of 1937—in part because Roosevelt had promised to balance the budget and slash the deficit spending of his first term. Unemployment rose again to 9.5 million by May 1938. The lesson was clear. The magic of deficit spending had been a temporary relief that could not inspire the private sector into steady and self-supporting growth. The confidence of private investors, who were grumbling at their higher taxes, remained desperately low. They and the banks that Roosevelt had saved proved strikingly reluctant to invest. What finally ended the Depression—unemployment topped 10 million again in the spring of 1939—was the coming of war in Europe, and the spate of arms purchases from Britain and France, and then, after the French defeat in 1940, from Britain alone.

Roosevelt was not blind to the threats from Japan and from Europe. In October 1937, after Hitler's reoccupation of the Rhineland and the outbreak of the Spanish Civil War, Roosevelt spoke in Chicago of the need for "quarantine . . . in order to protect the health of the community against the spread of the disease." It was a hesitant effort, and when the Gallup poll the following week asked whether the United States should join other nations to resist aggression, only 29 percent agreed. Roosevelt had difficulty enough raising the size of the armed forces from 243,000 in 1933 to 334,000 in 1939. His suggestion of a European peace conference in 1938 generated little response. When the king and queen of Britain visited the United States in June 1939, to feast on hot dogs and beer at Hyde Park, the king reported back to his government after a quiet talk that he believed that in the event of war, Roosevelt would do all in his power to help. Shortly after war broke out, Roosevelt amended the Neutrality Act, suspending the arms embargo to allow Britain (or any other power, but only Britain had command of the sea) to buy any war material they could carry away. Lockheed bought a tract of land on the North Dakota border with Canada and flew in their warplanes. They were then hauled the fifty yards across the border by horses. The law was satisfied. The planes had not left the United States under their own power.

Over the next two years, as Britain's plight become more perilous and the radio broadcasts of Edward R. Murrow from the London blitz brought the war into American homes with unprecedented intimacy, laws were bent further to make the United States into a nonfighting ally. The poet Archibald MacLeish wrote to Murrow, "You burnt the city of London in our homes, and we felt the flames." Fifty obsolescent but still useful American destroyers were provided to Britain in return for long leases on its Caribbean bases. The sympathies of the U.S. Navy were clear enough; the destroyers arrived stuffed with soap, luxuries, and presents gift-wrapped for the British sailors' children, and with scrawled messages of goodwill on the bulkheads: GIVE 'EM HELL! and KILL THE BASTARDS!

Roosevelt was under strong pressure from the 850,000 members of the America First group and from the traditional isolationists to stay out of the war, and he fought the 1940 presidential campaign with a promise: "Your boys are not going to be sent into any foreign wars." But from interventionists in both Democratic and Republican parties, and—after Hitler invaded Russia in June 1941—from the Left, as well as from his wife and many in his personal circle, he was under equally intense pressure to come to the aid of embattled democracy. The film star Douglas Fairbanks, Jr., a member of the Committee to Defend America by Aiding the Allies, went to Washington to lobby the president, and Roosevelt confided that he "had to be like the captain in front of his troops. If he got too far ahead in expressing his own sympathies and opinion, then he would lose the people behind. He could only be a little ahead—and it was our job to push public opinion."

Safely reelected, Roosevelt introduced the Lend-Lease bill in January 1941, under the reassuring title "A Bill to Promote the Defense of the United States," and his fireside chat used the homely metaphor of lending a garden hose to a neighbor whose house was on fire. "The best immediate defense of the United States is the success of Great Britain in defending herself," he maintained. Once the bill was passed, Averell Harriman was sent to London to administer lend-lease, and Roosevelt's parting orders were, "Recommend everything that we can do, short of war, to keep the British afloat." In April, Roosevelt ordered the navy to take over Atlantic convoy duties against U-boat attack up to the mid-Atlantic. In July, the United States took over the garrison duty on Iceland.

In August, Churchill arrived for his first wartime summit with FDR, and the Atlantic Charter, which they signed aboard the battleship *Prince of Wales,* set out the common war aims, which showed how far Churchill was prepared to go to secure the U.S. alliance. Clause three signaled the eventual end of the British Empire: "Respect the right of all peoples to choose the form of government under which they will live." Clause four signaled the end of Britain's closed trade system of Imperial Preference, with its guarantee to all nations of "access on equal terms to the trade and raw materials of the world." In September, after a U-boat attacked an American destroyer, the U.S. Navy provided military escorts to within aircraft range of British bases, and American merchant ships were armed. But in October, the Gallup poll found only 17 percent of Americans wanting war with Germany. Roosevelt, plunging billions of dollars into a crash program of rearmament and conscription, was trying to push public opinion further than it would go.

Finally, it was Japan that forced America out of isolation and into its destiny as the leader of the Free World. What Roosevelt called "a date which will live in infamy"—the attack on Pearl Harbor—and Hitler's subsequent declaration of war left no other option than to wage total war. The conflict itself, requiring unprecedented industrial mobilization and the mastery of the air and seas around the globe, left the country familiar and even comfortable with its new global role. It would take the Cold War to perpetuate the American leadership and global military presence into a time of nominal peace.

And if the war had left the United States the only unexhausted state, it also left it the overwhelming economic power, producing in 1945 half of the entire wealth of the planet. The war created modern America, and it also built upon the New Deal foundations to create the modern American state.

When Roosevelt was elected in 1932, the federal government collected $1.9 billion, just under 5 percent of the national income. In 1945, the year he died, it collected $45 billion, more than the entire GDP of 1932, and borrowed as much again because it spent more than double the $45 billion. The state had become the biggest employer, the biggest investor, the biggest debtor, and the dominant player in the economy. The gamble that Roosevelt had accepted in 1933, that a democracy could rescue itself from catastrophe by its own efforts while keeping its free institutions intact, had been won. The United States, like its British ally, had weathered the monstrous double test of Great Depression and global war and avoided the totalitarian temptation. America had provided the democratic answer to the ruthlessness of Soviet Russia, Nazi Germany, and militarist Japan.

And it had all been achieved by consent. Roosevelt established the dual consensus that was to guide the country through the rest of the century after his death: that it was prepared to shoulder the burden of leading the global military alliance of free nations, and that it was prepared to do so while taking public responsibility for the care of its elderly, its poor, and its unemployed. This was the very core of the Roosevelt compromise, that America would remain a broadly free-market economy, while the state would ensure that the kind of unbridled capitalism that had plunged it into the Great Depression would never again be allowed to fail the nation and its more vulnerable citizens. Roosevelt found an isolationist nation in desperate crisis and left it a world power, a nation with a thriving free-enterprise economy, and a modern state, first among equals in a new United Nations system that seemed the best hope that such a war would never come again. Above all, he had presided over the emergence of an America that had discovered a complete faith in itself, its abilities, and its free institutions to face any challenge and surmount any obstacle that destiny might bring.

13.
Katharine Hepburn and the American Star

O n the set during the shooting of Charlie Chaplin's *Modern Times,*
Katharine Hepburn was standing beside the Russian dancer Vaslav
Nijinsky as the greatest comic film star of them all waited to be
slapped in the face with a custard pie. They watched Chaplin's expression and
his timing, and the way that even though he knew what was coming for the ten
thousandth time, he refused to blink. "The nuance," whispered Nijinsky in
reverence, acutely aware of watching a master at work.

"It's a bunch of bunk. BUNK, BUNK, BUNK, BUNK!" thought Hepburn as she recalled the moment in an interview with Charles Higham over
forty years later. "A lot of hogwash is written about the business. It isn't all
that fancy. It's a craft. Spencer [Tracy] always said, 'Learn the lines and get on
with it,' and so does Larry Olivier and so does John Gielgud. Of all talents,
acting is the least. Acting is just waiting for a custard pie. That's all."

Katharine Hepburn and the American Star

Hepburn never took herself, or her acting, too seriously. In 1939, during the New York stage run of the play *The Philadelphia Story,* which was to make her rich and independent, Hepburn was invited to lunch at Hyde Park by President Franklin Roosevelt. She arranged for a pilot friend to fly her up. He landed on the riverbank below the hilltop estate, she disembarked, and he took off again. She trudged laboriously up the muddy hill, identified herself to a security guard, and then sat by a stream, took off her shoes and stockings, and began to wash her feet, just as Roosevelt was driving by. He stopped the car, looked down at the movie star, and began to laugh. They laughed all the way to lunch.

It was, Roosevelt said, what might have been expected from Katharine Houghton's daughter. He had known the actress's mother from the days of the suffragette movement, when she and Eleanor Roosevelt had campaigned together. And the actress and the president shared an American pedigree: Roosevelt could claim descent from the seventeenth-century Dutch families who had settled New Amsterdam in the years before it became New York, while Hepburn's ancestors had come to America aboard the *Mayflower.*

In an industry that became a byword for social mobility, in a country that asserted a cult of egalitarianism, Hepburn was the unmistakably polished embodiment of the American upper class. Her upbringing in Connecticut, her education at Bryn Mawr, her accent, her posture, and the confidence of her stride combined to make her an almost glaring example of that elusive species, the American aristocrat. Whenever she tried to step outside this natural role, as a hillbilly in *Spitfire,* or as a Russian pilot in *The Iron Petticoat,* or as a Chinese woman in *Dragon Seed,* the result verged on the grotesque. Whenever she played a character who shared her own social roots, in whatever period, from *Little Women* to *Bringing Up Baby,* from *The Philadelphia Story* to *Guess Who's Coming to Dinner,* she acted as if born to the role, as indeed she was. It was a style that translated easily to playing an Englishwoman of a similar class in *The African Queen,* or a European queen of the Middle Ages in *The Lion in Winter.*

Whether washing muddy feet before a president or refusing to be awed by Chaplin's comic timing, Hepburn was one of those unique creations of the film industry, a star. The word had never been used in this context before Hollywood, because it was not needed. There were famous actresses like Ellen Terry and Sarah Bernhardt, and there were famous opera singers like Nellie Melba who were known as divas or prima donnas, and there were women dancers like Isadora Duncan who had thrilled audiences around the world. But in their lifetimes, these celebrities played to at the most hundreds of thousands of people who saw them perform in the flesh. Hollywood created women who were seen on screen by hundreds of millions, in the curious blend of remoteness and intimacy of a darkened cinema.

The defining moment for a singer or a stage actress was the single aria or the great speech, a woman dominating row upon rapt row of an audience sharing her space and her intensity, and yet seeing her as part of a whole and surrounded by actors or sets or a live orchestra intent upon her every breath. The defining moment of the film star was the close-up, an image nearer, larger, and more compelling than anything to be seen or experienced in life, and yet forever distant and untouchable. A star, by definition, shone from the outer space of the screen, not the common space of the theater.

Hepburn became something more than a star. After her screen hit with *Little Women,* Hepburn was always as much symbol as actress. She foreshadowed by a generation the self-confident, assertive, and, above all, intelligent feminism that was to become a social and political force in the 1970s. She was always ready to take cinematic risks. *Sylvia Scarlett* (1936) saw the first overt flirtation with androgyny. This blurring of male-female roles was as old as the theater, but startling in a Hollywood still governed by a conventional code that insisted upon married couples being depicted in twin beds. "Katharine of Arrogance" became her Hollywood nickname, reflecting the spiky, uncompromising personality that matched the screen roles that enthralled, but also baffled, the cinema audiences of the 1930s.

When Hepburn's career began, Hollywood's women stars were sex goddesses like Jean Harlow, and if women were on occasion empowered to dominate, it was through Mae West's mocking burlesque of the vamp. Hepburn brought something else. It was partly a social assurance that came from a prosperous upper-middle-class upbringing, partly the cool intelligence honed at Bryn Mawr, which her suffragette mother had also attended. Partly, it was the resilience of a woman who succeeded on the stage and screen despite repeated setbacks, and who proved able to challenge and overcome the Hollywood studio system and chose her own films, her own roles, her own directors, and her own costars. In private, her self-confidence sometimes faltered, but never in public. Pride, and the traditions of her caste, would not permit it.

In a film career spanning sixty years, Hepburn won four Oscars. The first came in 1932, for her role in *Morning Glory,* the stereotyped part of a young understudy who becomes an overnight star when the leading actress falls ill. The fourth came for her role as the aged wife of the equally elderly Henry Fonda in *On Golden Pond,* forty-nine years later. In between, she won another for *Guess Who's Coming to Dinner* (1967), and then another for her role as Eleanor of Aquitaine, who had been the great beauty of her day and married in turn the king of France and the king of England, in *The Lion in Winter* (1968). The list of Oscars barely begins to sketch her career. It could as well be measured by the Oscars she inspired her costars to win, from Humphrey Bogart in *The African Queen,* to James Stewart in *The Philadelphia Story,* to Henry Fonda in *On Golden Pond.*

Her acting range was extraordinary, from the high drama of Eugene O'Neill's *Long Day's Journey into Night* with Ralph Richardson to the brisk repartee and comedy of *Bringing Up Baby.* Constance Collier persuaded her to take up Shakespeare with *As You Like It* on Broadway in 1950, and in 1955 she signed up for an Australian tour with London's Old Vic company, playing Portia in *The Merchant of Venice,* Kate in *The Taming of the Shrew* and Beatrice in *Measure for Measure.* She was particularly proud of her Cleopatra at Stratford in 1960. But she was also enchanted to play in a Western, *Rooster Cogburn,* opposite John Wayne. "When I leaned against him (which I did as often as possible, I must confess . . .), . . . it was like leaning against a great tree." He was "a simple and decent man," she recalled in her memoirs. But Wayne was also a consummate professional and one to be admired: "He is a very very good actor in the most highbrow sense of the word. You don't catch him at it." In historical epics, she played the grandest of grande dames in *The Lion in Winter,* and handled the most cutting-edge of contemporary themes in *Guess Who's Coming to Dinner,* in which the easy rhetoric of civil rights challenges the reality of racism on the most intimate of levels when a white girl brings a black boyfriend home.

She was and remained a star in youth, in middle age, in maturity, and in old age. On-screen, those incomparable cheekbones, sharp as axes, in an austere but intensely alive face made for remarkable close-ups. Her proud sense of self combined with a natural grace that survived the brilliant successes and humiliating failures of Hollywood, and the perilous ebbs and flows of political life. A lifelong liberal, she supported the right to free speech when the House Committee on Un-American Activities targeted the film industry and tried to restrict it, provoking so many outraged letters that studio head Louis Mayer had to stop putting her in MGM films. She succeeded stunningly with almost all of the great directors of the day, including Frank Capra, George Cukor, David Lean, Howard Hawks, John Huston, and John Ford.

And although Hollywood gossip claimed that she was a lesbian when she moved in with her friend Laura Harding, she had three striking and passionate love affairs with some of the most intriguing men of the day. The last, with Spencer Tracy, who was too devout a Catholic to divorce his wife, was to prove the love of her life, a decades-long devotion that was to endure his alcoholism and bring an almost tangible intensity of affection to their films together. But she also enjoyed a well-publicized affair with the billionaire Howard Hughes, and an almost equally luxurious relationship for several years with her agent, Leland Hayward. She once virtually stood up the heartthrob of the day, Douglas Fairbanks, Jr., pleading a headache to escape early from a dinner date. The besotted Fairbanks lingered outside, looking at her house, only to see a laughing Hepburn dance out to a waiting car and race off into the night with Hayward. She enjoyed men, but always on her own terms.

She treated Hollywood, the place and the industry, in the same imperious way. When the studios first became interested, after her 1932 New York stage success in *The Warrior's Husband,* she was earning $275 a week, but she held out for $1,500 a week for a four-week film contract, and, to her great surprise, she got it. Although she signed with RKO, she was wary of the then all-powerful studio system, insisting on contracts that gave her freedom to return regularly to the stage, which in effect allowed her to pick and choose her films. Her love for the stage was more than a devotion to the craft of acting. She supported the Theatre Guild, a cooperative that gave her her first, crucial break onstage, and which became her regular refuge from Hollywood set-backs. But it was also to be the key to her eventual independence. The Theatre Guild helped her turn a novel to which she had bought the rights, *The Philadelphia Story,* into a play, and the successful play became a potential hit movie, a property that was to give her extraordinary bargaining power in the bizarre economic structures that had developed in the film industry.

From the moment that Thomas Edison patented his Kinetograph (camera) and Kinetoscope (viewer) in 1893, an enduring battle began for control of the industry. It started with Edison and the inventors of the Biograph and the Vitagraph banding together, using their patent rights over the crucial technology of filming and screening the movies to control the production, distribution, and exhibition of films in the name of their Motion Picture Patents Company, which became known as "the Edison Trust." Hollywood itself first became an alternative filming center because small independent companies saw it as safely remote from the New York–based Trust, and handily accessible to the Mexican border in case of urgent lawsuits, as well as being climatically perfect for making films.

The Trust hated the idea of "stars," actors with sufficient name and drawing power to force higher salaries and shift the balance of power from those financing and making the films to those performing in them. The Trust sought a monopoly, but their dominance provoked the emergence of small independent challengers. These new independents deliberately created stars to challenge the Trust. Carl Laemmle, head of the Independent Motion Picture Company of America, bribed away "the Biograph Girl," Florence Lawrence. He then used the publicity techniques he learned from promoting her to build his next acquisition, Mary Pickford, into the first national movie star. At the same time, William Fox's small Greater New York Rental Company was challenging the Trust's distribution monopoly under the new antitrust legislation.

Adolph Zukor took up a different challenge, buying the rights to distribute a British-made film of Sarah Bernhardt in *Queen Elizabeth,* and then signing up established Broadway theater stars to make new films for his company, Famous Players. Again, the stars were a weapon in the battle for control against the Trust.

As the films grew longer than the pioneering twelve-minute *Great Train Robbery* and the plots fuller with D. W. Griffith's 1915 *The Birth of a Nation,* and movie palaces were going up to replace the cramped nickelodeons, the independents took over. Laemmle built Universal City. Mack Sennett started the Keystone studio to make comedies. Zukor's Famous Players and Jesse Lasky's company combined as Famous Players–Lasky, which later became Paramount. Famous Players–Lasky became a trust of its own, using the block-booking method to force the exhibitors to accept packages of poor films along with popular ones.

By this time, the stars were established enough to rebel, and Griffith, along with Chaplin, Pickford, and Douglas Fairbanks, broke away to form United Artists in 1919. The movie exhibitors set up their own rival purchasing system, First National, and then the Loew's movie house chain established its own production company, Metro-Goldwyn-Mayer. The Metro of the title came from the name of one of the companies owned by Loew's. Goldwyn came from Sam Goldwyn, brother-in-law and former partner of Lasky; Goldwyn had broken with Lasky and gone independent. Mayer came from Louis B. Mayer, who had made his fortune distributing *The Birth of a Nation* across New England and then decided to go independent in 1917. MGM's slogan became "More Stars Than There Are in Heaven."

By the 1930s, there were seven dominant studios: Paramount, Columbia, RKO, Metro-Goldwyn-Mayer, Warner Bros., Twentieth Century–Fox, and Universal. Columbia had been formed in 1920 by a group of defectors from Laemmle, led by Jack and Harry Cohn. Warner Bros. had started as a small nickelodeon company in Pennsylvania, took over First National, and then exploded into the front rank of studios in 1927 with the first real talkie, *The Jazz Singer.* RKO, which stood for Radio-Keith-Orpheum, began as a Milwaukee nickelodeon, which became the Mutual Film Corporation in 1917, then RKO in 1928. Twenty years later, it was bought by Howard Hughes. Twentieth Century–Fox traced its roots to the New Yorker William Fox, who had filed the original lawsuit to challenge the monopoly powers of the Trust.

The studios ran the industry from top to bottom, much as Henry Ford sought to control his business, from iron-ore mines to assembly line and showroom. The studios planned the films, made them, distributed them, and dominated the movie houses where they were shown. They developed a series of genres—historical dramas, Westerns, and mysteries—each with its own experienced directors and genre stars, to keep costs down and build audience loyalty. They rationalized the creative business of filmmaking into a kind of mass production, with centralized departments for scriptwriting, costumes, and special effects, as well as—highly important—a press agency to service the newspapers. Each studio found and developed its own stars, keeping them under strict contract, while developing its own house style, churning out almost a movie a week, fifty a year. By the 1930s, when the big studios made four out of every five films shown in the country, those films were seen by audiences of over 100 million each week.

Hepburn joined this system by entering a contract with RKO. Her first film, *A Bill of Divorcement* (1932), had been a hit. Her second, *Christopher Strong,* in which she played a female aviator, made its money back but little more. She won an Oscar in her third, *Morning Glory,* although the Oscars were then so much in their infancy that, according to Hepburn, only five members of the new Academy voted. Her fourth film was *Little Women,* a stunning success, even though at one point in the filming the director, George Cukor, slapped her hard across the face for spilling ice cream over an expensive dress. She was twenty-six. And then she made a flop, *Spitfire,* in which she tried to play a spirited hillbilly.

It was not easy to recover from a flop. Hepburn decided to return to the stage, but she made the mistake of agreeing in 1933 to appear in a new hit play from London, *The Lake,* directed by the imperious whiz kid of 1920s Broadway, Jed Harris. He was a gifted but most unpleasant man; Laurence Olivier claimed to have based his film performance of Richard III, Shakespeare's ultimate villain, upon Harris. Before Hepburn signed up, Helen Hayes warned her against him: "He will destroy your confidence," she said.

So it proved, producing a stage performance that inspired Dorothy Parker's famous review, in which she wrote, "Go to the Martin Beck and see K.H. run the gamut of emotion from A to B. . . . She has a red carpet running from her dressing room to each entrance . . . so that no one can see her. Who wants to?" Audiences dwindled away steadily. Harris insisted that the play go on tour, telling the wretchedly unhappy Hepburn, "My dear, the only interest I have in you is the money I can make out of you." She checked her bankbook and found that she had $13,675.75 in her account; she offered it all to Harris to buy herself out. He took the money.

She sank into her lowest period as an actress, and her personal life was unhappy. She sailed to Mexico to get a quick divorce from the young Philadelphia socialite Ludlow Ogden Smith, whom she had married in 1928 when she was a rising actress in New York. Then her agent and lover, Hayward, went off with another stage star, Margaret Sullavan. On his deathbed years later, after marrying Winston Churchill's daughter-in-law Pamela Churchill, Hayward asked for Hepburn. Pamela sent for her, saying, "He loved you more than any of us." It was during this lonely period that the equally solitary Greta Garbo came to visit Hepburn in Hollywood, toured the house, and detected the familiar shape of a hot-water bottle. Garbo patted it and sighed, saying, "Yes, I have one too. *Vot* is wrong *vid* us?"

Hepburn made a series of flops: *Sylvia Scarlett* with George Cukor and *Mary of Scotland* with John Ford, and *A Woman Rebels,* about a suffragette of the 1870s, a part she had taken in a kind of homage to her mother. She turned back to the stage, in an adaptation of *Jane Eyre,* which Hepburn disliked, but she was committed. As the play went on tour, it was followed from city to city by the infatuated Howard Hughes in his private plane, and by a growing posse of reporters. The subsequent notoriety, amid speculation of secret weddings and escaping from photographers down hotel fire escapes, filled the theaters and made the tour a financial success.

She was saved by the friendships she had made. There was Pandro Berman at RKO and Cukor. The fame from the affair with Hughes helped, along with the Oscar she had won for *Morning Glory.* Berman sent her a film script of an Edna Ferber and George S. Kaufman play, *Stage Door.* She loved it, took the part, and had another hit. Then Howard Hawks picked her for the role that established Hepburn as a great comic actress. *Bringing Up Baby* is now a classic, in which she plays a madcap, flighty socialite with a leopard as a pet, with Cary Grant as her foil. But on its release, the film played only moderately well in cities, and badly in rural areas. Harry Brandt of the Independent Theater Owners of America declared that Hepburn was box-office poison, placing her at the head of a list that included Joan Crawford, Greta Garbo, and Marlene Dietrich. Alarmed, RKO kept good scripts away from her, and in 1938, they finally offered her a role in a B movie, *Mother Carey's Chickens.* Her career clearly faltering, Hepburn bought herself out of the RKO contract. It cost her $200,000. Thereafter, by signing contracts to make individual movies rather than commit her services for years to a single studio, Hepburn took the risk of failure. Her track record was very mixed for such a gamble.

Then Cukor came to the rescue, offering her the starring role in *Holiday* with Cary Grant, produced by Harry Cohn at Columbia. The part might have been written with her in mind. She plays the rebel daughter of a rich Park Avenue father and falls for her sister's fiancé. Her powerful performance combined a subtle aggression with restraint and the perennial message that money isn't everything. It was a polished film, rather than a great one, and was helped by Cohn's defiant publicity campaign, which included billboards with the question: "Is it true what they say about Hepburn—that she's box office poison?" On the strength of this hit, RKO tried to sign her again. She refused, unless they bought the movie rights to the new best-selling novel *Gone With the Wind* and gave her the part of Scarlett O'Hara, with Cukor to direct. RKO declined. David O. Selznick bought the rights, and although Hepburn was given a screen test, the part went to the little-known British actress Vivien Leigh. "My dear, I can't see Rhett Butler chasing you for twelve years," Selznick explained to Hepburn. "Well, David, some people's idea of sex appeal is different from yours," she responded.

She went back to Fenwick, the family holiday home at the mouth of the Connecticut River, and the playwright Philip Barry came to see her with an idea for a play, which became *The Philadelphia Story.* She persuaded him to let the Theatre Guild perform it, and she and Hughes jointly financed half the production. Since she had just paid $200,000 to RKO, it seems likely that Hughes helped buy her share, and his greatest gift to her was to buy the film rights to the play, which allowed her to become a producer in her own right. The play, set among the upper class of Philadelphia, was written with her act-ing strengths as well as her own social background in mind. It was a perfect vehicle for her. It ran for 415 performances, grossing almost $1 million. It ran another 254 performances on tour, grossing over $760,000.

This success secured the future of her cherished Theatre Guild and made her rich. Armed with the film rights, she was in a position of power when she went to see Louis Mayer at MGM. She wanted Cukor to direct, and she got him. She asked for Tracy and Clark Gable, who both turned down the chance to play with a woman still known as box-office poison. Mayer offered Jimmy Stewart, whom he had under contract, and $150,000 to hire another male lead. This secured Cary Grant's services for three weeks, after Hepburn agreed to give him top billing over her, and he volunteered to donate his salary to the British War Relief Fund. She secured Joseph Mankiewicz to produce, and Joseph Ruttenberg as cameraman because she liked him and he knew how to light her from above to conceal the first signs of wrinkles on her neck, about which she was extraordinarily sensitive. In effect, she had control of the film, and it became an instant hit in 1940, grossing $100,000 a week in its first six weeks at Radio City Music Hall in New York, making her even richer.

Hughes may have been the godfather to Hepburn's Hollywood rebirth as an independent actress-producer, giving her a unique status and security in the industry, but the next step was entirely her own. It was to change her life. Word of her ability to deal with Mayer had spread. Ring Lardner, Jr., son of the sportswriter, had the idea for a film script based on the life of Dorothy Parker. He worked on it with Michael and Garson Kanin and offered it to Hepburn under the title *The Thing About Women.* She worked on it, changed the title to *Woman of the Year,* and took the project to Mayer. She persuaded him to pay a then-record fee for the property, $211,000, while she retained the right to choose director and costar. To direct, she picked George Stevens, whom she had dated after her affair with Hughes had ended amicably, and then she demanded that Tracy play opposite her. While making the film, they fell in love, thereby beginning a relationship that was to last until his death nearly thirty years later.

"We balanced each other's natures," she said of their film work together. "We were perfect representations of the American male and female. The woman is always pretty sharp, and she's needling the man, sort of slightly like a mosquito. The man is always slowly coming along, and she needles, and then he slowly puts out his big paw and slaps the lady down, and that's attractive to the American public. He's the ultimate boss of the situation, and he's very challenged by her. It isn't an easy kingdom for him to maintain. That—in simple terms—is what we did."

The great power of her films with Tracy, including *Woman of the Year* and *Adam's Rib,* stemmed from the way that this unusually self-reliant woman was fated to subordination by her own will. The great fascination of her personal life comes from the degree to which this film role was paralleled in her life with Tracy. They made nine films together. He died seventeen days after they finished *Guess Who's Coming to Dinner,* and she has never been able to watch it.

In Hepburn's autobiography, *Me,* she chronicles an extraordinary relationship. She reported that initially Tracy was reluctant to make a film with her, asking, "How can I do a picture with a woman who has dirt under her fingernails and who is of ambiguous sexuality and always wears pants?" His reluctance was short-lived. "After this he saw *The Philadelphia Story* and changed his mind," she recounted. Her own account of their affair chronicled her sleeping outside his hotel bedroom when he was on a drunken bender and saying her farewell at the funeral parlor, leaving him to be buried by the woman who was still his wife. "I always say Spencer grew me beyond my potential," was Hepburn's own summary in a film she made in 1995, *All About Me.* "I made it. I know a lot about life. I've been lucky. Thank you, Spencer."

This dignified farewell to her beloved partner has been challenged in a recent biography by Barbara Leaming, *Katharine Hepburn.* In this account, the Tracy-Hepburn relationship became a nightmare of a life with a man who beat up prostitutes and who believed his bout of venereal disease caused the deafness of his son. "Full of self-loathing as he was, he seemed to enjoy humiliating Kate by bringing her down to his own level; turning a woman of that calibre into his mistress, Tracy reminded himself and others of the moral depths to which he had sunk," Leaming writes. She presents Tracy as the antithesis of the Hepburn family and of its liberal and feminist values, and she chronicles a disastrous visit when Hepburn took him to the patrician family beach house on the Connecticut shore. "They [the Hepburns] did not argue with his conservative views or ask whether he intended to marry their daughter. Dr. and Mrs. Hepburn turned away because Spencer Tracy had failed to interest them; and in the Hepburn household, that was the greatest sin imaginable."

An ecstatic review of the book in the *New York Times* provoked bitter controversy. Dan Ford, grandson and biographer of John Ford, complained that Leaming was wrong in calling Ford a drunk and saying that he had had a grand affair with Hepburn. Leaming, he concluded, wildly exaggerated the relationship as "one of several convenient plot devices to add drama, mystery and a new twist to what is otherwise another ho-hum biography." Selden West, Tracy's authorized biographer, accused Leaming of bending the facts "to establish a romantic triangle that simply never existed"—Ford, Tracy, Hepburn in the middle. West added that there is no evidence for the venereal infection, and that it is "an utter falsehood" to assert that Tracy would visit Hepburn in the evening, have his drunken way, "and leave when he had finished." She cites not only Hepburn's own account but also the testimony of friends in making the argument that it was a loving relationship, filled with happy times of painting together, flying kites, walking beaches, and playing tennis.

This would be a predictable row between rival biographers, except for the bizarre reversal of the proud woman into the downtrodden handmaiden, and the complication involving John Ford, with whom Leaming suggests Hepburn began an affair during the filming of *Mary of Scotland.* But Dan Ford, despite his letter to the *Times,* wrote in his own account of John Ford's life that he and Hepburn "fell in love" and that his grandfather was "obsessed by Kate and found with her a degree of happiness and a peace of mind he had never known before." Still, the documentary record for the Ford-Hepburn affair is thin; five letters from him, of which only one is explicitly romantic, and sixteen from her, including postcards and telegrams. Her autobiography says only: "We became friends, and from time to time during his life we met." Whatever its flavor, the friendship with Ford took place during the most grueling phase of her career, before Hughes's money and her own drive and talents brought her independence within Hollywood.

Only Hepburn knows the reality of her relationships with men, and possibly, as gossip suggested, with women. She chose deliberately to tell and to control her own story, in an autobiography both in print and on film. "My privacy is my own. I am the one to decide whether it will be invaded," she maintained. As ever, she set her own rules and became the custodian of her own legend, refusing all comment on the Leaming biography, the twentieth book her extraordinary career had inspired. And controversy aside, what remains most significant is the constant public fascination with the woman and the era.

The key to this constant fascination lay in her almost unique ability to remain a star at every age. She defied all the usual stereotypes and pigeon-holes, of sex goddess and character actor, of "the older woman" and of the shrewish spinster of middle age. Her life was a refutation of that enduring Hollywood myth of Billy Wilder's *Sunset Boulevard* of the aging star whose own fantasy life of continuing beauty and fame echoes, even as it mocks, the fantasy lives of her fans, of Hollywood itself. Moreover, Hepburn commanded an enduring respect for her ability to force Hollywood and audiences to take her on her own terms. She remained as assertive off-camera as she was on the set, quite ready to bully any man, except Tracy. "She lectured the hell out of me on temperance and the evils of drink," recalled Humphrey Bogart after they made *The African Queen.* "She doesn't give a damn how she looks. I don't think she tries to be a character. I think she is one."

The nature of that character says a very great deal about America, and the way its attitudes toward women and sexuality changed through the course of Hepburn's life. It would be too much to claim that she was responsible for these changes, but foolish to assert that a career that kept her in the public eye decade after decade had no influence at all. She never set out to be a role model, but her constant screen appearances as a woman of spirit and ability, making her own decisions, succeeding in a world usually run by men, served as a recurrent commentary on the societal changes that her audiences were undergoing. A Hepburn fan was accustomed to women fighting wars, knocking inadequate men into shape, ruling empires, building corporations, fighting court cases, and grappling with fascism and racism.

There was a vital and endlessly relevant subtext to the roles she played and the way in which she won the financial freedom and Hollywood authority that let her play them. America changed with her, while watching her, and while continually fascinated by the most extraordinarily independent and assertive of the stars that Hollywood produced. There was, in the end, from the 1930s to the 1990s, no escaping the Hepburn experience. As her character says in *The Philadelphia Story,* "Oh, we're going to talk about me, are we? Goody!"

14.
Walter Reuther
and the American Worker

As the cold Michigan winter of 1936 gripped the sullen car-manufacturing plants of Detroit, a young red-haired tool and die worker who had been fired for trying to organize the workers at Ford borrowed three hundred dollars and found a job for his brother inside the Kelsey-Hayes plant, which made brakes for Ford cars. Walter Reuther could not get inside the plant himself; his name had been on the industry's blacklist since 1932, the year he was fired. But Victor Reuther got a job at 36.5 cents an hour, working a punch press, and began recruiting among workers angered by management's habit of speeding up the assembly line, changing work rules, and banning toilet breaks.

Victor found a young woman on the day shift in Department 49, which made the brake shoes in the giant factory of five thousand workers, who agreed to cooperate. When the assembly line was moving at its fastest, she pretended to faint. The foreman pulled the switch to stop the line, and then Victor and his handful of allies sat down and refused to continue working. Others spread the word elsewhere in the plant. The personnel director came down to the line, but he could not get the protestors back to work. Victor gave him a slip of paper with his brother's phone number and said, "Call Walter Reuther. He's the only guy that can get us back to work."

"What do you want me to do?" Walter asked when the personnel director called him on December 12, 1936.

"Put 'em back to work."

"How can I? Will they listen?"

"They listen to you on street corners."

"I can't talk to them from here. Will you let me in?"

The company sent a car to fetch Walter from his tiny rented office with its single battered typewriter and a phone on the rickety table. By the time Walter reached the brake-shoe building, rumors had spread throughout the plant that women had been collapsing from the accelerated pace of the line. Once inside, Walter climbed onto a pile of boxes and began to make a speech about the need to join the United Automobile Workers (UAW).

"What's going on here? You said you'd get them back to work," objected the personnel director, plucking at Walter's sleeve. Reuther's reply has gone down in Detroit and labor union legend.

"I can't put them back to work until I get them organized," he said. And as Victor and the tiny handful of UAW members inside the plant signed up new members, Walter began negotiating with management. He broke off when the shift changed in order to harangue the night shift. By morning, with the assembly lines still stopped, he claimed two thousand union members. Then the talks broke down over Walter's demands for a seventy-five-cent minimum wage, a 20 percent cut in the assembly-line speed, and recognition for the UAW.

Walter then gave a speech to the workers about the sit-down strike he had seen in a French factory, stressing, "The only way they can beat us is if they separate the workers from the machines. And they are our machines. Without us, those machines don't do a thing." He persuaded the workers to stay in the plant, and the sit-in strike lasted for ten days, while families brought parcels of food to the strikers. The Kelsey-Hayes management tried to sneak in some toughs to provoke the violence that would be required to call in the police to clear the plant. Walter and Victor were expecting that tactic, spotted the toughs, and had the strikers throw them out. Ford began leaning heavily on Kelsey-Hayes to settle the strike before the Ford plants had to close for lack of brakes. It was a race against time, because Walter feared that the sit-in strike would probably collapse soon, since the workers would want to go home for

America Reborn

Christmas Day. The final deal, reached December 23, was a compromise. The workers got the line slowed, a guarantee not to fire older workers, and a minimum wage of seventy-five cents an hour, plus overtime. But Kelsey-Hayes remained an open plant, where the union was not formally recognized and the company could pressure workers to stay outside the UAW. Walter had barely started.

That winter of 1936–1937 must have looked like the start of a revolution to America's industrial managers. In the six months before May Day 1937, 484,711 workers took part in sit-down strikes and occupied their factories and workplaces. Myra Wolfgang, an organizer for the American Federation of Labor's union of hotel and restaurant employees, recalled, "You'd be sitting in the office any March day of 1937 and the phone would ring and the voice at the other end would say 'My name is Mary Jones. I'm a soda clerk at Liggett's. We've thrown the manager out and we've got the keys. What do we do now?' " Saul Alinsky, biographer of the mine workers' leader John L. Lewis (the head of the CIO, the Committee for Industrial Organizations, later renamed the Congress of Industrial Organizations), interviewed many of the workers who took part in the factory occupations, recording their memories of bravery and solidarity. "It was like we was soldiers, holding the fort," one recalled. "It was like war. The guys with me became my buddies. I remember as a kid in school reading about Davy Crockett and the last stand at the Alamo. You know, mister, that's just how I felt. Yes sir, Chevy Number Four was my Alamo."

This was still the Great Depression, an industrial reality that was hard to discern in the accounts of the giant corporations like General Motors. In 1934, its net profit had been $167 million, which rose in 1936 to $227.9 million. The average yearly wage of the GM shop-floor workers was $1,150, just over $20 a week, and in the same year, GM president Alfred Sloan made $374,505. The mass unemployment of the Great Depression had cut the price of labor. In the boom year of 1928, the average pay on the assembly lines of the auto industry had been thirty-three dollars for a forty-four-hour week. The effect of the Depression had cut that pay by nearly 40 percent, while company profits boomed. The militancy of the workers should have come as no surprise. But there was another crucial factor in that decade of the New Deal. The Roosevelt administration had signed into law the Wagner Act of 1935, which gave workers the right to organize, free of company interference, and required employers to recognize and negotiate with any union freely chosen by a majority of the workforce. Although managers successfully fought part of this legislation in the Supreme Court, which gave companies some justification for refusing to follow it, the workers felt they had the government and the law as well as justice on their side.

As 1937 began, more than 112,000 of GM's 150,000 production workers were on strike, occupying their factories, or idle. Michigan governor Frank Murphy sent fifteen hundred National Guard troops to Flint, home of GM's Buick, Fisher, and Chevrolet plants, and advised city officials not to heighten the tension by issuing injunctions ordering the workers to leave. He managed to broker a compromise with Lewis, agreeing that the workers would leave the plants in return for a GM pledge to negotiate. But in Flint, where local newspapers published telegrams saying that GM was not bargaining in good faith but was trying to establish a tame company union, the workers stayed in. But it was cold, food and money were running out, and the motor-assembly plant, Chevy Four, was still operating, which meant that GM's cash flow was unaffected.

At this point, the Reuther brothers stepped in. The Kelsey-Hayes strike had just been Walter's first step. When that strike broke out, he was running a tiny local, or union branch, with just seventy-eight members. The Kelsey-Hayes victory swelled membership to over two thousand, many of them now devoted followers of the Reuther brothers. But there was a third brother, Roy, battling hard to save what looked to be the failing sit-in strike at the Chevrolet plant in Flint. On January 27, all the brothers met UAW strike leader Bob Travis and Powers Hapgood from the CIO (Lewis had provided a $100,000 fighting fund to get the Wagner Act enforced in the factories).

They planned an almost-military operation, outlined on a piece of cardboard Roy Reuther pulled from his freshly laundered shirt. The plan, as announced to the workers (and quickly revealed to management by spies among the strikers), called for a supreme effort to take over another plant, Chevy Nine. This, in fact, was a diversion, but it was made to look convincing. Victor Reuther took his loudspeaker truck, Walter took his volunteers from Detroit to join the UAW women's auxiliary, led by the tough Genora Johnson, and they marched on Chevy Nine, plunging into a free-for-all with police and factory guards as smoke from tear gas swirled over the plant and stones, bottles, and fists were thrown. And at the moment when the GM managers sent in their last reserves of guards to push back the marchers, the real attack was launched, led by Roy Reuther and Travis, against the crucial motor-assembly plant, Chevy Four. They took it easily, and held it.

The bargaining then began, with Lewis telling GM management that if they sent in armed guards to clear the plant, he would walk out of the talks and into Chevy Four. President Roosevelt appealed to Lewis to get the workers out of Chevy Four. Not until GM started to negotiate and recognized the UAW, Lewis replied. And for thirteen more days, the standoff continued, until GM surrendered and agreed to start talks with the UAW to end the strikes at seventeen of its plants. The United Automobile Workers had scored the breakthrough they needed, humbling the biggest of the auto giants after the forty-four-day sit-down strike at Flint, and their membership doubled overnight, exceeding 200,000 workers. The UAW turned to Chrysler, which quickly agreed to negotiate. But there was another target, even tougher than GM, and Walter Reuther volunteered to take on Ford at the massive River Rouge plant. Five years earlier, on March 7, 1932, local police and Ford guards had shot dead four demonstrators and wounded twenty more when the local Communist party led a march on the plant to demand a six-hour day.

Confident that the Wagner Act put the law on his side, Walter Reuther applied to the Dearborn authorities for a permit to distribute leaflets to the employees. He got it, but a city employee tipped off Ford management that the UAW campaign was heading their way. Dearborn was a company town, with Ford providing two-thirds of the tax base. Its chief of police, Carl Brooks, had been the head of Ford police at the Highland Park plant. Reuther chose for his leafletting the Miller Road Overpass, a footbridge that led across traffic to the plant's Gate Number Four. Ford security was run by Harry Bennett's Service Department, which had its own guards but which hired outside muscle for special occasions. Bennett maintained a close relationship with both J. Edgar Hoover of the FBI, to whom he sent lists of suspected Communists in the Detroit area and in the industry, and with Chester La Mare, the leading local gangster. La Mare, after making up to $2 million a year from bootlegging during Prohibition, was able to open some legitimate business operations with Ford, thanks to Bennett. He secured a Ford agency, the Crescent Motor Sales Company, and had the franchise to supply fruit to the Ford lunch stands. When Bennett wanted to hire thugs, La Mare was the contact.

The morning leafletting had passed without incident, and at midday, waiting for the shift change, Reuther was not expecting trouble. He was wearing a three-piece suit with a gold watch chain across its front. Three other UAW organizers were with him: Richard Frankensteen, later to become mayor of Detroit, Richard Merriweather, and Ralph Dunham, the latter two wearing spectacles. From a line of black cars parked beneath the overpass came a gang of fifty heavyset men in hats. One was a local boxing champion; two were professional wrestlers; and others were known gangsters. They set upon the four UAW organizers and beat them bloody and senseless. Dunham spent ten days in the hospital. Merriweather's back was broken. "Seven times they raised me off the concrete and threw me down on it," Reuther testified to the National Labor Relations Board. "They pinned my arms and shot short jabs to my face. I was punched and dragged by my feet to the stairway. I grabbed the railing and they wrenched me loose. I was thrown down the first flight of iron steps. Then they kicked me down the other flights of steps until I found myself on the ground where I was beaten and kicked."

But Bennett had barely begun. He realized that the real problem was not Reuther but the UAW as a whole, a new union that had only emerged in 1935 from the recurrent rivalries between the two wings of the American labor movement. There had been the old guard of the American Federation of Labor, based on the craft unions of men with specific and traditional skills, like carpenters, mechanics, and electricians. Their pay, status, and bargaining power had traditionally been higher, and they felt little in common with the semiskilled and often immigrant workers of the assembly lines. The other wing was composed of those like Lewis, who believed the future lay with industrial unions, with all the workers in a particular industry belonging to a single, powerful organization, irrespective of their craft or pay. In 1935, convinced that the introspective and jealous craft unions were wrong to remain small and exclusive, and that the Wagner Act created new opportunities for industrial unions, Lewis split away from the AFL and formed the CIO. It was an angry breach, symbolized by Lewis's roundhouse punch to the face of the carpenters' leader, Bill Hutcheson.

But a new industrial union like the UAW was barely established, and its new leaders, men like the Reuther brothers, were still rising through the ranks. So Bennett targeted the more moderate UAW leader, Homer Martin, and invited him to lunch with the old patriarch Henry Ford, who still posed as the workingman's friend for launching the five-dollar-a-day pay scale nearly thirty years earlier. Bennett set a double trap. First, he offered to negotiate with the UAW, but only if the union dropped its lawsuit before the National Labor Relations Board for the overpass assault. That lawsuit had been Reuther's best weapon, a virtual guarantee that the government-backed NLRB would order Ford to hold a ballot among its workforce to see how many wanted to join the UAW.

Then Bennett told Martin that under the Ford ethos, union men should be encouraged to become managers and businessmen, and he offered him contracts to buy components for Ford. Since this would mean some entertaining, Ford would provide Martin with a fully furnished house until his business was prospering. The second trap was to have Martin, by accepting Bennett's bribe, write him fulsome letters of thanks. Martin betrayed the union and himself. The UAW split, with Martin taking some remnants back to the AFL, and Reuther relaunching a new UAW within the CIO. Reuther continued the lawsuit, which the Supreme Court upheld, and the stage was set for the final confrontation.

Reuther found his pretext in a sudden strike at the River Rouge rolling mill in April 1941. To prevent a sit-in by the UAW, Bennett installed his own force of worker occupiers, mainly new black employees who were kept on full pay. It was a calculated act, which afterward did untold damage to race relations in Detroit. It also did a lot of damage to the plant, as the bored men smuggled in liquor and began holding drunken races with new cars. The deadlock was finally broken when Edsel Ford, the son of the founder, finally challenged Bennett and agreed to negotiate. The result was a ballot in May 1941, overwhelmingly won by the CIO. Walter Reuther had won the preliminary battle for public opinion by stressing the need to make the auto plants into the arsenals of democracy necessary to produce the tanks and warplanes to fight the coming war against Hitler.

Reuther knew about Hitler firsthand. When he had been fired from the Ford plant, after making a speech for the Socialist candidate Norman Thomas in the 1932 election, he withdrew his savings just before the Detroit banks crashed, then set off around the world with Victor. The brothers had been born in Wheeling, West Virginia, the sons of a German brewery worker who was a dedicated old socialist. Their grandfather Jakob had been a Social Democrat in the Kaiser's Germany until coming to the United States in 1892. His son Valentine joined the brewery, became a union man, and raised his sons in the family politics. Walter was born on Labor Day eve in 1907, and he worked as a machinist's apprentice before heading to Detroit in 1927, an apple-cheeked country boy. He and Victor worked an eight-hour day, earned high school diplomas, and then put themselves through Wayne University at night, still finding time to wage an antiwar campaign on campus against the Reserve Officers' Training Corps. Victor rose at dawn to study, went to class from 8:00 a.m. to 1:00 p.m., worked the late shift at Ford from 3:00 p.m. to 11:30 p.m. to make his skilled pay of twelve dollars a day, and then faced his homework.

Now the two brothers were embarking on an extraordinary journey. "We wanted to find out how the world was living," Walter recalled, "but it was also a tour in social engineering." They worked their way across the Atlantic on a ship, bought bicycles in England, and rode up to the coal mines of Durham and the cotton mills of Lancashire, talking to workers and union men and attending political rallies of the Labour party and Communists alike. They took a ferry across to France, then cycled twelve thousand miles through Western Europe in nine months, claiming to have slept only twice in hotels. They arrived in Berlin the day before the Reichstag fire, just after Hitler had come to power. Victor spoke German, but "with such a wonderful West Virginia accent that the Germans thought we came from some remote part of Swabia." The two brothers slept in student hostels and worked as miners in Gelsenkirchen. They went to labor union and Socialist meetings and began working with what became the anti-Hitler underground; they helped some students across the border into Switzerland just as the Nazis were tightening their grip on the working-class organizations.

Walter Reuther and the American Worker

The times were hard and becoming dangerous, so the Reuthers moved on to Poland and into "the workers' paradise" of the Soviet Union. They worked, and they traveled a total of eighteen thousand miles, visiting Samarkand in central Asia, the Caspian oil city of Baku, and the Donbas coal mines of the Ukraine, finding jobs at each stop. But mainly they worked at the auto plant built by Ford at Gorki, as the old Russian trading city of Nizhni Novgorod had been renamed. Walter became an instructor, teaching young Russians straight from the farm how to machine gasket dies to tolerances of 1/7,000 of an inch. Life was not too bad, once he and Victor learned that the cans of American food marked "corn," which the Russians would not eat, in fact contained pork and beans. "We lived like capitalists for a while," he said. It was also a delicate place for young Westerners to be, with Stalin's trials of "saboteurs" and "wreckers" being launched to justify his purges of the old party faithful. Among the earliest targets were Western engineers, and just as the Reuthers were thinking of leaving, a letter from brother Roy told them of the new UAW being formed after the breakaway of Lewis's CIO, urging them to come back to Detroit and join the union. They took the Trans-Siberian railroad to Manchuria, cycled through Japan, and were back in Detroit by 1936, ready to start organizing.

Just over twenty years later, in San Francisco in 1959, Walter Reuther brought up his Soviet experience in what became a famously heated exchange with the then Soviet leader, Nikita Khrushchev. Reuther accused him of "exploiting the workers of East Germany," and he was dismissed as "feverish." Reuther raised the question of the brutal Soviet repression of the Hungarian uprising of 1956, and claimed that "when I was in Russia, I was a member of a union, and it was what we would call a company union." He went on to ask, "Can you give us one single example in which one of your unions ever disagreed with government policy?" Khrushchev accused him of being "a capitalist lackey." At one point, Reuther tossed across the table a list of American wage rates and demanded, "How can we say these people are wage slaves exploited by capitalism, making these kinds of wages in America? How can he say they have nothing to lose but their chains?"

It was one of the almost-standard exchanges of the Cold War, a dialogue of the deaf, conducted through interpreters struggling to keep up. The two men were adversaries from the beginning. Reuther had been one of the founders of the International Confederation of Free Trade Unions, established by American, British, French, and West German labor unions after the previous international body was taken over by Communists at the time of the Marshall Plan. Reuther battled against Communists inside the American labor movement, where the Communist-dominated Farm Equipment Workers had tried to infiltrate the UAW through a merger plan. He campaigned hard against Progressive party candidate Henry Wallace's campaign for the presidency in 1948, which tried to rally a united front of the Left. "The liberal who succumbs to the united-front lure believes that Communists are simply democrats in a hurry . . . the American Stalinists may quote democratic scripture for their own purposes, but they are neither good democrats nor good Americans," Reuther maintained. He took his anti-Communist campaign abroad, to the developing world of India and Africa and to beleaguered West Berlin in the military stand-off in that divided city in 1959. "It is not your freedom alone that is being challenged by Soviet tyranny. It is ours as well," he told a cheering rally of 600,000 Berliners.

Khrushchev knew what manner of labor leader he was debating. And yet despite his job and his earlier devotion to Stalin, and despite the crushing of Hungary, Khrushchev was the most reform-minded of the Soviet leaders until Mikhail Gorbachev in the 1980s. It was Khrushchev who finally told the party in 1956 what a monster Stalin had been, Khrushchev who began to open the gates of the gulag, Khrushchev who authorized publication of Aleksandr Solzhenitsyn's seminal novel of the hitherto-secret gulag, *One Day in the Life of Ivan Denisovich.* There were times, in a Soviet context, when Khrushchev sounded almost like a dissident. And Reuther was a kind of counterpart, a controversial leader in his own land who found it impossible to be taken seriously by the other side in the Cold War. "Wall Street says I am an agent of Moscow. Moscow says I am an agent of Wall Street," he told Khrushchev ruefully.

Reuther was a social democrat of a peculiarly practical kind. He knew enough of the realities of working-class life in the West Virginia coal fields and on the assembly lines of Detroit to harbor no romantic illusions. He agreed with George Bernard Shaw that "the true socialist wants to abolish the working class," and he became a classically American labor leader who believed that a sensible labor union should use the power of the union to negotiate pay and working conditions and pension and medical rights that would haul the factory workers into the ranks of middle-class prosperity.

A visionary in much of his work, he believed, like the Keynesian economist John K. Galbraith, that America was heading (and so possibly was the Soviet Union) toward a mixed system that combined free enterprise at the industrial level with strategic economic planning at the national level by the government, in consultation with management and labor. He believed that the pension rights he negotiated for his members were slowly but surely building a new kind of worker capitalism, in which the pension funds would become the real controllers of American corporations. The raw capitalism of the 1930s had been tamed by the combinations of labor, law, and government, and capitalism now had to be civilized by a labor movement that could convince management and shareholders that it was in their common interest to work together. Sharing the pie more evenly, and turning workers into consumers, would make a far bigger pie.

Apart from the formative experience of organizing the UAW in Detroit in the 1930s, Reuther drew two more crucial lessons from his own experience. The first was World War II, which Reuther passionately supported. In December 1940, Reuther drafted the CIO plan to mobilize the underproducing auto plants for aircraft manufacture. "We need send no men to a future conflict with the Axis powers if we can supply enough machines now to our first line of defense in Britain," he urged in the proposal that was handed to President Roosevelt. "The auto industry could produce 8 million cars a year. It is producing approximately 4 million. . . . Adapted to plane production, this unused potential capacity (greater than the total motor plant capacity of England, Germany, France, Italy, Russia and Japan combined) would give us world plane supremacy within a short time." His advice was not taken then, but when the United States entered the war, the UAW threw itself into the war effort. Union rules and traditional contracts were suspended to bring women workers into the plants, to suspend free collective bargaining for wage controls, and to operate continuous shifts. The wartime combination of state investment and planning, with labor and management driven to cooperate under government guidance, struck Reuther as a vision of a sensibly organized future.

"The war has demonstrated to the American people that full employment is possible," he argued in the *New York Times* a month after the atom bomb fell on Hiroshima, then went on to outline how he thought it could be maintained. The secret was to understand that the modern economy was a system that demanded a consumer market as much as it required capitalist production. The more money the workers had, the more they could buy. The more the factories would then boom, and they could hire more workers, who would then spend more money in a vast virtuous circle of production and consumption. Reuther urged "reduction of unit cost by high-volume production and constant technological innovation, enabling the masses of workers to get their bigger cut out of a larger pie and providing industry with an expanding market." This was straightforward Keynesian economics. Reuther gave this a labor spin by arguing that prosperity could be spread nationwide and guaranteed by two further measures: "Industry-wide wage agreements based on the principle of equal pay for equal work, regardless of geographical area, and the introduction of guaranteed annual wage systems through collective bargaining between labor and management."

The second lesson for Reuther was his success after the war in persuading the big auto corporations that he was right. It did not come easily. In

1945–1946, there was a wave of strikes in the coal mines and steel mills. One at GM lasted for a hundred days, over a dispute that eventually came down to just one cent an hour on standard wage rates. That was eventually settled by a fact-finding commission appointed by President Harry S. Truman, which noted that GM and the auto industry could more than afford the money; it was by far the most profitable industry in the country, making a return of 25.54 percent on capital invested, compared with 16 percent for tobacco, 10.67 percent for oil refining, and 6.37 percent for department stores. Its average profits were greater than those of U.S. Steel, Standard Oil, and American Tobacco combined. The conclusion was that GM was fighting the strike in order to teach the UAW, its ranks swelling with returning army veterans, a lesson for peacetime.

But then Reuther, as the new president of the UAW, began negotiating directly with Charles E. Wilson, GM chairman and a man who became famous for suggesting (during his confirmation hearings to become Eisenhower's secretary of defense) that what was good for GM was also good for America. The two hit it off, as Reuther convinced Wilson that all that stood between GM and decades of future profits was labor unrest. Eventually, the so-called Treaty of Detroit was signed in 1948 and gave each man what he wanted. Reuther won job security for all existing workers and a wage increase, to be followed by guaranteed annual wage increases, linked to sales and productivity, and an automatic increase to match the future rate of inflation. In return, there was a UAW guarantee of no strikes during the contract, and cooperation over the introduction of new technology. "General Motors may have paid a billion dollars, [but] it got a bargain," commented *Fortune* magazine.

The two men had also enthusiastically discussed a new, low-cost GM "compact" car, which would be called the Cadet and would sell at less than one thousand dollars, so that GM workers would buy it. The project had to be shelved after GM accountants persuaded Wilson there would never be enough profit in such a car, since 300,000 would have to be sold for three years just to pay for the retooling to build it. GM's German subsidiary, Opel, later built the Kadet, at the suggestion of their own unions, after Reuther had converted them, and Opel made a success of it. The future success in the American market of Japanese and European compact cars suggests that Reuther and Wilson might have been right all along.

Reuther's career, which reflected his readiness to work with management, helps explain that extraordinary distinction of American political life—its persistent failure to establish a European-style socialist party. Karl Marx's colleague Friedrich Engels had predicted this would be so, in a letter he wrote to a German comrade who emigrated in 1851, stressing by way of explanation "the special American conditions: the ease with which the surplus population is drained off to the farms, the necessarily rapid and rapidly growing prosperity of the country, which makes bourgeois conditions look like a beau ideal to them." Thirty years later, Marx suggested that the time might at last be ripe, since capitalism in the United States had developed "more rapidly and more shamelessly than in any other country." But there was no feudal tradition in the United States to sharpen class distinctions. There were already two well-established political parties accustomed to absorbing new single-issue protest groups. The waves of immigration divided the working class along ethnic and religious lines; in the Pittsburgh steel mills of the 1890s, socialist agitators complained that they had to distribute leaflets in twenty different languages. Above all, there was great opportunity in America. In his 1906 book, *Why Is There No Socialism in the U.S.A.?,* Werner Sombart suggested that America was "the promised land of capitalism [where] on the reefs of roast beef and apple pie, socialistic Utopias are sent to their doom."

Walter Reuther believed in winning roast beef and apple pie for his UAW members. But he also wanted more. Some were prepared to return to the bloody tactics of the 1930s to stop him. In April 1948, shotgun blasts were fired at him as he stood in his kitchen, chatting with his wife. His right arm was almost severed, and while he was in the hospital, another attacker shot out the eye of his brother Victor, and others tried to dynamite UAW headquarters. He had more than enough enemies, from employers to racist bigots who opposed his early support of civil rights, from Communists who saw him as the key enemy in the unions to the gangsters against whose penetration of the unions he battled all his life.

The year after the shooting and the Treaty of Detroit, his address to the UAW convention of 1949 laid down the next demands beyond the pay packet: "We have to reassert the sovereignty of people above profits in America—we want the pension plans and the medical plans and the wage increase." The first victories in these areas had already been won by John L. Lewis for the mine workers after a strike that secured a five-cent levy on each ton of coal mined; the money would go to a pension fund, jointly administered with management, and a medical fund, run by the union. Again the role of government was crucial. During the strike, the government took emergency control of the mines, so Lewis negotiated the deal with the secretary of the interior, Julius Krug. Armed with this precedent, Reuther talked GM and Ford into similar funds, establishing a form of welfare capitalism, which made the autoworkers among the best protected as well as the best paid in the country. The long boom of the 1950s and 1960s followed, as median household income in America more than doubled in the twenty-five years between 1947 and 1972, from $18,564 to $39,884 (in constant 1993 dollars).

America Reborn

Reuther died with his wife in a plane crash in 1970, so he did not live to see the sudden stalling of that great rolling locomotive of American prosperity. American median household income barely grew in the seventeen years after 1973 as the OPEC price rise, inflation, and mounting global competition began to threaten the gains that Reuther's generation of labor unions had secured. A new economy was being born, one that made a mockery of the 1961 vow of his old adversary Khrushchev that within twenty years the Soviet Union would outdo the United States in the production of coal, steel, fertilizer, and cement. So it did, but only because by 1981 the United States and its Western partners were operating a different kind of economy altogether, based on plastics, silicon, and electronics, rather than on coal, steel, and raw power. This was to be the main cause of the long decline of American labor. In 1933, when the Reuther brothers left for their world tour, one American worker in ten belonged to a union. By 1950, the ratio had risen to one in three. By 1998, it was back to one in ten in the private sector, although significantly higher among public employees who were challenging the traditional authority of the big industrial unions like the UAW, the United Mine Workers, and the Teamsters.

Reuther lived a stormy life, filled with battles. He fought management and Communists, battled against gangsters and corruption in the unions, withstood Republicans like George Romney, the auto executive and future governor of Michigan, who called him "the most dangerous man in Detroit." He fought for the unification of the AFL and CIO, and then when he had achieved it, he fought with the AFL's leader, George Meany, and separated them again. He was always ready for a cause, whether joining the Americans for Democratic Action, the leftist pressure group in the Democratic party, or the National Association for the Advancement of Colored People. He marched arm in arm with Martin Luther King, Jr., through the streets of Detroit, invited him to address the 1961 UAW convention, and talked his autoworkers into starting integrated bowling leagues.

He never stopped talking and never stopped working. When he almost lost his arm after being shot, his doctors told him to keep exercising it, so he single-handedly turned his one-room summer shack into a two-story, eight-room cottage, and then he built the furniture, including the hi-fi set. The union bought him an armor-plated car after the shooting, but he refused to use it. He had known the heroic age of American labor in the 1930s, and the golden age of the postwar boom, marked by the new and responsible role for labor, which he had helped bring about. And while he foresaw and welcomed automation as a way to increase profits, which would boost workers' incomes and create new leisure time to enrich their lives, he never really envisaged the new industrial revolution, which slashed manufacturing to less than 20 percent of the workforce as the service sector thrived. While he dedicated his life to making labor into a comanager of a civilized capitalism, the capitalists were inventing an economy that needed fewer and fewer workers. Still, thanks to Reuther, many of those who remained came from America's minorities. Reuther's working class was color-blind. At his funeral, where those attending sang that haunting anthem of the labor movement, "Joe Hill," the eulogy was delivered by the widow of Martin Luther King, Jr.

15.
John Steinbeck
and the American Voice

L ate in November 1920, a young sophomore at Stanford University left a note for his roommate that read "Gone to China. See you again sometime," then took a bus to the San Francisco waterfront. No ship's crew would hire the gangling John Steinbeck, not yet nineteen and innocent of the sea, so he found a temporary Christmas job as a salesclerk in a department store. Thoughts of China were put aside; this was to be a decisive turn back to America for a writer who more than any other of his outstanding literary generation explored and relished the great sprawl of American life, and found it epic.

America had many voices in the twentieth century, from the rococo Anglicisms of Henry James at its beginning to the relentless and aggressive pounding of rap at its close. Its vocabulary and diction were to be inspired as much by sports reporters, the copywriters of Madison Avenue, and the lyricists of popular songs as by more celebrated authors. It was essentially a demotic voice, enriched by the sardonic humor and phrases of the old Jewish shtetls of Eastern Europe, by the rhythms and inventiveness of the descendants of slaves, and by the liquid vowels of Italy and hard Teutonic consonants. It was an English enhanced and at its ease, while sunk deep in the bedrock of Shakespeare and the King James Version of the Bible.

While the new American diction was exported to the world by radio and by Hollywood, its great force in the first half of the twentieth century was the extraordinary and international success of its writers. This was matched by the way America attracted to its shores so many of Europe's literary giants, from Thomas Mann to Aldous Huxley, Vladimir Nabokov to W. H. Auden. They came to America for refuge from Europe's tumults, but also because of literary and commercial opportunity. Auden defined the side of the Atlantic they were leaving behind:

> In the nightmare of the dark
> All the dogs of Europe bark,
> And the living nations wait,
> Each sequestered in its hate.

Meanwhile, in the United States, the publishers and colleges had vast appetites for European sensibilities, and fabled Hollywood was a lucrative lure.

In this context, the remarkable feature of American letters is how few of its greatest exponents sought to deploy their talents upon the broadest canvas of American life. James turned to the English and to expatriate longueurs. Ernest Hemingway, perhaps the most innovative stylist of them all, abandoned America after his incomparable short stories, writing of Americans in a Europe at languid peace and in an Italy and Spain during their different wars. William Faulkner stayed rooted in his incestuous South; F. Scott Fitzgerald in his equally incestuous decade of the 1920s; Henry Miller never grew out of Paris. Norman Mailer, after writing two of the most striking of America's post-1945 novels, *The Naked and the Dead* and *The American Dream,* employed his greatest gifts in documentaries. Gore Vidal, by far the most political of American writers and the finest historical novelist among them, left the country in fastidious distaste.

This left, of the giants, only Steinbeck to take on the vast and mysterious challenge of America, to plunge headlong into a singular mission, to relate America through the drama he perceived between its glorious catastrophes and its tragic triumphs. Steinbeck was the writer who stayed home. He also stayed the course; his first novel was published in 1929, and his last book, a free translation of Malory's *Morte d'Arthur,* was not published until 1976, eight years after his death. In 1991, a dramatized version of *The Grapes of Wrath* won the New York Drama Critics' Circle Award; the following year saw another film version of *Of Mice and Men.* He was a dominant figure in American letters for four decades, and his works stayed in print and were revived in film and drama for the rest of the century. *The Grapes of Wrath* sold 100,000 copies a year throughout the 1990s.

Moreover, Steinbeck took pride and pleasure in trying his hand at every literary form, even that of the scientific expedition in *The Log from the Sea of Cortez.* He was a fine documentary news reporter; witness the series he wrote for *The Nation* on the plight of migrant farmworkers. In the tradition of Ernie Pyle, the GIs' reporter who wrote about the individual "dogface" rather than grand strategy, Steinbeck was a brave and accomplished war correspondent in North Africa and Italy in World War II, and in Vietnam when he was over sixty. On the beach at Salerno, where the Allied invasion of Italy came perilously close to disaster, he experienced more raw combat than Hemingway and the rest of them combined.

Steinbeck wrote film documentaries and Hollywood film scripts, including the outstanding *Viva Zapata!* His unceasing pen poured forth successful plays and short stories; historical novels and light verse; enchanting light comedies and an endless correspondence. He invented a wholly new form, the play-novella, designed to be both read and performed. He wrote successful propaganda in wartime, and political tracts and travel books in peace. He never stopped trying to explore and to understand America—and he was a pioneer in establishing that this must include its Hispanic citizens—by describing and listening to it. He chose biblical parables and Arthurian myths and set them among the *paisanos* and hoboes of Cannery Row. He then moved briefly to England to try his hand at the real thing in the shadow of the mound where Arthur's castle might have stood. Above all, he wrote the most powerful American novel of an American reality to have been published in the century: *The Grapes of Wrath* was the *Uncle Tom's Cabin* of its time, a book that changed the way the country thought about itself.

No other American writer can match the broad reach of Steinbeck's work. He tried his hand at everything, and proved an honest craftsman at it all. His Nobel Prize attracted some derision at the time, for critics like those at the *New York Times* deemed him a popular novelist rather than a great one—popular at least in the sense of sales. Like Hemingway and Fitzgerald, he was regularly to dominate the best-seller lists of his day, and from his first success with *Tortilla Flat,* his books were regularly bought by the book clubs. Another literary generation was to come and go before powerful and ambitious novels were to be overwhelmed on the best-seller lists by books on diet and health. But his popularity came at the price of sharp controversy. *The Grapes of Wrath* provoked outrage in both California and Oklahoma.

Steinbeck was always a spiky and uncomfortable figure, probably because he was determined to root his work in his perception of the gritty reality of American life. His ear for its language was so acute that one of that handful of phrases that encapsulate something distinct about America, in its rich blend of defiance, duty, and monosyllabic wisdom, came from his pen in *The Grapes of Wrath:* "I know this—a man got to do what he got to do."

In his later years, increasingly baffled by what America was becoming, he

discovered that I did not know my own country. I, an American writer, writing about America, was working from memory, and the memory is at best a faulty, warpy reservoir. I had not heard the speech of America, smelled the grass and trees and sewage, seen its hills and water, its color and quality of light. I knew the changes only from books and newspapers. But more than this, I had not felt the country for twenty-five years. In short, I was writing of something I did not know about, and it seems to me that in a so-called writer this is criminal.

So he set off with his dog "to try to rediscover this monster land" on a tour of the country, an experience that resulted in *Travels with Charley in Search of America.* He was sufficiently self-conscious of the oddity and ambition of the venture that he called his truck "Rocinante," after Don Quixote's steed. It is a book of considerable charm, shot through with that respect for the common man and the instinctive human warmth that were Steinbeck's hallmarks, along with the deep conviction that America was a unique and fundamentally admirable nation. This in itself was a rare enough perception in the increasingly self-critical mood that gripped the country in the 1960s. He concluded:

For all of our enormous geographic range, for all of our sectionalism, for all of our interwoven breeds drawn from every part of the ethnic world, we are a nation, a new breed. California Chinese, Boston Irish, Wisconsin German, yes and Alabama Negroes, have more in common than they have apart. And this is the more remarkable because it has happened so quickly. It is a fact that Americans from all sections and of all racial extractions are more alike than the Welsh are like the English, the Lancashireman like the Cockney, or for that matter, the Lowland Scot like the Highlander. It is astonishing that this has happened in less than two hundred years and most of it in the last fifty. The American identity is an exact and provable thing.

Steinbeck was not a man to analyze this fact, at least not in the conventional manner of assessing the unifying roles of transport and media and countrywide marketing, of public schools and the mass conscription that came with wars. Once he had observed and stated the phenomenon, he moved on, because his interest was less in these proximate causes than in the organics of nation building. Some literary critics have suggested that Steinbeck was at heart a mystic. They cite the scene in *To a God Unknown* in which Joseph Wayne makes passionate, proprietorial love to his new land: "Deep down it's mine, right to the center of the world." The novel concludes with Wayne slitting his wrists, sacrificing himself on an ancient rock to water the parched land with his blood, to bring the rain the earth needed.

Yet much of the force in Steinbeck's work comes from his interest in natural science and evolution. His friend Ed Ricketts, a marine biologist, the model for Doc in *Cannery Row,* was his guide to the tide pools of Monterey, California, and to scientific literature. They had met in a dentist's waiting room when Steinbeck was newly married, living in his parents' cottage at Monterey, and struggling on a modest allowance from his patient father to write and to get by. Steinbeck grew vegetables, which he traded to Ricketts for fish, and they became intensely close friends. Ricketts, who had left college without getting a degree, was widely read—in philosophy, poetry, and psychology, as well as in science. He might today be called an ecologist, since Ricketts believed in the organic unity of everything that existed, that life itself could not be conceived in separation from its environment.

Steinbeck found this persuasive and congenial. It helped illuminate some of his own thinking about men as individuals and men in groups, an issue with which every novelist concerned with the dynamics of his characters must deal. Under Ricketts's approving eye, he wrote an essay entitled "Argument of Phalanx," which tried to consider men in groups not as a mindless mob or a drifting crowd, nor necessarily as a class in the Marxist sense, but as something distinct. He took the metaphor of the phalanx from the ancient Greek term for a military unit, drilled so that many could act as one.

> We have tried to study men and movements of men by minute investigation of individual men-units. We might as reasonably try to understand the nature of man by investigating the cells of his body. . . . Man is a unit of the greater beasts, the phalanx. The phalanx has pains, desires, hungers and strivings as different from those of the unit-man's as man's are different from the cells. . . . Within each unit-

man, deep in him, in his subconscious, there is a keying device with which he may become part of the phalanx.

This theme recurs constantly in Steinbeck's fiction, perhaps most clearly in the image of the great migration of the Okies from the Dust Bowl toward California. Steinbeck focuses on the individual family decision of the Joads, and he stresses that one of the few characters who stays behind does so from a kind of insanity. To leave for California is a logical as well as a personal—and family—choice, but it is one that is made by hundreds and thousands of people, in response not just to the widely issued handbills offering jobs as fruit pickers but to a deeper communal urge. When they can live and relate communally and in safety, as they prove at the sanctuary of the government's relief station, the disparate families become a unit, even a phalanx. It is to prevent that phalanx from forming that the California police and employers seek to divide them by setting them competitively against one another.

The book closes on the highly charged scene of the Joads' daughter Rose of Sharon, having lost her baby, offering the milk from her breast to a starving stranger, because finally the members of the phalanx realize that they are all one, that the imperative of phalanx is its own biological survival. This was important to Steinbeck, although his trusted editor, Pat Covici, gently suggested it needed rewriting. The stranger had to come from nowhere, insisted Steinbeck. The key fact was that "the Joads don't know him, don't care about him, have no ties to him."

For Steinbeck, this Okie migration, and other migrations before them, explain how the West was won, and how the nation was built. "We carried life out here and set it down the way those ants carry eggs," says Jody's grandfather in *The Red Pony*. "The westering was as big as God, and the slow steps that made the movement piled up and piled up until the continent was crossed . . . a whole bunch of people made into one big crawling beast. Every man wanted something for himself but the big beast that was all of them wanted only westering."

Steinbeck was a product of this westering process. His schoolteacher mother was a Hamilton, whose family had come to New York from Northern Ireland in the 1840s, moved to California in 1871, and established the farm near King City, sixty miles south of Salinas, which was to become the backdrop for so many of his books. His father came from German stock, from a family that was originally named Grossteinbeck, from the town of Düsseldorf. Steinbeck's grandfather left for Palestine in 1852 on a quixotic bid to convert the heathen Jews to Lutheranism, meeting his wife, the daughter of an American missionary, in the Holy Land. They moved to Massachusetts, and then to Florida on the eve of the Civil War, where he was drafted into the

Confederate army. He deserted, walked back to New England, and they moved to a small dairy farm outside Salinas immediately after the war ended.

One small particle of the great epic of the West, Steinbeck's parents were a respectable and even quietly prosperous couple, until his father's flour mill closed in 1910, when John was eight. His father put his savings into a feed store, an unwise decision when California was switching from the horse to the truck, and lost his money. A family friend found him an accountant's job in a local sugar plant, which lasted until he recaptured small-town gentility as the treasurer of Monterey County. This made for an interesting youth, in which prosperity gave way to hard times and Steinbeck's strong mother increasingly dominated his depressed father. But the vast enchantments of his grandparents' farm lay just down the road, and there was money enough for a solid and comfortable house in Salinas, and a cottage near the sea at Monterey. There were books in the house and a schoolmarm mother to ensure they were read, that the homework was done, and that young John did well at school.

In 1919, he enrolled at Stanford, and told his roommate, Carlton Sheffield, "I'm going to be a writer—I want to be the best writer in the world." He wanted to write far more than he wanted to study. He later recalled, "Once in college I went flibbery geblut and got to going to the library and reading what I wanted instead of what was required. I got so far behind that I could not possibly catch up." Constantly on academic probation, and under pressure from his mother, who would go up to Stanford to lecture him on the need for self-discipline, he was also under the spell of the writing life. Jack London's colorful career had helped romanticize the writer as hero, the kind of adventurer who knocked about the world in order to see it and write about its splendors and the deeds to be done.

If he could not drop out of college to go to China, there were adventures available at home. He took a series of jobs, most secured through his family and friends, as ranch hand and warehouseman, lab technician in a sugar-beet plant, a worker in fish hatcheries, and bus driver for a travel lodge. He went to New York via the Panama Canal, worked as a hod carrier on the construction of Madison Square Garden, as a news reporter at the *New York American,* and thought he had a contract to publish a collection of short stories. But when they were ready, the young editor who had raised his hopes had moved on. Steinbeck was broke, and he worked his way back to San Francisco as a ship's waiter.

The most congenial and useful to his writing career of his various jobs was to become a caretaker for a Lake Tahoe mansion, sustained by shipments of fresh eggs from home. It was beside Tahoe that he completed a draft of his first novel, *Cup of Gold,* a suitably adventurous fable of the pirate Sir Henry Morgan and his quest up the Orinoco River for a gold chalice that was his personal holy grail. The writing is louche and overblown, with one character saying, "I imagine great dishes of purple porridge, drenched with dragon's milk, sugared with a sweetness only to be envisioned." Merlin the Magician makes an appearance, and the thrills and memory of boyhood reading of the Knights of the Round Table glitter throughout the book, which he sent off to a college friend who was prepared to act as his literary agent.

It was at Tahoe that he met his first wife, Carol, who came to the fish hatchery for a tour. She had a strong interest in left-wing politics, and occasionally took Steinbeck to meetings where the works of Marx and Lenin were read and the imminent revolution was predicted. This was not, in the America of the 1930s, an impossible idea. *Cup of Gold* was published in August 1929, two months before the Wall Street crash. The novel, for which he was paid an advance of $250, sank almost without trace. Still, Steinbeck was emboldened to marry Carol in January. It was an event to which his parents were not invited, although he depended on his father's continued financial allowance, and on the family cottage at Monterey as a place to live as he began work on *To a God Unknown.*

In the month that Wall Street collapsed, Carol gave him a copy of Hemingway's "The Killers." The spareness and control of the writing stunned Steinbeck, and he told Carol that Hemingway must be recognized as "the finest writer alive." Hemingway was already a considerable figure, after the publication of *In Our Time* and *The Sun Also Rises,* and it is striking that Steinbeck was not familiar with him. Deeply influenced, Steinbeck wrote to an old college friend, Grove Day, that he was developing a new method of writing, which "reduced a single idea to a single sentence." The florid style of *Cup of Gold* began to be pared down, although not yet to Hemingwayesque leanness. He produced a series of connected stories, *The Pastures of Heaven,* again set in his familiar California; here, for the first time, the real talent of Steinbeck began to emerge. The themes are familiar, of families and their tensions, of the land and its demands, of the way ancient virtues and age-old dilemmas are played out anew on the stage of an American Eden. It is not yet Steinbeck as much as Steinbeck deeply impressed by Sherwood Anderson, whose *Winesburg, Ohio* he had been reading. He was casting around, learning his craft, and talking philosophy and Carl Jung's theories of the collective subconscious with Ricketts. He was not yet his own man; if another single writer's influence is clear in *To a God Unknown,* it is the mysticism of D. H. Lawrence.

These second and third books also failed to sell. He calculated that in seven years of writing, he had earned less than nine hundred dollars. But Carol was working, the garden of the cottage was productive, and the friendship with Ricketts and a congenial group around Monterey were all deeply satisfying. Then came a stroke of great fortune. The novella *The Red Pony* was published by *North American Review.* A Chicago bookseller named Ben Abramson read it, liked it, hunted down copies of Steinbeck's earlier books, and became convinced that a major writer had been born. Then into the Chicago store walked Covici, a New York publisher, who was persuaded to buy a copy of *The Pastures of Heaven.* Covici devoured it on the overnight train home, then immediately contacted Steinbeck's agent to sign up this stunning new talent.

Steinbeck had a new book ready to show him, *Tortilla Flat,* the delightful fable of the *paisanos* of Monterey, as seen through the enchanted eyes of a born storyteller who transforms them into the Knights of King Arthur's Round Table. It was published to serious and favorable reviews, and Steinbeck at last was an established writer, with a devoted publisher, all his financial worries behind him, and a new book under way. This was a powerful and deeply political novel of a strike and a cold-eyed Communist labor organizer, *In Dubious Battle.* Still perhaps the finest of American political novels, it is stunningly real, based on firsthand observation and research. It contains Steinbeck's characteristic jewels of detail, like the scene in which the party organizer tells a young recruit that he had better start smoking so that he can offer his tobacco bag to other workers and thus get to know them and start the process of indoctrination. Above all, it was taut with a passionate, controlled anger about the fate of the migrant farmworkers. The simple verities of *paisano* life in *Tortilla Flat* and his reportage of the strikes and wretchedness of the lives of migrant farmworkers led the way to the distinctive, subtle simplicity of Steinbeck's mature prose.

"Fascistic methods are more numerous, more powerfully applied and more openly practiced in California that in any other place in the United States," he wrote in a series of seven articles for the *San Francisco News.* "It will require a militant and watchful organization of middle-class people, workers, teachers, craftsmen and liberals to fight this encroaching social democracy, and to maintain this state in a democratic form of government."

These were not the words of the closet Communist whom the FBI was about to place under surveillance. They were the outraged response of an eyewitness to the effects of the combination of Depression, the desperate migration from the Dust Bowl, and the greed of the California farm industry. They led, directly, to *The Grapes of Wrath.* Published in 1939, it won him fame and fortune, the eager attention of Hollywood, and a Pulitzer Prize. It was a book in which the American myth of the West turns into a tragic epic, finally given the fleeting hope of redemption by the plain human solidarity of the downtrodden. And it opened the door to all the rest of his burgeoning career, to plays, film scripts, travel, and opportunity.

John Steinbeck and the American Voice

The more successful Steinbeck became, the more the strains grew in his marriage with Carol. It stumbled on until Steinbeck met a younger woman, a singer named Gwyn Conger. He divorced Carol in 1942, had two sons with Gwyn, and divorced her in 1946, shortly after the death of Ricketts in a car accident. In 1950, he met and married Elaine Scott, a Texan actress and theater director who had been stage manager for *Oklahoma!* Her marriage to the actor Zachary Scott was crumbling when she met Steinbeck, and the author finally found a lasting domestic happiness, along with the financial freedom to exercise his vast curiosity and sense of adventure about other books and genres, other forms of writing, other places to travel. After all, as he wrote to Covici, he had said all that he wanted to say about realism in *The Grapes of Wrath;* it was "a dead end for the novel."

Despite his Nobel Prize, it is not easy to define Steinbeck's place in American literature, in part because American writers themselves were so competitive about it. This may be an American trait. Whether in best-seller lists or baseball rankings, schoolchildren voted "most likely to succeed," or that middle-class initiation rite of the college admission system of SAT scores, America is a country that organizes itself by competitive ranking. There may be no other way to impose logic and order on a nation so vast and disparate and yet so utterly efficient when setting itself a great national goal. (The system of intelligence and aptitude testing was applied nationwide because of the need to create from scratch a vast civilian army in 1941.) But this competitiveness has had a curious impact on the way writers see themselves. In Lillian Ross's celebrated 1950 profile of Hemingway in *The New Yorker,* Hemingway defined it as a boxing tournament: Who was best? "I started out very quiet and I beat Mr. Turgenev. Then I trained hard and I beat Mr. de Maupassant. I've fought two draws with Mr. Stendhal, and I think I had an edge in the last one. But nobody's going to get me in any ring with Mr. Tolstoy unless I'm crazy or I keep getting better."

In a prolonged survey of his own self-consciousness, *Advertisements for Myself,* Mailer made a similarly brisk survey of the competition. He called it "Evaluations—quick and expensive comments on the talent in the room," and quickly followed it with the acknowledgment that those he listed, James Jones, Gore Vidal, James Baldwin, William Styron, Saul Bellow, and Jack Kerouac, were not fit to be in the same ring as the writers of the preceding generation. Mailer wrote:

> What a generation they were—how much more impressive than my own. If their works did not prepare us for the slack, the stupor and the rootless wit of our years, they were still men who wrote strong, original novels, personal in style—so many of us were ready

to become writers because of the world they opened. To call the roll today is depressing. Wolfe is dead and Fitzgerald is dead; both dead too early, one, a burned-out rocket, the other a gentleman blade who concealed his wounds too long and died lingering over them. Hemingway lost his will to work, or so it seems; Faulkner passed his zenith. . . . Steinbeck seemed to lose conviction, as well he might— the world became too complex and too ugly for a man who needed situations of Biblical simplicity for his art.

That is a characteristically perceptive observation. Biblical themes and great simplicities were dominant features of Steinbeck's work. *East of Eden* retells the archetypal myth of Cain and Abel, the warring brothers. *The Grapes of Wrath* is the odyssey of a people to the promised land (of California), finding trials, deserts, and crises of their faith along the way. *To a God Unknown,* the 1933 novel of the Wayne family of Vermont settling in California's long valley, begins with the biblical scene of the family patriarch recreating Abraham's blessing, his chosen son laying his hand on his father's genitals to receive it. The theme of *Cannery Row,* of Doc's friends preparing a surprise party to welcome him home, echoes the parable of the prodigal son. *Of Mice and Men* deliberately recalls the story of David and Jonathan, that other biblical tale of two inseparable men whose friendship ends in death. In a powerful and cold-eyed narrative that culminates in a sacrifice, *In Dubious Battle* describes a strike and the way Communist party organizers exploit it; the novel's hero dies so that the cause of the strike may live on. And in a grisly echo of the biblical crucifixion, the shattered body is put on display to strengthen the faith of the workers-disciples.

The Bible was one source of Steinbeck's attempt to create a distinctive American mythology. The other was the Arthurian legend, which fascinated him throughout his life. He delved into the libraries of Europe for original manuscripts, tramped the contours of Cadbury hill in Somerset, which remains one of the likeliest sites of King Arthur's Camelot, and translated Malory's original tales. Steinbeck made no secret of this source of inspiration. *Tortilla Flat* begins with Danny's house, which was "not unlike the Round table, and Danny's friends were not unlike the knights of it." They formed, as Mack and his friends were to create in *Cannery Row,* "a unit of which the parts are men, from which came sweetness and joy, philanthropy and, in the end, a mystic sorrow . . . this story deals with the adventuring of Danny's friends, with the good they did, with their thoughts and their endeavors. In the end, this story tells how the talisman was lost and how the group disintegrated."

Between them, the biblical and Arthurian myths impose a series of rules on the writer who chooses to plow them. The Arthurian echo says that there must be heroes, who are flawed by understandable human weaknesses, who must be challenged by the hero's own ethical code and his knowledge that the surrender to temptation undermines the very order and sweetness that he and his ethical code have wrought. The biblical echo says that there must be more to human fate than this, that each individual drama is played out against a canvas of wider spiritual meaning, and that redemption remains possible through grace. There is an inherent tension between the two forms, between the individual hero's ambition and his soul, between his fate and the wider fate of the chosen people, between the lifetime of a single hero and a single royal court and the eternal rhythms of a people.

Steinbeck's best work grappled with this tension and strove to explore it in a contemporary American setting. The great mysteries of American life obsessed him. The last book he published in his lifetime, *America and Americans,* was little regarded among literary critics, who saw it as a coffee-table book, some light text interspersed with the photographs. Steinbeck wrote it at a time of anguish, after the death of his lifelong editor, Covici, and his sister Mary, and as decent, ordinary Americans whom he instinctively trusted were behaving in the South like racist bigots. He ended the book on a despairing note that his America no longer lived up to the grand myths and destinies that he believed defined it. "No new path to take, no duty to carry out, no purpose to fulfill," he wrote of the nation that had created mass prosperity, built the world's first mass middle class, and now fretted over the dissatisfactions and hollowness of its new comforts. "Leisure came to us before we knew what to do with it," he grumbled.

Steinbeck's later work is shot through with this sense of loss, that in enjoying its postwar successes America had mislaid something essential to its well-being. In *America and Americans,* he suggested alternatively that what had departed was the founding myth of "equality and self-reliance," and the consensus around a common national goal. Once there had been a frontier to fill, then a war to be won, a Depression to be overcome, and then another war, as just in its mission to defeat Nazism as any war could be. There was, in the America of the 1960s, no shortage of great themes and causes, from civil rights to the space venture to Lyndon Johnson's war on poverty. There was also, although only a handful of espionage writers seemed to comprehend the squalid grandeur of it, the long, unheroic, and barely declared campaign to withstand and outlast communism, without resort to open war.

The cause that Steinbeck chose to take up was the disastrous war in Vietnam, to which—like so many of his generation—he brought the lessons of the dangerous folly of appeasement in the 1930s. Communism had to be stopped, just as Nazism had had to be defeated, an unconvincing parallel in what was for the Vietnamese a war of national liberation, in which Ho Chi Minh was no Hitler and the successive Saigon governments were no democratic institutions. Steinbeck instinctively knew this. In 1965, he wrote to White House aide Jack Valenti:

> There is no way to make the Vietnamese war decent. There is no way of justifying sending troops to another man's country. And there is no way to do anything but praise the man who defends his own land. . . . Unless the President makes some overt move towards peace, more and more Americans as well as Europeans are going to blame him for the mess, particularly since the government we are supporting with our men and treasure is about as smelly as you can get.

But Steinbeck also spoke and wrote of the need for the cosseted youth of the 1960s to learn the need to give something back to the land that nurtured them. He wrote privately to President Johnson after his own reporting trip to Vietnam, "We have here the finest, the best trained, the most intelligent and the most dedicated soldiers I have ever seen in any army and I have seen soldiers in my time. These men are the best we have ever had." (Among them was his son, Johnny, who volunteered to fight, grew deeply disenchanted with the war, and was to write a highly critical book about it.)

Steinbeck's controversial stand on the war was complicated by his relations with Johnson and with the Democratic party in general. Steinbeck had always been political without being a politician. In the 1930s, he had joined the League of American Writers, an antifascist Popular Front group that was attached to the Communist party, which is what led the FBI to place him under surveillance. In 1939–1940, the period of the Nazi-Soviet pact that set the stage for war, carved up Poland between the two totalitarian states, and turned most American liberals away from communism in disgust, he served as a vice president of the league.

Steinbeck was a New Dealer with a sentimental attachment to the Left, and an antifascist who had few illusions about Stalin's Soviet system but great hopes for Russia. He was not necessarily a convinced Democrat. In 1952, he confessed, he had been for Eisenhower, until he began to hear and then read Adlai Stevenson's election addresses, and then he became so convinced of the honest decency of the Democratic candidate that he wrote the introduction to Stevenson's collected speeches. He was briefly caught up in the Kennedy court, invited to the inauguration, and asked to undertake a cultural tour of the Soviet Union as part of Kennedy's hopeful thaw.

The politician to whom he grew closest was Johnson, who had been a

John Steinbeck and the American Voice

Texas schoolteacher in those Depression days where Steinbeck's own political instincts were rooted. Johnson wooed Steinbeck, invited him repeatedly to stay at the White House, while Johnson's wife would give Elaine Steinbeck her credit card and ask her to go shopping for her. Steinbeck both trusted Johnson and admired him for trying to complete in the 1960s the social and political agenda of the New Deal, and above all for the political skill and courage that went into the 1964 Civil Rights Act.

"In our history, there have been not more than five or six moments when the word and the determination mapped the course of the future. Such a moment was your speech, Sir," he wrote after Johnson introduced the bill to Congress. "Our people will be living by phrases from that speech when all the concrete and steel have long been displaced or destroyed. It was a time of no turning back, and in my mind as well as in many others, you have placed your name among the great ones of history."

Steinbeck revered Roosevelt and hailed Johnson for trying to complete Roosevelt's work at home. But the ills of America in the 1960s, despite the Civil Rights Act, were not to be resolved with a massive and determined state action like the New Deal, just as the Vietnam War was to be neither sustained nor won with the democracy-versus-dictators simplistics of the 1930s. The New Deal generation met its nemesis in the 1960s, and in this bafflement, Steinbeck's *America and Americans* sought to comprehend it. In the tension between the native-born duty of loyalty and the writer's obligation to judge, he discerned a classic American paradox. "We are able to believe that our government is weak, stupid, overbearing, dishonest and inefficient, and at the same time we are deeply convinced that it is the best government in the world, and we would like to impose it on everyone else. We speak of the American Way of Life as though it involved the ground rules for the governance of heaven."

Steinbeck believed in humanity in the same way that, and perhaps because, he believed in America. For him, the great organic development of the human species found its endlessly fascinating and deeply loved model in the American epic. Like America, humanity has the innate biological goal to aspire not just to the good life but to perfection. "The ancient commission of the writer has not changed. He is charged with exposing our many grievous faults and failures, with dredging up to the light our dark and dangerous dreams for the purpose of improvement," he declared in his Nobel Prize acceptance speech in 1962. Writing was too important to be left to any elite; it was the business and the voice of the common man:

Literature was not promulgated by a pale and emasculated critical priesthood singing their litanies in empty churches—nor is it a game for the cloistered elect, the tin-horn mendicants of low-calorie despair. . . . The writer is delegated to declare and to celebrate man's proven capacity for greatness of heart and spirit—for gallantry in defeat, for courage, compassion and love. In the endless war against weakness and despair, these are the bright rally flags of hope and of emulation. I hold that a writer who does not passionately believe in the perfectibility of man has no dedication nor any membership in literature.

16.
Albert Einstein
and the American Refuge

The last twenty-one years of Albert Einstein's life were spent in the United States, mainly at Princeton, and were defined by three crucial letters. The first was written to President Roosevelt in September 1939, as war broke out in Europe, warning him that an atomic bomb was intellectually feasible and that Nazi Germany could be expected to try and develop one. With the prestige of his Nobel Prize, and his reputation as the greatest scientific mind of the day, this was a warning to be taken seriously, and it focused presidential attention on the need for what became the Manhattan Project. The second letter, in October 1945, was public, and it warned that the use of the bomb at Hiroshima had "exploded our inherited, outdated political ideas." War, and the national, economic, and ideological rivalries that bred it, was no longer thinkable.

The third letter, in May 1953, was written to an obscure teacher in Brooklyn, William Frauenglass, warning that the anti-Communist witch-hunts of Senator Joe McCarthy were an attempt to intimidate and to demoralize "all those who do not prove submissive." It was an assault on the principle of academic freedom, a threat that had forced Einstein to take refuge in the United States nearly twenty years earlier: "Every intellectual who is called before one of the committees ought to refuse to testify, i.e., he must be prepared for jail and economic ruin, in short, for the sacrifice of his personal welfare in the interest of the cultural welfare of his country."

In none of the three letters did Einstein act alone. The first was inspired by another exile, the Hungarian Jewish physicist Leo Szilard, whose 1939 work on the interaction of fast and slow neutrons with uranium had convinced him and Einstein that an atomic bomb could be built. The second, public letter was written with the other best-known exile from Germany, the novelist Thomas Mann. The third, to the Brooklyn teacher, a personal letter, although Einstein clearly wanted it made public, sprang from Einstein's close involvement with concerned scientists and political liberals who were appalled by what the combination of the bomb, the Cold War, and McCarthyism was doing to their American refuge.

Einstein had appeared on Eleanor Roosevelt's television program to condemn McCarthy. During the war, he had been excluded from atomic research by Vannevar Bush, director of the Office of Scientific Research and Development, on the grounds that Einstein's "whole history" might make him a security risk. In his opposition to McCarthy, Einstein was following in the footsteps of Mann, who told the House Committee on Un-American Activities that he came before them "as a hostile witness. . . . [A]s an American citizen of German birth, I finally testify that I am painfully familiar with certain political trends. Spiritual intolerance, political inquisition, and declining legal security, and all this in the name of an alleged 'state of emergency'—this is how it started in Germany."

The United States found itself playing host, in the years after Hitler took power, not to the traditional flood of immigrants seeking economic opportunity and ready to blur their old cultural identities into a new Americanism, but to an articulate and highly educated group of independent thinkers. These were people who were not inclined to keep their political and social views to themselves and who had just been given the most brutal of lessons in the fate of those who did not stand up for their beliefs. Their devotion to America stemmed not simply from gratitude for the sanctuary they had found but also from their admiration for its ideals, its Constitution, and its rule of law.

The country acquired, within less than a decade, an instant European intelligentsia. Scientists and academics joined writers and artists. Lawyers and businessmen made their way across the Atlantic alongside filmmakers and ideologues. Musicians, political scientists, and architects talked and planned and bribed their way to the United States, bringing as many of their families as they could save from the nightmare engulfing Europe. "All of German literature had settled in America," wrote Mann. Rarely had such an intense brain drain taken place from a single nation. Nineteen Nobel laureates came as refugees. Of German academics in 1933, no less than 43 percent were exiled by the Nazis, and the loss of that scientific talent was to cost Germany dearly. Most of them, but not all, were Jewish, and saw themselves both as Germans and as patriots of an older and finer German culture. Some of them, and many of their fathers, had served loyally in the German armies of World War I. Richard Holbrooke, U.S. ambassador to Germany in the 1990s, placed on his desk a photograph of his grandfather in a German uniform, wearing the Iron Cross awarded him by the Kaiser.

In the six years between Hitler's assumption of power and the outbreak of war, some 300,000 German Jews fled into exile. Of a German population of 65 million, some 500,000 had been Jewish. Those who stayed had ignored the direst of warnings, not only in Hitler's own writings and speeches but in the mass firings of Jewish academics in the spring of 1933 and the book burnings in May of that year. The books of Marx, Freud, and Heine were burned because they were written by Jews; the works of Mann and Brecht were burned because their authors were anti-Nazi; Erich Maria Remarque's books were burned because *All Quiet on the Western Front* was deemed to be pacifist and critical of German heroism in the trenches where Hitler had won his Iron Cross. In 1935, the Nuremberg laws stripped Jews of their citizenship. In 1938, Kristallnacht, "the night of broken glass," saw Jewish shops, homes, and synagogues attacked and destroyed, and many of their inhabitants casually slaughtered or beaten. But by then, escape was almost impossible.

Most refugees went initially to European destinations, to Britain, France, Austria, and Holland. In all, 132,000 went to the United States, 78,000 to Britain, and 85,000 to Latin America, where visas were more easily available or could be purchased. Another 137,450 came to the United States after the war as "displaced persons," most of them concentration camp survivors. With the exception of Britain, where Sigmund Freud chose to remain, the European countries proved but temporary sanctuaries. The Nazis advanced into Austria in 1938, into Poland in 1939, into Holland and France in 1940.

Nor were the European countries entirely welcoming. In Switzerland, the chief of police wanted to stamp a large red *J* onto Jews' passports. Walter Benjamin, after months in Nazi camps and a brief exile in France, secured a Spanish visa in Marseilles in 1940 and crossed the Pyrenees, only to find that his visa was no longer honored; he committed suicide that night. Even after Kristallnacht, at an international conference at Evian, the other European countries decided not to increase their quotas for Jewish admissions. The United States insisted that refugees show proof of their financial independence. In June 1940, after the fall of France, the State Department decided to end immigration from Germany and Central Europe, and over ten thousand places on the quota went tragically unfilled.

It took some time, and the desperation of war, before America realized its luck. Rarely had any country enjoyed such an infusion of talent. This did not happen entirely by an accident of history; two American scholars played a crucial role—Abraham Flexner, the first director of the Institute for Advanced Study at Princeton, and Alvin Johnson, a founder of the New School for Social Research in New York. Both visited Germany in 1932 and found a country devastated by the Great Depression and political turmoil, with Hitler already jostling for power. Each saw the danger, but also the opportunity, and began approaching refugee scholars about working in the United States. Flexner offered places to Einstein and Mann. At the New School, Johnson established the University in Exile, and recruited an entire faculty of political scientists and labor specialists, most of them Social Democrats who were clearly sympathetic to the New Deal.

After the fall of France in 1940, a grant from the Rockefeller Foundation enabled Johnson to start another faculty for French exiles, the Ecole Libre des Hautes Etudes, which provided a temporary home for Claude Lévi-Strauss. A third group, the predominantly Marxist members of the Institute of Social Research in Frankfurt, made their own way to the United States and were given office space at Columbia University in 1934. They included the sociologists Theodor Adorno and Herbert Marcuse and the Christian theologian Paul Tillich, who found America "the ideal most consistent with the image of one mankind."

Despite the Depression, which was making it difficult for American academics to find university posts, the Emergency Committee in Aid of Displaced Scholars found places for 335 of the refugees in 145 schools and colleges. Other organizations, such as the Refugee Scholars Fund, provided other jobs. The writer Vladimir Nabokov went to Cornell and the historian Hans Kohn to Smith College in rural New England. The Library of Congress and the New York Public Library found jobs for more. The liberal economist Joseph Schumpeter went to Harvard and his conservative counterpart Ludwig von Mises to New York University. The Bauhaus group of designers and architects also prospered: Walter Gropius went to teach at Harvard, and Ludwig Mies van der Rohe to Armour Institute (now the Illinois Institute of Technology) in Chicago. Bruno Walter and Otto Klemperer found orchestras to conduct.

Others fared less well. The writer Hans Morgenthau was offered his first job running an elevator, and composer Paul Dessau tended chickens in New Jersey. Others, who probably shared Brecht's view that the bread tasted better and the air was spicier at home, also took to heart Brecht's words: "Everything changes. You can make / A fresh start with your final breath." Joe May, the Berlin theater and film director, opened the Blue Danube restaurant in Hollywood, which became the center of the exile community. The dramatist Carl Zuckmayer became a farmer in Vermont. The theater and film director Detlef Sierck raised avocados before finding Hollywood success as Douglas Sirk. On the whole, those who had professions maintained them. Some skills traveled relatively easily: science, architecture, photography, music, art, and film. The writers had a harder time adapting to the new language, although Hannah Arendt showed how fluidly the transition could be made. Teachers had their own difficulties adapting to the less formal style of American education. Observing one of his female students knitting during his lecture, Bruno Bettelheim informed her that this was a masturbation substitute. "You do it your way and I'll do it mine," she retorted.

From the tens of thousands of family griefs and personal epics, and amid the contribution made to American design, economics, business, and political life by the influx, three main currents of achievement stand out. The first was the matter of survival in an age that was foredoomed to become nuclear. The second was the sphere of entertainment, and particularly the impact of some of Europe's greatest filmmakers on Hollywood. The third was in the way that America looked at itself; newcomers with fresh eyes and the skill to publicize their observations and give them meaning imposed some introspection and self-questioning upon a young and ebullient society that had viewed its intellectuals with a touch of suspicion, if not disdain. Beyond their effect on science and the movies, perhaps the most enduring impact of Hitler's exiles was to make New York into the intellectual capital of the world. If the America of the nineteenth century had been the world's farm, and of the early twentieth century the world's workshop, in the second half of the century, it became the world's graduate school. The exiles played an essential role in that process.

There were two stages to the manufacture of the atom bomb. The first, the science, was almost entirely imported, from Britain and France and from the exiles from Nazi Germany and fascist Italy. The second, the monstrous and unprecedented task of engineering and devising various means to make the bomb that constituted the Manhattan Project, was very largely a homegrown American achievement. But the science was the key to it all. Two processes were crucial: establishing the critical mass of the radioactive elements required, then getting the chain reaction of the neutrons splitting atoms to take place almost simultaneously. The Hungarian Leo Szilard, who by 1936 had escaped to London, was given, under the auspices of the Royal Navy, a top secret patent on these two key processes. Two years later in Berlin, Otto Hahn and Fritz Strassman showed that uranium atoms would split when bombarded with neutrons. Two weeks after that, Frédéric Joliot-Curie in Paris showed that uranium could produce a chain reaction.

British, French, German, and Soviet military authorities all refused at first to heed the increasingly frantic warnings from their scientists. But by June 1939, Joliot-Curie's team had written a patent application for a uranium bomb and had designed on paper a workable reactor. The German education ministry finally heeded their scientists, called a secret conference, and the Third Reich's "Uranium Club" got under way. The British and French were each galvanized into action. The British arranged to buy the available stocks of uranium from the Belgian Congo. French intelligence, the Deuxième Bureau, sent its agent Jacques Allier to Norway to buy the available stocks of heavy water and ship them back to France. The German Luftwaffe diverted the plane on which he was booked, but he had switched planes at the last minute and went to Scotland. The heavy water crossed the Channel to France, and within three months it was shipped back again when France fell, to be stored in Windsor Castle.

Despite these secret dramas of the war's opening months, Szilard had been convinced by 1939 that the British would never let him into secret work, so he left for the United States, where he teamed up with Enrico Fermi at Columbia. Fermi had fled fascist Italy, and the two of them set up an experiment. "All we had to do was to turn a switch, lean back and watch the screen of a TV tube. If flashes of light appeared on the screen, it would mean that large-scale liberation of atomic energy was just around the corner. We just turned the switch and watched the flashes. We watched for a little while and then went home," Szilard recalled. He then contacted Einstein to write the famous letter of 1939. It took more letters and more pressure from two other Hungarian refugees, Eugene Wigner and Edward Teller, before the United States finally established the Uranium Committee under the National Defense Research Committee in the autumn of 1940.

Two more years of research followed—into both Szilard's design for a graphite reactor and the various methods of producing the essential fissile material, uranium 235 (U-235). Two other German physicists who had left for London, Otto Frisch and Rudolf Peierls, had established in theory that the more potent U-235 could be extracted from the basic element, uranium 238. This meant that a bomb weighing kilograms rather than many tons was now intellectually feasible.

The trick was how to extract U-235, and experiments were launched all across the United States. At Columbia, Harold Urey, the American Nobel laureate who had discovered heavy water, was trying a process called gaseous diffusion. In Pittsburgh, Eger Murphree was using a centrifuge to spin off the heavier U-235. In California, another Nobel Prize recipient, Ernest Lawrence, was using a magnetic process to extract the U-235. And in Chicago, yet another Nobel laureate, Arthur Compton, was trying a different route altogether, producing plutonium, an alternative material for fission, from a small nuclear reactor. Under the command of the U.S. Army engineer General Leslie Groves, the Manhattan Project pursued all these routes, except for gaseous diffusion. And by this time, the work of the exiles was done, and they were to be largely superseded in the manufacturing process until Edward Teller reemerged nearly a decade later as the father of the hydrogen bomb.

But the exiled scientists were not done. Having conceived the bomb, they began to dread its use. For Szilard, the main purpose was to have a weapon that could deter Germany from using one. Once the German defeat appeared inevitable, and with no sign of a German bomb (the Third Reich scientists were not even able to develop a working atomic pile), Szilard asked himself, What are we working for? In March 1945, he and Einstein wrote again to Roosevelt, in a letter that the dying president may never have seen, arguing against the use of the bomb or against publication of its secret, for fear of provoking the Russians into an arms race. Szilard went to see James Byrnes, about to become President Truman's secretary of state, but Byrnes told him that the bomb should be used—as a warning to Russia for the postwar world. Szilard rallied his colleagues at the University of Chicago, which had become the main theoretical center for the Manhattan Project, urging a public demonstration of the bomb over a desert, rather than its explosion over Japan.

"Our Air Forces, striking at the Japanese cities, are using the same methods of warfare which were condemned by American public opinion when applied by Germans to the cities of England," ran Szilard's petition of July 3 to the president. For Szilard, this was a moral issue, as urgent as the one that had confronted Germans under Hitler. But the cause was lost, first to the military argument that in August 1945 the alternative to Hiroshima would be a dreadful casualty list resulting from an invasion of Japan, and then by the gathering clouds of the Cold War. The scientists were not alone. The veteran secretary of war Henry Stimson, arguing that "the only way to make a man trustworthy is to trust him," suggested sharing the atomic secret with the Soviet Union.

The exile scientists said they had no doubt that even without American or British help, the Soviet scientists could develop their own bomb within five years. Groves laughed at the forecast, but the first Soviet atomic bomb came in 1949. This, in turn, spurred the Americans to proceed with the H-bomb, and the nuclear arms race was under way, along with intensive security screening that excluded the less militant scientists.

This issue of the moral responsibility of scientists was addressed by Brecht, another exile who found disappointment in America, in his 1947 drama *Galileo.* A Marxist, Brecht had come to the United States from Russia in 1941, arriving with wife and mistress, and took the precaution of tossing his copy of Lenin's works overboard before the ship landed. He was attracted by the presence in Hollywood of old friends from Germany who had made good, like actor Peter Lorre and conductor Lion Feuchtwanger, and by the prospect of work. In his last years in Europe, Brecht had received subsidies from the European Film Fund, which was financed by other successful exiles like director Fritz Lang.

But Hollywood and Brecht did not mix. He cowrote one film script that was made, *Hangmen Also Die,* about the assassination of SS leader Reinhard Heydrich. It was directed by Lang, but Brecht was not credited for the screenplay. Brecht and Feuchtwanger received a fifty-thousand-dollar advance for a film script titled *Simone Marchard,* about the French Resistance, but it was not made. Already being watched by the FBI, Brecht turned to Broadway, but with no more success, despite writing two classics, *The Caucasian Chalk Circle* and the improved version of *Galileo.* In 1946, he was called before the House Committee on Un-American Activities, where he denied being a Communist. Two years later, invited to run his own Berliner Ensemble theater in East Germany, he left the United States, grumbling, "In the States, there is as much and as little theater as in ancient Rome."

But there was Hollywood, which had proved from the beginning extraordinarily hospitable to American Jews. In a burst of creative empire building that outmatched the shorter-lived efforts of other Europeans to build colonial empires in Africa and Asia, the Goldwyns, the Mayers, and the Warner brothers had built Hollywood and the studio system. They were inclined, within commercial limits, to welcome the exiles of the German film industry, whose UFA studio and 1920s masterpieces had been both rivals and inspirations.

Some of the arrivals waited a long time for a breakthrough. Max Ophuls waited six years without work. Lang, already famous for *Metropolis* and the *Dr. Mabuse* films in Germany, fled as the Nazis came to power in 1933, just hours after Goebbels had asked him to head the German film industry. He went first to Paris, then to the United States, where he discovered the comic strip as his entry into the slang and attitudes of the new country. His first American film, *Fury* (1936), put the nightmare of mob rule into a universal setting, and established an emotional climate of complex moral ambivalence that carried through his career. Drawn to the Nevada desert (where he went first on arrival in the United States) and the American archetype of the Western, Lang made the vigilante movie his own. The balance between vengeance and private justice, or between vigilante law and no law at all, ran deliberately through his films, including his last Hollywood movie, *Beyond a Reasonable Doubt* (1956), in which a killer who is about to get away with murder is accidentally found out by his lover.

The émigrés brought not only a specific film style but also a determination to use film for a purpose that went beyond pure entertainment. This was more than just the desire to deliver a message, or to deploy the unsettling menace of film noir. It was the right to a directorial point of view. They warmed to America, but their affection was not blind, and they sought repeatedly to address the issue of race. Lang was overruled by the studio when he tried to make the target in *Fury* into a black victim of a lynch mob, a man accused of raping a white woman. The studio also cut a scene in which a black girl sings of freedom.

Billy Wilder went back to Germany as head of the U.S. Army's Psychological Warfare Division, rebuilding the German film industry, and the result was the bittersweet comedy *A Foreign Affair* (1948), which gently brought home the message that Americans and Germans were very similar. A visiting congresswoman, determined to ensure that American military manhood remained unsullied by German wiles, falls for an American officer who is himself "fraternizing" with a nightclub singer, played by Marlene Dietrich, who observes that "a woman changes her politics with her fashions." The Americans are shown as susceptible to German women and to the black market, and the congresswoman is portrayed as more than faintly ridiculous. On seeing the film, the outraged Pentagon issued a statement protesting this traduction of the U.S. Army, and Wilder was denounced in Congress.

Wilder had studied law in Austria, but he left the university after one year and became a reporter. He cowrote his first film in Germany at the age of twenty-three (*People on Sunday*), and left for France when Hitler came to power. He taught himself about America and learned the language through baseball and soap operas, then teamed up with *The New Yorker*'s former drama critic Charles Brackett to start writing film scripts, including *Ninotchka* (1939). His genius was to marry slapstick and satire, playing with gender and gangsters in the cross-dressing comedy *Some Like It Hot* (1959), and mocking the essential servility of the ambitious young executive in *The Apartment* (1960). No other director got as much from Marilyn Monroe as Wilder, possibly because he was less in awe of this American icon, possibly because he had directed Dietrich. But no Hollywood figure has ever provoked the outrage Wilder inspired with his merciless masterpiece *Sunset Boulevard* (1950). From the studio chiefs to the artifice of makeup, the film takes Hollywood apart in a twisted homage that even delves into the archives of the fast-talking wisecracks of the 1930s. The fans, with their manufactured idolatry and their eagerness to be fooled, are not spared.

If there is a common theme to the émigré movies, it is the way that American life is not depicted so much as coolly observed. The émigrés were in Hollywood and in America, but not wholly of it, preserving a detachment that in itself became a new kind of Hollywood genre. Moreover, the usual self-constraints of Hollywood were pushed steadily back, both in terms of race and the shadowy sides of America. Otto Preminger made *Carmen Jones* and *Porgy and Bess,* depicted a homosexual bar scene in *Advise and Consent,* and inspired a stunning performance from Frank Sinatra in a film about drug addiction, *The Man with the Golden Arm.* "I feel that our weapon is truth," Preminger argued. "I feel that showing America as it is will make it clear to foreign countries that we have freedom of expression."

So they did, but they also had McCarthyism, and Hollywood was one of the prime targets. In addition to Brecht, Lang was blacklisted for a year, and Brecht's musical collaborator Hanns Eisler, who wrote "The Comintern March," left the country when he was threatened with perjury charges. Most of the targets of McCarthyism, and most of those who at least temporarily fought McCarthyism, were American-born. But William Wyler, who had come to the United States from Germany via Paris in the 1920s, invited by his cousin Carl Laemmle, who ran Universal Pictures, bravely joined the brief flurry known as "Hollywood Fights Back." Most of the émigrés had learned something about survival, and about the different ways to maintain self-respect in hard times, long before they reached Hollywood. Their response, on the whole, was to devise in their films a method of social critique, and a choice of targets, that was, at least on the face of it, apolitical. "Refugees are the keenest dialecticians," suggested Brecht. "They are refugees as a result of changes, and their sole object of study is change." They held up a mirror to America, but the mirror was tilted at an angle that lent an ironic detachment.

There were other ways of adopting this technique of being engaged in America while observing it coolly from a certain distance. Paul Lazarsfeld, a sociologist and psychologist who was close to those émigrés of the Frankfurt school and who arrived in America in 1933, created an industry from his very detachment. A disciple of the psychologist Alfred Adler in Vienna, Lazarsfeld had already begun analyzing popular culture, and he offered his services "to promote the use of applied psychology among business." In the America of radio stations, soap operas, and pop songs, Lazarsfeld discovered a treasure trove of data and insights and was eventually to establish a new academic discipline when he founded the Bureau of Applied Social Research at Columbia.

Lazarsfeld began in the United States at the University of Newark, then set up the Office of Radio Research at Princeton and then at Columbia, where he remained. And while he briefly employed his old colleague Adorno, the theoretical Marxism of the Frankfurt school swiftly became an effective alliance between the university and commerce. The tools of the sociologist, from polling to questionnaires and interviews, could show the businessman, the advertiser, and the radio station what worked. Lazarsfeld's wife, the psychologist Herta Herzog, who had worked with Adorno on the social role of the soap opera, took the process to its logical conclusion by starting her own advertising agency.

Lazarsfeld offered business a method "to forecast and control consumer behavior . . . a systematic view of how people's marketing behavior is motivated." His work, scholarly and detached as it was, came to symbolize the consumer society manipulated by Madison Avenue. Social critics like Vance Packard were to attack the implications of this symbiosis between advertiser and researcher in his 1950s best-seller *The Image Makers*. Another émigré from the Frankfurt school, Herbert Marcuse, was to take the argument further in his book *One Dimensional Man* in 1964, suggesting that a society so manipulated could both stimulate and satisfy the material wants of a consumer society, while denying the deeper desires and freedoms of its members. Applied social science at the disposal of business had created an America of "repressive tolerance," in which rebellious individuals were not crushed or disciplined so much as marginalized and even humored into a harmless role, which thus "proved" that the consumer society was free and not repressive at all.

Highly fashionable on the radicalized campuses of the 1960s, Marcuse's theories were only on the most superficial and obvious level concerned with contemporary America. Their real core, like the political concerns of Einstein and like the social critiques of the Hollywood filmmakers, was that nightmare of civilized, intellectual Germany that they had fled, once it proved so vulnerable to the antirational madness of Nazism. Perhaps the grimmest fact of exile life was that their fellow Germans had voted Hitler into power, that he had become a dictator by wholly constitutional means, and that an apparently civilized society could take leave of its moorings and of its senses. This perhaps explains the stance that Einstein, Szilard, and Mann all took, calling on the America of the McCarthy years to hold fast to its liberties, because of their abiding fear that the madness could, amid Cold War spy scandals and nuclear tension, take hold even in their sanctuary.

17.
George Marshall
and American Power

Ge orge Catlett Marshall never allowed President Franklin Roosevelt
to call him by his first name. He was always "General," and always
formal, with an iron sense of duty. When first interviewed by Roosevelt as the probable next chief of staff of the army as a war in Europe
loomed in 1939, Marshall warned his president, "I have the habit of saying
exactly what I think, and that can be unpleasing. Is that all right?" Roosevelt
grinned and said it was. "I have to remind you again, it may be unpleasant,"
Marshall emphasized.

Within the year, the unpleasantness surfaced. War had broken out.
Poland, Norway, and Holland had fallen. France was collapsing before the
German panzer columns and Britain was facing defeat. Marshall, appalled at
American unpreparedness with an army of just under 165,000 troops, pre-
pared a crash program for an army of 280,000 and a National Guard of

another 250,000 men mobilized for foreign service. Most of the increase in the army would be for the training of new officers and NCOs, the core of future expansion, and it would cost $675 million, Marshall calculated. He won the support of Treasury Secretary Henry Morgenthau. Together, they took the plan to Roosevelt, who dismissed it "with a smile and a sneer," saying he could not possibly go to Congress with such a funding request at this time. Morgenthau said he ought to hear Marshall's strategic arguments.

"I know exactly what he would say. There is no necessity for me to hear him at all," Roosevelt replied. Marshall flushed brick red but kept his anger under tight control, saying, "Mr. President, may I have three minutes."

He took ten, speaking with rising passion of an army ill equipped, undermanned, and undertrained, and of a nation in mortal danger. There is no direct record of the conversation, not even in the oral-history tapes Marshall later made. But Morgenthau recalled him charging Roosevelt with "political timidity," stressing the president's duty as commander in chief, and he remembered Marshall's final statement: "If you don't do something, and do it right away, I don't know what is going to happen to this country."

Two days later, Roosevelt sent Marshall's military expansion program to Congress. He also increased the request to $900 million in emergency funds—at a time when federal revenues were just over $6 billion—and declared, "The possibility of attack on vital American zones has made it essential that we have the ready physical ability to meet these attacks and prevent them from reaching their objective."

Marshall's army career was punctuated by such moments of deliberate but dutiful insubordination. In the muddy French winter of 1918, he was a temporary lieutenant colonel on the staff of the First Infantry Division under Gen. William Sibert. The U.S. commander, Gen. Jack Pershing, came on an inspection visit, watched a mock attack on an enemy trench, and asked Sibert to explain and critique the exercise. Sibert, who had been out touring his troops all night and had only just returned, did a poor job. Pershing, a notoriously prickly man, lashed into him before his men as "a poor commander of an ill-trained division." Marshall stepped forward as Pershing strode away, seized his commander by the arm, and insisted, "General Pershing, there is something to be said here, and I think I should say it because I've been here longest."

Marshall explained the difficulties of training troops from scratch while manning frontline trenches, when they knew little drill and were using unfamiliar weapons, when medical services barely existed and food supplies were irregular, and when equipment depended on the kindness of French and British Allies. Pershing heard him out, then said that the frontline troops should appreciate "the troubles we have" at headquarters in trying to fashion a field army from an assortment of civilian conscripts shipped over to France. "Yes, General," Marshall replied. "But we have them every day and they have to be solved before night."

Marshall was convinced that he had done his duty but had ended his military career. In fact, Pershing made a note of his name, approved a recommendation for him to be promoted to full colonel, and summoned Marshall to join his own staff at American Expeditionary Force headquarters at Chaumont. He became Pershing's personal aide, and he remained at his side after the war, ghostwriting most of Pershing's memoirs. Marshall supplied the statistics and arguments to buttress Pershing's urgent but vain appeals not to scrap the great military machine the United States had built, but to preserve its core for swift readiness in what looked to be a tumultuous world after the Treaty of Versailles ended the war.

This tension between passion and duty also dominated Marshall's personal life. On graduation from the Virginia Military Institute (VMI) in 1901, where after a bad start he had become corporal of cadets and then captain of the school, he instantly married the belle of the district, Elizabeth Coles Carter, known as Lily. She had lived near the campus with her widowed mother, and rode by most days to watch the cadets at drill. On her wedding night, she confessed to Marshall that she had a heart condition, which meant she could never even risk having children. Their marriage was never consummated, but he remained devoted to Lily until her death in 1927.

He was already a young man of unusual will. He arrived late at VMI, where discipline was strict, after a debilitating bout of typhoid fever. Born in Uniontown, Pennsylvania, he arrived at this pride of southern military tradition with a Yankee accent. He was treated coldly, and subjected to worse than usual testing by his fellow cadets, including one particular rite of initiation in which a bayonet was placed on the floor with its point facing upward and the cadet had to squat above it for ten minutes, thighs quivering with strain. The other cadets did not know about the typhoid and Marshall was not about to tell them. He squatted over the point, refusing to give in, then after holding out for several minutes, collapsed onto the bayonet and sprawled on the floor, pumping blood. He was sewn up in the infirmary, refused to say how he had been wounded, and never had trouble with his fellow cadets again.

A week after his marriage, the newly commissioned second lieutenant was shipped out to the Philippines, leaving Lily to return to her mother's house. He went through a storm and near shipwreck, a cholera epidemic, a viciously fought guerrilla war, and learned about the command of troops. He was given an unruly platoon, whose members enjoyed testing their fresh-faced young lieutenant. On the first jungle patrol on Mindanao, they came to a river, cried, "Crocodiles," and trampled young Marshall into the mud as they raced to the far bank. He got up, crossed the river, formed the troop into a column, and led them back across the stream. Then he turned them about-face, again went to the head of the column, and marched them back across again. There was no insubordination after that.

There were instead the frustrating longueurs of military life in a peacetime army. Marshall mapped the vast spaces of West Texas in the grueling sun, went back to the Philippines, and sought in vain for a cure for Lily. The one moment of promise was his selection for a staff-training course at Fort Leavenworth. Despite promotion to full lieutenant, and fulsome reports from every commander under whom he served, in 1916, at the age of thirty-five, he was still stuck in that rank. Like many another frustrated young officer, he thought of leaving the service, and only the prospect of joining the European war kept him in the ranks.

He was finally made captain that year and assigned to the "preparedness" program, training young part-time volunteers in San Francisco. The camp commandant was Brigadier General Sibert, and when war came, Sibert was made major general and given the First Division. He asked to have Marshall on his staff, noting that the tall and rangy captain was so outstanding an officer, "I would prefer to serve under his command." With America's manpower almost inexhaustible, the priority in 1917 was to train, equip, and organize it for war. Staff officers were worth their weight in gold, and Marshall was an unusually good one. The myth later developed, and was assiduously promoted by that accomplished military politician Douglas MacArthur, who saw him as a rival, that Marshall had never commanded troops in combat. This was not so. As American attention focused on the stand of the marines at Château-Thierry, the First Division had been ordered to take and hold the village of Cantigny. Marshall broke his ankle when his horse slipped in the mud on the way to the battle, but he bound it up and stayed in the line, then remained in the village through repeated German shelling and counterattacks.

"It was not the ordeal of personal combat that seemed to prove the greatest strain," he later recalled. "It was the endurance for days at a time of severe artillery bombardment by shells of heavy caliber that proved the fortitude of troops. To be struck by these hideous agents without the power personally to strike back was the lot of the American soldier at Cantigny." After that battle, he was moved to Pershing's staff, where his celebrated feud with the heroic young commander of the "Rainbow Division," General MacArthur, began. MacArthur was a brave officer and an outstanding commander, but he was consumed by ambition. His career, he believed, was constantly being thwarted by the "Chaumont gang" of Pershing's staff, back-room boys who did not understand real combat and how to lead men.

America Reborn

In the final pursuit of the war, MacArthur sought and won the privilege of taking the French fortress of Sedan, site of one of the great battles of the Franco-Prussian War, and a place from which artillery could command the crucial railway line supplying the whole of the German Western Front. The order for the Rainbow Division was signed by staff colonel Marshall. But the French Fourth Army was itself resolved to take Sedan, and separate orders to Marshall's old First Division told them to capture the town, as well. The result was utter confusion, as two American and two French divisions, all heading in different directions, collided on the narrow roads. MacArthur strode forward in his usual informal uniform to sort out the traffic jam, and he was arrested by troops of the First Division until his identity could be established. The commander of the French Fourth Army told the Americans that any troops other than French trying to capture Sedan would be considered hostile and fired upon. MacArthur was finally released, fuming and convinced that it was all Marshall's fault, and Sedan remained in German hands.

MacArthur's resentment should not have affected the career of the brilliant young staff officer who had become General Pershing's right hand. But as the army was slashed back to its prewar size by 1921, its remaining units parceled off into little garrisons that had no need for staff officers accustomed to handling millions of men, Marshall found his career overtaken by the regimental officers. Wherever he served, he did well. In China, with a single regiment, he disarmed three entire divisions of demoralized Chinese troops who had threatened to loot Tientsin. He performed brilliantly as a lecturer at the National War College and then as assistant commandant and lecturer at the Infantry School at Fort Benning, where for five years he trained the rising young officers who would become the paladins of field command in World War II: the future generals Omar Bradley, "Vinegar Joe" Stilwell, Bedell Smith, Lawton Collins, and the paratroop pioneer Matthew Ridgway. But then came the recession, with Congress determined to cut the officer corps from twelve thousand to ten thousand. And General MacArthur as army chief of staff was in charge of promotions.

Appalled at the whittling down of the army, MacArthur persuaded the president to put the Civilian Conservation Corps, a job-creation program for the young unemployed, under military command. Still a colonel, Marshall was assigned to Fort Moultrie, South Carolina, in charge of 25,000 young civilians. Again, his command was exemplary. But time spent commanding nonregular troops did not count toward promotion and that essential step to brigadier general, without which he would be forced into retirement. So at the end of this tour, Marshall applied to be given a regular command. MacArthur assigned him instead to command National Guard troops in

Chicago, which again would not count toward promotion. Facing the end of his military career, Marshall appealed to the retired General Pershing for help, and Pershing wrote to MacArthur asking as a personal favor for Marshall to be given the promotion he deserved. MacArthur curtly refused, ordering Marshall to Chicago to watch for "incipient revolution," which the National Guard would be expected to suppress. Not until 1936, when MacArthur had become commander in chief of the forces of the newly independent Philippines, did Marshall get his promotion. The one consolation was that his personal life was now happy. After the death of his first wife, he had met and married Katherine Tupper Brown, a widow with two children.

MacArthur was replaced as chief of staff by a Pershing man, Gen. Malin Craig, who assigned his new brigadier to command the Fifth Brigade of the Third Infantry Division at Vancouver barracks near Seattle. After this essential taste of commanding regular troops, Marshall was brought back as deputy chief of staff in 1938, groomed to succeed Craig the following year. To do so, which meant promoting him ahead of thirty-four more senior generals, required President Roosevelt's personal approval. Perhaps Roosevelt relished having as chief of staff a general who would say no and who would insist on telling him the unvarnished military truth. He also had a regard for Marshall as the military man who had taken most seriously, and achieved the best results with, the Civilian Conservation Corps. Certainly Roosevelt knew that with war pending in Europe and a vast American rearmament plan to devise and fulfill, he needed an organizer and a staff officer, rather than a swashbuckler. There were other candidates clamoring and lobbying hard for the job, but whatever Roosevelt's motives, in picking Marshall, he chose the right man.

In 1940, the government spent a total of $9 billion. In 1944, it spent $91.3 billion, most of it to service the vast war machine that Marshall directed. Seldom has a public servant been more trusted. Congress voted him a personal budget of $100 million to use as he saw fit, which became the seed money to launch the Manhattan Project. Under Marshall, the army rose from 280,000 men to 8 million, and there were 14 million Americans in uniform by 1944 to be fed, clothed, armed, and trained. As Marshall explained in his final War Report to Congress in November 1945: "Out of our entire military mobilization of 14 million men, the number of infantry troops was less than 1.5 million Army and Marine. The remainder of our armed forces, sea, air and ground, was largely fighting a war of machinery. Counting those engaged in war production there were probably 75–80 million Americans directly involved in prosecution of the war. To technological warfare we devoted 98 percent of our entire effort."

America Reborn

Marshall was organizing a vast industrial empire, in which it took twelve officers and seventy-three men to service, maintain, load, arm, and refuel each B-29 bomber that lumbered into the air. In October 1941, there were only sixty-four American pilots qualified to fly four-engine aircraft. Four years later, after an extraordinary training program, there were over twelve thousand four-engine bomber pilots and another two thousand dead or in captivity. In the spring of 1941, for the first time in American history, Gen. George Patton put into the field as a training exercise the country's first armored division. It was laboriously put together from brigades here and cavalry troops there and requisitioned civilian trucks. By 1945, there were twenty-two American armored divisions in the field, each of them mustered, trained, assembled, and equipped at the giant new army bases that had been hurriedly built in the United States and then loaded onto ships that sailed in convoys that had to be guarded on the long voyage to Europe.

As chief of staff, Marshall ran the army and the Army Air Forces, not yet an independent service. In 1942, he established a new committee of the Joint Chiefs of Staff to run the war. This included Marshall and the Army Air Forces commander, Hap Arnold; the navy commander in chief, Adm. Ernie King; and Adm. William Leahy, as much political aide as career officer. Leahy had just returned from being U.S. ambassador to Vichy France. He was devoted to Roosevelt, an admirer of Marshall, and felt no great service loyalty to the irascible Admiral King. In short, with three votes of the four chiefs of staff, Marshall effectively ran the war from the American side. With astute diplomacy, he also came to run the Allied war, as the great weight of American manpower and resources first caught up with and then overwhelmed the British contribution.

This was a matter of the most delicate diplomacy. The British had been at war since September 3, 1939, when Hitler had defied the British ultimatum to cease his invasion of Poland. The British had fought on alone after the defeat of France, secured their homeland by retaining command of the air with the Battle of Britain, withstood the blitz of Luftwaffe bombers on London, and defeated the Italian armies in North Africa. Then they had to pour those victorious troops into the honorable but doomed attempt to save Greece from German invasion, and their weakened army in Egypt was then hard put to fend off the better-equipped German panzer divisions sent to North Africa under Gen. Erwin Rommel. The British fleet was straining every nerve to get the convoys across the Atlantic in the teeth of U-boat attacks, while also trying to retain command of the Mediterranean against a superior Italian fleet backed up by land-based German airpower. Like the Americans, the British had been ill prepared and ill armed for war in 1939. But by fighting on alone from the security of their island, by defying German airpower and taking the battle back to Germany with their bombing raids, the British had achieved a pride and seized a moral ascendancy in the war effort that would prove delicate to manage in alliance strategy.

Prime Minister Winston Churchill had become the embodiment of that British defiance and resolve: a symbolic figure of extraordinary stature in the United States as in occupied Europe. Marshall admired him unreservedly. But Marshall did not normally deal with Churchill. His counterpart was Gen. Alan Brooke, later Field Marshal and Viscount Alanbrooke, whose title revealed another difficulty in the Allied command. He was CIGS, chief of the imperial general staff. Britain was defending not just her own shores but the greatest empire the earth had ever known, which stretched from Egypt down through the length of Africa to the Cape of Good Hope, and east through the Suez Canal to the protectorates of the Persian Gulf and the oil fields of Iraq, and on to India, Burma, and Singapore; from there, it stretched north to Hong Kong, east to the scattered islands of the Pacific, south to Australia and New Zealand. Without their manpower and support, and the reinforcements from Canada, Britain would have been hard-pressed to fight on.

The British war aim, beyond survival, was to recover and maintain that empire, a colonial presence with which the Americans could never be wholly comfortable. And the habits and possession of that empire imposed on Churchill and the British a global perspective of the world after the war that the Americans found either baffling or too ruthlessly realist for comfort. Britain had declared war over Poland because it could not tolerate the dominance of Europe by the single hostile power of Germany. It did not intend to fight itself to exhaustion and bankruptcy in order to see that threat of German dominance replaced by that of Stalin's Red Army, however essential an ally the Soviet Union might be against the Wehrmacht. And aware that its own postwar strength would be critically diminished, the British pursued a geopolitical strategy that would ensure the United States remained committed to Europe's security after this war, rather than retreating into isolationism as it had after 1919.

To manage these difficult relations, Marshall had one supreme advantage in the person of a man who became his closest friend. Field Marshal Sir John Dill had been CIGS until almost the end of 1941, the period of Britain's supreme and lonely effort. Exhausted, he was replaced by Brooke, and Dill was then sent almost at once to Washington to be the British liaison officer with the Americans. Brooke later concluded that securing Dill's appointment to Washington was "one of my most important accomplishments during the war."

A professional soldier of iron duty and self-control, Dill was in many ways similar to Marshall, and the two men became fast friends. They devised their own secret code in order to communicate. Each man regularly went much further than his orders permitted in revealing to the other the deeper motives and ambitions of their respective politicians and planners. Their trust, at least for the first crucial years of the war, was complete. Their confidence in each other's judgment and their professional intimacy alarmed some of Marshall's colleagues, particularly after the Casablanca conference suggested that Brooke and the British planners were suspiciously well prepared to refute the American arguments. There are always differences between allies in wartime, where rival plans and operations can be matters of life and death. But the Anglo-American tensions never got out of hand until Dill's illness and subsequent death in Washington in November 1944. Heartbroken at the loss of a man on whom he relied so much, Marshall arranged for the signal honor of Dill's burial, with an imposing equestrian statue, at Arlington National Cemetery in Virginia.

There were three essential decisions of grand strategy that Marshall had to take. The first was whether the priority in the American war effort would be in Europe or the Pacific. The second, once it was agreed that the main thrust would be in Europe, was how best to take the war to the enemy. The favored American option was direct assault across the English Channel into occupied France and then driving on to the German heartland. The British, haunted by memories of the bloody attrition of trench warfare in northern France and Belgium in World War I, preferred an indirect approach. They wanted to attack through Italy and the Balkans, which Churchill dubbed "the soft underbelly," and knock away Germany's props one by one while the strategic bombing offensive destroyed German cities and factories. Such a course could have put Anglo-American armies into the Balkans and Central Europe and even Berlin before the Soviet troops could push back the main German armies from western Russia, the Baltic coast, and the Ukraine. Postwar Europe might thus find the Red Army at a safe distance. The third great decision that Marshall confronted was, therefore, whether the United States would wage war against Germany with a view to postwar tensions with the Soviet allies. This, he *and* his president were most reluctant to do.

The first decision was made long before the Japanese attack on Pearl Harbor finally brought the United States into the war. On January 6, 1941, Roosevelt's annual message to the nation announced the lend-lease campaign to provide war materials without payment (since British funds were now exhausted and all its holdings in U.S. stocks and companies already sold) "to those nations which are now in actual war with aggressors." Ten days later, Roosevelt convened his first grand strategy meeting with his secretaries of state, war, and the navy and with Marshall and Adm. Harold Stark, chief of naval operations. Marshall's memorandum on that meeting records the president concluding that there was "one chance in five" of a sneak attack on the United States by Germany or Japan. Marshall urged that the immediate policy should be to restrain Japan, while ensuring that Britain continued to fight. The president's final directive from that meeting, as recorded by a relieved Marshall, was crucial for the eventual grand strategy of the war:

> That we would stand on the defensive in the Pacific with the Fleet based on Hawaii; that the commander of the Asiatic Fleet would have discretionary authority as to how long he could remain based in the Philippines; that there would be no naval reinforcement of the Philippines; that the Navy should be prepared to convoy shipping in the Atlantic to England; that we should make every effort to go on the basis of continuing the supply of material to Great Britain, primarily in order to disappoint what he [the president] thought would be Hitler's principal objective of involving us in a war at this particular time, and also to buck up England.

The priorities could not have been more clear. The United States would go on the defensive in the Pacific, and even abandon the Philippines. The main effort had to be against Germany. When the Japanese attack came on December 7, Marshall summoned a fresh young general, Dwight Eisenhower, to be his deputy for operations and asked his view. Eisenhower replied that the Philippines had to be abandoned and Australia maintained as the crucial fortress. Germany had to be the main target, since it was the one place where all three Allies, Britain, the United States, and the Soviet Union, could exert maximum force together. This decision was complicated by the presence of General MacArthur with an American garrison in the Philippines. Marshall did his best to sustain the doomed fortress of Corregidor, and finally, in 1942, he ordered his old enemy to leave in order that he could become commander in chief at the new American base in Australia. The core decision, the Pacific or Europe, meant tension between the army and the navy, which was itching for revenge against Japan for Pearl Harbor and aware that an island-hopping war would give it the dominant strategic role. In the event, Hitler solved this problem by declaring war on the United States after his Japanese allies appeared to have secured command of the Pacific by sinking the American battleships at anchor.

The second problem, whether to invade France and Germany directly across the English Channel, was far more difficult to solve. To launch and sustain an unprecedented amphibious operation would require command of the air and sea over the Channel and invasion beaches. On the other side lay the German army, well trained and experienced, as well as equipped with constantly improving tanks that invariably enjoyed a technological edge over their American and British counterparts. Invasion would be a great gamble; the defeat of such a force would make it extremely difficult to mount another such attempt. The temptation was very strong to shift to the Pacific war and leave Germany to fight the Russians, while the Anglo-Americans continued their costly strategic bombing offensive and fought a holding operation in Italy. With German ingenuity producing awesome new weapons from jet aircraft to rockets, the eventual result could well have been a negotiated peace settlement that left Germany, with or without Hitler at the helm, dominating mainland Europe. For the British, this would have been a nightmare. Rather than take that risk, the British much preferred to attack "the soft underbelly" of Italy and the Balkans and aim for the strategic prize of seizing Central Europe before the Russians. Allied superiority in troops and material, the British argued, gave a near guarantee of success.

In July 1942, this debate came to a head. At Marshall's orders, Eisenhower, in charge of war plans, had drafted a proposal for an invasion of France in the autumn of that year, to be called Operation Bolero. Inevitably, at this stage of the American buildup, this would have required predominantly British troops. Marshall flew to London, where Churchill and Brooke flatly refused to back Bolero. Marshall, with the support of Admiral King and Secretary of War Henry Stimson, then cabled Roosevelt:

> If the US is to engage in any other operation than forceful, unswerving adherence to BOLERO plans, we are definitely of the opinion that we should turn to the Pacific and strike decisively against Japan; in other words, assume a defensive attitude against Germany, except for air operations, and use all available means in the Pacific.

This was a crisis of the war. Roosevelt asked for a detailed plan on such a shift in strategy. This was provided. He then wrote back:

> This is exactly what Germany hoped the US would do following Pearl Harbor. Secondly, it does not in fact provide use of American troops in fighting except in a lot of islands whose occupation will not affect the world situation this year or next. Third, it does not help Russia, or the Near East. Therefore it is disapproved as of the present.

Roosevelt was a better strategist than his chief of staff. But Marshall had a kind of revenge. Instead of Bolero, he agreed on a joint Anglo-American invasion of French North Africa—to seize command of the Mediterranean and thus save a million tons of shipping each year from having to be transported via the far longer route around the Cape. Roosevelt approved, but then he put his hands together in prayer and said, "Please make it before election day." Election Day was November 3. The invasion took place on November 8, and within six months, the Allies had cleared North Africa of German troops, and were planning the invasion of Italy.

In 1942, the British had the most troops and were doing the most fighting (although they were fighting only four German divisions in North Africa, while the Russians were battling over two hundred). The British view therefore prevailed. By the end of 1943, when the catastrophic losses of the B-17s over Schweinfurt in the disastrous attempts to halt German ball-bearing production had raised a large question over the strategic bombing campaign, the Americans were at least equal partners in ground troops and were becoming dominant. Ironically, the "soft underbelly" strategy was bearing fruit. Italy had been successfully invaded and had left the Axis alliance and at least nominally joined the Allies. The Mediterranean was an Allied lake. Twelve German divisions were tied down fighting Tito's partisans in Yugoslavia, who were being supplied with Allied arms. The Germans had been driven back by the Red Army into the Ukraine, so there was less need to launch a second front to relieve the pressure on the Russians. But a cross-Channel invasion in 1944 had now been firmly agreed, and Marshall hoped desperately that he would be chosen to lead it. Roosevelt, knowing his value as chief of staff, appointed Eisenhower instead.

Once the British and American troops were ashore in Normandy and the German armies of the west broken as the Allies raced to liberate Paris and then Brussels, the final great strategic question of war had to be decided: whether to conduct the final campaign in order simply to defeat Germany, or to seize commanding ground for the new strategic situation after the war. Roosevelt, Marshall, and Eisenhower insisted on the former, attacking slowly and steadily on a broad front, regardless of the postwar implications of a Soviet advance into Germany and Central Europe. The British wanted one powerful strategic thrust from France across the Rhine in order to end the war by the end of 1944 and to occupy Berlin before the Russians got there. The British took advantage of Eisenhower's need to capture the port of Antwerp to relieve his supply problems, and they advocated in September 1944 an attempt to cross the Rhine barrier at Arnhem. One British and two American paratroop divisions were dropped behind German lines onto the four successive bridges, at Eindhoven, Grave, Nijmwegen, and Arnhem, while the armored divisions on the ground raced the fifty miles to relieve them.

The strategic prize could not have been greater. To cross the Rhine in the autumn of 1944, cut off the Ruhr industrial belt, and race to Berlin by Christmas would not just have ended the war in Europe. It would have transformed the postwar situation. The Iron Curtain might never have fallen, and if it had, it would have dropped far to the east. Czechoslovakia and Hungary, what became East Germany, and possibly even Poland, where the Red Army was stuck on the far side of the Vistula River at Warsaw, might never have fallen under Soviet control.

But the Allies were defeated. The ground armies rolled forward to take the river crossings as Eindhoven, Grave, and Nijmwegen. But Arnhem was indeed "a bridge too far," as the historian Cornelius Ryan would detail memorably years later. The British paratroops had dropped onto two resting German SS armored divisions, whose presence had been reported by the Dutch underground but ignored by the British commanders. Reinforced by a brigade of Polish airborne troops, the British paratroops held out heroically for a week, but finally, out of ammunition, 2,400 of them pulled back across the river. Another eight thousand were dead or captive on the far side.

Churchill immediately arranged to fly to Moscow, in the hope that the traditional diplomacy of realism could secure what the paratroopers had failed to win. At 10:00 p.m. on October 9, Churchill met Stalin in the Kremlin and asked, "How would it do for you to have ninety percent predominance in Rumania, for us to have ninety percent of the say in Greece, and go fifty-fifty about Yugoslavia?" Churchill sketched out the figures on a sheet of paper, adding 50–50 for Hungary, and 75–25 in Bulgaria (in Stalin's favor). Stalin "took his blue pencil and made a large tick upon it, and passed it back to us," Churchill recalled. The British Foreign Office memorandum of the conversation also records that Stalin accepted that Britain after the war would be "the leading Mediterranean power." The famous sheet of paper contained no reference to Germany, Czechoslovakia, or Poland, the country for which Britain had gone to war in 1939, but which had become in Churchill's eyes a hopeless cause. Just before he left for the Yalta summit, Churchill confided to his personal secretary, "Make no mistake, all the Balkans, except Greece, are going to be Bolshevized, and there is nothing I can do to prevent it. There is nothing I can do for Poland either."

The war ground on through a dreadful winter, and then in February, Roosevelt, Churchill, and Stalin gathered for their final summit conference at the Crimean resort of Yalta, where Stalin's battle-won right to occupy Eastern and Central Europe was formally agreed upon, in return for his promise to hold "free elections of governments responsive to the will of the people." Roosevelt went on to explain his postwar aims. The Americans wanted peace and trade, and an amicable and democratic new order in Europe. But they also wanted to bring their troops home from Europe as fast as possible, partly because of the immediate priority of the war against Japan and partly because Congress was impatient. "Two years would be the limit," Roosevelt told a silently watchful Stalin and an appalled Churchill.

"If the Americans left Europe, Britain would have to occupy single-handed the entire Western portion of Germany. Such a task would be far beyond our strength," Churchill noted privately. The crushing of Germany created an opportunity that only Stalin seemed able to seize. At that moment, the hitherto barely foreseen results of the war crystallized. Nominally one of the outstanding victors of the Grand Alliance, Britain realized its triumph was Pyrrhic, bought at a price so high that its role as a Great Power could no longer be sustained. This meant that the cardinal principle of British policy thereafter would be to maintain an American military presence in Europe. The alternative would be Soviet domination of a hollow continent in which Britain was too weak to play its traditional role of balancing power.

It was to be Marshall's fate to confront the political implications of his wartime strategy. He was barely a week into his retirement in November 1945 when the new president, Harry Truman, called him back to be ambassador to China and to try to forge peace between Mao's Communists and the forces of Chiang Kai-shek. Marshall secured a brief truce, but he ultimately failed to prevent the civil war and Mao's subsequent success. This one shadow on his career provoked extraordinary attacks upon Marshall by Senator Joe McCarthy as "a traitor—he tricked us into war—he lost us China." These outlandish charges (although not denounced at the time by Marshall's friend, the Republican presidential candidate, Eisenhower) began the final discrediting of McCarthy's witch-hunting campaigns.

But with Soviet forces now installed in the heart of Central Europe and Chinese Communists poised to extend what looked like a monolithic Communist bloc throughout much of Asia, the West faced mortal peril. The hopes of Roosevelt and Marshall and, subsequently, Truman that the wartime alliance with Stalin would extend into the peace had not been fulfilled. Churchill's foreboding had become a grim reality as the Iron Curtain fell across Europe and America's most reliable public servant was recalled to the colors. In January 1947, Marshall was sworn in as secretary of state, and once again the fate of Europe was to be in his hands.

For one of the most significant moments of the century, Secretary Marshall made little immediate stir when he announced the European Recovery Program, subsequently known as the Marshall Plan, in his commencement speech at Harvard University on June 5, 1947. In the *New York Times* the following day, the headline read TRUMAN CALLS HUNGARY COUP "OUTRAGE." The second headline continued DEMANDS RUSSIANS AGREE TO INQUIRY, and only the third headline said MARSHALL PLEADS FOR EUROPEAN UNITY. Marshall's grand plan to rebuild the war-ravaged economies of Europe was almost humbly presented.

"It would be neither fitting nor efficacious for this government to undertake to draw up unilaterally a program designed to place Europe on its feet economically. This is the business of the Europeans. The initiative, I think, must come from Europe," Marshall said in the Harvard speech.

His deputy, Dean Acheson, ensured that it did, briefing three British journalists on its importance and advising them to tell their editors to send full copies of the speech to Ernest Bevin at the Foreign Office. Bevin heard the news from BBC Radio, immediately telephoned Georges Bidault, the French foreign minister, and within two weeks, they and the Russian foreign minister, Vyacheslav Molotov, were all meeting in Paris. Molotov was invited because the Marshall Plan's promise of American financial support to rebuild wartorn Europe was designed to be open to all. Marshall had stressed in his Harvard speech, "Our policy is directed not against any country or doctrine but against hunger, poverty, desperation and chaos. Its purpose should be the revival of a working economy in the world so as to permit the emergence of political and social conditions in which free institutions can exist. . . . Any government which maneuvers to block the recovery of other countries cannot expect help from us."

It was the task of Bevin and Bidault to ensure that Molotov understood the political implications of Marshall's phrase about "free institutions." But Molotov came to Paris with more than a hundred experts, including economists, transport and logistics consultants, and even nutritionists. Moscow, it was clear, was seriously interested in Marshall's offer, if the terms were right. Molotov began by saying each European country should add up its financial needs and send the combined list to the Americans. That, retorted Bevin, would be asking for a blank check. "Debtors do not lay down conditions," Bevin added. Molotov suspected that the Marshall Plan would be the Trojan horse of the American dollar, a way to infiltrate the Soviet Union and its sphere of influence in order to destroy it. He suggested that "only allied countries that had suffered from the ravages of war should participate." This would exclude both Italy and Germany. Bevin and Bidault said no. Molotov was then handed a telegram, only partially decoded, straight from Moscow. It reinforced Molotov's hard line; Stalin would not accept common planning, with its implication of American and British economists poring over the Soviet economy. In effect, the Paris conference was over.

The Marshall Plan, Molotov finally declared, "will lead to Britain, France and the group of countries that follow them separating from the rest of Europe, which will split Europe into two groups of states." In this, Molotov was absolutely right. But then Britain and the non-Communist parties in France and the other Western European countries had already chosen their sides. If the Iron Curtain was indeed falling across Europe, then all but the most loyal socialists and those to their left knew on which side they preferred to be. On July 4, two days after Molotov's departure, Bevin and Bidault invited twenty-two European governments, all except fascist Spain and the Soviet Union, to a wider conference in Paris the following week. The Czechs, Poles, and Hungarians all agreed to come, Bulgaria and Albania expressed interest, and only Yugoslavia and Romania said they would first consult with Moscow.

Moscow cracked the whip. The Czech premier, Klement Gottwald, and the foreign minister, Jan Masaryk, were summoned to Moscow on July 8, where they were threatened with grim consequences should they go to Paris. Masaryk glumly observed that he had gone to Moscow as the minister of a sovereign state and returned as a Soviet lackey. On Moscow's orders, Poland, Romania, Yugoslavia, Bulgaria, Albania, and Hungary all rejected the invitation, as did Finland. In retrospect, this has been defined as the moment when the Soviet boot crushed itself into the face of Eastern Europe. But for the U.S. Congress, it took the Communist-led putsch in Czechoslovakia in February 1948 to persuade them to vote the funds for European recovery. The final vote took place as the American and British airlift of food into blockaded West Berlin began.

The generosity of the American taxpayer was stunning. At a time when the American GDP was around $250 billion a year, the Marshall Plan devoted $15 billion over five years (the equivalent of nearly $450 billion in terms of today's GDP) to sending food and providing grants and loans for rebuilding what would become a major trade competitor. There were some shadows on the altruism. The insistence that American tobacco exports be included in the aid, and that Britain and France open their colonial empires to U.S. exports, provoked some resentment, including a vote in the French National Assembly to ban Coca-Cola. But there could be no doubt about the success of the plan. In Western Europe as a whole, industrial production rose by 62 percent in the two years after the desperately low point of 1947. Such a swift improvement on the previous year's economic figures was reassuring. Between 1949 and 1950, West Germany's foreign trade doubled, then rose another 75 percent the following year. In 1946, the Western zones of Germany had produced 2.5 million tons of steel, which soared to 9 million tons in 1949, and to 14.5 million tons in 1953. In France by 1954, industrial production was 50 percent higher than it had been in the year before World War II.

Alongside the Marshall Plan was built the North Atlantic Treaty Organization, NATO, the pivotal institution of what became an enduring Western alliance, with American troops based in Europe and committed for over fifty years to the common defense. Truman, Marshall, and his successor, Acheson, built the West and defined what became the ultimately stabilizing parameters of the Cold War. There were occasional differences among them. Marshall opposed Truman's decision to recognize the state of Israel, suspecting the Jewish vote for the 1948 elections weighed more heavily than long-term U.S. interests in the oil-rich Arab world. Indeed, he told Truman that because of this, were he to vote (which as a soldier he declined to do), he would cast his ballot for Truman's opponent. His resignation in January 1949 was prompted less by disagreement than by a serious operation to remove a kidney. The following year, he was recalled to duty, a call he could never refuse, as secretary of defense on the eve of the Korean War, for what became his final confrontation with General MacArthur.

The first direct clash between the West and the Communist world, the Korean War was also the first war to be waged from the beginning under the shadow of nuclear weapons on both sides. The successful testing of the first Soviet atom bomb was announced in September 1949. The initial North Korean attack in June 1950 overran most of the South, except for a small U.S.-held enclave around the port of Pusan. But then MacArthur launched an amphibious landing far behind the lines at Inchon, near Seoul, and the North Koreans were sent reeling back in disarray toward the Chinese frontier on the Yalu River. MacArthur gave chase, and the Chinese entered the war in overwhelming force. The American troops plunged into headlong retreat. Ordering his staff in Tokyo to start planning a major bombing assault on Chinese and Russian bases in the region, MacArthur spoke openly of the possible use of the atom bomb. Amid Allied panic, with British premier Clement Attlee flying to Washington to flourish a nonexistent veto over the use of atomic weapons, MacArthur was relieved of his command.

"George Marshall pulled the trigger," MacArthur concluded, the final act of a personal drama that had begun in the trenches of France in 1918. Certainly Marshall drafted the order that Truman signed, and conducted the review of MacArthur's repeated insubordination that concluded he should have been relieved much earlier. Marshall had tried to the end to resolve matters short of dismissal. But he was aware of both the domestic political complications of the action as well as the secret warnings being conveyed by the Central Intelligence Agency that the Soviets were preparing for all-out war in Europe if nuclear weapons were used against the Chinese.

The Korean War was allowed to drag on into a stalemate, whose one merit was that it avoided a wider war. That was one result of Marshall's wisdom. A second was that the West was now prepared, and equipped with the NATO alliance and a fast-recovering Western Europe, for the long haul of the

Cold War. The United States was also equipped with a Cold War plan, a secret national security document called NSC-68, which had been drawn up by Acheson and Paul Nitze before the Korean War broke out. It required a dramatic program of rearmament that would raise the U.S. defense budget from $13.5 billion to $50 billion a year, and the United States was to be prepared to maintain such an effort indefinitely. "The U.S. must lead in building a successfully functioning political and economic system in the free world," it said. It may be seen as the companion document, even the fulfillment, of the final report Marshall had sent to Congress at the end of World War II.

"We finish each bloody war with a feeling of acute revulsion against this savage form of human behavior, and yet on each occasion we confuse military preparedness with the causes of war and then drift almost deliberately into another catastrophe," Marshall had begun, recalling the bitter double lesson of American unreadiness in 1917 and 1941. "It no longer appears practical to continue what we once conceived as hemisphere defense as a satisfactory basis for our security. We are now concerned with the peace of the entire world. And the peace can only be maintained by the strong."

That peace, with allowance for the proxy wars in the developing world and the ill-fated war in Vietnam, broadly held. The American grand strategy, as devised by Marshall, Truman, and Acheson, maintained military readiness while building Western Europe and Japan into a prosperity that would help sustain the joint burden. In this lay its endurance, its genius, and its eventual triumph. This grand strategy, based on the experience of alliance politics that Marshall had sustained in the war against Hitler, forged the West as a new and incomparably prosperous economic system. In the end, the West prevailed because it could afford guns as well as butter, aircraft carriers as well as vacations abroad, a vast expansion of wealth that secured the political support of its democracies for the strategic long haul. Marshall, aware that he and Pershing had failed to persuade the country to maintain its defenses after 1919, was to help his country overcome its deep and abiding reluctance to shoulder such an unending global responsibility. Marshall not only built, deployed, and directed America's ascendance to global power; he convinced his presidents and his country of its need.

18.
William F. Buckley, Jr.,
and American Conservatism

In October 1951, a book was published by a young Roman Catholic recruit to the Central Intelligence Agency, William F. Buckley, Jr., who had recently graduated from Yale and was now based in Mexico City. The small and almost bankrupt conservative publishing house of Henry Regnery was based in Chicago and run by the man for whom the company was named. Regnery printed five thousand copies, unsure that he could sell so many of a work that his best editor had compared to Cardinal Newman's *Tracts.* Titled *God and Man at Yale,* it is a savage critique of the statist and even socialist teachings of the revered university's economics faculty at the time. This faculty was an intellectual redoubt of Keynesian ideas, solidly supportive of New Deal economics, and one of its stars was Paul Samuelson, whose best-selling textbook was to help make Keynesian economics into the orthodoxy of a generation.

William F. Buckley, Jr., and American Conservatism

Woven elegantly into this polemic, and expressed with all the assertive arrogance of the clever undergraduate, were two other themes. The first was that Yale had, to its shame, abandoned its traditional Christian faith and ethic. The second was a rather more thoughtful questioning of the moral relativism of a university that sought evenhandedly to present its students everything from communism to capitalism, Marx to Saint Augustine, and trust that a broad education equipped them to make up their own minds. This betrayed the duty of the university to uphold received and classical wisdom, the book argued. It made the eternal and the best into the hostage of the second-rate and the fashionable. It had, moreover, encouraged the growth of a dangerous new orthodoxy of laical liberalism, in which the conservatives and the devout were silenced. The liberal claim that the best ideas would prevail in an intellectual free-for-all was based upon a fundamental fallacy, since "the most casual student of history knows that, as a matter of fact, truth does not necessarily vanquish."

On the day of publication, Regnery received a panicky call from the Yale University bookshop. There was a long line of would-be buyers stretching outside the store and too few books for them to buy. Within the month, after a range of furious but still-respectful reviews had ignited a national controversy, the book was on the *New York Times* best-seller list. Within the year, over sixty thousand copies had been sold and Regnery's company had built a firm foundation for its conservative publishing program. Buckley resigned from the CIA, bade farewell to his friendly boss, Howard Hunt, who was later to run Richard Nixon's team of White House "plumbers," and resolved on a new career "to bring America back to herself."

Buckley's timing was perfect. The Korean War was under way and the Cold War had polarized political opinion. The Democratic administration of President Truman was demanding loyalty oaths from federal employees because Communists were seen as security risks. The wartime alliance with Soviet Russia had degenerated into a life-and-death struggle between America and an implacable communism. The rising stars of the Republican party were making their names by hunting down Communists and subversives in government and elsewhere. Communist spies had passed atomic secrets to Moscow, and the American monopoly of nuclear weapons had been betrayed. The republic was in mortal danger, and now one of the outstanding students of one of its most eminent universities had charged that the academics were an integral part of the peril.

The conservative cause could have had few more attractive enthusiasts. Intelligent and well-read, a gifted debater with extraordinary personal charm, Buckley was perfectly equipped for the new public stage offered by television. An essayist and columnist who swiftly won access to hundreds of newspapers, his own show, *Firing Line,* became an exemplar of the new televised political debate. He was clever, witty, and popular, even with liberal commentators, who opposed everything he stood for. Despite the often-convincing appearance of a dilettante, he worked hard for the cause, using his gift for celebrity to build institutions. The magazine that he founded, ran, and subsidized, the *National Review,* became the voice and the recruiting ground of the new conservatism. Over the half century after he burst onto the national scene with *God and Man at Yale,* he was called the high priest and patron saint of the conservatism that in the 1960s dominated the Republican party, and by the 1980s governed the country. He was, in the age of Madison Avenue, the cause's most engaging and relentless publicist, the figure who managed to weave the disparate strands of conservatism together and make them respectable again.

"*National Review* is to the West Wing of the White House what *People* magazine is to your dentist's waiting room," said longtime subscriber President Ronald Reagan at the magazine's thirtieth birthday party in 1985. He then turned to Buckley, smiled, and nodded his head in homage. "I want to assure you tonight: You didn't just part the Red Sea—you rolled it back, dried it up, and left exposed, for all the world to see, the naked desert that is statism. . . . Bill Buckley is perhaps the most influential journalist and intellectual in our era—he changed our country, indeed our century."

Buckley was far from the first to realize that the discredited cause of conservatism in America had found in patriotic anticommunism a new focus and new political glue that could bind its disparate parts together. But he had broadened the argument beyond the simple issues of Cold War loyalties to engage the intellectual establishment itself. His career, one of the most enthralling and public of postwar America, was to be dedicated to exploiting the potential of that glue to hold, while he enjoyed a most agreeable and entertaining life along the way. But the self-indulgent pleasures of inherited wealth were never allowed to compromise Buckley's strategic conviction that the intellectual moorings of a great democracy could be shifted.

Public life was in the end a battle of ideas as much as a contest of political wills. Buckley was convinced that the new anti-Communist core of the conservatives could be argued and marketed to accumulate an ever-growing constituency, until it could wrest the intellectual and political ascendancy from the liberal heresy. And the themes developed at Yale, the challenge to the intellectual orthodoxy of liberal politics and Keynesian economics, the insistence on the core importance of religious faith and of moral absolutes, were to run through Buckley's political life.

Conservatism had not died with the triumph of FDR, but had wandered off into different and often feuding directions. There was a gentlemanly nostalgia for Edmund Burke's eighteenth-century Toryism among the devotees of Russell Kirk's *The Conservative Mind.* A fiercer love of individualism and the free market could be found among the disciples of Ayn Rand and the far greater numbers who read her best-sellers, *The Fountainhead* and *Atlas Shrugged,* among them President Dwight D. Eisenhower. The doctrine of classic free-market economics revived around the Austrian school of Friedrich Hayek and Ludwig von Mises, which became Americanized as their disciple Milton Friedman came to dominate the University of Chicago economics faculty. There were libertarians and those nostalgic for the supposedly courtly ways of the Old South. And there were isolationists, anti-Semites, and conspiracy theorists who believed that Eisenhower himself was part of the Communist plot against American values, and who formed the John Birch Society, named after a Baptist missionary killed by Chinese Communists.

These were the fragments of a movement, but when Buckley's career began, there was no single conservative cause, because it had yet to recover from the searing discredit it had suffered during the Great Depression and World War II. The root of that discredit lay not just in capitalism's collapse but in the success of Roosevelt's New Deal despite the gloomiest predictions from the spokesmen of capital and of property. The defenders of the free market had been proved wrong and the advocates of state intervention and rational planning could claim to have been proved right, although their success was far more apparent during the war than it had been in the slow and bumpy economic recovery of the 1930s. That other traditional cause of American conservatives, the refusal to engage in foreign quarrels and military alliances since at least the defeat of Woodrow Wilson's League of Nations, was equally discredited by the war. Isolationism had proved a hollow recourse in the age of bombers and a sneak attack on Pearl Harbor.

The war had also undermined the traditional religious and moral codes of conduct that conservatives tended to support. Divorce had become easier and birth control commonplace, and social mobility was being revolutionized by the GI bill, through which over 10 million veterans received education grants. Twenty million Americans moved during the war, and 14 million more left home for the service. The racial and industrial geography of America was transformed by the war as southern blacks and whites alike moved to the traditional factories of the Northeast and Midwest and to the new ones of California. The new instant cities of Oak Ridge, Tennessee, and Hanford, Washington, between them attracted 100,000 people to build the components of the atom bomb. This kind of mass movement, which meant saying farewell to traditional churches, families, and ways of life, meant that conservatives faced a very different America after 1945, one that revered Roosevelt and broadly supported the New Deal and the government's role in the national economy. It was also a far more unionized economy, with the numbers in labor unions leaping from 8.9 million in 1940 to almost 15 million in 1945.

None of this meant that the Republican party could no longer win elections. Far from it; in 1946, the Republicans briefly won control of both houses of Congress for the first time since 1930. But it was a party in ideological disarray. Senator Arthur Vandenberg, an isolationist leader of the 1930s, helped craft a strikingly bipartisan foreign policy in support of the Marshall Plan as the Cold War took hold. The Republican party helped pass the Taft-Hartley Act to outlaw the closed shop and to bar federal employees from strikes, rallied behind a deliberately centrist presidential candidate in Eisenhower in 1952, and endorsed some of the crucial planks of the New Deal. The Republicans voted to lift price controls, then were appalled to see inflation rise more in the following year than it had throughout the war.

By 1948, the Democrats had regained control of Congress and embarked on Truman's Fair Deal. An extension of the New Deal, it widened the scope of Social Security, raised the minimum wage, and poured federal money into low-income housing, but it failed to enact national health insurance. Nonetheless, after Truman's second term, the United States had a recognizably social democratic system, similar in principle to, if more modest than, the welfare states established by the moderate socialist governments of Western Europe. And after the New Deal and the Fair Deal, the fundamental contours of this system were carved too deep to be abolished.

The Republican party may have contained many conservatives, but for the generation after World War II, it came to a broad accommodation with the Democrats. If there was a bipartisan consensus behind the Cold War in foreign policy, there was also an agreement that the Republicans would not seek to undo the domestic reforms of the New Deal. Indeed, the Eisenhower administration in its interstate highway program and the National Defense Education Act outdid any of Roosevelt's state investments. The United States was not alone in this. In Britain, this was the era of "Butskellism," named after the moderate conservative R. A. Butler and the moderate Labour party leader Hugh Gaitskell. On mainland Europe, conservative parties in France, Italy, and Germany called themselves Christian Democrats and built generous welfare states.

Genuine conservatives felt out of power and not really at home in what they saw as their own parties. This was the challenge that confronted Buckley as the Korean War broke out. Like the Kennedy family, with whose numbers and political ambition Buckley had much in common, the Buckleys were an Irish-Catholic family, although Buckley liked to claim that his ancestors had arrived as Protestants. Similar to the Kennedy patriarch, Buckley's father had made and lost one fortune as a lawyer and oil investor in Mexico during the

Mexican Revolution and then made another in Venezuela and Canada. The Kennedys went to Harvard; Buckley to Yale (and briefly to an English boarding school), acquiring the style and patina of the Yankee patrician. But whereas the Kennedys were brought up as Democrats with a lively sense of the Irish rebellions against the lordly British, Buckley was raised as a counter-revolutionary. His father never forgave the Mexican Revolution for the confiscation of his property, and he sensed a similar current in Spain in the 1930s. The family was firmly on the side of Franco, against Roosevelt's New Deal, and against intervention in the war.

Buckley did well at Yale, being asked to join that most elite of its secret societies, Skull and Bones (whose members included future president George Bush), and becoming the star of the debating team as well as chairman, which meant editor, of the *Yale Daily News.* He also forged an intense friendship with another student, Brent Bozell, who was to marry Buckley's sister and coauthor Buckley's next book. This new volume defended Senator Joe McCarthy of Wisconsin, the most outspoken and shameless of the politicians claiming that America faced mortal peril from the infiltration of Communist moles. The book, *McCarthy and His Enemies,* conceded that McCarthy's charges were exaggerated, but it argued that his intentions were both sound and vital to national survival. For all his flaws, McCarthy thus represented a lesser danger to America than his enemies, who, from left-wing ruthlessness or squeamish liberalism, would leave the moles still burrowing at freedom's vitals: "An Alger Hiss, critically situated, can conceivably determine the destiny of the West. . . . We cannot avoid the fact that the United States is at war with Communism and that McCarthyism is a program of action against those in our land who help the enemy."

The book was published in 1954, when McCarthy and his cause were on their last legs. His allegations had become outlandish—against former army chief of staff and secretary of state George Marshall, against the State Department, the army, and finally even tilting at the president. McCarthy, an unattractive figure and a drunk, increasingly discredited his own cause with these ever-wilder charges and a foolishly intemperate performance during the televised congressional hearings investigating Communists in the army. To support McCarthy at this time was not simply to take sides in the Manichaean struggle against communism (of course, many of McCarthy's liberal targets, including Marshall and Secretary of State Dean Acheson, had fought communism to far greater effect than McCarthy) but to nail one's colors to a visibly sinking mast. It was, quite deliberately, to assert a political place outside the American mainstream. It was also to partake of some of the foulness that accompanied McCarthyism, the readiness to intimidate and to victimize in a country whose laws required due process and whose essential distinction from communism was that its Constitution guaranteed all citizens freedom to think, vote, and agitate politically as they chose.

On August 3, 1948, with the Berlin airlift under way and Mao Tse-tung's Communists poised to seize power in China, the House Committee on Un-American Activities called a *Time* magazine editor, Whittaker Chambers, to testify under subpoena. Chambers said that he had been a Communist from 1924 until 1937 and in the course of his underground work had met a series of American officials. They had since risen to senior positions, he said, and he could identify them as Communist agents or resources. Among others, Chambers named Hiss, a State Department official who had attended the Yalta conference as an aide, had helped organize the conferences at Dumbarton Oaks, and had been the secretary-general of the founding sessions of the United Nations in San Francisco.

"So strong is the hold which the insidious evil of Communism secures upon its disciples," Chambers told the hushed congressmen as he described the moment he decided to leave the Party, "that I could still say to someone at that time 'I know I am leaving the winning side for the losing side, but it is better to die on the losing side than to live under Communism.' "

The confrontation between these two Americans, Chambers from the Communist underground and *Time,* and Hiss of Harvard Law School and the State Department, dramatized the issues of the Cold War for the American public in a striking and intensely personal way. Chambers and the broad cause of McCarthyism brought together the two essential figures of postwar conservatism: Buckley came late to the fray, and fed on the loyalties and resentments it had fostered; Nixon came early to the struggle, and built those resentments into a political career. Chambers was the key witness of Nixon, then a pugnacious young California congressman. Nixon had served in the navy during the war, then returned to his native state to run for Congress as an anti-Communist Republican. As a result of the Hiss case, Eisenhower introduced Nixon, his vice presidential running mate, to the Republican National Convention in 1952 as "a man who has a special talent and an ability to ferret out any kind of subversive influence wherever it may be found, and the strength and persistence to get rid of it."

Nixon had fixed upon a serious target, Hiss, about whom there was persuasive evidence of involvement in a Communist spy ring in the 1930s and subsequent lies to conceal that past. But Nixon's purpose was not simply to root out and crush the Communists. It was also to intimidate their potential sympathizers among the liberals. "Hiss was clearly the symbol of a considerable number of perfectly loyal citizens whose theaters of operation are the nation's mass media and universities, its scholarly foundations, and its government bureaucracies," Nixon concluded. "They are of a mind-set, as doctrinaire as those on the extreme right, which makes them singularly vulnerable to the Communist popular front appeal under the banner of social justice. In the time of the Hiss case they were 'patsies' for the Communist line."

Nixon and Buckley were at one in their anticommunism and their urge to crush the liberals. Where they differed, in addition to the timing of their plunge into McCarthyism, was that Nixon saw his future in the political mainstream, which meant edging to the center, while Buckley took his stand on the Right and challenged and chivied the party to join him. His vehicle was the *National Review,* a conservative magazine whose first issue claimed, "It stands athwart history, yelling Stop."

It was financed with $100,000 of Buckley family money, which had also helped subsidize the publicity tour for *God and Man at Yale,* and also by some wealthy conservative backers, who raised another $200,000. These supporters included the textile magnate Roger Milliken (a member of the John Birch Society), the Houston oilman (and a former editor on the *Yale Daily News*) Lloyd Smith, and a Wall Street financier, Jeremiah Milbank. Perhaps the most unusual backer was the former left-wing screenwriter for the Marx Brothers, Morrie Ryskind, who had been converted to conservatism during Hollywood's struggles with McCarthyism. Buckley's financial backers in the 1950s were to become Goldwater's bankrollers in the 1960s and Reagan's supporters in the 1970s and 1980s. The *National Review*'s lawyer, Bill Casey, was to become Reagan's head of the CIA.

Lively, irreverent, and catholic in the sense that it was hospitable to most causes on the Right, the *National Review* took some time to prosper. Its circulation rose swiftly to eighteen thousand a week, dropped back to fourteen thousand in late 1956 as Eisenhower was being triumphantly reelected, and then began a steady climb to success. By 1961, its circulation was 54,000, chicken feed to *Time* magazine's weekly sale of 4 million, but growing steadily thanks to such ploys as sending sample copies to everyone who wrote a condolence letter to Senator McCarthy's widow. In 1961, the rising star of the Right, Senator Barry Goldwater of Arizona, wrote an appeal that brought another seven thousand new subscribers. By 1964, the *National Review* had a circulation of ninety thousand.

There were some limits to Buckley's conservative tolerance. Anti-Semitism was one, and after a long silence, he finally condemned the "crackpot" leader of the John Birch Society. His friendship with Bozell began to disintegrate after he refused to publish Bozell's call for a preemptive nuclear war against the Soviet Union. And yet as the ghostwriter of Goldwater's bestselling and influential book *Conscience of a Conservative,* Bozell embodied the influence the clever young men of Yale were to have on the wider politics of conservatism. Bozell, who developed mental problems, also helped pioneer what was to become another salient feature of the modern Right, violent attacks on abortion clinics.

The *National Review* became a nursery of literary as well as conservative talent. Joan Didion and Garry Wills were first published in its pages. An array of speechwriters came from its stable, from Bozell to Buckley himself (who wrote speeches for Goldwater) to Tony Dolan, who was to write Reagan's "Evil Empire" speech. George F. Will, the magazine's Washington columnist in the 1970s, went on to become the laureate of the Reagan White House. When Reagan won the 1980 election, Will noted, "All great Biblical stories begin with Genesis. And before there was Reagan, there was Goldwater, and before there was Goldwater there was the *National Review,* and before that there was Bill Buckley with a spark in his mind, and the spark in 1980 has become a conflagration."

"Buckley was the spiritual father of the movement," recalled Pat Buchanan, who served both Nixon and Reagan in the White House before running for the presidency himself. "To the conservatives of the silent generation, he was a real beacon. He was as responsible as anyone else for my being part of the conservative movement. I read TNR, and that's the first magazine I took an interest in. It expressed, with a sense of humor and intelligence and wit, exactly the things I felt I believed."

The conservative triumph required more than Buckley and his magazine. Perhaps the most important development came during the 1948 Democratic convention, when the radical young mayor of Minneapolis, Hubert Humphrey, forced into the party platform a firm commitment to civil rights. The delegations of Mississippi and Alabama marched out of the convention, brandishing a Confederate flag, and instantly formed the new Dixiecrat party, led by Strom Thurmond of South Carolina as their presidential nominee. Truman held most of the South, but in an ominous foretaste of the future, the Dixiecrats carried Alabama, Mississippi, Louisiana, and South Carolina. This threatened the very base of Roosevelt's grand coalition of labor, the South, and the industrial states. If the southern white vote could be seduced from the Democratic loyalties that had lasted since the Civil War, the Republicans could hope for a dominant and lasting political majority.

The Democratic administrations of the 1960s, to their great credit, enacted the civil rights legislation that gave southern blacks the real, rather than the nominal, right to vote, and lost their electoral bastion as southern white voters began to abandon the Democratic party. Some of them, like George Wallace, argued that with the desegregation of schools and civil rights legislation, they had been abandoned by the Democratic party. No instant landslide resulted; rather, the slow, jolting movements of a tectonic plate. In 1964, Georgia, South Carolina, Alabama, Mississippi, and Louisiana went to

William F. Buckley, Jr., and American Conservatism

Barry Goldwater. In 1968, George Wallace won Georgia, Alabama, Mississippi, Louisiana, and Arkansas. In 1972, all the southern states went to Nixon. The Democratic vote remained more loyal in state and congressional elections, but by 1994, the Republicans had a majority of the congressmen, senators, and governors of the Old South.

This process was due not simply to racism on the part of white voters. There was also a deep religious current at work. The ban on school prayer, the legalization of abortion, the spread of pornography that followed the erosion of censorship, and then the acceptance of gay rights were all endorsed (like the South's desegregation) by the Supreme Court. All these liberal reforms helped to push Baptists and fundamentalist Christians into the conservative camp and created the Christian Coalition. "It is the great successes of secular and liberal forces, principally operating through the specific agency of the courts, that has in large measure created the issues on which the Fundamentalists have managed to achieve what influence they have," noted Harvard professor Nathan Glazer, who was himself to embody the third important tributary that swelled the conservative tide.

A handful of New York intellectuals, most of them Jewish and graduates of City College of New York, where they had been Communists and Trotskyists in the 1930s, moved decisively to the Right in the course of the late 1960s. The heated rhetoric for Black Power, which broke the traditional civil rights alliance between blacks and Jews, was one factor. The extremes of the anti-Vietnam movement on the campuses, blocking free speech for supporters of the war and holding the universities hostage to their demonstrations, was another. The threat to Israel by the terrorism of the early Palestine Liberation Organization was yet another. Perhaps advancing age also played a part, along with the palpable failures of the classic government interventionist policies of the 1960s Great Society programs to eradicate poverty. But the rightward drift of intellectuals like Nathan Glazer, Irving Kristol, Seymour Martin Lipset, Norman Podhoretz, Daniel Bell, and Daniel Patrick Moynihan not only strengthened the intellectual firepower of the Right; it demoralized many liberals, as well.

Buckley was not a part of this movement, which in a way made him redundant as the thinking conservative. But he had already begun to withdraw from the fray. After Buckley was squeezed out of the Goldwater campaign by the candidate's jealous Arizona loyalists, he became more gadfly than leader. He ran, rather flippantly, for the New York mayoralty in 1965, and when asked what his first act would be if elected, he replied, "Demand a recount." Offered the chance to run for the Senate from New York as a conservative in a three-way race with a Democrat and a liberal Republican, he passed the chance to his brother, who was elected. He became a television personality, the quick-witted and sharp-tongued man of the Right, always a guarantee of entertainment in his public mud-slinging matches with left-winger Gore Vidal. "No other act can project simultaneous hints that he is in the act of playing Commodore of the Yacht Club, Joseph Goebbels, Robert Mitchum, Maverick, Savonarola, the nice prep school kid next door, and the snows of yesteryear," quipped Norman Mailer.

It was better showbiz than politics. But then in a sense, Buckley had won, or at least accomplished what he had set out to achieve. By 1964, the conservatives dominated the Republican party, routing the traditional liberal patricians of the Northeast, and by 1968, Nixon had won the White House. Buckley was influential, as a networker who had helped arrange the inclusion of Henry Kissinger in the Nixon team, and remained influential when Reagan won in 1980, at which time he was offered several jobs, including ambassador to the United Nations and head of the U.S. Information Agency. He turned them down, preferring to write spy novels and languidly waspish diaries and accounts of his sailing trips. A project he had launched in 1960, to write the great book on modern conservatism, has never been completed.

In a fundamental sense, Buckley's victory was hollow. The Reagan revolution was a fiscal fraud. Having assaulted the Democrats as the party of "tax and spend" and having vowed to reverse the tide, Reagan's Republicans became, as Senator Barry Goldwater mourned to Buckley, "the party of borrow and spend." The debt of the federal government was just under $1 trillion when Reagan was elected in 1980. When he stepped down eight years later, it was almost $3 trillion, and the annual interest on that debt was beginning to rival the defense budget as an annual charge on the taxpayer. In many ways, despite the courting by Republican presidents, Buckley's life was a long defeat. By the time America had elected the kind of president for whom he had yearned, abortion was legal, illegitimate births commonplace, states' rights had been crushed by a Supreme Court intent on equal treatment under the law, and the placid universities where his career had begun had been rocked by riots and tear gas.

By the time the conservative tide turned and the Democrats recaptured the White House in 1992, the Soviet Union had disappeared. And without that anti-Communist glue, the new Republican coalition that Buckley had done so much to build confronted its own deep divisions, between its Christian fundamentalists and its socially liberal patricians, between Wall Street and Main Street, between its populist protectionists like Buchanan and its free-market free traders. It had become a party with one foot in the country club and the other in a redneck chapel, and Bill Buckley was too fastidious, and also too self-indulgent, to feel at home in either one.

19.
Richard Bissell
and the American Spy

On July 2, 1956, the amateurish, cowboy style of the young Central Intelligence Agency changed fundamentally when President Eisenhower gave Richard Bissell approval to send the new U-2 spy plane on flights across Soviet territory. It was a cautious decision. The White House authorization was for ten days only.

"That's ten flying days, right?" Bissell asked. No, ten days from today, he was told. Two days later, having won approval from British prime minister Anthony Eden to base the planes at England's RAF Lakenheath airfield as the "First Provisional Weather Reconnaissance Squadron," the first U-2 spy flight took off to overfly and photograph Moscow and Leningrad from a theoretically invulnerable seventy thousand feet. Four days later, on the third U-2 mission over Soviet territory, Marty Knutson, a former Strategic Air Command pilot who had been trained to attack Leningrad, found to his horror that Soviet radar was tracking him, and fifteen Russian MiG fighters were following him. But they could come no closer than 55,000 feet as he flew "right over a bomber base called Engels airfield, and there lined up and waiting for my cameras were thirty Bison bombers."

This was exactly the kind of information the U-2 had been invented to acquire, hard evidence that there was "a bomber gap" and that the Soviet Union had the same numerical superiority in strategic bombers that the Red Army enjoyed in tanks, guns, and troops. But as the U-2 flights continued, each one photographing a swathe of country 200 miles wide and 2,500 miles long, it became clear that there were no other Bisons deployed at any Soviet air base. The belief that there were vast fleets of nuclear bombers had come from appalled Western diplomats who watched endless squadrons of Bisons fly over Moscow's Red Square during the May Day parade; in fact, that belief had been the result of deliberate disinformation by the Soviets. They had flown their only two squadrons around and around the same route over Red Square. There was no bomber gap.

"It was as if the scales had been lifted from our eyes and we could now see with clarity exactly what it was we were up against," recalled Richard Helms, later to be director of the CIA. "It really was as if we in the intelligence community had cataracts removed, because previous to those splendid U-2 missions our ability to pierce the Iron Curtain was uncertain and the results were often murky. We were forced to use defector information and other unreliable clues—the U-2's cameras leapfrogged us into another dimension altogether. For example, those overflights eliminated almost entirely the ability of the Kremlin ever to launch a surprise pre-emptive attack against the West. There was no way they could secretly prepare for war without our cameras revealing the size and scope of those activities."

For the next four years, until the Soviet air defenses developed the SA-2 ground-to-air missile that shot down the U-2 piloted by Gary Powers, twenty-eight missions were flown, scanning over a million square miles of Soviet territory. The plane was developed by the "skunk works" of Lockheed in the Los Angeles suburb of Burbank, under the leadership of Kelly Johnson, a brilliant and irascible engineer, whose team went on to develop stealth technology in the 1970s. (Ironically, the initial idea for stealth, which made aircraft almost invisible to radar, came when a skunk-works engineer read a technical paper published in the Soviet Union by Dr. Pyotr Ufimtsev, chief scientist of the Moscow Institute of Radio Engineering.) Built like a glider with enormous wings, the U-2 was so light and fragile that during takeoff, the wingtips had to be supported by disposable wheels. Bissell's crucial role, apart from seeing at once the potential of the idea, was to take the risk of committing $22 million from the CIA's secret funds to the skunk-works project, and to manage the project from the secrecy of his own tight-knit Development Project staff. The result, a prototype plane in eighty-eight days and operational flights within eighteen months, brought in below budget, was unprecedented in the laborious history of American military procurement.

The U-2 reflected an extraordinary example of America's industrial prowess. Edwin Land of Polaroid had to develop the special cameras, and the Shell oil company had to devise a special fuel that could work at high altitude. Extraordinarily close in its chemical composition to a popular antimosquito spray called Flit, whose chemical suppliers suddenly found their stocks bought up by the Pentagon, the first manufacturing process of the fuel led to a national shortage of the spray. The U-2 flights amassed 250 miles of film, overwhelming the capacity of the aerial-reconnaissance analysts, and transformed the nature not only of intelligence gathering but of America's intelligence structure. When the U-2 first flew, about two-thirds of the CIA's budget was allocated to covert operations. By 1990, only 5 percent of the annual intelligence budget of $30 billion went to the covert arm that produced the soft data from spies and defectors and that sought to buttress friendly, and to subvert hostile, regimes. The vast bulk, well over 80 percent, was allocated to spy satellites and signals intelligence and analysis of the hard data they produced.

Bissell, the man who achieved this great transformation, was a former assistant professor of economics at Yale. In the 1930s he was an early Keynesian and a political liberal. He had attended the elite prep school of Groton, and then Yale. He did not really fit in at either place. Although he was a keen and expert sailor, and let off steam by making difficult nighttime climbs of the college roofs and spires, he was not at all the classically dashing upperclass athlete who went off to a secret war with a martini in hand and Yale's "Whiffenpoof Song" on his lips. That was how many of the young members of the CIA were recruited, in the same way that those in the wartime Office of Strategic Services (nicknamed Oh So Social) came from a small group of corporate lawyers and Wall Street bankers, and from the Ivy League colleges. There was little alternative. Except for the counterespionage operations of the FBI, the United States had never fielded a professional civilian intelligence service until World War II. The military services had their specialized intelligence operations, good enough to be breaking the Japanese naval code on the eve of Pearl Harbor. But the war emphasized the dependence of the Americans on the British, whose own intelligence tradition dated back almost four centuries to the days of Queen Elizabeth I. The British had utterly penetrated the network of German agents in their country, then used them to convey false information to Berlin. They had also, through the Ultra system, broken the German codes and devised a complex and closely guarded way to use the intelligence thus garnered without compromising the source. Impressed and dependent, the United States based its own embryonic intelligence system on the British model, which itself reflected the hierarchies and clubbishness of the British class system. Thus, social intimacy and caste loyalty were seen as good security. Yale's rowing coach, Skip Walz, became one recruiter for the new CIA when the Cold War provoked its establishment, and Princeton's then dean of students, William Lippincott, was another. "The actions of the men who ran the CIA during the early Cold War cannot be understood without examining the web of friendships, class, and culture that made them," suggested one historian of the CIA.

Bissell was different. He did not fight with Chinese troops in the jungle like Desmond Fitzgerald, nor had he been dropped into occupied France with the OSS Jedburgh teams. Nor did he romance the exiled wife of fascist Italy's foreign minister into giving him her husband's diaries, as Tracy Barnes did. Fitzgerald and Barnes were two CIA colleagues who had gone from Harvard to Wall Street law firms. Bissell spent World War II running the merchant shipping schedules, which probably had a far greater effect on the overall war effort. After the war, his numerate and intricate mind and easy familiarity with card indexes and flow charts won Bissell an invitation to join the staff running the Marshall Plan. Then in 1952, while sailing with Tom Braden, an old Yale friend who had joined the CIA, Bissell saw the way the Agency successfully closed ranks against Joe McCarthy, who was trying to attack yet another institution by claiming to have found security risks. Cord Meyer, a young liberal and Yale graduate, had spoken on the same platforms as known "leftists" and written letters in support of groups on the subversive list. That was enough for McCarthy. But the CIA fought back and defended Meyer, who went on to become the CIA station chief in London in the 1970s. Warming to this camaraderie, Bissell joined the Agency as an aide to its director, Allen Dulles, and was then assigned to work on a covert project with an old schoolmate from Groton, Barnes, who had joined the CIA from the OSS.

The project was Guatemala, where a left-leaning reformist president, Jacobo Arbenz Guzmán, had been elected in 1950 on a pledge of land reform, which included nationalizing some of the American-owned sugar plantations. In these years before the U-2, the CIA was heavily dependent on clandestine political operations for any kind of success. Its efforts to foment unrest in the Soviet Union, Eastern Europe, and China had been humiliatingly unsuccessful. It tried to emulate the wartime effectiveness of Britain's Special Operations Executive in supporting partisan and guerrilla movements, but it was constantly outmaneuvered by the veteran Soviet counterintelligence teams. One such CIA effort, the WIN group in Poland, turned out to have been penetrated from the beginning by Soviet agents, and all the agents and airdrops fell straight into Soviet hands. Time after time, the radios of the small teams parachuted into the Ukraine and China fell regularly, hauntingly silent.

When opportunity came, as it did with the Hungarian uprising of 1956, the CIA could do nothing, even though its propaganda radio service had given the Hungarians the tragically mistaken impression that the West would not let them down. Soviet military power, and the risk of escalation to war, forced the West to hold back, even as it listened to the final appeals that turned into curses from the radios of the Hungarian freedom fighters. Frank Wisner, the CIA's deputy chief, who had boasted that his propaganda service was "a mighty Wurlitzer," stood helplessly by in Vienna, confronted by the utter amateurism of his service. He had not a single Hungarian-speaking case officer at hand, no guns to send, no idea of where or to whom they might be sent, and orders from Washington "not to incite to action."

When the CIA did manage to sustain a secret army in the field to sabotage and attach Communist regimes, it found new embarrassments. The force commanded by Li Mi, a local warlord on the Burmese-Chinese border, made two ineffective forays into Yünnan province, each time betrayed by his radio operator in Bangkok, a Chinese agent who worked for the CIA's covert airline, Overseas Southeast Asia Supply Company. Disheartened, Li Mi's men turned to the safer and more lucrative work of producing opium.

Most of the intelligence the CIA was able to provide came from its liaison with allies, particularly the British, and from its subsidies to Reinhard Gehlen's organization based in Pullach, West Germany. Gehlen had run the Wehrmacht's military intelligence operations against the Red Army, and in April 1945, he arranged to sell his files and his services to the Americans in return for protection. The first independent success that the CIA could claim was its hastily organized propaganda effort with covert cash subsidies to friendly parties that helped prevent the Communists from prevailing in the 1948 Italian elections. The CIA was never short of money in Europe, using unvouchered slush funds from the $200 million a year in local currencies that Europeans repaid to the United States under the rules of Marshall Plan aid. But with Communist regimes installed in a solid Eurasian belt from the frontier of divided Germany across Russia and China to the Pacific, Italy's manipulated election was but small consolation.

Then came a breakthrough. In 1951, a nationalist reformer, Mohammed Mossadegh, became premier of Iran, tried to reduce the power of the Shah (who later fled the country), and nationalized Britain's main oil supply. Britain's Labour government failed to get American support for some traditional gunboat diplomacy against Iran. Dean Acheson, then secretary of state, refused the support, warning of the dangers of Soviet intervention, Communist coups in Tehran, and disturbances throughout the Middle East, and virtually forced the British to continue fruitless negotiations with Iran. But when Eisenhower won the 1952 election, he appointed as his secretary of state John Foster Dulles, brother of the CIA director. A Cold War hawk, Dulles spoke of "rolling back" the Soviet dominance of Eastern Europe.

So Britain tried again, in the person of C. M. "Monty" Woodhouse, a senior official in British intelligence, who reckoned that the new administration would be more amenable. "The Americans were more likely to work with us if they saw the problem as one of containing Communism rather than restoring the position of the Anglo-Iranian Oil Company," he explained. So it proved. With the support of Dulles and the CIA, an Anglo-American covert operation succeeded in toppling Mossadegh and restoring the Shah. The spoils were subsequently divided in accordance with the new realities: Britain's monopoly of Iranian oil concessions was cut to 40 percent, American companies were given an equal amount, and Royal Dutch Shell and French interests shared the rest.

The Tehran coup was run by Kermit Roosevelt, grandson of Teddy Roosevelt, and was hailed in Washington and London as a triumph of the covert arts, and a success the CIA needed. In fact, it had been a confused and almost comic opera affair. The young Shah had assumed Mossadegh was an American agent all along, largely because he had been on the cover of *Time* magazine. Assured by Roosevelt that this was not so, the Shah said he would try for a constitutional dismissal of Mossadegh by the National Assembly, but he got cold feet and fled to Rome. Convinced that all was lost, Allen Dulles cabled Roosevelt to get out "at the earliest possible moment." Before he could do so, one of the bribes Roosevelt had passed around bore fruit. A team of circus strongmen started a pro-Shah demonstration, as they had been hired to do. It somehow exploded into a full-scale riot. Mossadegh panicked and fled in his pajamas. The Shah was restored and Roosevelt and the CIA were hailed as heroes.

Then came Guatemala, where the CIA first recruited a small force of 150 men. They were based and trained just across the border in Nicaragua, on a plantation owned by the right-wing dictator Gen. Anastasio Somoza. The Agency then put together a small air force and a clandestine radio station (which broadcast from the roof of the U.S. embassy in Guatemala) and began to destabilize the regime. Panicked, Arbenz ordered a shipload of arms from Eastern Europe, which convinced Washington and most of the Guatemalan officer corps that a Soviet takeover was imminent, and the Pentagon began shipping more arms to the "rebels." The *New York Times* cooperated by transferring an overly nosy correspondent, who had begun probing the reality of the rebel army, and the CIA sent Barnes and Bissell down to assess the prospects for the coup. Confident that victory was within its grasp, the CIA sent in its tiny air force to drop makeshift and ineffective bombs on the presidential palace and dispatched its army across the border. It moved six miles and stopped. The Guatemalan people failed to rise against Arbenz, and instead, he moved against his opponents in the city so effectively that the CIA's own history of the coup reported that there was "nothing left to organize" of their agent network.

Downhearted, Bissell began assembling ships to evacuate his rebel army, and Dulles informed President Eisenhower that their chances of success were down to 20 percent. Impressed by this honesty, Eisenhower authorized further covert measures, and the CIA bought two P-51 fighter-bombers for President Somoza of Nicaragua. He leased them back to Barnes's rebel air force, which began a three-day bombing campaign. The CIA's radio station stepped up the war of nerves with news of two rebel armored columns closing on the city. Convinced that the United States was about to send in the marines, Arbenz ordered the distribution of arms to the people, which, for his army officers, was the last straw. The next step was hardly subtle. Col. Elfegio Monzon was recruited when John Doherty, the CIA head of station in Guatemala City, turned up at Monzon's home, identified himself, and announced that the CIA wanted him to form the next government. The officers persuaded Arbenz to step down, and the CIA had achieved its second triumph, replete with the seductively dangerous lesson that their covert operations worked.

They had indeed succeeded, but as much by luck as judgment, and against minor players. In the process, they had radicalized an entire generation of young Latin Americans, including Fidel Castro and Ernesto "Che" Guevara, who were to inflict their own revenge on the CIA within the decade. But the CIA in particular and the West in general were doing far less well against the main enemy, the Soviet KGB. Britain's Secret Intelligence Service (SIS), sometimes known as MI6 (to distinguish it from the domestic counterespionage and security service known as MI5), had been seriously penetrated by Soviet moles since the 1930s. Kim Philby, who served as SIS liaison with the CIA in Washington and rose to become deputy head, was perhaps the best known. Donald Maclean, a senior British diplomat who furnished details of the atomic bomb to the Soviet Union, may have been more important. In 1951, with the counterintelligence operations of the FBI and Britain's MI5 closing in on Maclean, Philby helped organize his escape. While Philby's own guilt could not be proved, he was forced to resign, and the U.S. and British intelligence communities had to confront the depth of their penetration. Nor was the process over. Another senior SIS official, George Blake, who was probably recruited while a prisoner during the Korean War, remained in place until the 1960s, and later escaped from a British prison to Moscow. Blake revealed to the KGB one of the few operational triumphs the

British and Americans thought they had achieved—the tunnel dug beneath the border into East Berlin through which they could tap Soviet military telephone lines.

Perhaps because it never became hot, the Cold War drew much of its drama—and its one indisputable art form—from the duels of the espionage agencies. The spy thriller and spy film came of age during the Cold War. In retrospect, this may have had as much to do with the lifestyles of the heroes as with their exploits. With his golf clubs, health farms, and vodka martinis shaken, not stirred, James Bond summed up the glittering essence of the capitalist West with the spy as consumer and lifestyle model. The reality, best caught in the gloomy betrayals and disillusions of the characters in John le Carré's novels, was far more bureaucratic, prosaic, and complicated.

First, the espionage agencies were not very good at overall intelligence. The CIA in the 1970s and 1980s repeatedly overestimated Soviet economic prowess, and in 1983, the KGB was mistakenly convinced that the West was about to launch preemptive nuclear war. Both sides were taken by surprise when the East Berlin workers launched their spontaneous uprising (initially against increased output requirements) in 1953. Second, both sides were handicapped by the remorseless logic of intelligence, where hard choices must be made between using intelligence and betraying its source. (Blake revealed to the KGB the secret of the famous tunnel into East Berlin before it was even built. But the KGB was unable to do much about it, including using this potential conduit for disinformation, for fear of exposing Blake.) Third, the spies were the victims of their own bureaucracies. The CIA in Berlin fought its own paper war with U.S. military intelligence, to the detriment of proper coordination. And while the CIA's relationship with SIS was highly fruitful, it came with the high price of Philby and Blake. The alliance politics with the West Germans were even trickier: Heinz Felfe from the Gehlen organization, who was the liaison officer between West German counterintelligence and the CIA in Berlin, had been a KGB mole from the beginning.

The Soviets had their own difficulties, including a sharp bureaucratic rivalry between the KGB and the GRU, Soviet military intelligence, and suffered badly from political interference. The Soviets might have been more alert to the dangerous signals of worker dissatisfaction in Berlin in 1953 had the head of Soviet intelligence, Lavrenti Beria, not pulled out "all residents and operational staff" as part of the Moscow power struggles after Stalin's death. This mass recall also helped Western agencies identify almost an entire generation of Soviet intelligence officials. The Soviets were also betrayed by their own spies. Philby's treachery was balanced by the CIA's mole in the GRU, Col. Pyotr Popov. He identified more than 650 GRU agents and—in that era before U-2 spy planes and satellites—is said to have saved the Pentagon over $500 million in its scientific research programs. With extraordinary courage, he was able after his arrest to alert the CIA in Moscow that he was now being controlled by his captors. Blake's betrayals were more than balanced by Col. Oleg Penkovsky of the GRU, recruited by SIS. He provided important intelligence, particularly during the Cuban missile crisis of 1962, on the surprisingly modest scale of the Soviet missile arsenal.

On balance, and because of its repeated success in penetrating the West German government and NATO, the KGB probably won the espionage war. They were helped by the ease of inserting and recruiting agents into the open societies of the West and the difficulty of doing so in the high security states of the East. But then the sheer unpleasantness of life in the closed police states of the Warsaw Pact countries became a central factor in their eventual collapse. The price of the KGB's victory in the espionage sideshow may have been defeat in the big match. If so, it was because after Bissell's achievement with the U-2 spy plane, traditional espionage had indeed become a sideshow. The hard evidence from aerial photographs was far more useful and reliable for western policy makers than the informed assessments of spymasters. Bissell went on from the success of the U-2 to develop an even more advanced plane, the SR-71 Blackbird. It flew at three times the speed of sound and at over ninety thousand feet, and it generated such an intense heat that it had to be built of titanium, a rare metal whose main source was inside the Soviet Union. The aircraft's manufacture required the CIA to make clandestine purchases without alerting the KGB. By the time the Soviets had developed anti-aircraft missiles capable of reaching the Blackbird, the plane was being replaced by Bissell's final legacy to the CIA, the first spy satellites.

But Bissell is remembered less for the success in Guatemala and for bringing America's technological and industrial skills to bear with the U-2 and spy satellites than for the humiliation of the Bay of Pigs. To the anguish of the veteran spymaster Helms, and the surprise of most of the CIA's espionage professionals, Bissell's success with the U-2 meant that he, rather than Helms, won promotion to become DD/P (deputy director, plans) in 1959. Probably not the best man for the job, Bissell at least saw his duty clearly: "There will be no communist government in Latin America while I am DD/P," he vowed. The challenge was to repeat the success of Guatemala against the new and suspect regime of Castro in Cuba. The means were broadly similar: a secret army of exiles backed up by a clandestine air force and a radio station. But the opposition on the ground was very different. Unlike Arbenz, who had won an election and thus inherited an existing army and security system, Castro seized power after a guerrilla campaign. Castro's army was loyal as well as experienced, and it was also forewarned by the lesson of Guatemala. Moreover, as an island, Cuba would have to be invaded from the sea.

America Reborn

Initially approved by the Eisenhower administration, JMARC (the code-name for the Cuban project) was to be launched in the first months of John Kennedy's presidency. It was difficult to keep secret a project of such size and ambition. The *New York Times* first reported in January 1961 that a secret army of Cuban exiles was being trained in Guatemala. The entire plan was based on the assumption that Castro was already so unpopular that the twelve thousand men of "La Brigada," landing near the port of Trinidad, would be joined by double their number of volunteers within the first three days. If the landing failed, Trinidad was close enough to the Escambray mountain range for the force to disperse and take up a guerrilla war, supplied from the air by the CIA. On his first review of the plan, President Kennedy grumbled that the invasion sounded too much "like D-day," and he suggested landing somewhere more remote and less noisy. The landing site was moved to the Bay of Pigs, separated from any mountainous shelter by an impenetrable swamp. Deeply concerned about the diplomatic and propaganda effects of a U.S.-backed invasion, Kennedy also changed the initial plan, sharply reducing the use of B-29 bombers to destroy the Cuban air force on the ground.

Renamed ZAPATA, the transformed operation was an utter disaster. The men of La Brigada were killed or captured on the beach, while a U.S. naval task force steamed impotently by. It was one of the most humiliating defeats of the Cold War, appalling America's allies. Worse still, by convincing both Castro and the Kremlin that the Kennedy administration was intent on invasion, it persuaded Castro to accept the risk of deploying Soviet medium-range nuclear missiles on the island. The White House learned of this from U-2 overflights. When Kennedy asked how the CIA knew the missile sites were manned, a magnifying glass was brought to show the president a soldier sitting in an outdoor latrine, reading a Russian newspaper. The consequent Cuban missile crisis was the closest the world came to a nuclear confrontation, the very thing that intelligence agencies are supposed to prevent, rather than provoke. Kennedy fired Dulles, and although he had planned to install Bissell as director of the CIA when Dulles retired, Bissell had to go, too. The CIA had to be brought back firmly under White House control.

At least the other secrets of the Cuban operation had not leaked. The earlier efforts by Bissell to arrange the assassination of Castro by the Mafia remained hidden for another decade, until the CIA saw its most embarrassing secrets made public through congressional inquiry. They were already known to J. Edgar Hoover, who in October 1960 sent Dulles a memo warning that Sam Giancana, the Mafia chieftain in Chicago, was boasting to his intimates that he was involved in a plot to murder Castro and restore the Mafia's lucrative gambling revenues from prerevolutionary Cuba. The CIA provided the poison pills, but the Mafia was unable to deliver them. Bissell also arranged for poison to be sent for the assassination of the Congolese leader Patrice Lumumba, but again the operation failed. There is little doubt that Bissell believed he was acting under the orders of his president, however disguised the wording, and that he had been bedazzled by the success of Guatemala and the U-2 into believing that his CIA could perform any kind of miracle, abiding by no rules.

The results were not just a defeat for the CIA but the kind of humiliation that did the anti-Communist cause desperate harm by making the United States appear as ruthless and as morally indefensible as their Soviet opponents. The Cold War was not just a secret war between spies or a struggle to the death between two political and industrial systems; it was also a contest for world opinion. The West's freedoms of speech, thought, and rule of law should have permanently dominated the moral high ground, just as its U-2 planes and its spy satellites dominated the skies. The CIA's defeats and self-inflicted wounds, along with the wretched and disastrous war in Vietnam, were prime exhibits in that crisis of self-confidence that gripped America in the late 1960s, when its cities were periodically swept by race riots and its campuses roiled by antiwar demonstrations. The CIA, to its great discredit, became a focus of suspicion and abuse.

This had operational implications. Under political pressure, the CIA shifted its focus, relying more and more on the reliable "technical means" of satellites and signals intelligence and downplaying the human intelligence of spies and covert operations that had brought them so much grief. In the 1970s, its directors James Schlesinger (a Republican appointee) and Adm. Stansfield Turner (appointed by President Jimmy Carter) fired or retired hundreds of veteran officers. The esprit de corps of "the Company" was savagely battered, which helps to explain the later spate of mercenary moles inside the CIA, like Aldrich Ames, betraying secrets for money.

But the dependence on the hard evidence of the spy satellites carried its own problems: The intelligence obtained was only as good as the human analysis of the data. Cowed and browbeaten, the CIA came under pressure to tailor its analysis to the White House and Pentagon needs of the time. If the CIA appeared to the hawks to be underestimating the strength of the Soviet regime and its defense forces, then the politicians demanded a second opinion from outside sources. At the end of the 1970s, when the United States was humiliated by the seizure of its diplomats in the Tehran embassy and appeared to have been taken by surprise both by the fall of the Shah of Iran and the Soviet putsch in Afghanistan, the CIA took a great deal of the blame. So after the 1980 election, the Reagan administration, already hawkish toward the Soviet Union, installed a veteran of the wartime OSS and an implacable anti-Communist, William Casey, to run the CIA on the old aggressive lines. This led to massive embarrassment in Central America, where a Bissell-style secret war against the leftist Nicaraguan regime led to the new embarrassment of Iran-Contra. This seemed at times more likely to topple Reagan than the Sandinista government. The outstanding success of Casey's term, the arming and support of the Afghan mujahideen against the Soviet forces, imposed its own costs in the future when mujahideen volunteers like Osama bin Laden turned their fundamentalism back against the United States.

The intelligence services of a democracy have four main functions. The first is to gather information on the intentions and capacities of potential enemies. Thanks to Bissell's technological revolution, the CIA proved extraordinarily good at this, albeit at a current price of almost $30 billion a year. The second is to use that data to give its political leaders the information required for good policy making. At times, for example in Cuba on the eve of the missile crisis of 1962, the CIA did well. In Vietnam, when it consistently gave far more pessimistic assessments than the Pentagon, it was right, although sufficiently discredited in the Washington bureaucracy that its views held less weight than they should have. The third task of good intelligence is to support the country's friends and frustrate its enemies, and overall, the CIA has a mixed record on this score. It succeeded in helping keep Italy, Greece, and South Korea in the non-Communist camp, and it helped detach Yugoslavia from the Communist bloc. But in much of the developing world, the CIA blocked leftist governments at the price of installing unsavory, authoritarian, and often military regimes. The final duty is to protect its own service from penetration, and the CIA proved no worse at this than its British and Soviet counterparts, although the relentless mole hunts of counterespionage chief James Angleton were damaging to the Agency's morale.

In the end, the CIA can claim to have helped win the Cold War, and by reassuring both President Eisenhower and President Kennedy that the Soviet capacity to wage nuclear war was very limited, it ensured at crucial moments that the Cold War did not become hot. This was Bissell's real achievement, and it probably outweighs the damage he did to the name and reputation of the service that, but for the Bay of Pigs, he would have led. Bissell's story is the stuff of Greek tragedy. A man of great gifts, and confident like so many of his generation that a sufficient input of American men, money, and know-how could achieve anything, Bissell had a flaw: He was overconfident, thinking that what had worked in Iran and Guatemala should succeed in Cuba. And even as Bissell went to work for an insurance agency, the broader lesson of his disaster was lost on that generation he had so impressed, as they embarked with equal confidence on the disastrous operation to shore up a supportive but desperately unpopular government in South Vietnam.

20.
Billy Graham
and American Religion

Billy Graham heard the call to become a preacher beside the eighteenth green of the campus golf course of the Florida Bible Institute in Tampa in 1938. He had just been jilted by his first love, a fellow student named Emily Cavanaugh. On a solitary late-night walk, he fell to his knees by the carefully tended turf and said, "All right, Lord, if you want me, you've got me. I'll be what you want me to be and go where you want me to go."

The Florida Bible Institute also boasted a hotel, popular with the faculty of Wheaton College in Illinois, the Harvard of the Christian fundamentalist world. Having heard the young student preach at the Tampa Gospel Tabernacle, a group of them asked Graham to caddy for them the next day. He impressed them so much that they offered to finance his first year at Wheaton and then use their influence to secure him a scholarship. So again golf did the

Lord's work, helping recruit the most charismatic and effective preacher of modern Christianity.

A quarter of a century later, in the course of his long courtship on and off the golf course of the then vice president, Richard Nixon, Graham felt their relationship was sealed when Nixon sent him a set of three "Mr. Vice-President" golf balls. "How thoughtful of you. No wonder you are one of the youngest vice-presidents in history," Graham wrote back. It was one of a series of letters in which the role of pastor merged with that of political consultant and fellow cold warrior, ever watchful of the Communist menace.

"Governor Dewey said to me a few weeks ago that you were the most able man in the Republican party. He has great confidence in you but seems to be a little fearful that you may be taken over unwittingly by some of the extreme right-wingers. I think he's right!" Graham wrote in 1955. "You will have my constant prayers and I will put in a word here and there and use my influence to show people that you are a man of moral integrity and Christian principles."

"I think your political advice was right on the beam, and as you have probably noted, I have been trying to follow the course of action you recommended," Nixon replied, in a correspondence that had already reached the stage where the two participants addressed each other as "Dick" and "Billy." "Very frankly, you are in need of a boost in Protestant religious circles," Graham wrote back, and he offered to arrange a lunch for Nixon at his home in Montreat, North Carolina, with the president of the Southern Baptist Convention, the moderator of the Presbyterian Church, and a Methodist and an Episcopal bishop. He proposed to put Nixon up in a three-room suite with air conditioning, and for him to golf at an exclusive club.

Politics and golf are not normally associated with the pastoral mission, but along with an astute sense of the media and marketing, and the politics of the Cold War, they were to be the hallmarks of Billy Graham's extraordinary career. The most effective and beguiling preacher of his time, he was the first to understand fully and to exploit the new possibilities of film and television. His two crucial breaks came from that celebrated sinner William Randolph Hearst, who sent two telegrams that guaranteed him media celebrity. The first, when Graham had just been hired by an evangelical organization called Youth for Christ, went out to all Hearst newspapers and said simply, "Puff YFC," on the principle that any patriotic and God-fearing Christian movement that could bring tens of thousands of young people to its services was good for America and thus good for Hearst newspapers. YFC was duly puffed, with full-page stories wherever YFC rallies were held.

Hearst's second telegram, when Graham had become the star of the YFC team of traveling preachers, said simply, "Puff Graham." It happened in Los

Angeles, which Graham dubbed "a city of wickedness and sin" in his opening meeting, just two days after the announcement that the Soviet Union had tested its first atom bomb. This was the devil's work, preached Graham, and the great confrontation was at hand. "Western culture and its fruits had its foundation in the Bible, the Word of God, and in the revivals of the seventeenth and eighteenth centuries. Communism, on the other hand, has decided against God, against Christ, against the Bible, and against all religion. Communism is not only an economic interpretation of life—Communism is a religion that is inspired, directed, and motivated by the Devil himself who has declared war against Almighty God." And in the front line of that war would be California's City of Angels, since "the Fifth Columnists, called Communists, are more rampant in Los Angeles than any other city in America. In this moment I can see the judgment hand of God over Los Angeles. I can see judgment about to fall."

Heated as his rhetoric was, Graham's crusade in Los Angeles was at first a disappointment, with bad weather keeping the crowds away, and the local support committee suggested it might be time to fold the tent. Graham's subsequent prayers have gone down in legend among his followers as producing a miracle, a sudden change in the weather. Equally important was Graham's success in bringing back to God a hard-drinking local radio personality, Stuart Hamblen, who came to Graham's apartment drunk and left a new man. "I heard the heavenly switchboard click," Hamblen told his radio audience, and he encouraged them and his Hollywood friends to attend the meeting. Hamblen's friend John Wayne remarked on the change in his character, and Hamblen replied, "It's no secret what God can do," which he then turned into a successful country-music song. After Hearst's newspapers ran their stories, the AP and UPI news wires followed, and then came big features in *Time, Newsweek,* and *Life.* The revival became a massive success. Hollywood stars Gene Autry and Jane Russell turned up, and Cecil B. DeMille offered Graham a screen test. His career was never again in jeopardy.

Graham was a particularly attractive and articulate young man of military age as millions of American servicemen came home from the war with good reason to thank Providence for their lives, and as the country was undergoing a religious revival. Church membership rose by 40 percent during the 1940s, and Bible sales doubled between 1947 and 1952. Churches of all denominations were being built at a rate unknown before or since, spurred by the great wave of population migrating from the cities to the new suburbs, where a church became the natural and familiar focal point for a fledgling community.

"Old-fashioned Truth for up-to-date Youth" was one slogan of the barnstorming team of YFC preachers. Another was "Geared to the Times, but

America Reborn

Anchored to the Rock." They dressed in aggressively modern clothes, with neon socks and jazzy ties, sometimes wearing bow ties that lit up. Their services were infused with all the tricks of show business, with choirs of up to five thousand voices, three-hundred-piece orchestras (including "a consecrated saxophone"), and a trained horse named MacArthur, which would kneel before the cross and had learned to paw the ground three times when asked the nature of the Trinity, twelve times when asked the number of the apostles. There were pageants and exhibition races by the world-champion miler, Gil Dodds. For the welcome-home rallies for the troops, there were patriotic marches with four hundred white-clad nurses, the national anthem, drum solos amid appeals to buy war bonds, and searchlights and sirens in the sky until the arena fell into darkness for the benediction, concluded by the flaring of a great sign that read JESUS SAVES. "We used every modern means to catch the attention of the unconverted—and then we punched them right between the eyes with the Gospel," Graham recalled.

Graham had another message to deliver after his first evangelical trip to Britain and war-battered Europe in 1946—he began punching them right between the eyes with the politics of the Cold War. "Communism is creeping inexorably into these destitute lands, into war-torn China, into restless South America," he declared on his return to his hometown of Charlotte, North Carolina, for a revival meeting. "You should see Europe. It's terrible. There are Communists everywhere. Here, too, for that matter. . . . Unless the Christian religion rescues these nations from the clutches of the unbelieving, America will stand alone and isolated in the world."

It made for a heady cocktail of showbiz and politics, youth and energy, God and Armageddon. He warned "how sleek Russian bombers are poised to drop death upon American cities; how Communism and Catholicism are taking over Europe; how Mohammedanism is sweeping across Africa and into Southern Europe." And with the coming of the state of Israel in 1948, Graham's technique of using events in the news, "preaching with a Bible in one hand and a newspaper in the other," as he put it, gave him the perfect platform for warning that the end of the world was nigh. The return of the Jews to the Holy Land meant that the Second Coming was near, just as the Bible had foretold.

Although deliberately founded as a modern nation with its Constitution requiring the separation of church and state, America was unusually receptive to such appeals. It remains to this day the most devout of the Christian societies, far more constant in its churchgoing and in its religiosity than the traditional Roman Catholic lands of Europe. Nine out of ten Americans told the Gallup pollsters in 1989 that they never doubted the existence of God. Eight in ten still believed in miracles and knew that they would answer to God for their sins on Judgment Day. Four in ten claimed to have been "born again." Fifty percent believed in angels. Almost seven out of ten, 68 percent, said in 1994 that they were members of a church or synagogue, and 42 percent had been to a place of worship during the previous week, compared with 14 percent in Britain, or 12 percent in France.

In part because church and state are legally separate, America never went through the anguished strife between the clerical and the secular that marked France for more than a century after the Revolution. It never experienced the edgy tension between the papal lands and the nation that marked Italy for seventy years after the risorgimento. Americans have never suffered the persecutions that marked the church in Ireland or the fate of Catholics in England until the 1820s, or of believers in the Communist bloc, and never endured the Kulturkampf between church and state that Bismarck inflicted on his new Germany.

In a sense, the country was founded by fundamentalists, the Puritans who fled England in 1607 for the religious tolerance of Holland, and who then in 1620 joined with more Puritans from Britain for the expedition of 102 people to seek freedom in the New World. Their ship, the *Mayflower,* lost its way. Instead of reaching Virginia, where the Puritans had the promise of a land grant, they landed in what was to become Massachusetts and established the Plymouth Colony. The Pilgrims were the pioneers of wave upon wave of sects and freethinkers.

In 1687, Governor Thomas Dongan of New York reported that his city "has first a Chaplain belonging to the Fort of the Church of England; secondly a Dutch Calvinist; thirdly a French Calvinist; fourthly a Dutch Lutheran. Here be not many of the Church of England; a few Roman Catholics; an abundance of Quaker preachers; Singing Quakers, Ranting Quakers; Sabbatarians; Anti-Sabbatarians; some Anabaptists; some independents; some Jews; in short, of all sorts of opinions there are some." But the common experience of escape to a land of free religious observance did not engender a wide sense of toleration of others. The historian Richard Hofstadter, in his magisterial book *America at 1750,* sums up the Puritan experience in Massachusetts: "Harried out of England as victims of persecution, they themselves became persecutors who harried out Quakers, or worse, put them to death, who suppressed Anglicans and Baptists, until they were forced to relent by pressure from London."

The eighteenth-century religious map of the New World was a great mosaic, with French Catholics in Canada and northern New England, Puritans in Boston and Massachusetts, with William Penn's tolerant Quaker state of Pennsylvania to the south, and an established Church of England in Virginia. Scattered among them, like raisins in a pudding, were German Anabaptists and Mennonites and other fundamentalist sects, from Shakers to Ranters. It was a great achievement of the Constitution to establish the firm principle of state neutrality with regard to these religions. The state guaranteed the rights of all to worship as they chose, without endorsing the theology of any. In this, the American state was running with the current of religious development, as the children of the Puritans eased the rigors of their religious rule and the passions of zealotry slowly expired in the vastness of the new land.

"Persecution, religious pride, the love of contradiction are the food of what the world commonly calls religion," suggested Hector St. John de Crèvecoeur in his 1782 book, *Letters from an American Farmer.* "These motives have ceased here; zeal in Europe is confined; here it evaporates in the great distance it has to travel; there it is a grain of powder enclosed; here it burns away in the open air, and consumes without effect." The price of the state's neutrality, and the absence of religious wars between the sects, was the tolerance of any religious group or cult, no matter how idiosyncratic or bizarre, so long as it did not challenge the authority and prerogatives of the state itself.

Consider the curious "Mormon campaign," or the "Utah war," of 1857. President James Buchanan ordered the Mormon leader Brigham Young to be deposed as governor of the Utah Territory and sent federal troops to fight a short and nasty guerrilla war in the Utah Valley. The war ended in 1858 when Young accepted the new governor, and the president gave pardons to all concerned. One Mormon militant, John Doyle Lee, was later shot by a firing squad for his part in the massacre at Mountain Meadows, when a party of 137 emigrants from Arkansas, Missouri, and Illinois were slaughtered by Paiute Indians and Mormon guerrillas. After the Mormons at least officially eschewed polygamy in 1890, Utah was accepted into the union as a state in 1896, and an odd theocracy it remains, with one of its current senators, Orrin Hatch, a bishop of his church. The Mormon church still owns the two dominant newspapers in the state, a television station, the biggest department store, banks, and insurance companies. The abundant language schools to equip young Mormons for their overseas missionary work means not only that the Mormons are the most polylingual of Americans but that their patriotic ranks also provide a hugely disproportionate share of CIA agents.

The Mormons have made their peace with the U.S. government. Other more recent cults have not. In the Selkirk Mountains of northern Idaho, pastor Carl Franklin of the Church of Jesus Christ Christian-Aryan Nations preaches that "Adolf Hitler was simply a son of God." One of Pastor Franklin's worshipers was a former Green Beret named Randy Weaver, who lived with his family in a remote and well-armed cabin in the woods above the

Nazi church. In October 1989, Weaver sold two sawed-off shotguns to an undercover informer for the Bureau of Alcohol, Tobacco and Firearms and was arrested. When Weaver refused to turn up for his trial in 1992 U.S. marshals began stalking his cabin. They were spotted, and Weaver fired. So did a friend and fellow worshiper, Kevin Harris, killing a U.S. deputy marshal. A firefight ensued. Weaver's fourteen-year-old son was shot dead. After a night of siege and shooting, Weaver's wife, Vicki, was shot in the head and killed, with her ten-month-old baby in her arms.

The siege ended when Weaver agreed to surrender to his old Green Beret commander, Col. Bo Gritz. And in a bizarre and troubling scene, Weaver came out and requested that his old superior officer give him the Nazi salute. Colonel Gritz complied, to an ominous silence from the force of three hundred armed federal agents who had established a base below the cabin, and to cheers from a watching band of skinheads.

"You have the tyranny of a Zionist occupation government coming foursquare against a Christian, American white family," Pastor Franklin later announced in a statement after the siege. "When the Feds blew the head off Vicki Weaver, I think symbolically that was their war against the American woman, the American mother, the American white wife. This is the opening shot of the second American revolution."

Consider another curious scene, which took place in the same year in the Church of Jesus Christ in the hills above the West Virginia town of Jolo. As pastor Dewey Chafin chanted, "We are saved, sanctified and filled with the Holy Ghost," his worshipers sang, danced, jangled tambourines, and opened black boxes carved with the inscription "Jesus Saves." Inside each box was a deadly timber rattlesnake, black and sinuous but strangely calm as the chanting worshipers picked them up and brandished them before the congregation. Chafin handled two at once and began to chant in strange tongues, letting the Holy Spirit take over his voice as he fulfilled the biblical definition of those who are saved and can handle serpents, safe in the hand of the Lord.

"And these signs shall follow them that believe," says the Gospel of Mark (16: 16–17). "In my name shall they cast out devils, they shall speak with new tongues. They shall take up serpents and if they drink any deadly thing, it shall not hurt them. They shall lay hands on the sick, and they shall recover."

Gracie McAllister, her gray hair pinned up in a bun above her pink jersey, her floral skirt swaying as she danced with her rattlesnake, chanted her devotion and passed the snake to her husband, Roy. The church founder, Bob Elkins, then drank from a jar containing a solution of deadly strychnine. "Thank God, thank God," said the pastor as the serpents were returned to their boxes, and he anointed Gracie with oil as one of the saved. There was cause to be grateful: Two worshipers had died from snakebites in this church since 1945.

This is a scene that is repeated throughout the hill country of the American South. In revivalist tents across the land, preachers in the grip of the Lord lay hands upon the sick, and in the surpassing power of faith and the intoxication of religious devotion, some seem to be healed. The snake-pit Church of Jesus Christ is as legal, and as protected by the panoply of American constitutional freedoms, as the Church of the Christian-Aryan Nations, or those of Roman Catholics and Episcopalians. They are as legal as the People's Temple of Jim Jones, who moved his fundamentalist congregation from California to Jonestown in the Guyanese jungle and then took 911 followers to death with him in a mass suicide by poisoning.

These varieties of the American religious experience are the dark Christian echo of the Muslim fundamentalism that horrifies America when it condemns them as the Great Satan, or when it brought its own devout and implacable sense of divine justice to bear by bombing New York's World Trade Center. The deadly combination of guns and God are not uniquely American. They are universally human, a mark of Cain that stretches from Belfast to Beirut. But what lies at the heart of the American pathology is the unique constitutional accommodation that America has made with its own religiosity. Muslim fundamentalists, Christian fundamentalists, God-fearing Nazis, polygamous Mormons, and the Branch Davidian cult of Waco, Texas, which in 1993 lost the bulk of its members in armed confrontation with federal forces, are all free to think what they like. They may arm to the teeth, and if the state feels menaced, it is then free to blow them away with guns bought with a currency inscribed "In God We Trust." That is the American way, or at least one of its stonier paths.

The more customary course is for America's churches to cooperate with the state in a common purpose, from the education of children to the relief of poverty at home, and more generally in foreign policy. Billy Graham, whose crusades took him to Africa and India, and later to Russia and China, was almost from the beginning of his mission an important asset to his country's leaders. In the promotion of God, he was also fighting communism. He took his mission to the Korean War battlefront, where he was given VIP status by the army, to West Berlin, to Yugoslavia in 1967, to Hungary in 1977, and to Poland the following year. In the early, hot years of the Cold War, his anti-Communist rhetoric was uncompromising, and so was his political activism. When South Korea was invaded by North Korea in 1950, Graham sent a cable to President Harry Truman that read: "Millions of Americans praying God gives you wisdom in this crisis. Strongly urge showdown with Communism now. More Christians in Southern Korea per capita than in any part of the world. We cannot let them down. Evangelist Billy Graham." Shortly afterward, he sent a letter urging "total mobilization to meet the Communist threat, at the same time urging the British Commonwealth of nations to do the same."

In the course of 1951, with the presidential election a year away, Graham began to sketch out what became the political strategy of the Religious Right. "The Christian people of America will not sit idly by in 1952. They are going to vote as a bloc for the man with the strongest moral and spiritual platform, regardless of his views on other matters. I believe we can hold the balance of power," and he told a UPI reporter that he reckoned he could swing some 16 million votes.

Truman, after inviting Graham to a meeting in the White House during a Washington crusade, was not impressed. "He's one of these counterfeits I was telling you about," Truman wrote to a friend years later. "He claims he's a friend of all the Presidents but he was never a friend of mine when I was President. I just don't go for people like that. All he's interested in is getting his name in the papers."

He did, however, become a friend of President Eisenhower, after giving discreet support to his campaign, and writing a private letter to Eisenhower while he was still supreme commander in Europe, urging him to run. He then called on Eisenhower in Europe to repeat the plea. He lost few opportunities to snipe publicly at Truman. "When Mr. Truman went to war in Korea, you and I went to war in Korea whether we liked it or not," he told his congregations, conveniently forgetting his earlier telegram to Truman calling for war. "It is time for a change to clean up the mess in Washington, time for a new foreign policy to end this bloodletting in Korea." Graham did not openly call for Eisenhower's election, but on the eve of the vote, he told the press that his own survey of religious opinion showed 77 percent for Eisenhower. Once elected, Eisenhower asked Graham to participate in the ceremonies for his inauguration, which led to Eisenhower becoming the first president ever to lead a prayer in the event; the two then repaired to the White House, where Graham baptized the new leader.

This may have been the peak of Graham's political access and influence, although most future presidents took care to cultivate him. Nixon, of course, had become a close personal friend. Gerald Ford played golf with him. George Bush had Graham to stay at the White House and lead the National Security Council in prayer as the decision was taken to launch the Gulf War. John Kennedy, aware of Graham's open support for the Protestant Nixon in the 1960 campaign, kept his distance. He took Graham aback at one meeting, asking if he believed in the Resurrection and life after death. "Of course," replied Graham. "So does my church," said Kennedy, adding pensively that he didn't hear much about it in the Catholic services he attended.

The three most controversial political stands that Graham took were his campaign against the Roman Catholic candidate Kennedy, his staunch support for Joe McCarthy, and his long equivocation over civil rights. Each was in a way understandable, given the prejudices of Graham and of his main constituency at the time. Graham was not a sophisticated political thinker. He was a fundamentalist who believed literally in the truth of the Bible and in the existence of hell, and when carried away, he would preach joyously of "gravestones popping" on Judgment Day. His cosmology was simple: Communism was the Devil's work, so a fighter against communism was doing the Lord's work, even if that might require amending the Constitution to scrap that First Amendment right to freedom of speech, which the Devil's agents could use for cover.

"While nobody likes a watchdog, and for that reason many investigation committees are unpopular, I thank God for men who, in the face of public denouncement and ridicule, go loyally on in their work of exposing the pinks, the lavenders and the reds who have sought refuge beneath the wings of the American eagle and from that vantage point, try in every subtle, undercover way to bring comfort, aid and help to the greatest enemy we have ever known—Communism," he declared in a 1953 sermon on his *Hour of Decision* television series. McCarthy, the man he was defending, was to be censured by the Senate the following year.

His attempt to defeat Kennedy in 1960 was inspired in part by self-defense. Graham had been condemned by the Catholic Church as "a danger to the faith" on the eve of his New York crusade in Madison Square Garden, and the Catholic National Welfare Council forbade their faithful to attend. In a letter to Nixon, which Graham wanted destroyed but was not, he wrote, "No matter what concessions you make to the Catholic church or how you play up to them—even if you had a Catholic running mate, you would not even crack five or ten percent of the Catholic vote. . . . It is imperative that you have as your running mate someone the Protestant church can rally behind enthusiastically."

In another private letter, this one to Eisenhower, urging him to campaign more vigorously for Nixon, Graham warned that if Kennedy were elected and Lyndon Johnson then became vice president, the Catholic senator Mike Mansfield would probably become Senate majority leader, and Massachusetts Democrat (and Catholic) congressman John McCormack become Speaker of the House. "The Roman Catholic church will take advantage of this," Graham warned. Like many other Protestant evangelists, he became almost irrationally feverish over the issue, writing to Nixon repeatedly, saying that it might do more harm than good to campaign openly for him but that he would "if I feel it would help your cause." He urged Nixon to mention "the twenty countries that went Communist" under previous Democratic presidents. He drafted, but finally withheld, a lovingly supportive profile of Nixon—"the epitome of warmth, affability, and sincerity"—for *Life* magazine. When Nixon lost, Graham wrote to commiserate: "Dick—there are few men I have loved as I love you."

A crucial factor in that election was the black vote, 70 percent of which went to Kennedy, while only 60 percent had gone to Eisenhower in 1956. Kennedy's famous telephone call to the wife of the imprisoned Martin Luther King, Jr., was an important factor in that shift, in that period when the civil rights movement was exerting its electrifying moral force upon American public life. Graham responded slowly and hesitantly but finally decisively. He had initially, like most evangelists, accepted the segregation of his meetings. But then he said, as a fundamentalist Christian, he read his Bible, and concluded, "There is no scriptural basis for segregation. It may be there are places where such is desirable to both races, but certainly not in the church." In 1951, he won praise from the Christian press for a sermon in which he said, "The ground at the foot of the cross is level, and it touches my heart when I see whites stand shoulder to shoulder with blacks at the cross."

But then he went to Mississippi, where he told the *Jackson Clarion-Ledger:* "I feel I have been misrepresented on racial segregation. We follow the existing social customs in whatever part of the country in which we minister. As far as I have been able to find in my study of the Bible, it has nothing to say about segregation or non-segregation. I came to Jackson to preach only the Bible and not to enter into local issues." He anguished over the matter, but in 1952, he declared that Baptist seminaries should be desegregated, and then in Chattanooga, Tennessee, finding that his local committee insisted on segregated seating in the revival tent, he went down and removed the dividing ropes himself. By the time of the bitter 1957 crisis in Little Rock, Arkansas, he was urging the White House to enforce the law of desegregating the schools with troops, if necessary. It had taken him some time, but he got there. He was, after all, a southerner, with a grandfather who had fought at Gettysburg.

Graham was born in Charlotte, North Carolina, just four days before the armistice that ended World War I. He was the son of a devout and reasonably prosperous dairy farmer, although in later life Graham would write of "the hard red clay where my father eked out a bare existence." Both his parents were born-again Christians of a strict Calvinist type, who prayed at every meal and required their children to learn a biblical verse each day. His father also joined the Charlotte Christian Men's Club, formed after the visit of the fire-and-brimstone evangelist preacher Billy Sunday, and sometimes hosted revivalist meetings at the farm.

It was at a local revivalist campaign by Mordecai Ham that Graham and his lifelong friend Grady Wilson went forward to declare themselves born again, at the age of sixteen. At the time, this did not seem to run deep. The Charlotte Church's Life Service Band turned him down for membership as "just too worldly." It was the example of Wilson, already starting to give powerful sermons, that set Graham on his course. "I'd give anything in the world if I could stand up in front of people like Grady did and preach. That'll never happen to me, I know," he said, and went home to start practicing sermons in front of his bedroom mirror. Although Graham wanted to attend North Carolina State University, his mother insisted on a fundamentalist college. After a lucrative summer as a Fuller Brush salesman, during which time he became the top salesman in North and South Carolina, he went to Bob Jones College in the fall of 1936. It was then a nonaccredited Bible school, run on strict lines, and Graham did not much like it. Jones made an effort to keep him. "You have a voice that pulls," he told the young student. "Some voices repel. You have a voice that appeals. God can use that voice of yours. He can use it mightily." But Graham left, following his friend Wendell Phillips to Florida Bible Institute and its golf course.

From Florida, he moved to Wheaton, fell in love again, and married Ruth Bell, daughter of medical missionaries in China, whose goal in life was to evangelize Tibet. He was hired to be the pastor of a small Baptist church in nearby Western Springs, Illinois, and his reputation as a magnetic and energetic preacher won him a place on a Chicago radio station. He had to find $150 a week to pay for the airtime, but the listeners sent contributions, and more money began to come from sales of sheet music of the gospel songs he broadcast. This led to an invitation to preach at a Chicago Youth for Christ rally in June 1944, Graham's first taste of a mass audience. He had volunteered to be an army chaplain, but just before beginning the course at Harvard Divinity School, he contracted a serious case of mumps. While convalescing, with the war clearly coming to an end, he took a salaried post as a preacher and field representative with Youth for Christ International, stumping the country to organize meetings and preaching with such energy that he logged 135,000 miles and became United Airlines' leading civilian passenger.

There were three remarkable aspects to Graham's personality that help explain his meteoric rise to national prominence. He was a powerful and effective preacher; after one spellbinding address to the Georgia legislature on the demon drink, they voted to reintroduce prohibition. He was a genuinely charming and humble man, who made a habit of calling on local church leaders whenever he planned a crusade and politely seeking their help. If they opposed him, he courteously called on them to ask why, to pray with them, and usually to bring them around. He was particularly effective at this in Britain, where the established Church of England was initially suspicious of this outlandish Holy Roller, but he ended up charming archbishops and the royal family. His humility meant that he was always ready to learn, and to grow, from recognizing the moral evil of racial segregation to accepting the need to work with both Protestants and Catholics in Northern Ireland, where he was denounced by another alumnus of Bob Jones College, the Reverend Ian Paisley. "The church which has Billy Graham in its pulpit will have the curse of the Almighty upon it," thundered the voice of militant Protestantism.

Above all, Graham was honest and frugal. When he began the YFC International crusade, he called his fellow preachers together and they agreed upon his draft of what came to be known as the Modesto Manifesto. Since many revivalists had won reputations for greed and for skimming the collections, he insisted that all money raised should be audited by the local organizing community, which then paid to YFC (and later to the Billy Graham Evangelistic Association) an agreed share for administrative costs. The preacher got a fixed annual salary. He fixed his own, in 1950, at fifteen thousand dollars, a good middle-class income, standard pay for the pastor of a big urban church. The large sums that came from his television shows and his publications and the millions of dollars that came in book royalties went to his mission, which subsidized other preachers and crusades. The only occasions on which he took some of his royalties were to pay for the college education of his children and grandchildren. The Modesto Manifesto noted that the other greatest temptation to a traveling preacher was sex, and one rule stipulated that Graham and his fellow preachers should never be alone with any woman but their wives. Like Caesar's wife, God's messenger had to be seen to be above suspicion. The charges of hypocrisy that were justifiably leveled at some other evangelists never stuck to Graham.

In retrospect, his career appears to have had a greater political effect than a religious one. Despite repeated claims of stunningly successful crusades, with record numbers of people declaring themselves born again, there was little sign of any mass return to religion or the ways of godliness. Indeed, Graham's crusading life span coincided with the great American boom in pornography. He was no prude about these matters, and he was able to praise the acting in one film he saw, *Dangerous Liaisons,* some of whose scenes he found "steamy." But America had not become a noticeably more godly nation through Graham's work, and in many important ways his career paralleled a serious national religious decline. From 1965 to 1998, the number of Catholic parish priests fell sharply, from 35,070 to 21,030. In 1997, Cardinal Bernard Law of Boston proposed to close sixty of the city's 387 Catholic churches because church attendance had been declining by 2 percent a year for the previous five years. In that period, twenty-two new churches had opened in the city, all Pentecostal, serving predominantly Nigerian, Korean, and Zairean congregations. Moreover, the strikingly high figures for church attendance came under question in a 1998 survey by *Christian Century*, which compared the claims people made to pollsters with the reality in eighteen Catholic dioceses. Although half of registered Catholics claimed to have gone to church the previous week, only 28 percent had actually done so. A parallel survey among Protestants found 20 percent going to church, although 40 percent claimed to have worshiped. A Gallup poll of the same year found that among Jews, only 18 percent claimed to have gone to synagogue the previous week, a decline from 22 percent over three years.

The aspect of American religion that did prosper was the mobilization of the godly as a political force, whose power Graham had seen back in 1951 when he was musing about being able to sway 16 million votes. Religious forces animated both Left and Right. Churchmen, although not Graham, were prominent in the opposition to the Vietnam War and in the campaign against nuclear weapons in the 1980s. The Left strongly backed the Sanctuary movement of the 1980s, when hundreds of Presbyterian and Catholic congregations risked prison terms for defying the Immigration and Naturalization Service by giving Christian shelter to illegal immigrants who were refugees from the wars of Central America.

But these movements on the Left were dwarfed by the growth of the Moral Majority and the Christian Coalition, which organized openly and professionally to elect conservative candidates. And with the Reverend Pat Robertson, who had learned the lesson of Graham's television mission and built a Christian network, Graham's heirs had their own presidential candidate. There were two final ironies to this process of religious commitment to politics in a land with a constitutional requirement to separate church and state. The most charismatic and certainly the finest speaker among the Democrats ranged against Robertson was the Reverend Jesse Jackson. And the political priorities of the Christian Coalition, which campaigned so powerfully on the wickedness of abortion, required a tactical alliance with the Roman Catholic Church. Perhaps Graham's most potent legacy was that in American religion, the political need for alliance could triumph over the prejudices of doctrine.

21.
Walt Disney
and American Entertainment

On July 17, 1955, the ABC-TV network, riding on the crest of the post-war boom, ran a live two-hour broadcast, hosted by Ronald Reagan, of the opening of the Disneyland theme park in Anaheim, California. It was a glorious mess. The new freeways were jammed. Women's stiletto heels sank deep into the hastily laid asphalt. The unfinished Tomorrowland was draped in concealing balloons. Fantasyland had to be closed because of a gas leak. Restaurants ran out of food. A plumbers' strike forced Walt Disney to choose between providing toilets or water fountains. The toilets were judged more essential, and in the midsummer heat, thirst-crazed passengers on the old Mississippi steamboat staged a near mutiny to get back to dry land and buy soft drinks at the Frontierland saloon as Fess Parker rode in dressed for his television role as Davy Crockett, risking heatstroke in his coonskin hat.

America Reborn

Opening day was, thanks to ABC, and to the Disney employees with their families stationed at strategic points to wave and cheer for the cameras, a triumphant success. Within six months, Disneyland had attracted a million people. By 1960, it had 5 million visitors a year, 10 million in 1970. In the first surveys, over 98 percent of the visitors said they thought they had gotten their money's worth and 83 percent said they would come back. It was more than just fun; it was a magnificent marketing exercise, delivering the customers into a series of familiar settings from the backlist of the Disney imagination. There was the Dumbo ride, from the Disney film of the flying elephant; Davy Crockett canoes from the Disney television series and films; the Treehouse from the movie *The Swiss Family Robinson;* and rides through the best-known scenes from the Disney movies *Snow White and the Seven Dwarfs, Peter Pan,* and *Alice in Wonderland.*

Mickey Mouse and Pluto strolled through the park to greet visitors while the familiar tunes "Heigh-Ho, Heigh-Ho, It's Off to Work We Go" and "Davy, Davy Crockett, King of the Wild Frontier" played through the speakers. More than a fun fair, more than a conventional entertainment, it was designed to be a complete leisure experience. It was also a total and deeply comforting immersion into the wonderful world of Disney, which was itself rooted in profound pride in the American way of life. Its great themes came together in heavy-handed architectural symbolism. Main Street, USA, with its train station, its drugstores, its Abe Lincoln exhibit, and its ice-cream parlors, paved the way to Frontierland, Tomorrowland, and Adventureland, and it all culminated in Fantasyland, with the palace of Sleeping Beauty as its focal point. "Nostalgia jammed up against the needle-pointed promises of the future," noted *Look* magazine of that opening-day ceremony when the marines led the parade and the air force staged a flyby overhead.

"There's an American theme behind the whole park," Walt Disney told journalist Hedda Hopper in an opening-day interview. "I believe in emphasizing the story of what made America great and what will keep it great." The film to promote Disneyland, which went to every theater showing a Disney movie, boasted that such a cultural icon "could only happen in a country where freedom is a heritage and the pursuit of happiness a basic human right."

It could only have happened in California, home to the movie industry and the fastest-growing state in the nation since the explosion of the military aviation industry during World War II. While California's boom was breeding a new generation of free-market conservative ideologues, for whom Reagan and Disney were both symbols and inspirations, the industrial strategies of state and federal governments had in reality created the wealth that produced the mass middle class that was to guarantee Disneyland's success. California's power and water came from the federally funded dams along the Colorado River. Its thriving aerospace industry prospered under government research and manufacturing contracts during World War II and the Cold War alike. In the decade after Disneyland opened, California received 34.6 percent of all federal expenditure for research and development, and 36.3 percent of all Pentagon spending for the same. In 1960, the state began a mammoth public works project to ensure water supplies, and it embarked on a dramatic expansion of the state university system, which grew to nineteen campuses with over 300,000 students by the late 1970s. Until the end of California's great period of public investment with the taxpayer revolt of Proposition 13 in 1978, the state routinely spent 25 percent more per head on education than the national norm.

Disney understood part of the point when he boasted that Disneyland could only happen in a vibrant and booming capitalist economy, and in 1960, he wanted to show it off to the visiting Soviet leader Nikita Khrushchev. The U.S. government turned the idea down "on security grounds." Khrushchev was sent to the Twentieth Century–Fox studio instead, but he was so disappointed to miss Disneyland that he made an empty vow to erect an even better "Miracleland" in Moscow. The Soviet system might have built it, but it could never have re-created the essential corporate infrastructure that made Disneyland thrive. Franchising and sponsorship deals lured Bank of America, Eastman Kodak, Carnation Foods, Fritos, Pendleton Woolen Mills, and Pepsi-Cola into monopoly partnerships. TWA sponsored the Rocket to the Moon ride; Monsanto sponsored the House of the Future, all in plastic; Kaiser Aluminum sponsored the giant telescope. It was, noted the marketing industry's trade press, "A Wonderland of brand names with a captive viewing audience of 5 million."

ABC-Paramount held 35 percent of the shares in the Disneyland venture, and it had provided start-up loans and guarantees of $5 million. The combination of a television and film studio with a theme park that featured characters and modern fairy tales from the world's preeminent cartoon and animation factory produced a critical mass that exploded American culture into new forms. It marked at one and the same time both the industrialization of entertainment and the creation of a single brand that could be marketed collectively through a series of different media. It both recognized and represented the crucial fact that postwar prosperity had created a mass market with the time and the disposable income to sustain a leisure industry.

Disneyland was a giant gamble. Disney overrode the advice of his bankers, his business manager brother, and most potential investors to forge ahead and build his dream. He had to sell property, borrow on his life insurance, and mortgage himself to the hilt to do it. Even then, he would not have succeeded without the support and financial backing of ABC. So there was something fitting in the corporate dynastic heritage, as well as something telling about the direction of the American leisure industry, when a generation after ABC helped build Disneyland, Disney bought ABC in 1995.

The real meaning of Disney was defined in 1991 in a seminal *Foreign Policy* essay entitled "Soft Power" by Harvard professor Joseph Nye, who went on to become the Pentagon's main policy theorist in the Clinton administration, and the intellectual architect of its Asian policies. "Soft power," Nye suggested, "occurs when one country gets other countries to want what it wants, in contrast with the 'hard' or coercive power of ordering others to do what it wants."

From Levi's jeans to Coca-Cola, McDonald's hamburgers to Disney movies, the essence of America's new global hegemony was that the United States was not only the unique military superpower but also the dominant soft superpower, which invented the world's dreams and defined its aspirations. Nowhere was that soft power more thoroughly assembled and deployed than by the new Disney Corporation after its decision to pay $19 billion to purchase the television and cable network Capital Cities/ABC. The day he announced the deal, Disney's Michael Eisner went onto the top-rated current affairs show *Nightline* on ABC, where he commented, "Frankly, we have to be strong to be able to compete against everybody."

At the time of the purchase, Disney had revenues of $5 billion from the box office, another $3.5 billion from its theme parks in Florida, California, Japan, and Paris (not then profitable). It earned another $2 billion selling Disney merchandise in four hundred stores across the world—videos, storybooks, cheap Mickey Mouse hats, and $399.95 Mickey Mouse leather jackets.

The ABC purchase brought in eight of the country's most profitable television stations, the ABC network with its news division and its hit shows, including *Home Improvement,* the ESPN sports cable channel, and a CD-ROM publishing house. Above all, it brought synergy. When Disney's movie *The Hunchback of Notre Dame* was not doing as well as expected at the box office, Disney pulled a thirty-minute film about the film from the Disney Channel and told ABC to run it on the network, at such short notice that *TV Guide* still had the old listing. And to ram home the implications of the new management to the diehards of independent journalism at ABC News, Disney installed two vast cutouts of Quasimodo in the lobby of the ABC News building in New York.

But the toughest adaptation for ABC was to conform with the most rigorous system of central planning since Mikhail Gorbachev dismantled Stalin's old Gosplan system, which had devised and run the Soviet five-year plans. Disney required each of its divisions to develop five-, ten-, and fifteen-year plans, in keeping with the ethos of a corporation that is based on the assumption that reality can be reshaped at will by the power of imagination. Nothing, literally, is sacred. Visitors to the now-profitable Disney World outside Paris could for an extra six dollars get a Disney-guided tour of the cathedral of Notre Dame, by special arrangement with the Archdiocese of Paris, and see the very spot where the hunchback had rung the bells.

The Disney Corporation has become the heartland of soft culture's colonial realm. It is unmatched at pillaging the cultures of others to repackage them in Disney's universal vocabulary. Inevitably, much is lost in the translation. The hunchback Quasimodo became cuddly. *Crossbow* sought to reshape the Swiss resistance hero William Tell into Davy Crockett. Then came the Disney version of *Aïda,* which gave the customarily inventive Disney treatment to Verdi's music and characters. Disney stores offered *Heigh-ho! Mozart,* a CD subtitled *Favorite Disney Tunes in the Style of Great Classical Composers,* played by the English Chamber Orchestra. This included "Beauty and the Beast" à la Rachmaninoff and "Wish Upon a Star" in the manner of Richard Strauss.

"A lot of brands talk about being global," commented Raymond Perrier of Interbrand, a marketing group that specializes in brand building. "But Mickey Mouse's ears may be more recognizable than the Pope."

This global dimension was clear from the corporate earnings. In 1994, not quite a quarter of Disney's $10.1 billion in revenue came from outside the United States. By 1996, overseas earnings just topped 30 percent. That year's ten-year plan required half of the revenues to come from the rest of the world by 2006, and the ultimate market of China's 1.2 billion potential customers was one key to that process. Another was the international marketing structure that Disney has built. It invested in buying the rights to distribute Fox's *Die Hard with a Vengeance* outside the United States, a deal that earned more than $100 million in revenues. Another crucial component was global alliances with other giant corporations. By 1996, 13 percent of the sales of top toy maker Mattel came from Disney characters. Eastman Kodak estimated that 5 percent of all snapshots taken in America are snapped at Disney theme parks. Burger King's revenues rose by $80 million with the free toys and tie-ins to Disney's *The Lion King,* and McDonald's followed suit with its own linked promotion with *101 Dalmatians.*

"No company has ever had such a cradle-to-grave influence on American consumers," commented Gerald Celente, publisher of *Trends Journal.*

Put this into perspective. Include the figures from Capital Cities/ABC, and the Disney revenues were $19.3 billion in 1995, which put it at number forty among America's biggest corporations, just ahead of Boeing but behind United Parcel Service. The real giants, like General Motors, Exxon, and Ford, had revenues of over $100 billion each. But who can put a price on dreams, as packaged and sanitized by Disney, a corporation so sure of its future that it snubbed the geriatric materialists of Beijing?

Mickey Mouse faced down the Chinese dragon when the world's two most inscrutable empires staged a curious power game. Despite Beijing's threats against the Disney Corporation's ambitions to expand into the world's biggest market, that of the Inner Kingdom, the Magic Kingdom held firm and insisted it would go ahead with its controversial Martin Scorsese film about the Dalai Lama and his life in exile from Chinese-occupied Tibet. The last time the United States took on Asia, the motto of the First Air Cavalry Division in Vietnam was, "If you got them by the balls, their hearts and minds will follow." The Magic Kingdom planned to do better, by going for the hearts and minds directly. When the Beijing government in 1999 authorized a Mandarin version of the latest Disney movie *Mulan,* the soft power of Disney showed its force.

In the United States, the Southern Baptist Convention took up the cudgels, leading a boycott of Disney products for what they deemed a series of cultural offenses. The Baptists' Ethics and Liberty Commission listed twenty-three reasons "to beware the Magic Kingdom." They included Disney's support of homosexual rights campaigns, its payments of spousal benefits to gay partners, and the marketing by its subsidiaries of sexually explicit films like *Pulp Fiction, Priest,* and *Chicks in White Satin.* The Baptists also complained that Disney had dropped its annual TV show *Glory and Pageantry of Christmas* for the less overtly Christian *Tropical Santa.* The sixth annual Gay and Lesbian Day at Disney World provoked more outrage, after Disney allowed a cartoon to be screened portraying Mickey Mouse and Donald Duck as gay lovers. The boycott had some success, the Baptists claiming to have cut by 3 million the number of homes subscribing to the Disney Channel, and the Texas School Board divested its holdings of Disney stock. But Disney shares continued to be a wonder of the stock market.

This vast cultural empire, with its theme parks, its range of film, television, music, publishing, and marketing outlets, seemingly impervious to pressure from lobbies at home or governments abroad, had begun in the small Missouri town of Marceline, population 2,500. Walt Disney was born in Chicago in 1901, his father a carpenter and devout lay preacher of the Congregational Church, who bought a small farm outside Marceline when Walt was four. His family lived there for four years of Walt's idyllic, if hardworking, boyhood, until his father contracted pneumonia, sold the farm, and moved to Kansas City, Missouri. Walt's father was a stern disciplinarian and a follower of the American Socialist Eugene Debs; some of the first cartoons young Walt drew depicted the greedy capitalist in top hat pitted against the sturdy workers.

Marceline, as a golden memory and inspiration for Disneyland's Main Street, had a treasured place in Walt's imagination. "Main Street U.S.A. represents the typical small town in the early 1900s—the heartline of America," Walt explained, in that curious nostalgia common to so many of the American tycoons whose industry had overwhelmed that bucolic past. His Main Street echoed Henry Ford's Greenfield Village in Dearborn and John D. Rockefeller's restoration of Colonial Williamsburg. When Disney later built his own workshop at his Beverly Hills home, it was a replica of the family barn he recalled from Marceline. In Kansas City, he delivered newspapers, went to high school, and enlisted in the Red Cross Ambulance Corps in the last weeks of World War I. He arrived in France after the armistice, but he claimed to have gotten "a great education" in ten months with the Ambulance Corps in France. He learned something of business, obtaining a stock of German steel helmets, simulating a bullet hole in each one, and selling the helmets as war souvenirs.

Back in Kansas City at the end of 1919, he tried and failed to get work as a newspaper cartoonist, settled for work as a commercial artist, and met Ub Iwerks, who was to become a lifelong collaborator. They joined a local film advertising company, producing crude cartoon shorts, and then Walt began experimenting in his spare time with brief animated stories, Laugh-O-Grams, which encouraged him to start his own company in 1922. It slowly failed, but one project survived, the *Alice* movies, featuring a little girl filmed amid cartoon settings. He had interested a New York distributor in the idea, and with bankruptcy looming, Disney struck out for California and borrowed just enough money from his brother to send *Alice's Wonderland* to New York.

It worked. With capital of five hundred dollars, the Disney Brothers—Walt and Roy—Studio was formed in 1923, with a contract to produce an *Alice* series, of which fifty-six were made by the end of 1926, and an option to buy two more Disney series. The *Oswald the Rabbit* series began in 1927, and the New York distributor, Charles Mintz, who was backed by Universal Pictures, realized he had a hit on his hands. But Mintz, who owned the *Oswald* copyright, hired away most of Disney's staff and then offered Walt a job as an employee, take it or leave it. Walt left it, and in 1928 with Roy and Iwerks, he dreamed up a new character they called Mickey Mouse, whose distinctive voice was provided by Walt.

The first film, *Plane Crazy,* inspired by Charles Lindbergh, featured Mickey as pilot. The second was *Gallopin' Gaucho.* The third, *Steamboat Willie,* took the bold but brilliant risk of synchronizing the action to the music of the new sound technology. Back in New York to sell the idea, Walt made a deal with the distributor Pat Powers, who owned the Cinephone sound system. They launched *Steamboat Willie* at the Colony Theater, and, fighting off an attempt by Powers to poach his animators (Powers had already lured away Iwerks) and buy him out, Walt never looked back. Mickey Mouse was taken immediately into the hearts of the American public and the film industry. Mary Pickford named him as her favorite actor, and Marion Davies wanted to make a movie with him. Mickey appealed to adults as much as to children, to intellectuals as much as to working men and women, rich and poor alike. One celebrated cartoon of the day showed a crowd in evening dress emerging disconsolately from a Broadway theater and grumbling, "No Mickey Mouse."

"We have found out that they want most to laugh," Disney said in 1931. "We learned after hard lessons, too, that the public wants its heroes. Most of all we learned that the American public loves dance music." He provided all three, but emphasized the tunes, knowing that the early sound technology reproduced music better than speech. Minnie Mouse became a heroine in her own right, from the girlfriend in *Plane Crazy* and *Touchdown Mickey* to torch singer in *Blue Rhythm.* The Mickey Mouse cartoons were endlessly inventive. In *The Opry House,* made in 1929, Mickey played classical piano, Minnie sang "Yankee Doodle," and a varied animal choir mangled grand opera. In *The Castaway* (1931), a chorus line of seals danced to Mickey's piano, and a giant gorilla showed him how to play it with both hands and feet.

This relentless drive to invent new characters and new styles was driven by Disney's early lesson, from the loss of *Oswald the Rabbit,* of the need to diversify. Not that America was tiring of Mickey Mouse, who was appearing in two thousand cinemas each week and whose nationwide club had 3 million children meeting every Saturday morning. Walt had no time for the occasional critic who complained of the pernicious effect of loose dancing and suggestive scenes. "It is not our job to teach, implant morals, or improve anything except our pictures," Walt wrote in *Overland Monthly* in 1933. "If Mickey has a bit of practical philosophy to offer the younger generation, it is to keep on trying. That's what we do who make animated cartoons." Still, the rules of the Mickey Mouse Club required its members to swear, "I will be upright and fair in all my dealings with my playmates. I will obey my father and mother . . . my teachers, and strive for high marks in my studies."

Invention came also from the very cartoon form itself. Once new characters were introduced, Disney's insistence that each had to have a distinctive look and personality led easily to new cartoon heroes, from Pluto to Donald Duck to Dumbo. Whatever item was drawn had to pull its cinematic weight. Subordinate characters, and even furniture and clothing, had to learn to dance and add their voices to the carnival on-screen. So the next step was the *Silly Symphonies* series, film shorts that emerged from an argument between Disney, who felt that the action should lead the music, and his old Kansas City collaborator Carl Stalling, who thought it should be the other way around.

"The whole idea of the Symphonies was to give me another street to work on, you know," Walt later recalled. "Getting away from a set pattern of a character. Each Symphony, the idea would be a different story based on music with comedy and things." The first, *The Skeleton Dance,* came out in 1929. An enchanting macabre comedy, with skeletons' ribs used as xylophones and cats' tails as guitar strings, it offered a new artistic freedom. From its spiders playing Schubert and pelicans performing grand opera to the next Silly Symphony of the more stately *Four Seasons* Quartet, the extraordinary potential of the animated form led Disney's artists to explore ever further.

The movies were one industry whose growth and profits were left almost untouched by the Great Depression. A cheap form of escape and entertainment, and a new art form that was just entering its golden age with the talkies, the movie industry was booming amid disaster. Technology forced the pace, with Disney releasing the first two-strip color cartoons in 1931, and full three-strip Technicolor by 1935. His studio, thanks to Iwerks's tinkering, also developed the first multiplane camera, which allowed real depth and perspective into the animated form.

These new possibilities, and the soaring popularity of Disney products, led Walt to rationalize his production system and invent the cinematic equivalent of the assembly line. Instead of the simple planning session where a loose plot was devised and then a single artist assembled a team to put the cartoon together, he developed a strict hierarchical system. The old, informal Hollywood studio in which everyone worked together and where Walt claimed "anyone could run down the hall and shout 'Eureka!' " gave way to a new purpose-built plant in Burbank. A separate story department devised the plots and created the storyboards, which had to be strictly followed. Low-paid staff on long periods of probation did the hackwork in strictly defined work areas, with separate departments for coloring and for backgrounds and assembly, with little recognition or artistic challenge. Some complained they had no idea which film they were working on.

"A greater degree of specialization was setting in. The plant was becoming more like a Ford factory, but our moving parts were more complex than cogs—human beings," Disney wrote in the *Journal of the Society of Motion Picture Engineers.* The studio had become "an entertainment factory" where the inkers worked a six-day week, eight hours a day, with individual charts to record how many of the cells (celluloid frames) they had churned out each day. This stored up trouble for the future. Walt was furious when a studio party to celebrate the completion of *Snow White* degenerated into an open-air orgy as the staff let off steam after months of intense work and overtime. There was never any shortage of recruits. The Disney name saw to that, as well as the challenge of working for a studio that was constantly expanding the possibilities of both film and animation. Most of all, the Depression meant that jobs were scarce.

It was, Disney wrote in 1933, a time of "the wolf eating the Fuller Brush man at the door and good men sleeping three deep on the benches of Pershing Square." This was a curious image, inspired by the project featuring a wolf that he was to launch in May 1933. *The Three Little Pigs* was a Silly Symphony that was to enjoy a dramatic international success. Launched just as the New Deal was promising a way out of the Depression, its cheery tune "Who's Afraid of the Big Bad Wolf?" caught a national mood with its promise of a happy ending. Together with the nursery-rhyme plot of the thoughtful pig building his brick house and the weak banding together to defy the menacing wolf, it provided a potent and reassuring symbolism in its eight brief minutes.

It became a cultural phenomenon, the inspiration for newspaper editorials and political speeches, and the shared experience of over 100 million Americans. Dance floors filled when the tune struck up. Just by whistling a few bars from "Who's Afraid of the Big Bad Wolf?" or by repeating a phrase three times as the little pigs did, a common reference point was established. Coming hard on the heels of Mickey Mouse and Donald Duck, the creation of yet another national icon made Disney a unique figure. His own life, from a wholesome Missouri farm, through hard work and talent, to fame and riches, became a constant parable. For the *New York Times,* he was "the Horatio Alger of the cinema." *Fortune* magazine noted in 1934, "Enough has been written about Disney's life and hard times already to stamp the bald, Algeresque outlines of his career as familiarly on the minds of many Americans as the career of Henry Ford or Abraham Lincoln."

Popular culture and film studies were just beginning to be topics of scholarly study when Disney brought them a new focus. Marxists could discern capitalists, proletariat, and petty bourgeoisie in the three pigs. Psychologists could weigh the power of nursery archetypes. Sociologists could marvel at a form of entertainment that transcended race, class, and national boundaries. Disney took most of this with a pinch of salt, but in an article for the *Christian Science Monitor,* he wrote with approval of a newspaper cartoon that labeled the wolf as the Depression and the three pigs as Confidence, Recovery, and Hope. It was all splendid publicity; moreover, Walt was a New Deal supporter and great admirer of Roosevelt. And it brought in the money that was needed for the next great project—Disney's dream of breaking out from the subsidiary world of shorts to produce a full-length animated feature film.

Snow White and the Seven Dwarfs was three years in the making. Roy warned against the massive investment in animators. At twenty-four frames a second, a full-length feature required sufficient artists to produce more than 100,000 separate drawings. Even with the factory-style assembly line that Walt established, this was an unprecedented and costly effort, from which no revenue could be expected for three years. But once launched, Roy demonstrated his own inventiveness by crafting a series of marketing and franchise deals with other companies—based on the Mickey Mouse watch, which had saved the fortunes of the Ingersoll-Waterbury clock company—to ease the cash flow.

The result was worth it, with the songs of the Seven Dwarfs' "Heigh-Ho, Heigh-Ho, It's Off to Work We Go" and "Whistle While You Work" striking the same popular chord as "Who's Afraid of the Big Bad Wolf?" The mythic power of the old fairy tale worked its traditional magic as good struggled valiantly against evil and the little people rallied to the honorable cause. It was a plain and simple moral universe that Disney films portrayed, and all the more approachable for that. Like *The Three Little Pigs,* the film was a world-wide success, which undermined the solemn cultural portents some critics sought to invoke of a uniquely American return to the emotions and comforting myths of childhood.

There was nothing specifically American in the films he made and tales he told, Disney insisted in a 1933 essay about the nature of the Mickey Mouse audience. He aimed instead for "that deathless, ageless, absolutely primitive remnant of something in every world-wracked human being which makes us play with children's toys and laugh without self-consciousness at silly things. . . . You know, the Mickey in us."

Because film was the first mass and universal art form, and cartoons easily penetrated the language barrier, Mickey became an international phenomenon. In one jocular article, Walt noted that Mickey's fans included the king and queen of England and Benito Mussolini, but found one bastion of resistance. "Mr. A. Hitler, the Nazi old thing, says that Mickey's silly. Imagine that! Well, Mickey is going to save Mr. Hitler from drowning or something one day—Then won't Mr. A. Hitler be ashamed." In fact, Hitler was to watch and rewatch *Snow White,* whose sentimentality he far preferred to the grandiose Wagnerian operatics he hailed in public as the essence of German culture. It was to be a remarkable feature of World War II that the various leaders, Hitler, Stalin, Churchill, and Roosevelt, would all relax to Disney.

As war broke out in Europe, Disney was offering more than humor and fairy tales. In 1940, two films were released that took the animated form to new heights. *Pinocchio* was technically a more accomplished film than *Snow White,* although less popular, possibly because of what *Time* magazine called its "savage adult satire" of the greedy villain, the fox J. Worthington Foulfellow. With the unforgettable Jiminy Cricket playing the role of Conscience, it was another of what Disney's best biographer, Steven Watts, was to call "the Populist Parables." They were tales that caught the mood of the New Deal era, with its claim to be the era of the common man. The common sense and decency of Disney's heroes and heroines outmatched the wicked rich, and the underdog always beat the odds. These age-old but heartening themes may have helped explain the phenomenal success of *The Three Little Pigs* and *Snow White,* and perhaps *Pinocchio* did less well at the box office because the New Deal era was coming to a close.

In a sense, Disney was getting ahead of his audience, which became clear with the second 1940 film, *Fantasia,* a hugely ambitious project that combined classical music with stunningly inventive animation. The sequence of Mickey Mouse as the Sorcerer's Apprentice, menaced by the marching brooms, or the opening movement of Bach's Toccata and Fugue in D Minor set to flowing abstract designs that echoed the paintings of Kandinsky or Miro remain marvelous and arresting art today, sixty years after the film's release. In the same way that grand opera combines music and drama, Disney seemed to be aspiring to a new creative form.

No other Disney production aroused quite so much controversy. Most outlandish was the attack by prominent journalist Dorothy Thompson, who called it "Nazi" for its "brutal and brutalizing performance of Satanic defilement . . . the perverted betrayal of the best instincts, the genius of a race turned into black magical destruction." Walt rejected the outraged claim that he was demeaning the great art of classical music. In an address to the New York Metropolitan Opera in 1942, on "Our American Culture" (a theme he had chosen), he stressed that art was too important to be left to the professionals. "If we are to have a true and honest culture, we must be aware of the self-appointed tyrant who puts a fence around painting or art or music or literature and shouts 'This is my preserve, think as I do or keep out.' "

Despite his deliberate cultivation of the down-home, farm-boy image, Walt had become a figure of considerable sophistication. Two paintings hung in his office, a predictable Norman Rockwell and a startling Salvador Dalí. Walt liked and admired Dalí and invited him to spend time at the studio, and he delighted in taking the Spanish Surrealist, waxed mustache and all, for a ride on the miniature train at his home. Artists like Thomas Hart Benton and Frank Lloyd Wright and the novelists Thomas Mann and Aldous Huxley, recognizing a fellow spirit, gravitated to Walt's studio. Walt began hiring designers with art school training, and *Fantasia* owed much to the conductor Leopold Stokowski.

Because of its high costs, low box-office receipts, and the closure of many foreign markets when war broke out in Europe in 1939, *Fantasia* plunged the studio into crisis, just as the working conditions and increased labor organization in Hollywood provoked a strike. About a third of the studio staff struck, Disney fired some activists, including a key creative figure, Art Babbitt, and there was some violence and much bitterness. One lasting result was that some of the strikers broke away to form their own company, United Productions of America, which developed a looser artistic and more hard-edged style. Mr. Magoo and Howdy Doody were to emerge from this stable. The other development was that it transformed Disney's New Deal populism into a fervent anticommunism. Combined with the patriotism of World War II, when Disney became the most productive of all the Hollywood studios in churning out training and other films for the war effort, this suspicion of Reds at home and the Communist menace abroad proved to be a heady brew when the Cold War got under way.

In 1947, Disney testified before the House Committee on Un-American Activities that, with the 1941 strike, "throughout the world all of the Commie groups began smear campaigns against me and my pictures. . . . I feel they ought to be smoked out and shown up for what they are." He offered the FBI the full use of his studio and its facilities and was listed as an "SAC contact," an essentially honorific title that was often awarded to chamber of commerce worthies, clerics, and civic leaders. (SAC stood for special agent in charge, the head of each regional office of the FBI.) There is no evidence in his FBI file that he acted as an informer. Indeed, the FBI listed their suspicions of some of the "leftist" events he had attended in the New Deal years.

But the HUAC appearance and the FBI connection, however loose, established for some suspicious Disney critics a political pattern that they then discerned throughout his work. Cynics interpreted the American patriotism and pride that ran through so many of his films as a gigantic and artful form of American Cold War propaganda. They saw a subtle political-social agenda in the way African-Americans were depicted. Indeed, the 1946 movie *Song of the South,* now remembered mainly for the enchanting "Zip a Dee Do Dah" sequence of Uncle Remus and the bluebirds, offended many blacks. One columnist in *The Afro-American* called it "as vicious a piece of propaganda for white supremacy as Hollywood has ever produced." The National Association for the Advancement of Colored People condemned its "dangerously glorified picture of slavery." Moreover, Disney films were explicitly targeted at the family audience and portrayed an utterly orthodox view of women as dutiful wives and mothers. These social "messages," and the way patriotic themes and conventional behavior were promoted to children in the Mickey Mouse Club, made Disney an obvious target in the late 1960s when so many Americans began to question the supremacy and wisdom of the American way.

Certainly the adventure films, like *Davy Crockett—King of the Wild Frontier, Westward Ho the Wagons,* and *Johnny Tremain,* that Disney began producing in the 1950s reflected a profound self-satisfaction with the American way of life and its revolutionary and frontier traditions. And Disney's nature films, such as *Bambi* and *The Living Desert,* not only anthropomorphized the animals but also virtually turned them into so many churchgoing, child-rearing midwesterners with fur. But this was what Disney had always done. In the Depression years of the 1930s, his films reflected the mainstream populist progressivism of the time. In the Cold War era, Disney enthusiastically embraced the patriotic suspicions of communism and the cheerleading for freedom that were the commonplace political rhetoric of the day. And he did so in much the same instinctively patriotic way that he had made *Victory Through Air Power* during World War II.

Disney's political views followed the same path from New Deal liberal to Cold War conservative that was taken by many of his contemporaries, including Ronald Reagan and John Steinbeck. It was almost predictable that the politics of a young man making his way in the world of the Depression would give way to the pride and conservatism of an aging man who had achieved much and built a fortune that he wanted to protect as America enjoyed its postwar economic boom. Indeed, Disney did not change much; he described himself to his family as "a true liberal," hewing firmly to the freedoms of the Constitution, and remained a steadfast supporter of Social Security.

But these were not the passions that drove Disney. He was, let there be no doubt, a true artist, whose canvas spread steadily until it included the American way of life in which he believed so firmly. Clearly, he wanted to build an entertainment empire, and to take advantage of each new medium and possibility that emerged, from the feature films that his studio had learned to make with actors in World War II, to the pioneering films of nature, to the new possibilities of television. And since so much of his revenue came from overseas, he was a strong supporter of an American foreign policy that pushed open doors for his and other American products, as well as one that defended the free world to make it safe for American enterprise. What he really wanted to do was to make money in order to make films that would make more money, which would eventually let him build his dream of the greatest amusement park of all, "the happiest place on earth."

Walt Disney and American Entertainment

Perhaps the psychological driving force came from the boyhood memories of Marceline, and his instinctive understanding of the universal charm of childhood innocence. Perhaps also his genius to industrialize and to market nostalgia for a mass audience contained a hint of the authoritarian. His dream of the bigger and better Disney World in Florida always included plans for a residential community, whose civic rules were to prove as old-fashioned as its architecture. The essence of Disney lay in his remarkable ability to harness and develop the latest in technology in order to re-create and sustain his concept of that more wholesome and virtuous American past. In the robotics and the gee-whiz technology of Tomorrowland, in the Disneyland exhibits, and in the "Carousel of Progress" and the Skyway his engineers developed for the 1964 New York World's Fair, Disney was as much in love with America's future as he was with its past.

22.
Richard Nixon
and the American Retreat

The United States suffered few important defeats during the Cold War.
The apparent military setbacks at the Chosin Reservoir in Korea in
1950 and in Saigon during the 1968 Tet offensive were swiftly stabilized, if not reversed. But the decision Richard Nixon took amid the leafy
Maryland hills at Camp David on August 15, 1971, was one of three strategic
disasters that marked his presidency. The last of these, the 1975 fall of Saigon,
with its humiliating television images of the last, overloaded helicopter abandoning the roof of the U.S. embassy, followed his departure from office, but it

was a direct result of his policies and his weakness. The second, the blow to American prestige and self-confidence that came with the Watergate scandal and his abdication, hours before impeachment, was wholly his responsibility. The first great defeat, the admission that the United States could no longer afford to maintain both its prosperity and its global leadership, was in a profound sense the precursor to both Nixon's demise and the fall of Saigon. Moreover, it plunged America into the recurrent economic crises of the 1970s. At the time, it did not seem that way at all.

"We knew that we would very soon have to confront a major crisis concerning the international economic position of the United States," Nixon recalled in his memoirs, referring to a weekend session of his senior economic advisers at Camp David. The cost of the Vietnam War, combined with America's appetite for imports, had produced a balance of payments crisis that had drained the country's reserves to a critical degree. Significantly, Henry Kissinger was not invited to attend. This was perhaps the last time when an American financial crisis would not be seen at once to have strategic and diplomatic considerations requiring the presence of the national security adviser.

After two days of consultations at Camp David, Nixon announced "the new economic policy." He unveiled a stunning package, the most dramatic extension of state powers over the economy in peacetime throughout its history. He imposed a freeze on all wages and prices, a tax on all imports, and effectively took the United States off the gold standard and the world off the dollar standard. The United States would no longer make gold available for dollars for other countries' central banks. Having become the world's one reserve currency, after the 1967 devaluation of the British pound, the dollar was, in its turn, now devalued.

The result was the great inflation of the 1970s, not only because Nixon had abandoned the gold standard and devalued the dollar but also because this launched the institutionalized anarchy of floating exchange rates. Within a month of his announcement, the Organization of Petroleum Exporting Countries (OPEC) had adopted a resolution in which it agreed to joint action to restore the real value of its oil revenues, paid in devalued dollars. This was somber news for the United States, which had just seen its domestic oil production pass its peak of 11.3 million barrels per day, and which could no longer count on any surplus from its own wells. The United States was increasingly dependent on oil imports, and thus on OPEC. Imports rose from 2 million barrels a day in 1967, or 19 percent of total consumption, to over 6 million barrels a day by 1973, or 36 percent of consumption. The United States was becoming more vulnerable to OPEC pressure just as its dollar was becoming less acceptable to OPEC as payment.

America Reborn

In August 1971, the crisis was thrust upon America by its closest ally, when the British ambassador, Lord Cromer, called upon the U.S. Treasury to request that $3 billion of Britain's reserves be converted into gold, or their equivalent in exchange-rate guarantees. The significance of Britain's decision of that year to join the European Community became suddenly, acutely plain. Britain's European commitment was one thing; its apparent conversion to the long-standing French suspicions of the dollar was quite another. Britain's entry in Europe and the new financial crisis that dramatized American economic vulnerability were like the movements that precede an earthquake.

The motive of Nixon, and his treasury secretary, the Texas Democrat John Connally, was largely political: to free the American economy from the balance of payments restraints and open the way for reflation to ensure the economy was growing comfortably in time for Nixon's reelection campaign the following year. The one dissenting voice at Camp David was that of Arthur Burns, chairman of the Federal Reserve Board, America's central bank. He warned that this degree of state intervention was a mistake in itself, that the destabilizing effect on the global economy would be incalculable. But he was outnumbered. The immediate reaction of American economists was enthusiastic. "I applaud ending the fiction that the dollar is convertible into gold," Professor Milton Friedman, yet to become famous as the father of the new monetarism, told the *Wall Street Journal.* Paul Samuelson, author of the standard textbook of the day, wrote in the *New York Times,* "At last, devaluation . . . if the dollar depreciates 7 to 15 per cent relative to the currencies of the surplus countries, there will be a movement from disequilibrium to equilibrium." This was correct, as far as it went, and Wall Street rallied with a rise of thirty points.

Wall Street's relief is explained by the statistics. In 1971, for the first time since World War II, the United States recorded a deficit in the trade of manufactured goods. The 1971 federal budget deficit was $23 billion, back up to the figure that had forced President Johnson into a tax increase in 1968. The balance of payments deficit on official settlements had reached a record $10.7 billion in 1970. Europe was once more awash with dollars, which meant that the United States was exporting inflation, to the anguish of the West Germans, who found themselves with over $13.5 billion in their reserves. The Bundesbank wa 1so convinced that the United States would eventually be forced to devalue, which ould mean heavy losses for its own account. In the first hour of trading on May 5, 1971, another $1 billion had sloshed into the Bundesbank, effectively forcing the deutsche mark to float. The flood of dollars provoked the disruption in European currency markets that had led Lord Cromer to make his request.

Richard Nixon and the American Retreat

"To be perfectly frank," Treasury Secretary Connally told a restive audience of bankers in Munich, "no longer will the American people permit their government to engage in international actions in which the true long-run interests of the U.S. are not just as clearly recognized as those of the nations with which we deal."

Finally, on December 17, the major industrial nations met at the Smithsonian Institution in Washington and agreed on a wholesale revaluation of currencies. The yen was increased in value by 16.9 percent, the deutsche mark by 5 percent, and the dollar was devalued some 8 percent against gold, the price rising from thirty-five to thirty-eight dollars an ounce. This was a purely notional price, since it was no longer to be sold, even to other central banks. On the commercial market, its price immediately rose to forty-four dollars an ounce. President Nixon called this "the most significant monetary agreement in the history of the world." It lasted just eighteen months. By 1973, the world had entered the roller-coaster era of floating exchange rates. The removal of the traditional gold-dollar discipline led directly to an explosion in global money supply. The growth of global money had begun in the 1960s, when the United States profligately printed dollars to finance its deficits (which is to say the Vietnam War) without increasing taxes. The enforced dollar devaluation of 1971 made matters worse. With the Smithsonian agreement, the great inflation of the 1970s began. Between January 1, 1970, and September 30, 1974, international monetary reserves increased by 168 percent.

"In this short span of three years, world monetary reserves increased by more than in all the previous years and centuries since Adam and Eve," commented Professor Robert Triffin. In 1973, as the inflation rate climbed sharply to almost 9 percent, a new record for the postwar era, the Nixon administration began to dismantle the wage- and price-control system that had been imposed in 1971. Adding to the OPEC effect, this gave inflation another impetus, and in 1974, American inflation rates rose above 12 percent as the economy sank into serious recession. Industrial production declined by almost 15 percent, and unemployment rose to a peak of over 9 percent. Even after this recession—which saw a cumulative GDP decline of 6 percent—inflation still remained at the historically high base level of over 5 percent. A new word—*stagflation*—had to be coined to describe this theoretically improbable combination of inflation and economic stagnation.

Nixon had surrendered the dollar's grip on the gold standard and had dismantled the Bretton Woods financial system that had safeguarded America's economic predominance since the 1940s. In retrospect, it was doubtless the most important measure of his presidency. It eased an immediate crisis, but it guaranteed far more trouble for the future. Aside from the inflationary implications, and the way it provoked the OPEC oil price rise, it also deeply soured America's relations with its allies. The Europeans and Japanese felt that their own hard-won prosperity was now being put at risk to sustain an American foreign policy in Vietnam with which they did not agree. After a dramatic export drive, the German central bank saw the value of the dollars received for these exports collapse in value by almost half between 1970 and 1974, because of the steady decline of U.S. currency.

Wealth is power, as the Americans had learned and enjoyed in the golden years after 1945. After 1971, the Europeans were learning the same lesson, and using that wealth to explore a greater freedom of strategic action, even while fretting at the new American policy of paying their way through both domestic devaluation and exporting inflation. West Germany's policy of Ostpolitik, seeking to make its own settlement in Eastern Europe with Moscow, can be traced directly to the crisis of faith in the Atlantic alliance that followed this shift in American economic policies. The long, slow process toward a single European currency, because of their loss of faith in the dollar, can be traced to this moment. The clearest sign of this new European independence came with the warning of a new nuclear confrontation that helped convince both Moscow and Washington that superpower détente was not only desirable but essential.

The Yom Kippur War of 1973, between Israel, America's closest ally in the Middle East, and the Soviet-equipped armies of Egypt and Syria, suddenly exploded into a new crisis between the superpowers. The Israeli military superiority that had been so dramatic in the 1956 and 1967 wars had since been eroded. Soviet antitank missiles blunted the Israeli counterattacks as the Egyptian tanks thrust across the Suez Canal. Faced with defeat and dwindling stocks of planes, antiaircraft missiles, and artillery ammunition, Israel appealed desperately to the United States for resupply. The European allies, with the exception of Portugal, bluntly refused to let American supply planes use their airfields. For the first time since 1945, America was not able to persuade its allies to acquiesce.

This was a more dramatic example of Europe's strategic independence than the refusal to send troops to support the United States in Vietnam. This time, the Europeans refused to allow even the use of the American air bases on their soil. Their fear of an Arab oil embargo outweighed their support of American policy. At the last minute, thanks to Portugal's permission for its Azores bases to be used, the American munitions arrived in Israel. The Israeli counterattacks encircled the Egyptian army in Sinai, threatening to cut it off. The Soviet Union insisted on a cease-fire and suggested that American and Soviet troops be deployed to enforce it. But Kissinger was determined to keep Soviet forces out of the region.

Richard Nixon and the American Retreat

To warn Moscow that U.S. vital interests were at stake, the first nuclear alert since the Cuban missile crisis was declared. This was DefCon 3, the highest state of alert short of war. It involved prelaunch checks of nuclear-tipped missiles and required B-52 bombers to fly in holding patterns to be refueled by air tankers, awaiting the final order to invade Soviet airspace. This move to the very brink of war was ordered by Kissinger alone, without consulting the president, who was distracted by the latest turn in the Watergate scandal, which would topple him.

On October 20, 1973, Nixon had ordered Attorney General Elliot Richardson to dismiss the Watergate special prosecutor, Archibald Cox, who had issued subpoenas for the tape recordings of the president's Oval Office conversations. Richardson refused, then resigned. Richardson's deputy also refused when given a similar order. Resolutions calling for the president's impeachment were immediately introduced in Congress. Nixon suffered something close to a nervous breakdown, telling Kissinger that he was being attacked "because of their desire to kill the President. And they may succeed. I may physically die."

The symbolism of this moment is acute. The presidency was virtually vacant, and the national security adviser took over. Kissinger declared a nuclear alert as a diplomatic weapon in a regional crisis that was perceived purely in terms of diplomacy, strategy, and the balance of power. In fact, the real importance of the Yom Kippur War was its economic impact, which seems not to have troubled Kissinger at all, at a time when the most serious long-term threat to American interests and strategy was its cumulative economic enfeeblement. Kissinger had no peers in the media promotion of the great game of superpower diplomacy and his own masterly role within it. But in his obsession with power politics, Kissinger ignored the far more serious shift in the economic balance of forces that was under way.

The period from 1963 to 1980, bracketed by the assassination of President Kennedy and the disastrous failure of the attempt to rescue the American diplomats held hostage in Tehran after the fall of the Shah of Iran, was an extraordinary and dispiriting phase of American defeat, retreat, and domestic crisis. Its political institutions seemed unable to tackle the challenges. The politicians who tried, Martin Luther King, Jr., and Robert Kennedy, were assassinated. It was the crucial phase of the Cold War, because throughout these years the United States and the West seemed repeatedly on the verge of losing it. The postwar boom ended, the Great Inflation began, and the wondrous American prosperity machine seemed to have lost its way. In city after city—Los Angeles, Newark, Detroit, Washington, D.C.—racial riots broke out and neighborhoods burned. Campuses were in turmoil from antiwar demonstrations, strikes, and riots that themselves escalated from tear gas to the shooting deaths of four protesting students at Kent State in May 1970, after Nixon had expanded the Vietnam War into Cambodia.

The misbegotten war in Vietnam, in which neither America's allies nor, increasingly, its own people believed, was the constant, draining presence of this period of American decline. Nixon was elected in 1968 after promising a secret plan to end the war and vowing also to restore "law and order" after the campus and urban riots that had rocked the country. But the war went on, and so did the campus unrest, even after Nixon limited the reach of the draft, scaled down American participation in the war, and finally moved to a wholly professional army, recruited only from volunteers. This eventually brought an uneasy calm to the colleges, but at the expense of abandoning any serious hope of sustaining, let alone winning, the war in Vietnam. By Nixon's second term, defeat in Vietnam—and the consequent setback to American international prestige and the loyalty of its other allies—was becoming plain. The combination of economic, domestic, and military weakness provoked a crisis in foreign policy that Nixon sought to address with his strategy of détente with the Soviet Union. Henry Kissinger later concluded in his 1994 book, *Diplomacy:*

> In the Vietnam period, America was obliged to come to grips with its limits . . . the age of America's nearly total dominance of the world stage was drawing to a close. . . . Although in a strict sense, the only dominoes which fell were Cambodia and Laos, anti-Western revolutionaries in many other areas of the globe began to feel emboldened. It is doubtful that Cuba would have intervened in Angola, or the Soviet Union in Ethiopia, had America not been perceived to have collapsed in Indochina, to have become demoralized by Watergate, and to have afterward retreated into a cocoon. . . . Perhaps the most serious, surely the most hurtful, domino which fell as a result of the Vietnam War was the cohesion of American society.

Détente was an admission that the Soviet Union had reached strategic parity with the United States, and that the relations between the two superpowers had now to be stabilized and codified by treaty. The Anti-Ballistic Missile Treaty of 1972 became the cornerstone of this new international order in the wake of Vietnam, and also the first of a series of arms-control treaties that sought to manage the nuclear arms race. At the same time, Nixon sought to make up for the decline in American strength by putting pressure on the Soviet Union's other flank and opening diplomatic relations with China. This represented an extraordinary shift for Nixon, hitherto a solid supporter of the Republican party's long refusal to acknowledge the existence of "Red" China.

Richard Nixon and the American Retreat

It is explained by Nixon's perception of American weakness. The United States could no longer stabilize the world alone. It had to return to that traditional British policy of maintaining, and, if necessary, intervening to maintain, the balance of power.

"The only time in the history of the world when we have had extended periods of peace is when there has been balance of power," Nixon told *Time* magazine in an interview on January 3, 1972. "It is when one nation becomes infinitely more powerful in relation to its potential competitor that the danger of war arises. So I believe in a world in which the U.S. is powerful. I think it will be a safer and a better world if we have a strong, healthy U.S., Europe, Soviet Union, China, Japan, each balancing the other, not playing one against the other, an even balance."

Such a strategy was highly congenial to Kissinger, a professional historian of the balance of power of nineteenth-century Europe. For Kissinger, the Sino-Soviet border disputes were an opportunity for American diplomacy:

> America needed breathing room in order to extricate itself from Vietnam and construct a new policy for the post-Vietnam era, while the Soviet Union had perhaps even stronger reasons for seeking a respite. The buildup of Soviet divisions on the Chinese border implied that a Soviet Union faced with tensions on two fronts thousands of miles apart might well be ready to explore political solutions with America, especially if we succeeded in the opening to China—which was a keystone of Nixon's strategy.

Kissinger and Nixon both argued later that their strategy was succeeding and that the United States was well placed to benefit from this readjustment to its reduced circumstances, except that the Watergate crisis and the subsequent four years of the Carter presidency demoralized the country. Whatever merit the argument may have founders on the direct responsibility of Nixon for the Watergate saga, and its draining effect upon the presidency and America's international standing, as well.

Nixon is known to history as the only American president forced to resign in disgrace, after the House of Representatives, the Senate, and the broader American public all declined to swallow the most pathetic protestation ever uttered from the Oval Office: "I am not a crook." He was also the one international figure who could claim to have played an important role in both the birth and the death of the Cold War. The vengeful anti-Communist who led the witch-hunts in Congress in the 1940s had, by the 1990s, secured some rehabilitation as an elder statesman by leading the campaign for magnanimity and generosity in financial aid for the prostrate Soviet Union.

America Reborn

Born in 1913, in Yorba Linda, California, in the orange groves to the east of Los Angeles, Nixon was the second of five sons, two of whom died in childhood. His Quaker parents made a precarious living from their oranges, and in 1922, they moved to the inner suburb of Whittier to run a small gas station and grocery store. His mother's favorite, he was given piano and violin lessons and encouraged to join acting classes and the local debating club. Driven to succeed in all things, he forced his slight frame onto the football team, and in later years he would often cite his mother and his football coach as his greatest influences. He majored in history at Whittier College, a Quaker institution, and paid his way by part-time work at his father's store. He won a scholarship to Duke University Law School in North Carolina, returned to practice law in Whittier, and then became an assistant city attorney and a member of the Republican party. He also failed in his one business venture, an attempt to market frozen orange juice.

He met his wife, Pat, a high school teacher of business studies, in an amateur dramatics group. He convinced her of his determination to marry her by his readiness to chauffeur her to dates with other swains. A shy and reticent woman in public, she was a loyal political wife and a dutiful mother to their two daughters. After her death in 1993, Nixon went into a depression from which he never really recovered. They married in 1940, and by August 1942, he was in the navy, bound for the Pacific. He served in the supply and legal services, learned to play highly profitable poker, and returned to political life as a war veteran, one of "the new generation vowing to lead in peace as we did in war."

In 1946, he won a California congressional seat with this message, and in Washington he served with distinction on the committees that laid the groundwork for the Marshall Plan to rebuild Western Europe and for the wider foreign aid program. As the leading Red-baiter of the House Committee on Un-American Activities, he launched the persecution of Alger Hiss as a Communist agent.

"The Hiss case brought me national fame," Nixon recalled in his early autobiography, *Six Crises*. "I received considerable credit for spearheading the investigation which led to Hiss's conviction. Two years later I was elected to the U.S. Senate and two years after that General Eisenhower introduced me as his running mate to the Republican national convention." Nixon was the first politician to save his career through television. Almost dropped from the Eisenhower ticket after being accused of taking money from California businessmen to pay some of his expenses while in the Senate, he brought his wife, children, and family dog, Checkers, before the cameras to deny the charges. Nixon blustered in characteristic populist style that Pat "does not have a mink coat. But she does have a respectable Republican cloth coat."

And he insisted that Checkers was a gift to his daughters that he would not, as a devoted father, return. This mawkishness succeeded. The next time they met, Eisenhower put his arm around him publicly, saying, "Dick, you're my boy."

The Republicans were then perceived as the party of privilege and the country club, rooted in the upper-middle classes of the Northeast and Midwest. Nixon brought a social resentment of the patrician elite to his political career that helped make the Republicans into an acceptable party for the rising lower-middle classes just moving to the new suburbs. Taking command of the administration during Eisenhower's recurrent illnesses, Nixon became the most visible vice president of modern times. He acted as Eisenhower's roving ambassador abroad, facing down angry mobs during a Latin American tour and challenging Khrushchev over the respective quality of life of Soviet and American people in the celebrated "kitchen debate" in Moscow. Nixon's later profitable relationship with Pepsi-Cola may have owed something to his ensuring that the Soviet leader was holding a bottle of the soft drink as they spoke.

This traveling played a crucial role in one of the lesser-known aspects of Nixon's life: his strong Anglophilia, and his close personal relationship with the future British foreign secretary and prime minister, Alec Douglas-Home. They met in Africa in 1957, during the independence celebrations for the former British colony of Ghana, shortly after Britain's humiliation at Suez. Partly under Home's influence, Nixon came to the view that decolonization should not proceed too fast and should involve safeguards for Western access to strategic minerals, particularly in southern Africa. This proved important in Nixon's presidency after 1969, when the United States and, after 1970, the Heath government in Britain closely coordinated their policies toward Zimbabwe, South Africa, and Portugal's colonies in Africa.

After his defeat in the 1960 presidential election, Nixon ran for governor of California in 1962. In defeat, he snarled at the press, "Thank you, gentlemen. You won't have Richard Nixon to kick around anymore." Almost a broken man, he flew to London, where Lord Home threw a lavish banquet for him at the Carlton Club, seat of the Tory grandees, and encouraged him to stay in politics. Home persuaded Nixon to the view that a natural sympathy should develop between the Republican and Conservative parties.

Nixon's defeat in 1960 had been a narrow one, by 118,574 votes out of almost 69 million votes cast. He carried twenty-six states to Kennedy's twenty-four. Nixon, the first politician to understand television, did not woo the cameras as well as Kennedy. On the air, he sweated, failed to use makeup, and, inhibited by the secret knowledge that a CIA-backed invasion of Cuba was in preparation, sounded far less hawkish on the Cold War than did

America Reborn

Kennedy. He lost those television debates, but for his next presidential election bid in 1968, he put his image and his campaign into the hands of his supporters from the California advertising industry, the future White House aides H. R. Haldeman and John Ehrlichman. But it was the Democratic party's internal agonies and divisions over the Vietnam War and the riots at home that were most responsible for Nixon's victory in 1968.

His "secret plan" to end the war amounted to changing the color of the corpses—by bringing home American troops and replacing them with South Vietnamese—and dramatically increasing the American bombing campaign. He invaded Laos and Cambodia in the vain hunt for North Vietnamese sanctuaries, and subjected "neutral" Cambodia to merciless and secret bombing. By ending the military draft, he achieved enough of a promise of peace, and enough dilution of the student rage on campuses, to face the 1972 reelection year with equanimity. Nixon had much that was impressive to campaign on, and he faced an enfeebled Democratic party led by the dovish Senator George McGovern, who could not attract much support from the traditional Democratic sources of trade unions and patriotic blue-collar families.

The achievements of Nixon's first term were signal and in several instances historic, at home as well as abroad. He ended the diplomatic isolation of China, established the policy of détente and the structure of arms-control negotiations with the Soviet Union, and pursued what amounted to an almost-liberal agenda for domestic reform. Until President Clinton's abortive call for health care reform, Nixon was the last president to send to Congress a bill for a national health insurance system. He hired Daniel Patrick Moynihan, later a Democratic senator from New York, as a domestic policy adviser to develop a Family Assistance Program and provide a minimum federal stipend to every needy family with children. The plan was defeated in Congress, but Nixon was able to enact a revenue-sharing scheme that spread federal funds among the states, enabling them to finance their own locally run welfare systems. Under the cumbersome label of the New Federalism, it was the great domestic reform of his first presidential term.

Lyndon Johnson may have invented the American attempt at fashioning a welfare state with the Great Society plan, but Nixon was the president who maintained it, extended it, and financed it—in part by tax reforms that closed several gaping loopholes much exploited by the big oil corporations. Nixon also established the Environmental Protection Agency, the first institutional attempt to take pollution and ecology seriously. He signed the legislation that launched the Public Broadcasting Service, and despite his attempt to place two highly conservative and possibly racist judges on the Supreme Court, the federal government's affirmative action programs for hires began in his presidency.

Richard Nixon and the American Retreat

It would be tempting to describe Nixon as the last liberal president, but there was a deliberate pattern to these reforms, reflecting the one book that Nixon read twice while he was president. This was Lord Blake's biography of Benjamin Disraeli, the British prime minister of the 1860s and 1870s. Another parvenu who rose against the odds to lead the party of the rich, Nixon identified strongly with Disraeli. Above all, he was entranced with Disraeli's theory of Tory Democracy, in which the party of wealth and privilege could win democratic elections by playing the patriotic card and displaying a decent regard for the improvement of the condition of the people. In modern political terms, this made Nixon a most unusual Republican, one who believed firmly in governmental economic intervention.

In 1972, Nixon campaigned as a world statesman. He visited China for eight days and the Soviet Union for nine days, twin diplomatic triumphs that overshadowed the continuing slaughter, and the unfolding American disaster, in Vietnam. McGovern's ineffective campaign made his reelection almost a foregone conclusion, but Nixon's aides left nothing to chance. Their attempt to bug the Democratic party offices in the Watergate complex in Washington, D.C., and their dirty tricks campaign to destabilize the Democrats were probably politically superfluous. And their discovery was to prove politically lethal. Through the investigations of the *Washington Post,* then the rest of the press and the investigating committees of Congress, it emerged that a special unit of "plumbers" had operated from the White House, involved in clandestine operations. They became involved in the 1973 military coup in Chile to overthrow the elected Marxist government of Salvador Allende; in the burglary of the office of the psychiatrist of Daniel Ellsberg, who leaked the Pentagon Papers; and in the operations against the Democrats, using funds improperly diverted from CRP, the Committee to Re-elect the President.

Three startling developments turned Watergate into a national scandal. The trail the reporters uncovered from the original Watergate burglars led deeper and deeper into the White House, and *Washington Post* reporters Bob Woodward and Carl Bernstein, leaders of the journalistic pack, claimed to have found a source in the still-murky person of an informant known as Deep Throat. Various names have been floated regarding the identity of Deep Throat, from Nixon's military aide (and later secretary of state) Alexander Haig to leading Pentagon or FBI officials, or some amalgam of them all. Deep Throat's crucial advice was "follow the money" and pursue the payments to the burglars. That led back to CRP, which in turn raised the new criminal matter of misuse of campaign funds. Then Congress took up the matter, with special investigating committees pursuing their own inquiries. It emerged, almost by accident, that a tape-recording system had been installed inside the White House and that crucial conversations between Nixon and his staff in the days after the burglary might be available. Nixon refused to surrender the tapes, stonewalled the courts and the Congress, and fired Archibald Cox, the special prosecutor. This led, in turn, to the resignation of the attorney general and to the beginning of impeachment proceedings by Congress.

Nixon's presidency lingered on, his credibility evaporating as the evidence gathered that would fuel his formal impeachment. He finally resigned in August 1974. By then, his vice president, Spiro Agnew, had been forced to resign, pleading no contest when accused of taking bribes. The damage to the fabric of the American political system, and to the public's faith in the decency of its government, has never been fully repaired, even though the system worked to the degree that Congress brought Nixon's obstruction of justice into the open and forced him out of office.

In American mythology, the memory of Nixon's presidency is poisoned by his ruthless policies in Vietnam, and by the Watergate machinations, which went far enough to justify Ellsberg's claim that they amounted to "a slow coup" against the Constitution. Nixon's desperate use of his office to deflect attention from Watergate, from nuclear brinksmanship during the Yom Kippur War to a hastily arranged summit in Moscow, was shamelessly self-serving. Nixon left office still a touch defiant, although widely despised. He was soon pardoned by his successor, Gerald Ford. And in his irrepressible way, with all the tenacity of a cornered rat, Nixon began the long campaign to redeem his reputation. He began producing statesmanlike books on the United States and the world, along with self-serving memoirs. Endlessly available to his presidential successors as a discreet go-between to Russia and China, he slowly began to make himself useful, then grudgingly respected, and finally an important source of advice for Presidents Reagan and Bush.

Nixon never outlived his disgrace, but he lasted long enough to see the historians bring balance to the demonology. He also saw Reagan fulfill his own political strategy of building an American version of Disraeli's Tory Democracy, a new source of blue-collar support to widen the Republicans' appeal beyond the prosperous suburbs. And in his own contacts with Gorbachev and Boris Yeltsin, he played a minor role in ending the Cold War, which he had waged so viciously as a domestic Red-baiter when his political career began.

It was an American life that had come full circle. The self-improvement, self-reliance, and utter determination that took him from the ranks of the respectable poor to the presidency carried with it a fatal flaw. Like so many of his class and generation who benefited from the long boom of the 1950s and 1960s, the success once achieved proved hollow. Driven by some internal demon, Nixon always pushed for more. In Vietnam, he wanted peace with honor and at least some spurious claim to victory. In the 1972 election, victory was not enough; McGovern had to be crushed. In the Watergate cover-up, an early admission of error and responsibility was never an option; he wanted a blameless innocence. Instead, he plumbed a shame deeper than any other American politician, a humiliation only moderately redeemed by time and effort and a new acknowledgment of his diplomatic gifts. Even that was little consolation in his busy retirement. There was an inherent sadness to a man so self-controlled that he went walking on the beach in a suit and laced-up shoes, a sadness that accompanied an inner meanness of spirit that, in office, betrayed all the rest.

His real achievement was to have understood the degree to which the United States had been weakened by the Vietnam morass, in psychological as well as in military and economic terms. He devised a new strategy of retreat and accommodation to adjust to this weakness, hoping to use it to create a new era of stability that might endure as long as his model, the Pax Britannica of the nineteenth century. But his own faults and follies exacerbated that weakness, demoralized the nation to the degree that it could not sustain his strategy, and encouraged America's enemies to take such advantage of America's setbacks that the détente strategy itself collapsed.

The key to the enfeebling disasters he inflicted upon the country in the 1970s lay in his implacable determination to win reelection in 1972. Not only did it lead him to the political excesses that became the Watergate scandal but it also accounts for that disastrous weekend of economic policy making at Camp David in August 1971, when the global financial structure that had sustained American economic dominance since 1945 was coldly and deliberately put to death. The American median household income, which had doubled in the twenty-five years before that Camp David weekend, was to be stalled for the next twenty years. America paid a high price for its decision to elect Nixon twice to the White House.

23.
Martin Luther King, Jr.,
and American Sainthood

Martin Luther King, Jr., did not initially see, nor did he immediately seize, the opportunity that came on December 1, 1955, to transform the civil rights movement. Rosa Parks, a seamstress, was arrested in the segregated southern city of Montgomery, Alabama, for refusing to give up her seat to a white passenger. This was the cause that a handful of local activists, mainly male preachers and women teachers from Alabama State University, had been waiting for in order to launch a boycott of the city's bus service to protest its segregation. Another woman had been arrested a month earlier for the same offense, but the activists had quietly paid her fine when they realized that as an unwed mother with an alcoholic father she would not represent the image they wanted. Parks, a quiet and respectable married woman and churchgoer, who was also the secretary of the local branch of the National Association for the Advancement of Colored People, was far more suitable.

The first person in the community to be told of the arrest was E. D. Nixon, a Pullman porter in an era when that was a prestigious job for an African-American. A powerful figure in the local branch of the NAACP, Nixon had recently warned a new young preacher in town against running for branch president. He had already chosen his candidate, Nixon told the young King, who should be content with his appointment to the local NAACP support committee. (King had learned of his appointment in a letter signed by Parks.)

After Nixon heard of Parks's arrest, he made a list of local community leaders to call. King's was the third name on the list. Nixon asked if King would host a meeting the next day at his centrally located Dexter Avenue Baptist Church. "Brother Nixon, let me think it out for a while. Call me back," said King, and then called his friend the Reverend Ralph Abernathy of the First Baptist Church, Parks's pastor, whose name had been the first on Nixon's list.

King had reason for caution. With a newborn baby in the house, his wife had already advised him against taking on any new responsibilities at the NAACP. The other pastors of Montgomery were a difficult group, often personally quarrelsome and politically quiescent. "The apparent apathy of Negro ministers represented a special problem," King later recalled. But he decided to go along to the meeting. As a new figure in town with few enemies, and young enough to make another career elsewhere if this protest went disastrously wrong, and probably because of some resentment of Nixon by the other pastors, King was then surprised to find himself drafted as president of the new protest organization, the Montgomery Improvement Association (MIA). A learned and impressive son of the black middle class of Atlanta, the son and grandson of preachers, with a glittering academic career behind him and a bright future, King, at the age of twenty-six, was already a leader of the community.

"Since it had to happen, I'm happy it happened to a person like Mrs. Parks, for nobody can doubt the boundless outreach of her integrity. Nobody can doubt the height of her character. Nobody can doubt the depth of her Christian commitment. And just because she refused to get up, she was arrested. And you know, my friends, there comes a time when people get tired of being trampled on by the iron feet of oppression," King told the mass meeting that filled Montgomery's Holt Street Church and spilled into three blocks surrounding it. "The only weapon that we have in our hands this evening is the weapon of protest. If we were incarcerated behind the iron curtains of a communistic nation, we couldn't do this. If we were trapped in the dungeons of a totalitarian regime, we couldn't do this. But the great glory of American democracy is the right to protest for right. . . . We are not wrong in what we are doing. If we are wrong, the Supreme Court of this nation is wrong. If we are wrong, God Almighty is wrong."

This was the moment when the new civil rights movement began. It was rooted in Americanism, in Christianity, and in the utter conviction that whatever the local statutes of Alabama and Montgomery might say, the real law, both the law of God and the law of a righteous nation, was on the side of racial justice. This spirit, profoundly loyal to the Constitution and to a faith in an America that would live up to its ideals, infused both the strategy and the immediate tactics of the movement. And the campaign and the movement could not have happened except for a crucial decision the previous year that justified King's faith.

The Supreme Court on May 17, 1954, in the case of *Brown v. the Board of Education of Topeka,* had ruled: "We conclude that in the field of public education, the doctrine of 'separate but equal' has no place. Separate educational facilities are inherently unequal." President Eisenhower had immediately ordered the schools of the District of Columbia to be desegregated. President Truman had earlier desegregated army posts; Eisenhower now applied the same rule to all navy facilities. The signs that said WHITES and COLORED over lavatories and drinking fountains were removed. The first black secretary for the White House secretarial staff, Lois Lippman, was hired, followed swiftly by the first black executive assistant to the president, E. Frederic Morrow.

The change was as sudden as it was profound. Two years before the Supreme Court decision, Ralph Ellison had published *Invisible Man,* the classic novel of the black predicament. His hero, an idealistic young southern black who goes north to become a political activist and finds himself ignored, concluded: "I am an invisible man. . . . Invisible, understand, simply because other people refuse to see me. . . . I can hear you say, 'What a horrible, irresponsible bastard!' And you're right. . . . But to whom can I be responsible, and why should I be, when you refuse to see me?" That was the first essential point about desegregating American public schools. Black children, even in the South, would no longer be invisible.

Both the Supreme Court decision and the Montgomery bus boycott were pivotal moments. The one put the law on the side of racial equality and justice; the other evinced the readiness and the skill of a southern black community to challenge the circumstances of their own humiliation. The boycott of the transit system lasted for over a year, with King and his helpers raising money to buy station wagons for a taxi service, and maintaining the solidarity of the boycott among Montgomery's fifty thousand blacks, who normally provided 75 percent of the bus company's revenue.

The hostility of the leaders of the seventy-thousand-member-strong white community of Montgomery was intense, even though some of its finest citizens were volunteering their own time and cars to help the boycott. The civic leaders issued a statement that said: "The City Commission, and we know our people are with us in this determination, will not yield one inch but will do all in its power to oppose the integration of the Negro race with the white race in Montgomery, and will forever stand like a rock against social equality, intermarriage and mixing of the races under God's creation and plan."

Victory was finally secured by another Supreme Court ruling, which declared that segregation of public transport was also against the Constitution, which required for all citizens "the equal protection of the laws." Before the Montgomery victory was won, King's home was dynamited twice, and he was arrested, first on a spurious speeding charge and then on a charge of conspiracy in restraint of trade. The home of a white pastor, Robert Graetz, who joined the board of the MIA, was bombed twice. The constant threat of violence and the aggressive statements of the local white citizens forced King to put into action the theories of nonviolence that he had studied in divinity school. From the steps of his dynamited home, with trigger-happy police holding their guns as they nervously eyed the gathering crowd of King's dismayed supporters, he declared, "We believe in law and order. Don't get panicky. Don't do anything at all. Don't get your weapons. He who lives by the sword will perish by the sword. Remember, that is what God said. We are not advocating violence. We want to love our enemies. We must love our white brothers no matter what they do to us."

The precepts of Mahatma Gandhi, who had used nonviolent civil disobedience to challenge the British Raj in India, suddenly assumed a central relevance half a world away in the Deep South. Where a fundamental rule of law obtained, where the press was free, and where the ultimate governing authority depended upon democratic votes, nonviolence became a strategy of extraordinary power.

Evening courses were held in the churches of Montgomery. A seventeen-minute film, *Walk to Freedom,* with a commentary by King, was shown to every congregation. Leaflets were distributed around the city, with the rules of the new political game: "If cursed, do not curse back. If struck, do not strike back, but evidence love and goodwill at all times. If another person is being molested, do not arise to go to his defense, but pray for the oppressor." Reinforced by the deep familiarity of the Gospel, in which the doctrine of nonviolence directly echoed the Sermon on the Mount, the impoverished and barely educated black community of Montgomery rose to the challenge and achieved a stunning victory. Money came in from across the country and from around the world; the United Automobile Workers sent $35,000, to help keep the taxi transport running. But the organization of the routes and the pickup points that allowed blacks to go to work and to church and to lead a customary life—except for the boycott of the buses and the self-discipline displayed—was a community achievement.

Montgomery became a source of black pride that reached far beyond Alabama, and far beyond the black community, at a time when the Cold War and the gathering movement of colonial independence in Asia and Africa were imposing a new and politically charged context around the private grief of America's racial complexities. The American ambassador to Italy, Clare Booth Luce, who was married to the founder of *Time* magazine, wrote to King in January 1957: "No day passed but the Italian communists pointed to events in our South to prove that American democracy was a 'capitalist myth.' . . . No man has ever waged the battle for equality under our law in a more lawful and Christian way than you have."

Luce's admiration assumed practical force when *Time* then published a laudatory cover story on King as the American Gandhi. The *New York Times Magazine* swiftly followed, and King became only the second black American to appear on the prestigious television show *Meet the Press*. Although he had been christened Michael, King told *Time* that he and his father had chosen to name themselves after Martin Luther, the father of German Protestantism. "Perhaps we have earned our right to the name," he suggested. More than that, he had received the accolade of American celebrity, not simply as a media star but as the lead player in a subplot of the Cold War.

The Cold War was a global confrontation that took on the characteristics of a morality play enacted before a global audience. As King had been winning his doctorate in the spring of 1955, twenty-nine nations, mainly from Asia and Africa, had gathered in Bandung, Indonesia, to raise the banner of nonalignment, a kind of watchful neutrality in the Cold War. The neutrality seemed to have a pro-Soviet bent, in part because the Bandung conference supported the Soviet doctrine of peaceful coexistence between East and West, but also because of its rousing denunciation of racialism and colonialism. The United States was vulnerable on both counts, at home because of racial segregation, abroad because its key European allies in NATO, France and Britain, were both fighting hard to cling to their old empires and colonies. Although China loomed heavily over the proceedings, Bandung was also a celebration of the new nations that had lately won their freedom: India from the British, North Vietnam from the French, and Indonesia from the Dutch.

Bandung ended with a statement of solidarity for the Algerian National Liberation Front, fighting for independence from France.

With American newsstands still displaying the February 18, 1957, issue of *Time* magazine with his face on the cover, King received an invitation to attend the birth of another new nation. Ghana was the first African colony to be granted its independence within the British Commonwealth. Part of the Gold Coast of West Africa, whence so many slaves had been brutally wrenched to the horrors of the Middle Passage and lives of wretched servitude in the American colonies, Ghana's freedom had a special resonance for African-Americans. The leader of the new nation, Kwame Nkrumah, recently released from a British jail, had studied at Britain's London School of Economics and at the University of Pennsylvania, where he had been influenced by the "Back to Africa" movement of the Jamaican-born Marcus Garvey. Nkrumah invited to Ghana's independence celebrations a range of prominent African-Americans, including Congressman Adam Clayton Powell, Jr., Ralph Bunche of the United Nations, the union leader A. Philip Randolph of the Brotherhood of Sleeping Car Porters, and King. Vice President Nixon, the official U.S. representative at the event, made a point of cultivating the young preacher from Montgomery, and he invited King to the White House for private talks on civil rights.

The issue was becoming heated. On the one hand, King returned from Ghana convinced that things were changing, as he preached to his Dexter Avenue congregation on his return: "An old order of colonialism, of segregation, of discrimination is passing away now, and a new order of justice and freedom and goodwill is being born." On the other hand, when the school season opened at the end of that summer, the governor of Arkansas, Orval Faubus, sent his Arkansas National Guard into the city of Little Rock to prevent the racial desegregation of its schools. President Eisenhower eventually, after deep hesitation, sent paratroopers of the 101st Airborne into the city to enforce the desegregation law and prevent the ugly mobs from intimidating black children. Like the Anglo-French invasion of Egypt at Suez the previous year, it served to blur the moral lesson of the brutal Soviet suppression of the Hungarian uprising. And those in Eisenhower's White House knew it.

"The crude practice of racism in the self-styled sanctuary of freedom," wrote Emmett John Hughes, one of Eisenhower's speechwriters. "The tale carried faster than drum signals across black Africa. It summoned cold gleams of recognition to the eyes of Asians, quick to see the signs, in the heartland of America, of the racial enmities that had helped to make colonialism through the generations so odious to them. . . . To all peoples, in all lands, the trained and instructed voice of Soviet propaganda could relay, in almost affectionately fastidious detail, the news of Little Rock."

America Reborn

The essential feature of desegregation was that it forced a political crisis that was to transform the electoral geography of the United States. In the seventeen states where segregated schools had been required by local law, and the four states where it was permitted, the local politicians had to choose between reluctant enforcement of the new law or resistance. Those states were overwhelmingly loyal to the Democratic party, and had been since the Civil War, when Republican president Abraham Lincoln had emancipated the slaves. The Democratic South, with their solid block of votes in the House and Senate, was also the most solid building block of a Democratic majority that could win the presidency. In the South, the white power structure used every available means, from literacy tests to qualifications based on the amounts of taxes paid, to prevent nonwhites from registering to vote. Democratic presidents from Woodrow Wilson to Franklin Roosevelt had, with varying degrees of discomfort, tolerated this vicious system as the key to their election.

If King had seemed to both the publisher of *Time* and the vice president to be a useful symbol in America's wider strategic purpose in the moral confrontation of the Cold War, they had missed the point of both his radicalism and the tectonic political forces that desegregation was unleashing. Had they been in the Dexter Avenue congregation when King preached on his return from Ghana, they would have been left in little doubt of the revolutionary purpose, the militancy, and the conviction of doing God's work that now inflamed him.

He told his congregation:

Ghana reminds us that freedom never comes on a silver platter. It's never easy. Ghana reminds us that whenever you break out of Egypt you better get ready for stiff backs. You better get ready for some homes to be bombed. You better get ready for some churches to be bombed. That's the way it goes. There is no crown without a cross. I wish we could get to Easter without going through Good Friday, but history tells us that we got to go by Good Friday before we can get to Easter. That's the long story of freedom.

In one of the most powerful and challenging sermons of his life, he concluded by saying:

That's the beauty of this thing. All flesh shall see it together. Not some from the heights of Park Street and others from the dungeons of the slum areas. Not some from the pinnacles of the British Empire and some from the dark deserts of Africa. Not some from inordinate, superfluous wealth and others from abject, deadening poverty. Not some white and some black, not some yellow and some brown, but all flesh shall see it together. They shall see it from Montgomery. They shall see it from New York. They shall see it from Ghana. They shall see it from China. For I can look out and see a great number, as John saw, marching into the great eternity because God is working in this world, and at this hour and at this moment. And God grant that we will get on board and start marching with God because we got orders now to break down the bondage and the walls of colonialism, exploitation and imperialism, to break them down to the point that no man will trample over another man, but that men will respect the dignity and worth of all human personality. And then we will be in Canaan's freedom land. Moses might not get to see Canaan, but his children will see it.

King had become a preacher of remarkable and mesmerizing power, his cadences combining the stately English of the King James Version of the Bible with the vibrant rhythms of his flock. And he began to build a movement that brought a kind of beauty to the often-squalid world of politics. Blacks and whites, rough-handed union men and New York intellectuals, determined old ladies from the sharecropping fields and Jewish students, disillusioned Communists and hopeful young idealists—all came together in what became one of America's finest hours. King had warned them that it would not be easy. But if few had suspected the vicious force and the dogs and the fire hoses and the guns that white supremacists would deploy to protect their segregating traditions, even fewer could have expected the sublime determination with which the Freedom Riders and the campaigners put their bodies on the line for the cause of civil rights.

In retrospect, it seems easier and more inevitable than it really was. America had tried and failed after the Civil War to give the nominal equality of emancipation an economic and social reality. This attempt had foundered on the determined rock of southern white opposition, the ruthlessness of the Ku Klux Klan, and the skill with which their politicians bartered their block votes in Washington to dilute the purposes of Reconstruction. Those southern defenses remained in place, and they were buttressed by a new development, the mass migration of southern blacks to the cities and factories of the North and West. Accelerated by the production demands of World War II, the migration had a double and paradoxical effect. First, it meant that there were now new audiences, new sources of funds and political support for the civil rights campaign, and a new political potential in a black electorate that could register in the North with little harassment. But second, it meant that the phenomenon of American racism could no longer be dismissed as a distinctive problem of the Deep South and its history.

Moreover, the broad coalition of the civil rights movement suffered from its own internal tensions and rivalries. The NAACP had been the core organization since its genesis by white northern philanthropists, black preachers, and the outstanding black academic W. E. B. Du Bois in 1909 in the wake of a major race riot in Atlanta in 1906. King's grandfather, the Reverend A. D. Williams, a slave preacher's son who assumed the leadership of Atlanta's Ebenezer Baptist Church when its congregation numbered fourteen souls, was a founding member. What became the King family home on Atlanta's Auburn Avenue was bought cheaply during this period, after the riots provoked a white flight from the downtown area.

The NAACP believed in slow and steady improvement through the law and constitutional process, a frustrating experience when white southern senators for decades had proved capable of preventing an anti-lynching law being enacted. But the NAACP repeatedly proved its worth, and secured the crucial Supreme Court victory of 1954. The NAACP was torn in different directions. In 1956, the reluctance of the Democratic presidential candidate, Adlai Stevenson, to put civil rights in the forefront of his campaign provoked the NAACP's Roy Wilkins to denounce him in terms so severe that the venerable Eleanor Roosevelt threatened to resign from the NAACP board. At the same time, Wilkins felt pressure from the young and radical King, who was raising funds from traditional NAACP donors and also proposing a massive voter-registration campaign, the kind of work the NAACP felt was its own preserve. In cofounding the Southern Christian Leadership Conference (SCLC), King mounted a rival institution, which was seen by the NAACP as a challenge. The feud was to rumble on for years, maintained by King's increasing radicalization.

No sooner had Eisenhower won reelection than the NAACP was lobbying for congressional and White House support to enact the 1957 Civil Rights bill, which was meant to guarantee the right of blacks to register to vote. The act that was finally passed was fatally weakened by the Senate majority leader, the Texas Democrat Lyndon Johnson, who advocated allowing jury trials of state officials accused of blocking black voters. Southern juries were most unlikely to convict in such cases. King, who had his promised meeting with Vice President Nixon as the Senate bill was being fought, confided to Nixon that he and his colleague Ralph Abernathy had both voted Republican in 1956.

Many blacks voted Republican, reacting against the traditionally solid block of southern white Democrats. But the irony was rich, because King was starting to work with a group of radicals who had earlier flirted with the Communist party. It began with Bayard Rustin, an exotic figure who had joined the Young Communist League in Harlem in the 1930s, become a disciple of Gandhi's nonviolence, and served a prison term as a conscientious objector in World War II, as well as another for homosexual activity in California. An activist with the Congress of Racial Equality who ranged from Gandhi's India to Ghana and from South Africa to the bars of Greenwich Village, Rustin joined the Montgomery bus boycott and became a devoted King supporter. His connections among white radicals and fund-raisers included Stanley Levison, a socialist lawyer who had worked closely with Communists who were persecuted in the McCarthy era. He was to become King's closest white friend, until the wiretapping and anti-Communist obsession of J. Edgar Hoover forced a breach between them.

Voting Republican, working with alleged Communists, building an organization with black preachers, squabbling with the NAACP, traveling over 750,000 miles a year to give lectures and raise funds and galvanize black and white college students, all while raising a family and running a church, King was buffeted in the contrary political winds of his mission. He was stabbed in the chest by a deranged woman in New York when signing copies of his book *Stride Toward Freedom,* arrested briefly in Montgomery for "loitering" at a courthouse, and arrested again on charges of tax evasion (of which he was proved innocent) in the state of Alabama over the money raised for the Montgomery bus boycott. Prepared to go to jail rather than pay the fourteen-dollar loitering fine, he found it had already been paid by an anonymous donor, almost certainly the embarrassed police chief. Every arrest of the most prominent black leader was now a major news story.

Exhausted and frustrated by the failure of SCLC to make a breakthrough in voter registration, he decided to respond to the appeal of his ailing father to resign from the Dexter Avenue church in Montgomery and take over his father's and grandfather's Ebenezer Baptist Church in Atlanta. On the day that the Dexter congregation organized his service of farewell, in February 1960, the next stage of King's odyssey began in Greensboro, North Carolina. Four young black students had decided to sit at the whites-only lunch counter at the local Woolworth's. By the next day, there were twenty students. By the third day, there were eighty, braving the menace of the local Klan; and suddenly in other cities around the state, other sit-ins began at other segregated lunch counters. Soon there were over eighty such protests in seven southern states.

The NAACP, not yet accustomed to taking student protests seriously, did not mobilize its legal defense fund. King, realizing that the students had found a way of provoking a confrontation in which nonviolent tactics could work, hailed them in his sermons and speeches and visited the sit-in in Durham. "If the officials threaten to arrest us for standing up for our rights, we must answer by saying that we are willing and prepared to fill up the jails of the South," he declared. Then he was served with a warrant in Georgia for the tax evasion felony charge in Alabama. He was in the headlines again, just as the cities across the South began to erupt in student protest, and he appeared in the public eye to be the ringleader that he was not.

In Montgomery, where thirty-five students had gone to the whites-only cafeteria in the state capitol and left calmly when refused service, Governor John Patterson ordered the head of Alabama State College to expel them all. He then sent armed police to occupy the campus, saying, "The citizens of this state do not intend to spend their tax money to educate law violators and race agitators." Friends of King ran a full-page ad in the *New York Times,* which conflated his arrest and the show of force at Alabama State as a common strategy "to behead this alternative movement, demoralize Negro Americans and weaken their will to struggle." The police chief sued the *Times* for libel and lost, in what would become a landmark case before the Supreme Court over the rights of a free press.

The student sit-ins were spreading, with marches and demonstrations across the South, and white volunteers coming down from northern colleges. In April, King gave the keynote speech at what became the founding conference of SNCC, the Student Nonviolent Coordinating Committee, hailing them for "moving away from tactics which are suitable merely for gradual and long-term change." And as the students fanned out to foment more confrontations, King went back on *Meet the Press* to defend the mounting wave of protests. It was as though long-glowing embers had suddenly burst into vibrant flame, and it was 1960, an election year, that changed everything.

Nixon and Kennedy were neck and neck in the opinion polls, with the election campaign in its final weeks, when King was arrested with thirty-five students at an Atlanta department store. President Eisenhower instructed his attorney general to join the legal appeal against the arrest. Kennedy telephoned King's wife to commiserate, and his brother Robert called the judge to ask for bail. The Kennedy election campaign printed 2 million copies of a leaflet called "the Blue Bomb," relating all this on blue paper, and distributed them in black churches around the country. A loyal old Republican, the Reverend Martin Luther King, Sr., informed his flock, "I had expected to vote against Senator Kennedy because of his religion. But now he can be my President, Catholic or whatever he is. It took courage to call my daughter-in-law at a time like this. He has the moral courage to stand up for what is right. I've got all my votes and I've got a suitcase and I'm gonna take them up there and dump them in his lap."

Martin Luther King, Jr., and American Sainthood

In 1956, the black vote had gone Republican by a margin of 60 percent to 40; in 1960, it went Democrat by 70 percent to 30. This swing in the vote was sufficient to win Kennedy the states of Michigan, New Jersey, Pennsylvania, Illinois, and the Carolinas, and to put him into the White House. American politics had shifted, and in place now were all the explosive forces that were to produce the extraordinary phenomenon we know as the sixties. The currents were moving: Kennedy, student protest, sexual revolution, state intimidation, assassination, Black Power, mass demonstrations, the Freedom Riders. Their power was gathering, from the first stirrings of urban riot to a small military support operation in one of those parts of the developing world that had begun to impose itself on the planetary conscience at the Bandung conference: South Vietnam.

In each of these varied phenomena, King was to play a central and ultimately tragic part. It began with disappointment, the reluctance of the new Kennedy administration to move as fast and decisively to enact civil rights legislation as King had hoped. It grew worse as the increasingly militant students of SNCC demanded that he join not just the sit-ins but the Freedom Riders, whose campaigns were now coordinated so that when the police arrested the local demonstrators, a new wave of Freedom Riders would arrive to bring the media and galvanize more local support. In Anniston, Alabama, one of two Freedom Rider buses was stopped and set alight by an angry white mob. The second bus reached Birmingham, where the students were savagely beaten. The next day in Montgomery, a mob of hundreds of whites attacked another Freedom Rider bus, beating SNCC organizers, *Time* correspondents, and White House aide John Siegenthaler.

"The cause of human decency and black liberation demands that you physically ride the buses with our black Freedom Riders," cabled the fiery student leader Robert Williams to King's Atlanta church. "No sincere leader asks his followers to make sacrifices that he himself will not endure. You are a phony. Gandhi was always in the forefront, leading with his people. If you are the leader of this nonviolent movement, lead the way by example."

It was a classic example of the respectable revolutionary being overtaken and challenged by the passions he had unleashed. King's constituency was made up not just of the militant students but of the powerful figures in the White House, of the voters in Congress, of the public opinion of the North, and of the large proportion of the white South that was ready for change. It was impossible simultaneously to satisfy the expectations of them all, to court the public, challenge the police, bargain with the White House, raise funds for the struggle, and sit in jail, too. He tried, desperately hard, and stuck to his friends even when President Kennedy took him into the Rose Garden to tell him that the FBI had "incontrovertible" evidence that Communists had infiltrated his organization and the price of White House support was to get rid of Levison. Learning of the pressure on King, Levison selflessly took himself out of the picture. The FBI wiretaps gathered other evidence, which was then leaked with calculating incontinence, of the sexual solace that King took on the endless campaign trail.

There were a series of defeats, in Albany, Georgia, and in St. Augustine, Florida, where all the energy and arrests and the passion of the volunteers seemed unable to crack the white bastions. But there were triumphs that would echo down the years: the bravery of the schoolchildren of Birmingham who took up the cause, and King's letter from a Birmingham jail, a classic text on a nonviolence that went beyond passive protest in the face of injustice to aggressive confrontation.

"I am here because injustice is here," King wrote on the margins of a newspaper and on scraps of paper smuggled to him by another black prisoner. "Non-violent direct action seeks to create such a crisis and foster such a tension that a community which has constantly refused to negotiate is forced to confront the issue. . . . The purpose of our direct-action program is to create a situation so crisis-packed that it will inevitably open the door to negotiation."

As the jails of Birmingham filled and President Kennedy put the military on alert to intervene, the businessmen of Birmingham settled. They agreed to integrate the public facilities, to release and grant bail to all those arrested (with funds from the labor movement arranged by Attorney General Robert Kennedy), and to upgrade black civic employees. Birmingham was a triumph because King had managed to juggle the various impossible tasks, to control the militants and hold the moral high ground, to be in prison and to dominate in his absence the meeting in the White House at which the president accepted that unless the city of Birmingham fulfilled its agreement, black America in the South and elsewhere would become, in his words, "uncontrollable."

But the storm had not passed. There were killings on top of the beatings, explosions, and shootings. The murder of Medgar Evers of the NAACP in Jackson, Mississippi, on the night that President Kennedy declared in a televised address, "We face a moral crisis as a country and a people," reignited the feud with the NAACP just as the student militants of SNCC were denouncing King's readiness to compromise. The shooting of Evers came in a two-month period that Taylor Branch in his magisterial book *Parting the Waters* recorded as experiencing 14,733 arrests in 658 racial demonstrations in 186 American towns and cities. The country was in something frighteningly close to a revolutionary situation when King organized an event that could have been the ultimate confrontation but that became instead a great moment of healing.

Martin Luther King, Jr., and American Sainthood

There was much bickering about the 1963 march on Washington, much argument with the NAACP on the one side and the student militants on the other, much anguish from a White House that was trying to push a real civil rights bill through a bitterly divided Congress. But in its peace and its moving dignity, in its rallying of white opinion and of black purpose, that day when King told America "I have a dream" was one of those tremulous moments that justified its subsequent place in the national memory. The television networks dropped their usual programming to broadcast it live. President Kennedy was watching from the Oval Office and murmured, "He's damn good," even as he had winced when an earlier speaker, United Automobile Workers leader Walter Reuther, had said, "We cannot defend freedom in Berlin so long as we deny freedom in Birmingham." Mahalia Jackson was standing to one side of King, crying out "My Lord, my Lord" as his cadences soared, urging him, "Tell them about the dream, Martin." And he did, starting with a bow to Abraham Lincoln, in the shadow of whose monument he stood, the president who had ended slavery a hundred years earlier.

"But one hundred years later, we must face the tragic fact that the Negro is still not free," said King. "One hundred years later, the life of the Negro is still sadly crippled by the manacles of segregation and the chains of discrimination. One hundred years later, the Negro lives on a lonely island of poverty in the midst of a vast ocean of material prosperity. There will be neither rest nor tranquillity in America until the Negro is granted his citizenship rights. The whirlwinds of revolt will continue to shake our nation until the bright day of justice emerges."

America chooses now to remember the dream, the emollient and comforting assurance that the country would come to its senses, heal, cleave to justice. So, eventually, it did. But not before an anguished season of blood sacrifice had been unleashed. King spent the remaining five years of his life knowing that a media event, the prestige and eminence of the Nobel Peace Prize that he was awarded in that year of the dream, a catharsis, and even a Civil Rights Act finally voted by a Congress stricken with grief and guilt at the assassination of their young president, were not enough. Racial justice was not enough; it was ultimately but another symptom, although the most grievous and most compelling, of a deeper ailment that cut to the heart not just of America but of humankind.

The first warning of King's new preoccupations came in the speech at which he accepted his Nobel Prize. "I refuse to accept the cynical notion that nation after nation must spiral down a militaristic stairway into the hell of thermonuclear destruction," he said. The next warning came in Chicago, aiming at a completely different target: "Where Negroes are confined to the lowest paying jobs, they must get together to organize a union in order to have the kind of power that could enter into collective bargaining with their employers." Then another and wholly different kind of warning, opening yet another political front, came at New York's Riverside Church. He said, "The Great Society has been shot down on the battlefields of Vietnam—it would be inconsistent for me to teach and preach non-violence in this situation and then applaud violence when thousands and thousands of people, both adults and children, are being maimed and mutilated and many killed in this war, so that I still feel and live by the principle, 'Thou Shalt Not Kill.' "

The dream was not enough. Beyond racial justice, there were issues of poverty, of war and peace, and of human survival in a nuclear age. "I am much more than a civil rights leader," King told his young assistant Julian Bond that year. "There must be a better distribution of wealth," he told his Atlanta congregation. "We can't have a system where some of the people live in superfluous, inordinate wealth while others live in abject, deadening poverty." The battle for black freedom went on, but in a context transformed as some of the student militants he most loved and admired moved on in that feral season after Kennedy's murder to a black nationalism that he could not condone and an absolutism of Black Power he could not share. At the bridge in Selma, Alabama, he drew the marchers back from a confrontation with armed police that threatened to become apocalyptic, and the militants never forgave him. In Chicago, he reached an agreement to desegregate public housing with Mayor Richard Daley that the militants denounced as a betrayal.

In Los Angeles, where the black suburb of Watts exploded in riot after a man named Marquette Frye was arrested for drunken driving, he was stunned to find that many of the young blacks he met had never heard of him, and few wanted even to hear his offers of mediation. With his aides Andrew Young and Bayard Rustin, he tramped disbelievingly through the ruins, and a group of young men called out to him, "We won." He stopped and gaped, almost lost in his bafflement, and finally asked, "How can you say you won when thirty-four Negroes are dead, your community is destroyed and whites are using the riots as an excuse for inaction?" They laughed. "We won because we made them pay attention to us."

Black America, stirred and awoken and then unleashed, was moving into different and startling political terrain. But then so, in a rather different direction, was King. From labor unions to housing to the war in Vietnam, his agenda was broadening. It was evidently becoming more radical and in some ways more ambitious, but it was also becoming more politically conventional, as if the great moral victory of the 1964 Civil Rights Act had transformed him from the great preacher into something less incandescent. He never became just a politician, or just a community leader. And if some of the currents of the age had flowed swiftly past him, he always retained the power to surprise. In Memphis, Tennessee, during his last campaign, supporting a strike by sanitation workers, he jolted the black middle class by insisting that this was as much their struggle as the cause of civil rights: "There is a need to move beyond class lines. Negro haves must join hands with the Negro have-nots."

He spoke of the plans for a Poor Peoples March on Washington, to do for economic justice what the 1963 march had done for racial justice. But militant young blacks in Memphis, calling themselves the Invaders, had no patience with this. "All this stuff about marching downtown. All these bourgeoisie wanting to march downtown to get their pictures on national TV doing their civil rights thing. Man, that's nothing. That ain't going to help my brothers—if you expect honkies to get the message, you got to break some windows." Windows were duly broken. A sixteen-year-old boy was shot dead, 120 people were arrested and 50 injured, and King was whisked away in a car. Roy Wilkins of the NAACP suggested that the Poor Peoples March be called off, since King could no longer arrange a peaceful rally.

It was in Memphis, at the Mason Temple, that he gave his last, prophetic sermon. "It really doesn't matter with me now. Because I have been to the mountaintop, I won't mind. Like anybody, I would like to live a long life. Longevity has its place. But I'm not concerned about that now. I just want to do God's will. And He's allowed me to go up to the mountain. And I've looked over, and I've seen the promised land." He returned to the Lorraine Motel, where he had a pillow fight with Abernathy and Young, a final moment of laughter before he walked onto the balcony and was shot. He was thirty-nine years old. The telephone call from E. D. Nixon to tell him of the arrest of Rosa Parks had been but thirteen years and another America away.

The country erupted in flames and riot, another spasm from a people who had been shown a promised land but had seen the incomparable guide ripped from them. And then slowly, the nation proceeded to reinvent him, to name schools and roads and public buildings in his honor, and to declare a public holiday in his memory. When Gen. Colin Powell stepped down as President Reagan's national security adviser and took up his new post as the first African-American commander of U.S. forces, he installed in his office a large poster of King, signed by his widow and carrying King's words: "Freedom has always been an expensive thing." There was no irony in this display of a pacifist icon in a military headquarters. King had moved beyond the labels that had defined him in life. The resolution to name a national holiday in his honor was proposed by the conservative Republican senator Barry Goldwater, who had in 1964 condemned him as an agitator: "As long as people are told they are allowed to break the law, as Dr. Martin Luther King is doing, urban riots will continue." Powell and Goldwater embodied that sublime selectiveness of memory that encouraged America to revere a lost leader as a secular saint.

"We do not honor the critic of capitalism, or the pacifist who declared all wars evil, or the man of God who argued that a nation that chose guns over butter would starve its people and kill itself. We do not honor the man who linked apartheid in South Africa with Alabama; we honor an antiseptic hero," said Julian Bond, a student in King's philosophy class at Morehouse College in Atlanta and an activist in his cause. "We have stripped his life of controversy, and celebrate the conventional instead. We remember half of a man. We have realized only half of his dream."

24.
Betty Friedan
and the American Woman

In 1957, fifteen years after she had graduated from Smith College, a young married mother and magazine writer sent detailed questionnaires to all her classmates to see if they shared her unease. She could not precisely define her disquiet. There was a sense of waste, that the education she had received at Smith, and later as a graduate student at Berkeley, had equipped her for more than raising children and running a home. But there was also a touch of guilt that homemaking was not enough to fill her life, as the surrounding culture assured her it should be. Betty Friedan felt it "as a question mark in my own life—a strange discrepancy between the reality of our lives as women and the image to which we were trying to conform, the image which I came to call the feminine mystique."

It was summed up in part by the commencement address that Adlai Stevenson gave to the Smith graduates of 1955. Their future would not be in business or in the academy, he assumed, but in the home, where woman's duty was a nobler one, to the husband and sons within in it, "to inspire in her home a vision of the meaning of life and freedom."

Demographically, the 1950s cult of motherhood was logical enough. In that fifteenth year after graduation, when Friedan began working on her book *The Feminine Mystique,* over 4.4 million babies were born in the United States. This was and remains a record; the American birthrate of 25.2 per thousand in 1957 was higher than it had been in 1910, and higher than in India in the 1980s. That 1957 figure has never been exceeded, even though the American population has grown by almost 100 million since then. The average American woman in the 1950s married at the age of twenty, according to the official census reports, and one-third of marriages involved teenage girls. And whereas all of the countries that had fought in World War II had undergone a baby boom as the soldiers returned home, the United States was unique in the way that the baby boom continued for twenty years after the war's end. Not until 1965, when the oral contraceptive pill became widely available, did the birthrate drop below twenty per thousand, to settle in the 1990s at around fifteen.

The cult of motherhood was gushingly portrayed in a special issue of *Life* magazine in 1956, "The American Woman." The archetype was a suburban housewife, a mother of four, aged thirty-two, "pretty and popular," who had graduated from high school and married before she was twenty. She sewed her own clothes and entertained fifteen hundred guests in the course of a year, many of them at coffee mornings for young housewives like herself. "A conscientious mother, she spends lots of time with her children, helping with their homework, listening to their stories or problems. . . . In her daily round she attends club or charity meetings, drives the children to school, does the weekly grocery shopping, makes ceramics and is planning to learn French." With a car, a home in the suburbs, a refrigerator (how else could she shop but once a week?), and her guest lists, she also happened to be the perfect consumer for *Life*'s advertisers.

It all sounded, to Friedan and many of the women she interviewed, too irritatingly good to be true. Part restlessness, part dissatisfaction, the feeling that set Friedan on her research was that despite the assurances of women's magazines and conventional wisdom, she did not feel fulfilled as a wife and mother in the prosperous suburbs. At the same time, she felt only limited satisfaction in her career as a writer: "half-guiltily and therefore half-heartedly, almost in spite of myself, using my abilities and education in work that took me away from home."

The questionnaire she had distributed had originally sought to disprove the popular theory, which had been promoted in earlier best-selling works by the Kinseys, the psychoanalyst Helen Deutsch, and Marynia Farnham and

Betty Friedan and the American Woman

Ferdinand Lundberg (*Modern Woman: The Lost Sex*), that the more education a woman had, the higher the prospect of "sexual disorder." But the questions she posed to her classmates ranged more widely: "What difficulties have you found in working out your role as a woman? What are the chief satisfactions and frustrations of your life today? What do you wish you had done differently? How do you visualize your life after your children are grown?"

Of the almost five hundred in her graduating class, two hundred replied. All but six were married—most had married by the age of twenty-five—and six had divorced. All but twenty-two were housewives. Twenty wrote that they felt "martyred" by motherhood. A majority—121—replied that they did not find the housewife's role "totally fulfilling." Even greater majorities wanted to continue their studies or get a job, since their children were grown, and almost all regretted that they were not using their education. This was less an anguished cry for help than a troubled expression of disappointment and deep unease that combined with self-doubt. Was there something wrong with a woman who could not be wholly fulfilled by a home and children, when every magazine, broadcast, publicist, and advertiser was telling her that this was the essence of modern American contentment? This was the American way of life that had been fought for, and hard-won, and was now the envy of the world.

The dissatisfaction that Friedan and many of her Smith classmates felt was not unique to women in the 1950s. It was a decade of extraordinary unease, despite the soaring prosperity of the postwar boom as manufacturers raced to fill all those new suburban homes and garages with cars and furniture and kitchen appliances and baby carriages. In 1950, David Riesman and Nathan Glazer had published *The Lonely Crowd,* which suggested a deep sense of alienation among the outwardly contented and prosperous conformists who were submerging their individuality into the received ethics of the day. The following year, C. Wright Mills published *White Collar,* which saw the affluent new mass-middle-class male as purposeless and adrift, fearful to ask whether there could be more to life than the accumulation of material goods and status. William H. Whyte's *The Organization Man* in 1956 and Vance Packard's *The Status Seekers* in 1961 made the same best-selling point in different ways: Americans were achieving what had beckoned from the wretchedness of the Great Depression and the war as the good life, but it was not making them happy.

Friedan's book was in some ways inspired by these other books, and it treated the similar theme of malaise among the American affluent. But it met an altogether different response. At first, she could not get it published. Initially, she turned the results of her questionnaire into a magazine article, only to have it rejected by *McCall's* as "unbelievable," by *Redbook* as a conception for "only the most neurotic housewife," and rewritten by the (male) editors of *Ladies' Home Journal* "to deny its evidence so I wouldn't let them print it," Friedan wrote. In 1960, *Good Housekeeping* ran a rather tame version, under the title "Women Are People Too." Meeting Packard, she learned that he had experienced a similar difficulty in publishing his own pioneering critique of the advertising industry in magazines, so he had turned it into a book, *The Waste Makers*. She resolved to do the same, but her conclusion, in deliberately overheated tones, was dynamite:

> The feminine mystique has succeeded in burying millions of American women alive. There is no way for these women to break out of their comfortable concentration camps except by finally putting forth an effort—that human effort which reaches beyond biology, beyond the narrow walls of home, to help shape the future. Only by such a personal commitment to the future can American women break out of the housewife trap and truly find fulfillment as wives and mothers—by fulfilling their own unique possibilities as separate human beings.

The Feminine Mystique (1963) started selling slowly, although the reviews were more than respectful. The novelist Pearl S. Buck wrote that the book had "gone straight to the heart of the problem of the American woman." *Life* magazine called it "an angry, thoroughly documented book that in one way or another is going to provoke the daylights out of almost everyone." Then the sales mushroomed, and it became a publishing phenomenon, selling 3 million copies within three years. The women's magazines that had rejected her articles clamored to publish extracts, so Friedan happily realized that her ideas and arguments were reaching 15 million women. The book sold steadily throughout the 1960s and 1970s, becoming the organizing text of the women's liberation movement. The prominence the book brought her, along with the mounting evidence of a groundswell of agreement among women across the country who wrote to her and attended her lectures, inspired her in 1966 to help found the National Organization of Women (NOW).

Organization was second nature to Friedan. The image she had cultivated as just another, if well-educated, suburban mother was economical with the truth. She was born in Peoria, Illinois, in 1921, a year after women won the right to vote. Her father was a jeweler, a Russian Jewish immigrant who became steadily more prosperous, and her mother worked on the local newspaper. At Smith, Friedan edited the student newspaper, writing strident editorials on the need for America to join the war and the fight against fascism. She graduated with honors in psychology in 1942, and after a year of graduate school at Berkeley, she was offered a scholarship to pursue a doctorate. In one account, she has claimed that she shrank from the prospect of becoming a dedicated academic and spinster. In another, she cited the impact of her scholarship offer on her then boyfriend, who was not so honored. Her local newspaper in Peoria suggested in 1943 that she turned it down because "she wanted to work in the labor movement." Doubtless all three factors played a role.

She moved to New York to become a radical young writer in the labor movement, working in particular for the UE, the United Electrical, Radio and Machine Workers. This was by far the most radical of the postwar labor unions, and one that was largely run by Communists. From 1943, when she left Berkeley, until 1946, she worked in New York for the *Federated Press,* a left-wing agency that specialized in labor stories. Then, losing her job to a returning veteran, she joined the staff of *UE News,* the union's own publication, and remained there until 1952. She considered herself and the friends with whom she lived, she wrote in 1974, as part of "the vanguard of working class revolution," going from strikes to union halls to Marxist discussion groups, passionately engaged in the arcane theologies of Stalinism and Trotskyism. She was kept busy organizing abortions (then illegal) for friends, and when one couple decided to get married quickly instead, she wryly noted that it was harder to find an emergency minister to perform the ceremony than to find an abortionist.

Marriage in 1947 to Carl Friedan, a returning veteran who had been an actor in a soldiers' troupe in Europe and was then to move into advertising and public relations, brought that intense period of Greenwich Village activism to an end. But she was a participant and witness to a long, inexorable defeat, as the mainstream labor unions, the FBI, and the anti-Communist witch-hunts of Nixon and McCarthy, all in their different ways, combined to crush that flowering of American communism that had attended the war. The leaders of the UE, which claimed over 600,000 members in 1946, refused to sign the anti-Communist declaration required by the Taft-Hartley Act, a prerequisite for dealing with the National Labor Relations Board, and in 1949, its link to the Congress of Industrial Organizations was severed. Its members thus became fair game for poaching by other unions. By 1953, its numbers had dwindled to just over 200,000, and to barely 70,000 in 1957. Although Friedan was never formally a member of the Communist party, she, along with other union activists, was targeted in that highly charged period for investigation by the FBI.

Her own politics could best be described as Popular Front. She was prepared to work with Communists and any other progressive movement or body that shared her broadly left-wing objectives. She welcomed the launch of the Progressive party and supported Henry Wallace in the 1948 presidential election. But her articles in this period reflect little interest in the wider strategies of the Cold War and communism, and far more on the immediate issues of pay scales and making ends meet, and ending discrimination against women, Jewish, and African-American workers. A second theme of her work was the gathering clouds of an anti-Communist campaign, in industry, politics, and the media, that was ominously spreading to attack the progressive movement as a whole and roll back the achievements of the New Deal.

On the one hand, the union work gave her a distinct and classically socialist perspective on the problems of women as underpaid workers who were victims of a particular kind of exploitation because of their gender. Under her maiden name, Betty Goldstein, she wrote the union's recruiting and organizing pamphlet, *UE Fights for Women Workers,* which remains a classic text for activists fighting wage discrimination. She reported one meeting where the women took the stage, raising their own consciousness with the perception that they were "fighters—that they refuse any longer to be paid or treated as some inferior species by their bosses, or by any male workers who have swallowed the bosses' thinking." But she noted privately how difficult it was to alert the male-dominated union to the specific problems of women workers. On the other hand, she learned from personal experience that even the movement of the Left did not see sexual equality as a priority. When pregnant with her second child, she was fired, a common experience in those days before the mandatory granting of maternity leave. Her own union, the Newspaper Guild, would not stand by its own written commitment to pregnancy leave and job security.

Soon, with another child on the way, Friedan turned to housewifery, interspersed with writing for mainstream magazines, which became the inspiration of her book. But she was never a typical housewife. Beyond her journalism, she remained an activist. Moving from the Upper West Side of New York to the Parkway Village apartment complex in Queens, developed to house United Nations staff, she became the campaigning editor of the community newsletter and led a rent strike against a commercial redevelopment scheme. She and some friends planned at one stage to set up a rural commune, before she and her family moved to the country outside New York. Not only her circumstances but also the political environment had changed. "McCarthyism, the danger of war against Russia and of fascism in America, and the reality of U.S. imperial, corporate wealth and power" had all taken their toll, she recalled in 1974. The effect was to make her, and people like her who had planned with youthful enthusiasm on "making the whole world over, uncomfortable with the Old Left rhetoric of revolution."

In short, *The Feminine Mystique* did not suddenly emerge from nowhere, or from the "comfortable concentration camp" of the suburban housewife. It came from a strong radical tradition, rooted in her personal experience of discrimination at work and of the lives and struggles of women too poor to know the gilded restraints of the suburban middle class. Although the book was written for a general audience, rather than as a didactic political tract, its progressive credentials peep through the text. She does not dismiss the idea that there was a corporate conspiracy to keep the American housewife locked in the gadget-filled home and released only to fulfill her economic duty as consumer. "The perpetuation of the housewifery, the growth of the feminine mystique, makes sense (and dollars) when one realizes that women are the chief customers of American business. Somehow, somewhere, someone must have figured out that women will buy more things if they are kept in the underused, nameless-yearning, energy-to-get-rid-of state of being housewives."

Her other arguments, however, are more subtle and perceptive. She noted that the American tradition of pioneer women, helping to open the frontier, was far more sturdy than women's postwar condition would suggest. She analyzed the contents of the main women's magazines for the previous two decades, and she identified a trend in the fiction of the 1930s for a "New Woman" heroine, who had an education and her own career and goals, as well as a sense of self-worth that was not rooted solely in home and family. In writing about the end of the 1940s, she said, "Suddenly the image blurs. The New Woman, soaring free, hesitates in mid-flight, shivers in all that blue sunlight and rushes back to the cozy walls of home." Her explanation for this is persuasive, recalling those years of studying psychology before she joined the labor movement.

"There was, just before the feminine mystique took hold in America, a war, which followed a depression and ended with the explosion of the atom bomb," she wrote. "The lonely years when husbands or husbands-to-be were away at war, or could be sent away at a bomb's fall, made women particularly vulnerable to the feminine mystique." She also sought intuitively to comprehend what these experiences had done to men. "In the foxholes, the G.I.s had pinned up pictures of Betty Grable, but the songs they asked to hear were lullabies. And when they got out of the army they were too old to go home to their mothers. . . . We were all vulnerable, homesick, lonely, frightened. A pent-up hunger for marriage, home and children was felt simultaneously by several different generations; a hunger which, in the prosperity of post-war America, everyone could suddenly satisfy."

This illuminates the fundamental paradox of *The Feminine Mystique*. She diagnosed a national malaise, which almost by definition is a series of millions of individual subjective states, all different in their particulars, if similar in their causes. This is a national predicament, which, irrespective of the biological fact that women bear children and alone have the natural equipment to feed them, is very hard to quantify. Her diagnosis is essentially psychological, and owes much to her education. Her remedy is eminently practical, and owes much to her radical work: Women should get educations, careers, interests, and lives that take them beyond the confines of the home and maternity ward. This remedy can, in a way, be measured. It is amenable to the intervention of public and governmental policy, through encouraging education for women, equal access to jobs and professions, equal pay, and the right to return to careers after having children.

The psychologist had conceived and defined the problem; the labor activist then found ways to address it. But there was a hole in this solution. If the problem was that many American women were made unhappy by the limitations of the housewife's role, there was no guarantee that work, careers, or outside interests would make them any more content than their working menfolk, whose own alienation had been explored by some of the books that helped inspire her own. As Thoreau had argued a century earlier, "Most men lead leaves of quiet desperation." Within a generation of the publication of *The Feminine Mystique,* a new generation of educated and well-paid professional women (many of them raised by suburban mothers who stayed home to do so) found a new concern: whether their own children were being properly raised by the nanny or the au pair, while mother pursued her career.

The second paradox that attends Friedan's work is that at the very time her book was published, the problem was already inspiring an official response. Friedan was not the only observer to note that all was not well with American woman. In October 1961, almost two years before her book was published, President Kennedy created a president's commission on the status of women, chaired by Eleanor Roosevelt, "to develop plans for fostering the full partnership for men and women in our national life." Its report, in 1963, echoed Friedan's conclusions in more sober tones, arguing that for women "aspiration must be fostered, beyond stubbornly persistent assumptions about 'women's roles' and 'women's interests.'" The political system responded. In the year her book was published, Congress passed an Equal Pay Act and the first federal law against sex discrimination (although it took much agitation to get it even spasmodically enforced). Moreover, President Kennedy had issued an executive directive that instructed all federal agencies to prohibit sex discrimination in hiring and promotion.

So as Friedan was writing, the problem was starting to solve itself, or at least to change its demographic shape. The cult of maternity was ending as the furious birthrate slackened and American women started going back to work in greater numbers than their mothers had in World War II. The trend is clear. Throughout the nineteenth century, women never numbered more than 20 percent of the labor force. Then the figures start to rise, and never stop.

YEAR	FEMALE PERCENTAGE OF LABOR FORCE
1900	18.1
1910	20.0
1920	20.4
1930	21.9
1940	24.6
1950	27.8
1960	32.3
1970	36.7
1980	42.6
1990	45.1
1995	46.0

Source: U.S. Bureau of Labor Statistics.

The sharp rise gathered force as Friedan was leaving the Upper West Side for Parkway. It took off as her book was written and published. The phenomenon she was describing, at least insofar as it can be measured by whether or not women had lives outside the home, was shrinking measurably. In 1960, just over 21 million women were fully employed outside the home. By 1970, the number had risen to 30 million, and by 1980 to 42 million, almost exactly the number of men who had been fully employed in 1960. This was a revolution, not only for women but also for the American workforce, and it still shows few signs of slackening. By 1990, 53 million women were working outside the home.

This was the real sexual revolution of the period, an economic transformation, rather than an erotic one. And it both accompanied and predated the women's liberation movement, which gathered force in the late 1960s. It is not easy to identify any single moment of the movement's birth. The establishment of NOW in 1966 was a crucial date, with its powerful campaign for abortion rights, which triumphed in 1973 when the Supreme Court effectively ruled in *Roe v. Wade* that there should be no restrictions on abortion in the first three months of pregnancy. The launch of *Ms.* magazine in 1972 was also significant. And the change in the divorce rate provides some clue to the fast-moving social trends in which women's lib emerged. From 1948 to 1967, it was roughly stable at between nine and eleven divorces each year per one thousand couples. In 1968, it began to climb sharply, reaching twenty-two per one thousand in 1978, a level where it has remained. There was also a significant change in college enrollment. In 1960, young men were far more likely to go to college than women. By 1988, women were more likely to go to college than men.

YEAR	PERCENTAGE OF MALES ENROLLED IN COLLEGE	PERCENTAGE OF FEMALES ENROLLED IN COLLEGE
1960	54.0	37.9
1965	57.3	45.3
1970	55.2	48.5
1975	52.6	49.0
1980	56.7	51.8
1985	58.6	59.9
1990	57.8	62.0
1994	60.6	63.2

Source: Statistical Abstract of the United States, 1996.

Women's march into the colleges and the workplace was accompanied and probably reinforced by a host of cultural factors, from improved contraceptive techniques like the pill to the sudden stagnation in the American median household income. After doubling in the twenty-five years after 1947, it suddenly stagnated in 1973, and remained stalled for the next two decades. This was partly because, with divorce more common, there were now more households, and the median income was dragged down by the rise in the number of households headed by women, which tended to be disproportionately poor. But this income stagnation also encouraged married women to go to work, to maintain with two paychecks a prosperity, or even a sufficiency, that hitherto had been maintained by one wage earner.

These economic and cultural factors, giving women a direct interest in pay, working conditions, and the public provision of family services, helped drag the focus away from the question of Friedan the psychologist—Why were women unhappy?—to the remedies proposed by Friedan the labor activist—What could and should the country do to improve women's lot? The political implications of the changing role of women were striking. In 1960, women were slightly less likely to vote than men. By 1976, they were more likely to vote, and from 1980 on, they were clearly voting with a marked Democratic bias.

The women's vote was clearly affected by their economic status. In 1992 (and 1996), Bill Clinton won strong majorities among women who were

Betty Friedan and the American Woman

YEAR	PERCENTAGE OF MALES VOTING DEMOCRATIC	PERCENTAGE OF FEMALES VOTING DEMOCRATIC
1976	52	52
1980	38	46
1984	38	42
1988	42	49
1992	41	45
1996	44	54

Source: American Enterprise, Demographic Report, Jan.–Feb. 1993, pp. 90–91.

employed full-time or part-time, or who declared themselves unemployed. In 1992, Clinton lost only among women who declared themselves "homemakers," winning 36 percent of their vote, while George Bush won 45 percent. Married women voted 41 percent for Clinton, 40 percent for Bush. But single women preferred Clinton over Bush by a stunning margin of 55 to 29, and divorced or separated women preferred Clinton by 49 to 32. Paradoxically, while women's participation in electoral politics increased, and more and more women stood for and achieved electoral office, the largest nationwide political campaign that NOW undertook, for the Equal Rights Amendment to be enacted, failed to win sufficient state ratifications, despite heroic efforts by Friedan, who, after leaving the presidency of NOW, campaigned full-time for the amendment.

At the same time, Friedan was concerned by some of the trends in the women's movement. When helping to found NOW, she had brought some sympathetic men into the leadership. Richard Graham, head of the Equal Employment Opportunity Commission, was appointed vice president. But just as Martin Luther King, Jr., in the civil rights movement had found his determination to include whites in the leadership challenged by young black nationalist radicals, so Friedan was confronted by her own militant followers, who maintained that the issue was not to reform society in order to improve opportunities for women. The problem was men and the male hierarchy itself. Friedan fought what she called "female chauvinism."

"Feminism means a woman's right to move in society with all the privileges and opportunities and responsibilities that are their human and American right. This does not mean class warfare against men, nor does it mean the elimination of children," she maintained in her 1976 book, *It Changed My Life*. Her next book, *The Second Stage* (1981), took the argument further, suggesting that the radicals were making the mistakes of the Old Left in dividing into factions, and making new mistakes of their own through inward-looking preoccupations with sexual and identity politics. For Friedan, the bottom line remained political and economic inequalities, and the women who now had choices, power, and influence had an obligation to use them to improve the opportunities for the less fortunate. The call to action remained, demanding that the women's movement now use its weight to require the economic system to adjust to families, through flexible work time, job sharing, and day-care centers at the workplace.

She was saying, in effect, that the war had been won, even if there were still some battles to fight and a great deal of mopping up to be done. Not only had America acknowledged women's demands and brought women into the decision-making process; it had developed a political culture, which would, slowly but eventually, respond to democratic pressure. The system was improvable. But indefatigable radical that she was, Friedan had developed a new cause, that of the elderly. Her 1993 book, *The Fountain of Age,* argued that just as America had falsely labeled and undervalued its housewives (when she was a housewife), so it undervalued and wrongly labeled its increasing number of elderly as irrelevant and unable to contribute, just as she had become a highly active elderly woman. "There is a mystique of age more pernicious and pervasive than the feminine mystique," she maintained.

This was perhaps the key to her career. She was a situationist revolutionary, responding to whatever circumstance she was experiencing at the time. As a student, she was a radical and a campaigning campus newspaper editor. In New York in the 1940s, she became a labor movement revolutionary. Raising her children at home, she identified and publicized with brilliant force and conviction a genuine psychological malaise with which generations of women could identify, and also stressed the sheer human waste of millions of talented and able women stuck in what felt like a backwater of life. As she aged—but went on Outward Bound courses in her sixties to test herself and her capacities—she became almost equally outraged by the similar waste of talent among the retired and the elderly. Wherever she found herself, she discovered a cause and a way to fight for it. In the women's movement, her talents and the time and gathering social trends all came together with extraordinary force. If she did not change America, she was one of the few not just to notice but to articulate and define the way that it was changing, and she gave it a crucial and ultimately deeply humanist nudge.

"Some worry that we'll lose our femininity and our men if we get equality," she wrote in 1976. "Since femininity is being a woman and feeling good about it, clearly the better you feel about yourself as a person, the better you feel about being a woman. And, it seems to me, the better you are able to love a man." For Betty Friedan, the cause was never women against men, but people against the system.

25.
Alan Greenspan
and the American Banker

The dominance of the global economy that the United States enjoyed as the twentieth century drew to its close had many roots, from the fortunes of climate and geography to its productive experience in two world wars. But one crucial aspect of financial hegemony was born in the Harry Jerome Swing Band of 1947. America's central banker Alan Greenspan, who is sometimes assumed by corporate America to sit at the right hand of God, played bass clarinet. Alongside him in the rhythm section was Leonard Garment, who went on to a slightly blemished legal career as White House counsel to Richard Nixon. In 1974, in the heat of Nixon's losing battle to save his presidency, Garment persuaded Nixon to nominate his old band mate as chairman of the Council of Economic Advisers.

This was not an obvious choice. Greenspan, who made his name after 1954 as a private financial consultant on Wall Street, had only been awarded his doctorate in economics two years before getting the White House post. Before that, he preferred to sit at the feet of Ayn Rand, that extremely conservative laureate of the utterly free market. She had left Russia after graduating from the University of Petrograd in 1924, then became a Hollywood screenwriter and a best-selling novelist. Passionately anti-Communist, she extolled the virtues of the individual against the collective. Honest selfishness, she preached, was a moral good, and the only moral society was purely capitalist. Every couple of years, Greenspan confided when installed as chairman of the Federal Reserve, America's central bank, he still reread her novel *Atlas Shrugged.* A political tract lightly disguised as fiction, the plot concerns gold-loving entrepreneurs who decide to go on strike, withdrawing their labor and their wealth-producing talents until Americans saw the error of their socialistic ways.

Confirmed in his chairmanship by the Senate after Nixon's resignation, Greenspan stayed on in Gerald Ford's administration, where he presided over a jump in inflation to within a whisker of 10 percent and a recession that helped Ford lose the next election to Jimmy Carter. In 1987, Greenspan was appointed chairman of the Federal Reserve Board by Ronald Reagan, and his swift decision to raise interest rates helped precipitate the stock market crash in October of that year. Having made the mess, he helped the economy clamber out of it by a promise to make available whatever liquidity the market needed, and the inevitable result was that the economy began to overheat.

No problem, Greenspan assured the new president, George Bush. He would engineer a "soft landing," an exquisitely crafted squeeze on interest rates that would slow the economy without going too far, thus enabling it to continue strong and stable growth. Bush lost the 1992 election because he believed his central banker. The recession of 1991 may have been mild, as such things go, but it dismayed enough voters to trigger the Ross Perot phenomenon and secure the election of Bill Clinton in a three-way race.

But with the reelection of Clinton in 1996, it seemed to be third time lucky for Greenspan. After two disasters, America's central banker had finally gotten the economy right. At least Greenspan delivered an extraordinary bonanza for shareholders, and what appeared to be a stable-state boom based on strong GDP and productivity growth, low inflation, and unemployment stable at an unusually low 5 percent. In the process, he also delivered the most socially divisive American economy since the 1930s. The Institute for International Economics, an establishment think tank run by a former assistant secretary of the treasury, in June 1997 defined those steepening divisions in an arresting way. During the previous twenty years, the ratio of wages for the best-paid 10 percent of workers to those of the bottom 10 percent rose from 360 percent to 525 percent.

The figures were for wages before taxes, and tax cuts for the wealthy had been implemented over the same period, particularly during the administration of President Reagan. This meant, for example, that Jack Welch, chief executive of General Electric, in 1997 took home 300 times the earnings of his shop-floor workers. Thirty years ago, Welch's predecessor took home thirty times more than his shop-floor workers.

This may be a good thing for the American economy, narrowly defined. But it may be a damaging process to inflict on American society as a whole. Laura D'Andrea Tyson, who could claim some of the credit for the 1990s boom from her time chairing the Council of Economic Advisers in Clinton's first term, warned of "the economic disaster that has befallen low-skilled workers, especially young men." There were other casualties of the Greenspan boom, beyond the warning signs of unprecedented numbers of bankruptcies and soaring consumer debt. The growth in employment included temporary and part-time jobs, many of them deliberately crafted to spare employers the extra costs of health care and pension schemes.

Alan Blinder, the liberal academic economist who served alongside Greenspan at the Fed, suggested rather glumly that the United States and much of the rest of the developed world had seen a historic and strategic victory for wealth in their own societies, a domestic echo of the defeat of the Soviet Union in the Cold War. "I think when historians look back at the last quarter of the twentieth century, the shift from labor to capital, the almost unprecedented shift of money and power up the income pyramid, is going to be their number one focus," suggested the historically minded Blinder.

He was echoing a debate that was as old as the republic, and one that had long polarized its politics. There have always been two essential aspects to sovereignty, whether of monarchs or of nations: the power to declare war and the authority to issue money. The Constitution is clear on the first but vague on the second. Alexander Hamilton, the first secretary of the treasury, had no doubt that a national bank was required in order to fund the public debt left over from the War of Independence, and to provide a common means of exchange. Thomas Jefferson was equally convinced that Hamilton was wrong and that such a bank would be both unconstitutional and pernicious. He saw it shifting power to the urban bankers and men of finance, and away from the states and rural farmers whom he saw as the backbone of the republic. This was the issue that carved the great political dividing line of America, between Jefferson's Democrats and Hamilton's Federalists. Hamilton won the first battle, and Congress authorized the charter of the Bank of the United States in 1791. But it was a private rather than a government institution, in which the federal government held 20 percent of the stock. The charter lapsed twenty years later, and was too unpopular to be renewed.

America Reborn

The issues were simple. On the one hand, people who have property want to safeguard it. If they have money, they want it to be safe and backed by a strong and reliable authority like a national government, and to know that the coinage can be trusted to be sound rather than adulterated metal. They want their money to be as good as gold, which means it will be expensive to borrow. On the other hand, people who do not have money, but who need it to buy land, or seeds for next year's harvest, or a new cart to take crops to market, want money to be easily and cheaply available. They also want it available nearby, preferably from a local banker who knows them and local conditions. The established and propertied classes of the coastal cities and trading ports of the young republic wanted sound money. Those driving inland to the West and seeking to make their fortunes needed cheap money. It is the choice between growth and stability, and the real job of a central bank is to balance the two.

From 1811 to 1816, the constituency for cheap money held off the central bank. They might have held out longer, but for the War of 1812, which collapsed the finances and the credit of the government, with no central bank to sustain it. In 1816, the forces wanting sound money secured a new charter. The cheap money faction renewed the assault, and in 1831, President Andrew Jackson put the issue clearly in his veto of the bill to renew the charter of the Bank of the United States:

> It is to be regretted, that the rich and powerful too often bend the acts of government to their selfish purposes. Distinctions in society will always exist under every just government. Equality of talents, of education, or of wealth can not be produced by human institutions. In the full enjoyment of the gifts of Heaven and the fruits of superior industry, economy and virtue, every man is entitled to equal protection by law; but when the laws undertake to add to these natural and just advantages artificial distinctions, to make the rich richer and the potent more powerful, the humble members of society—farmers, mechanics and laborers—who have neither the time nor the means of securing like favors to themselves, have a right to complain of the injustice of government.

The bank war between Jackson and Nicholas Biddle of Philadelphia, president of the Bank of the United States, became the great political drama of the age. Henry Clay and Daniel Webster fought for the bank, while Jackson claimed to fight for the people. Congress passed the charter again, despite Jackson's veto. The presidential election of 1832 was fought on the matter, and Jackson won by a landslide, despite the plentiful funds that the bank steered to his opponents. Even the election verdict was not sufficient. Jackson, who had to fire his treasury secretary to do it, banned the deposit of any government funds in the bank. For the bank, Biddle responded by calling in loans and plunging the country into a crisis of credit. Henry Clay spearheaded a congressional motion of censure that was passed on the president, but Jackson held firm, and Biddle finally had to surrender.

Eighty years were to pass before the country had a central bank again, years in which the question of cheap or sound money continued to divide the nation and inspire its politicians. William Jennings Bryan won his party's nomination in 1896 with a speech in which he declared, "You come to us and tell us that the great cities are in favor of the gold standard. We reply that the great cities rest upon our broad and fertile prairies. Burn down your cities and leave our farms, and your cities will spring up again as if by magic; but destroy our farms and the grass will grow in the streets of every city in the country. . . . You shall not crucify mankind upon a cross of gold."

But by 1896, the frontier had closed. The great emptiness of the American West was occupied, if never entirely filled. Most Americans lived in cities, and many of them lived by trade. The great state banks were grand institutions, and those of New York and Pennsylvania were quite the match of the national banks of some European countries. But the case for a national bank for a national economy, with the power to control the national money supply, was a powerful one. The question became less whether the country should have one, but who would control it.

In his address to Congress on June 23, 1913, the newly elected Woodrow Wilson insisted that banking was too important to be left to the bankers; control must be "public, not private, must be vested in the government itself, so that the banks must be the instruments, not the masters of business." By the end of the year, after furious lobbying on both sides and splits in each party, the Federal Reserve Act was passed. It was and remains a compromise between centralized government and regional influence. There are twelve federal reserve banks, in New York, Boston, Chicago, Dallas, St. Louis, Minneapolis, Atlanta, San Francisco, Richmond, Cleveland, Philadelphia, and Kansas City (Kansas). Each of these is a private institution, required by law to serve the public interest. Each is run by a board of nine members, six of whom are elected by the local member banks and three of whom are appointed by the board of governors of the Federal Reserve System.

Two fundamental changes have modified the system signed into law by Wilson on the eve of the Great War in Europe. The first was the experience of the Great Depression, which transformed the Fed's concept of its task. The second was the simultaneous challenge of America's role as the preeminent Great Power and leader of the West in the Cold War, combined with the coming of the interdependent global economy. This forced the Fed into a new dimension, as the leading central bank of a global system, and custodian of the globe's dominant currency.

Wilson's act had tried to decentralize financial power, thereby shifting it away from New York to the autonomous regional banks. But in the course of the 1920s, the weight of Wall Street and the prestige of New York brought these other banks back under the dominance of the New York Reserve bank, which was run by a veteran of the Morgan finance house, Benjamin Strong. "What this system requires is protection against misled public opinion," Strong told a bankers' conference in 1921. The way he achieved this was to persuade all the regional banks to let New York coordinate, and in effect handle, all purchases and sales of government bonds.

In a process only partially understood at the time, this buying and selling was itself a critical factor in the American money supply. And Strong and his banking colleagues wanted sound money, low inflation, and lower taxes. This meant higher interest rates and lower prices for farmers, whose share of the national income plunged from 15 percent to 9 percent between 1920 and 1928, and the extraordinary 63 percent growth in industrial productivity during the 1920s resulted in less than half that much growth in industrial wages. The beneficiaries were the already-propertied classes, and stock market prices. Strong wanted this to happen, but he saw the process getting out of hand. Shortly before his death in 1928, after doubling the Fed's discount rate to 6 percent, he called on the banks to cut back lending for speculative investment, warning, "The problem now is so to change our policy as to avoid a calamitous break in the stock market."

A year after Strong's death, the calamitous break came. When stock prices plunged, the nightmare of the margin process began. Buying on margin meant investors putting down 16 percent of a stock price and borrowing the rest, confident they could pay the money back when the stock rose. When the stock fell, they suddenly owed money they could not repay. The banks lost about $7 billion, and over the next five years of crisis, almost ten thousand commercial banks failed.

One that did not was the First National Bank of Ogden, Utah, although it only survived a run on its money in 1931 by paying out its cash, counting dollar bill by dollar bill with painful slowness, until a panic call for more funds brought an armored car from the Federal Reserve branch in Salt Lake City. The Ogden bank's president was Marriner Eccles, a Mormon who had been raised in orthodox banking ways. But the experience of the Great Depression puzzled him. Orthodox banking, which meant calling in the loans of a farmer in arrears or a company that could not pay, was making the problem worse. It was causing factories to close and workers to be laid off and was forcing bankrupt farmers to put more unsellable farms on the market, which meant fewer paychecks and fewer customers, which in turn meant less business and less money to go around. The puzzle led this devout and straitlaced Mormon to suggest a curious metaphor drawn from the gambling saloon: "As in a poker game where the chips are concentrated in fewer and fewer hands, the other fellows could stay in the game only by borrowing. When their credit ran out, the game stopped."

The point, Eccles realized, was to get the game started again, which meant making credit available. This meant the government, or its central banker, issuing and lending more money, which would drive down interest rates and revive the economy. He was not alone in this insight. In Britain, John Maynard Keynes was developing the same idea for his book *The General Theory of Employment, Interest, and Money* (1936). And in Washington, Eugene Meyer, who was about to buy the bankrupt *Washington Post* at an auction held on the newspaper's front steps, was urging a similar course from his seat on the Federal Reserve Board. The regional Federal Reserve banks hated this idea, because lower interest rates mean lower earnings on their holdings of U.S. Treasury bonds.

Orthodox bankers saw sound money and more thrift as the way out of the Depression. As treasury secretary throughout most of the 1920s, Andrew Mellon (of the Philadelphia banking family) argued that a recession would "purge the rottenness out of the system. People will work harder, live a more moral life."

It was because so many Americans found it hard to lead any kind of life at all in the Great Depression that Franklin Roosevelt won the election of 1932, albeit on a promise to balance the federal budget. This was precisely the wrong thing to do at a time when the nation was crying out for money that only the authority of the federal government could create. Roosevelt's distinction was that he was prepared to change his mind when he listened to Meyer and to the young Mormon banker whose articles, speeches, and testimony before Congress insisted that there was a better way.

Money had to be pumped back into the economy and the unemployed had to be fed, and perhaps even given work by the government if private enterprise failed. A public works program and unemployment pay would do both, and a federal guarantee of all bank deposits would stop runs on the banks and keep business moving. A minimum wage law would ensure that those who worked would have the money to become customers in their turn. The economy did not have to be seen as a contest between labor and capital, and in setting interest rates, banks did not have to choose between the propertied classes and the poor. The economy was an interdependent whole. Just as banks needed borrowers and lenders, production needed both workers and customers. The more customers, the more production.

Roosevelt asked Eccles to draft the legislation for a reform of the Fed and, in 1934, asked him to become the first chairman of the newly centralized system. The board based in Washington now had authority over the regional reserve banks, but the regional votes were still important in the Fed's Open Market Committee, which in effect regulated the national supply of money. There were two main ways to do this: by buying and selling the Treasury bonds that were financing the job-creating New Deal program that Eccles had sketched out before Congress and by changing the interest rates at which commercial banks could borrow money from the Fed.

Eccles stressed one rule: The program of public spending was an emergency measure. The New Deal was financed by money the government was not able to raise by taxes. Instead, the government borrowed the money by issuing Treasury bonds, thus increasing the national debt. Once the crisis had passed and America was back to work, the borrowing had to stop. And when economic recovery was fully under way, it was then the Fed's duty to stop growth from going too far. The task was, said Eccles, "to assure that adequate support is available whenever needed for the emergency financing involved in a recovery program, and to assure that a recovery does not get out of hand and be followed by a depression."

Eccles's successor, William McChesney Martin, said the job made him the person "who takes the punchbowl away just when the party gets going." The Fed had to go against the prevailing current of the economy, pumping in money when it slowed and taking money out when it began growing too fast. This carried a revolutionary political implication, so dramatic in its contrast to the traditional American system that only an event as traumatic as the Great Depression could have produced it. The federal government was now the biggest single player in the economy, with a permanent and strategic role in defining how the economy should perform. The tactical management of this new power of government was left to the Fed, whose board of governors were presidential appointees. The Fed had a considerable degree of independence, enough to let Eccles ignore political complaints when the recovery stalled and the economy turned sour again in 1938. But an event was looming in which the Fed had little choice but to defer to the administration.

Far more than the New Deal, World War II carved into stone the new power of central government, and sealed into place the Eccles system of growth through federal debt. When Roosevelt was elected, the national debt stood at $22 billion. Eight years later, when Japan attacked Pearl Harbor, it had more than doubled to $48 billion. By the time peace was restored in 1945, it had grown again fivefold, to $240 billion. War was expensive. In 1940, the federal government had spent 9.9 percent of America's GDP. In 1944, it spent almost half of it.

But the war had produced a vastly larger economy. In simple terms, it doubled the size of the economy in less than five years. From a GDP of $41 billion in 1932, the American economy recovered to deliver a GDP of $95 billion in 1940. By 1945, even with 12 million of its youngest and most productive citizens in uniform, the nation boasted a GDP of $212 billion. It was able to achieve these feats of growth because there was never any shortage of money. Eccles at the Fed held down interest rates throughout the war, so that long-term Treasury bonds always delivered interest of 2.5 percent. Short-term loans could be had for as little as 0.5 percent interest a year. The new aerospace plants in California and Georgia, the new tank and armored car factories around Detroit, and the new shipyards up and down both coasts were all built with deliberately cheap money, and after the war, these modern plants were available for relatively easy conversion to civilian output.

This booming new economy was not only a miraculous transformation from the dismal 1930s; it meant that the United States alone now accounted for about half of all the wealth produced on the planet in that year. Its homeland untouched by the devastation of war, the United States was not only militarily dominant but economically vastly more powerful and productive than any other country. Britain was broke, and thus dependent on American loans. France was shattered by the war and the years of Nazi occupation. The enemy nations of Germany and Japan were prostrate, bombed flat and exhausted. But if one war was over, another was about to begin. And while the Soviet Union had also been devastated by the war, its armies dominated half of Europe and loomed over the rest. Almost destroyed by the war against Japan and the Japanese occupation, the Chinese government of Chiang Kai-shek fell before Mao's Communist armies.

The United States accordingly shouldered another burden, not only maintaining its own armaments but also financing the recovery of Western Europe through the Marshall Plan. There was altruism in the great generosity of the Marshall Plan, which saw the United States investing 2 percent of its GDP every year for five years into its European allies, but also hard strategic calculation. A Europe recovered was a Europe that could support the United States in the West's defensive alliance, and so Germany was rearmed as well as rebuilt. And with the outbreak of the Korean War in 1950, a lesser-known aid package, known as the Pentagon Special Procurement Fund, put more money into the new strategic base of Japan than West Germany had received under the Marshall Plan. American funds rebuilt the railways, and even financed the first Toyota truck assembly line so that Japan too could play its part in the Cold War.

America Reborn

In retrospect, the grand strategy of the United States in the Cold War was to create the tripartite economy of the modern West—of North America, Western Europe, and Japan. American credits and investments poured out, financed by the great productive machine of postwar America, financed in effect by the Fed. The Eccles system, as refined and promulgated by the academic reputation of John Maynard Keynes, became the economic ideology of the West. At the mountain resort of Bretton Woods, New Hampshire, as World War II drew to a close, Keynes helped draw up the plans for the postwar economic system of the World Bank and the International Monetary Fund (IMF), institutions that would prove as strategic to the West as NATO.

The long postwar boom in the West appeared to justify the title that Herbert Stein, of President Nixon's council of economic advisers, chose for his seminal book, *The Fiscal Revolution in America.* But having been nursed back to health, Japan and the Western Europeans proved to be formidable competitors, and as its share of global GDP shrank from 50 percent in 1945 to just over 20 percent by 1990, America's costly global role came under repeated strain. The financial crisis of the Vietnam War, when the federal budget went $25 billion into deficit in 1968, showed that even the world's richest economy could not indefinitely afford both guns and butter.

Politicians knew that prosperity bought votes and assumed that the new Keynesian economics had delivered a permanent prosperity machine. They forgot the Eccles rule, that deficit spending was for emergencies. Otherwise, deficit spending provoked inflation. Lyndon Johnson learned the lesson in 1968, when he had to impose a 10 percent tax surcharge. Richard Nixon did not learn it. He appointed a compliant new Fed chairman in Arthur Burns who proclaimed, "The Federal Reserve System is a part of the government," and who obligingly kept interest rates down to ensure a wave of prosperity to help reelect Nixon.

But the damage had already been done as the continuing hemorrhage of dollars to the Vietnam War combined with the growing trade deficit. On August 15, 1971, Nixon and treasury secretary John Connally announced from that weekend retreat at Camp David the most sweeping range of economic powers any U.S. government has assumed in peacetime, which led to the OPEC rise in the oil price. (See chapter 22.) The decade of inflation began as the Treasury and the Fed simply lost control. Between 1970 and Nixon's resignation in 1974, international monetary reserves increased by 168 percent.

Once unleashed, the inflation was very difficult to stop. And it fell to Paul Volcker, the Fed chairman who replaced Burns, to stop it. His task was made the harder by the election of Reagan in 1980, on a promise of tax cuts and an end to the inflation that had reached an annual rate of 20 percent, combined with a pledge to spend whatever it would take to restore the national defense.

Alan Greenspan and the American Banker

The price of these incompatible goals was a severe recession, whose pain was justified by the apparent bankruptcy around the Western world of the (misused) policies of Eccles and Keynes. The monetarist theories of Milton Friedman, which held that inflation was the result of the government and the Fed allowing too much money into the economy, became the fashion, even though it proved dauntingly difficult to ascertain what the relevant monetary supply should be, or how to measure it.

No wonder economics was dubbed "the dismal science." The policies of Eccles and Keynes had shown how to get out of a recession but not how to manage steady growth. Nor had monetarism, although it had squeezed inflation out of the system. The one fixed fact of economics appeared to be that a serious recession or a stock market slump has invariably been preceded by a rash of predictions that the economic cycle has been flattened and that the key to the endless boom has at last been found.

There was the historic prediction by the legendary financier Irving Fisher of "a permanent plateau of prosperity" in 1929, just before the Wall Street roof fell in. He was in good company. President Hoover ran in 1928 on the promise of "the new slogan of prosperity, from the full dinner pail to the full garage." There was the glorious IMF pronouncement of 1959 that "in all likelihood, inflation is over," and the famous conference of economists in 1969, under the benign gaze of Federal Reserve chairman Burns, with the comforting title "Is the Business Cycle Obsolete?" Then there was George Bush's rosy scenario in the 1988 campaign, as the fans of Reaganomics claimed the new wonders of just-in-time production and computerized inventory controls had finally smoothed out the roller coaster of the business cycle. In the summer of 1990, with a recession already gathering force, Federal Reserve chairman Greenspan assured Congress that "the likelihood of a recession seems low."

In the 1990s, as the stock market reached new peaks, a new theory became fashionable in America, that a quantum change had taken place in the nature of economic life with the productivity opportunities brought by computerization. Just as the world had moved from the agrarian age to the industrial era, now it was in transition to the information age. At the G-7 summit in Denver in 1997, President Clinton bragged to his fellow world leaders of "the new economic paradigm," and he told *Business Week* that after tutorials from his central banker, Greenspan, "I believe it's possible to have more sustained and higher growth without inflation than we previously thought. . . . The globalization of our economy, the impact of technologies, improved management, increased productivity, and a greater sophistication among working people about the relationship between their incomes and the growth of their companies—all are giving us a greater capacity for growth."

The ebullience of mature capitalism was flying as high as the stock market, and it proved catching. "Are Recessions Necessary?" asked the cover of *U.S. News & World Report.* "Capitalism Without Limits" proclaimed the cover of Rupert Murdoch's *Weekly Standard. Wired* magazine hailed the role of computers in bringing "the Long Boom." Presidential candidate Steve Forbes declared in his eponymous magazine that "this new era will be liberating and inspiring. It will enrich us not only materially but spiritually and culturally."

Perhaps happy days were finally here to stay, just in time for the millennium. Perhaps governments and central banks had finally learned how to deregulate, to cut taxes, to curb spending, and to control their debts, just as the baby-boom generation reached its peak earning years and started to save for retirement. Perhaps, despite all the false starts and disappointments of the past, the economics profession had at last gotten it right and Greenspan had finally found the philosopher's stone. Indeed, he had persuaded Clinton that "the new paradigm" represented the third revolution that America's central bank had faced, after the Great Depression and the global responsibilities that came with the Cold War.

Greenspan was said to study an extraordinary range of economic indicators. The Fed staff used to track five thousand data series. Under his reign, they began to track over fourteen thousand. He received special briefings from key sectors. The National Association of Home Builders gave him an early peek at their housing starts, and Detroit provided advance sales figures for the auto industry. But he was also fascinated by the transformation of the system itself, where he saw global competition and the benefits of the free-trade agreements reached during the Clinton presidency combining with the productivity benefits of computerization in creating a new kind of economy.

But if globalization was such an important component of the new American economy, then there was obvious room for alarm in the difficulties so many other parts of the global economy began to suffer at the peak of the American boom. The Asian miracles collapsed. Japan's financial sector fell into desperate straits. The tiger economies of Thailand, Malaysia, and Indonesia began whimpering in their lairs. At the same time, the countries of the European Union, whose combined GDP equaled that of the United States and whose share of world trade was markedly greater, finally launched their Euro, the single currency of which they had dreamt since their economies began to be sharply disrupted by the dollar diplomacy of the Johnson and Nixon administrations in the late 1960s. Greenspan may or may not have presided over the coming of a new economy, but he was certainly the American banker who saw the dollar's lonely and undisputed reign as the world's currency draw to a close.

26.
Bill Clinton
and the New America

When Bill Clinton first went abroad, to take up his Rhodes Scholarship at Oxford in 1968, America barely needed to trade with other countries. It was self-sufficient in almost everything except oil. Imports and exports together amounted to about 8 percent of the GDP. By the time Clinton started on his second term as president, trade in goods and services and financial transactions accounted for almost 30 percent of a much larger GDP. The United States had been the world's leading exporter in each year of the Clinton presidency; it had become an export-dependent country. Exports accounted for just 9.5 percent of Japan's GDP in 1997, but over 12 percent of that of the United States.

This slow revolution in the economy was spurred by the fastest-growing sector of American trade, its exports of services, including computer software, movies, insurance, royalties, financial services, and telecommunications.

America Reborn

In 1986, the American surplus on this trade was $11 billion. By 1992, the surplus on services had swollen to $64 billion, and just nudged $100 billion in 1997. Not just the nine-hundred-pound gorilla of international trade, the United States had also become the most nimble at developing the smart exports of the future.

This is a matter of quality as much as quantity. Of the world's three great exporting nations, the classic image of number three is the Mercedes-Benz car, a splendid piece of basically 1930s technology. The classic image of number two is the Sony Walkman and the VCR, cleverly marketed products of 1970s technology. The classic image of number one is the Windows 95 computer operating system, or a Boeing 747, or Hollywood's latest global megahit movie. Most of the world's consumers, and those endless immigrants seeking to enter the United States legally or illegally, know which economy they would prefer to join.

This extraordinary shift from self-reliance to far-reaching dependence on world trade began with America's grand strategy for the Cold War. The Marshall Plan, of course, and the Pentagon Special Procurement Fund budgets in the late 1940s and 1950s were used deliberately to rebuild the war-battered economies of Western Europe and Japan so that they could share the burdens of the West's collective defense. The total volume of world trade and foreign investment grew with the happenstance of the free market and boardroom decisions combined with the growing attraction of the world's ever more prosperous export markets. But throughout the 1990s, the process of intensifying world trade was nurtured by political design. President Bush began the process, negotiating the North American Free Trade Agreement (NAFTA) and the basics of the General Agreement on Tariffs and Trade (GATT). But the Bush administration shrank from promoting this grand project before a reluctant Congress. Clinton, by contrast, defied his party leadership in Congress and split his party to pass NAFTA and GATT with Republican votes.

Reaching far beyond Bush's initial vision, Clinton then defied the skeptics to convene in Seattle in 1993 the first trade summit of the Pacific Rim, the Asia-Pacific Economic Conference, and propose a regional trade pact. One year later, the agreement to develop a Pacific Rim free-trade area was signed in Indonesia. Clinton flew almost directly from that meeting to Miami to convene a summit of the western hemisphere (with the sole exception of Cuba), which agreed to form a Free Trade Association of the Americas.

In December 1995, Clinton flew to a far less reported meeting in Madrid. There he signed with the European Union the framework agreement for the Transatlantic Free Trade Agreement (TAFTA). Half of all American investment overseas was in Europe, and more than half of Europe's was in the United States. Europe was America's biggest export market, and one in every twelve American workers was employed by a European firm. The scale of U.S.-EU trade was so large that it dwarfed other trading relationships; for example, in 1997, the growth in American exports to the EU was greater than the entire sum of American exports to China. Above all, unlike the giant trade deficits that Japan and China enjoyed with the United States, the European trade was roughly in balance, and the mammoth scale of mutual investment made the relationship mutually advantageous. The growth in U.S.-European trade and investment had already become the first trillion-dollar economic relationship in history.

U.S.-EU TRADE
(1997 FIGURES, IN $ BILLIONS)

U.S. exports to EU	$306
EU exports to U.S.	$335
U.S. investments in EU	$369
EU investments in U.S.	$382
Total	$1,392

Source: US Mission to the European Union.

That total of almost $1.4 trillion had leapt by 50 percent in the first five years of the Clinton presidency. But then, so had American trade in general. The country exported $743 billion in manufactured goods and services in 1992; it exported $1,168 billion in 1997. Whatever the footnotes of history may say about Gennifer Flowers, Paula Jones, and Monica Lewinsky and the narrow vote in the House of Representatives to impeach him, Bill Clinton's real place in history is secure. He will be known as the free-trade president.

For the steady resolve with which he has pursued this grand strategy of geoeconomics, it might fairly be called "the Clinton Doctrine," because its implications reach far beyond trade. In 1990, at the G-7 summit of the leading industrial nations in Houston, Margaret Thatcher warned that the world was in danger of congealing into three trade blocs, each based on a single currency: the yen, the dollar, and the deutsche mark. Recalling George Orwell's nightmare vision in his book *1984* of the three warring blocs of Oceania, Eastasia, and Eurasia, she was troubled that trade rivalry could easily degenerate into strategic antagonism. The Clinton Doctrine was designed to preclude such an outcome by locking the dominant economy of the United States into each of the trading blocs.

When Clinton came into office, he was confronted by the slow implosion of the foreign policy consensus around an American global military leadership that had guided his country since 1941. The long tradition of American isolation, secure behind its two-ocean moat, had been destroyed by the Japanese attack on Pearl Harbor. The country had no choice but to assume the leading role in the defeat of German Nazism and Japanese militarism, and after the war, this responsibility continued to the protection of the freedom of the seas and the freedom of trade, taking over from the exhausted British. The coming of the Cold War sealed the new American responsibility. The crucial moment came in January 1947 when President Truman, Secretary of State George Marshall, and his deputy Dean Acheson went to Capitol Hill to persuade the Republican-dominated Senate Foreign Relations Committee that the United States had to take over from Britain the responsibility for supporting Greece and Turkey against Soviet subversion and aggression.

"I knew we were met at Armageddon," Acheson recalled in his memoir of those pivotal years, *Present at the Creation.* "Soviet pressure on the Straits, on Iran and on Northern Greece had brought the Balkans to the point where a highly possible Soviet breakthrough might open the continents to Soviet penetration. The Soviet Union was playing one of the greatest gambles in history at minimal cost. We and we alone were in a position to break up the play."

"Mr. President, if you will say that to the Congress and the country, I will support you and I believe that most of its members will do the same," said Senator Arthur Vandenberg, the old isolationist who was chairman of the committee, and the bipartisan foreign policy was securely launched. Broadly speaking, with the occasional political storm over Korea and a rather deeper crisis over Vietnam, that American consensus was to endure for over forty years, with American commitment to the NATO alliance never seriously in question. For over forty years, an American garrison of more than 300,000 troops stood guard in Europe.

The end of the Cold War in 1989, and the subsequent collapse of the Soviet Union in 1991, brought that consensus to an end. The Clinton Doctrine was to be its replacement. Thanks to the support of Senator Robert Dole and Speaker of the House Newt Gingrich for his free-trading strategy, Clinton was able to replace it with a new consensus on America's place in the coming century in a free-trading global economy of democracies, with the United States as linchpin and guarantor in a new architecture for the post–Cold War world.

There was grandeur in his second-term ambitions for foreign policy, where Clinton and his new national security team felt they had grown experienced and comfortable with the uses of American power. They all shared the conviction that theirs was "the indispensable nation," the superpower without whose leadership and involvement nothing serious could be achieved internationally. Clinton and his colleagues were raised as students in the shadow of that great post-1945 generation of Americans who launched the Marshall Plan and NATO, all to contain the Soviet Union without all-out war.

The new Clinton team, not to be outdone, saw their mission in almost equally ambitious terms. They aspired, if not to a new creation, then to be present at the solution; to go down in history as the wise men and women who resolved the outstanding difficulties of the post–Cold War era and launched the world on a new millennium of peace and goodwill. Secretary of State Madeleine Albright set her own tone for the next four years by telling the Senate Foreign Relations Committee at her confirmation hearing that "we must be more than audience, more even than actors, we must be the authors of the history of our age." Her entire budget for foreign aid, diplomacy, the United Nations, and all the other international organizations to which the United States subscribed, amounted to barely 1 percent of the federal budget—"but that will be used to write fifty percent of the history and legacy of our times," she said.

She then explicitly compared the challenges ahead to those that faced the United States when she first arrived as a little girl, a refugee for the second time in her short life. The first time, she had fled her native Czechoslovakia for Britain in 1939, and still recalls sheltering in the air raid shelters of Notting Hill Gate during the London blitz. Eight years and one "liberation" later, she fled Soviet domination for an America that was already girding for the long Cold War struggle that Acheson had envisaged. So when Albright invoked Acheson's name before the Senate as she prepared to be the first women to join the ranks of his successors, one of the wheels of history had come full circle.

"Senators, you on your side of the table and I on my side have a unique opportunity to be partners in creating a new and enduring framework for American leadership," she concluded.

One of my predecessors, Dean Acheson, wrote about being present at the creation of a new era. You and I have the challenge and the responsibility to help co-author the newest chapter in our history . . . to answer a prayer that has been offered over many years in a multitude of tongues, in accordance with diverse customs, in response to a common yearning. That prayer is a prayer for peace, freedom, food on the table, and what President Clinton once eloquently referred to as "the quiet miracle of a normal life."

The second Clinton administration shared four grand international ambitions. The most immediate, according to the new national security adviser, Sandy Berger, was to assert that America remained a European power, which planned "to build an undivided, peaceful and democratic Europe." The goal was to do for Central and Eastern Europe what the Cold War generation had achieved for Western Europe. The administration was determined, one way or another, to persuade Russia to accept an enlarged NATO alliance advancing right up to Russia's borders, while devising new mechanisms to draw a compliant Russia into an American-led transatlantic trade and security system. In this, with Russia's decision to join a Permanent Joint Council with NATO, and to send Russian peacekeeping troops to serve under American command in Bosnia, they broadly succeeded.

Clinton's second goal, rooted in America's parallel claim to be an Asian-Pacific power, was "to cement America's role as a stabilizing force in a more integrated Asian-Pacific community," in which China would be engaged and cajoled into becoming a cooperative power. The third was to build on the global free-trade strategy of the first term and "build an open regional economy in the Western hemisphere," with presidential visits to widen the North American Free Trade Agreement to include Chile and Argentina. The last objective was finally to resolve America's wretched relations with the United Nations and pay off the $1.4 billion in arrears. These were formidable dreams for a team that had four years earlier bungled the petty squabbles of Somali warlords and were now embarked on the grandest reordering of the global order since the Treaty of Versailles.

It all seemed possible. For the first time since the 1920s, the United States in the late 1990s appeared to be ending the century while enjoying the rare combination of peace and prosperity. From the Great Depression of the 1930s until the end of the Cold War, the country had been in economic recession, at war, or maintaining its defense budgets and its large standing armies on a quasi-war footing. But since 1992, when Clinton entered the White House, the economy and the stock market had boomed and the United States was able to enjoy an unprecedented state of military security at almost painless cost.

There is no parallel in modern history for the global military hegemony that the United States enjoyed in 1999 on land, on sea, and in space. Its defense budget was the same as the next ten significant military powers put together, and its weaponry was a technical generation ahead. No other nation could challenge at sea any one of the twelve aircraft carrier task forces by which America ruled the waves. No other nation could defy the power of America's stealth warplanes, invisible to radar, able to inflict aerial bombardment of devastating precision with virtual impunity. And it all cost just $250 billion a year, a mere 3.5 percent of the GDP. The last time the United States had spent so tiny a portion of the national wealth on defense was 1940.

Throughout the Cold War, the United States usually spent 8 percent of the GDP on defense, rising to 11 percent during the height of the Vietnam War, and to a grueling 15 percent of the GDP during the Korean conflict. The 1999 level of defense spending, and the unmatchable military supremacy it brought, could be sustained indefinitely with minimal political pain.

America had become the modern Rome, its garrisons still standing watch on the Rhine as the legions had two thousand years earlier. But its 1.3 million troops and two hundred bases around the world also uphold the Pax Americana in Japan, Korea, and the Persian Gulf. Its language is the modern Latin, just as the American-developed communications satellites, phone links, and Internet are the modern age's equivalent of Roman roads. The Americans even share the Roman obsession with the export of decent plumbing and central heating.

There are two extraordinary features of the way the country ended what has come to be called "the American century" (a phrase coined at the end of World War II by *Time* magazine founder Henry Luce). The first is that this awesome power is now wielded by a new generation, which came of age and learned many of its political instincts during the bitterly divisive era of the Vietnam War. Clinton, his national security adviser, Berger, and his deputy secretary of state, Strobe Talbott, not only avoided military service, like the majority of their generation, but actively opposed the war. This helps to explain not only the tension between the civilians of the Clinton administration and the professional military establishment in the Pentagon but also the curious reluctance of modern America to wield the power it commands. Bush boasted after the short, sharp victory of the Gulf War against Iraq that "the Vietnam syndrome is finally over." But this syndrome, the public dismay at the loss of American lives in overseas conflicts, returned with a vengeance when eighteen Rangers were killed in a single day in Somalia in 1993. Clinton hesitated for nearly three years before finally taking the risk to deploy American troops to end the Bosnian war in 1995. The United States may be the world's only superpower, but it is locked in a strategic paradox; never has so much overwhelming force been so constrained by political hesitation.

The second remarkable feature of America's peace and prosperity in the 1990s is how quickly it had come, and how suddenly the national mood had changed. As late as 1988, Bush won the presidential race with a campaign that stressed the Cold War was not over, with an ominous campaign ad that stressed "the bear is still in the woods." As late as 1992, the consensus was that America had paid a desperate price for its Cold War victory. The most pungent sound bite of the 1992 election campaign came from the late Senator Paul Tsongas: "The Cold War is over, and Japan won." He was talking about the massive federal budget deficits of the Reagan-Bush years, which took the government's debt—as cited earlier—from barely $1 trillion when Reagan entered the White House to over $4 trillion when Bush left it. But the real economic failure had begun much earlier, just as the baby boomers began leaving their colleges and their antiwar demonstrations for the real world.

Between 1947 and 1972, the median family income in the United States doubled, from $18,000 to $36,000 a year in today's dollars. From 1972 to 1994, it barely rose. Some of this is explained by the increase in the number of households, spurred by rising divorce rates and the poverty of single-parent households. But the fact that the number of women in the workplace had more than tripled in the previous thirty years meant that for most American families, two wages were needed to sustain living standards that one paycheck used to provide. Through the great inflation of the 1970s and the ravening deficits of the 1980s and the downsizing of the old labor-intensive corporations in the early 1990s, this stalling of the great American prosperity machine dominated the politics and the mood of the nation. It fueled the fashionable (and wrongheaded) theories of American decline and of imperial overstretch, and accelerated the economic and jobs crisis of the inner cities, which in turn steepened crime rates and racial tensions. Then came what may with fairness be called "the Clinton boom." The median family income in 1998 exceeded fifty thousand dollars. Unemployment was below 5 percent, and GDP growth was over 4 percent and inflation below 3. Above all, this prosperity came from a transformed American economy, the way the United States had become the world's biggest exporter, unprecedentedly dependent on the global economy that it dominates.

And yet Clinton had won the 1992 election on the slogan "The economy, stupid!" The country had been in a mild recession and a rather deeper psychological depression. Clinton had campaigned on the need for a stimulus package to get the economy moving again. But as he awaited his inauguration, sobering news came from the outgoing Office of Management and Budget (OMB). Its revised estimates of the budget deficit suggested that the structural problem was very much worse than even Clinton thought it would be—$20 billion higher. Without new taxes, and even assuming optimistic assumptions for growth and employment, the deficit would be $60 billion higher than envisaged by 1997, and it would exceed $400 billion by the end of the decade.

Perhaps the most important meeting Clinton held before assuming the presidency, certainly the one that arranged the economic circumstances of his reelection, took place in Little Rock on December 3, 1992, when he met Alan Greenspan. Greenspan's Fed set short-term interest rates and governed the money supply. Its constitutional role was designed to spare the Fed day-to-day political pressures from the White House or from Congress. Greenspan's term would last most of Clinton's first term, and there was nothing Clinton could do about that. The two men had never had a serious conversation before. Clinton knew Greenspan was a conservative who believed passionately in free markets, hated inflation, and was massively unsympathetic to the Keynesian views that Clinton instinctively upheld. Clinton assumed he could expect little help from the Fed in fulfilling his election pledge to stimulate the economy.

The conversation between the two men had been expected to last for two hours or so, but it extended far longer and through lunch, as Greenspan explained the predicament that he and the new president now faced. Something unusual was happening to interest rates, Greenspan said. The recession was ending, and recovery well under way, thanks to the Fed's steady reduction of short-term interest rates from 7 to 3 percent. But long-term interest rates for ten to thirty years ahead were not following the short-term rates down. They were stuck much higher, at around 7 percent, which meant that the markets feared future inflation. The markets were dominated by the scale of a federal budget deficit of over $200 billion a year, which had now become a structural fixture of the American system. That amount of regular government borrowing left less money available for investment in the real economy. This was a crisis of confidence; the markets did not trust the politicians. The only way to bring down the long-term rate was to convince the markets that the era of budget deficits would end. Once convinced, lower interest rates would improve the prospects for the economy incomparably more than any short-term stimulus.

"We can do business," Clinton told Al Gore after the meeting, which had left him fascinated and impressed, as well as optimistic. Clinton had referred to his campaign pledge to halve the budget deficit by growing the economy. If that could be credibly put in motion, Greenspan had told him, the long-term rates would drop and the economy would grow at a strong sustainable rate in 1997 and after. If not, then any short-term stimulus could result in a renewed recession in 1995 or shortly thereafter. Greenspan did not have to spell out the key date in Clinton's head—his reelection in 1996. The message was clear enough, and Clinton filed away the crucial implication for his economic plans; deficit reduction would do the economy—and him—more good than the immediate stimulus package he had been planning.

Clinton had promised in the campaign to pass an economic-stimulus bill in his first hundred days in office. But now that was simply to be the beginning. He decided that he wanted an overall economic plan for his entire first term. The first planning meeting took place on January 7, 1993, and was dominated by two statistics. The first was offered by OMB director Leon Panetta, who said the deficit was heading out of control and by fiscal 1997 (the target date of the end of Clinton's first term) would be $360 billion a year. The second was from Gene Sperling, thirty-four, a graduate of Yale Law and the University of Pennsylvania's Wharton School of Finance who had worked for Governor Mario Cuomo in New York and then had joined the Clinton team to help draft the economic plans in Clinton's campaign manifesto, "Putting People First." Now a deputy to Robert Rubin in the National Economic Council, Sperling was a workaholic. Sperling, who knew the plans better than anyone else, had costed them out—they would come to $88.8 billion in the first year.

For Clinton, the meeting contained only bad news. Laura D'Andrea Tyson, chairing his Council of Economic Advisers, said that she did not expect robust growth from the current recovery, no more than 3 percent a year. Her new deputy, the Princeton economist Alan Blinder, warned that deficit reduction might sound politically popular and reassure the markets, but it would reduce the rate of economic growth. To cut the deficit by 1 percent of the GDP, roughly $60 billion, meant taking that much money out of the economy, and that would cut the year's growth rate by 1.5 percent. A crash program to balance the budget would take 4 percent of the GDP out of the economy. This would cause obvious hardship for the pensioners, welfare recipients, defense industries, and others whose access to federal funds would be cut. The reward for this virtue would come much later, Blinder went on. It could come faster, if the markets believed that the deficit cuts were genuine and the Fed visibly shared that confidence and lowered long-term interest rates. But the markets, after the roller-coaster years of the 1980s and the accumulation of deficits, would be extraordinarily hard to convince.

"You mean to tell me that the success of the program and my reelection hinges on the Federal Reserve and a bunch of international bond traders?" asked Clinton. Precisely so. Or as Clinton said later in the meeting: "So we have to pick up the tab for the Reagan-Bush deficits. They got elected by wrecking the economy and I lose reelection by fixing it." Again, Clinton was correct. The presidency he had fought so hard to win from Bush was a poisoned chalice. Unless—and this was to be the essential perception that shaped all the forthcoming battles over his stimulus package and his budgets—he could take advantage of the one way out. It meant relying on Greenspan. Blinder thought the markets would take years to drop interest rates. Greenspan had suggested, rather than promised, that their reward might in certain circumstances come much sooner.

It came very soon indeed. Clinton's first speech to a joint session of Congress, shortly after the inauguration, revealed his new appreciation of Greenspan. Hillary Clinton thoughtfully invited him to sit beside her as the new president spoke. Common courtesy required that he rise to join a standing ovation whenever the First Lady did, and a great deal of courtesy was required of him. But he looked visibly cheered by what he heard: the promise of a shrunken stimulus package and a pledge of a determined assault on the deficit, promising $490 billion in spending reductions over the coming five years. Greenspan applauded, and the bond market rose the next day. The day after that, Greenspan appeared before a congressional committee to praise the Clinton plan as "serious and plausible," an endorsement that was widely reported. The following week, the interest rate on thirty-year bonds dropped below 7 percent for the first time since they had been issued, fulfilling Greenspan's promise at Little Rock that stringent economic virtue could bring its own reward with some speed.

By breaking his campaign pledge to stimulate the economy and by following Greenspan's advice to curb the deficit, Clinton secured the best stimulus of all, a sustained fall in interest rates. This, in turn, stimulated new investment, which meant new jobs, which meant higher tax receipts and fewer payments of unemployment and welfare benefits, and the virtuous circle began. By the start of his second term, the deficit, which had once threatened to reach $400 billion, had virtually disappeared. By 1998, the federal budget was in surplus and unemployment was below 5 percent.

America's renewed domestic prosperity brought with it some happy social effects: plunging rates of murder and violent crime; a job-creating economy that was easing the transition to what Clinton and the Republican majority in Congress called the "reform" of the welfare system; and a baby-boomer sensibility that was civilizing the discourse for women and gays. Above all, the prosperity seemed finally to be helping the country to ease its historic anguish over race. The United States and its foreign critics had been accustomed to focusing grimly on that 40 percent of young black males who were in prison, on bail, or on probation, caught up in a violent and vindictive penal culture that had almost 1.5 million Americans behind bars. But there was a bright side to the picture, one that would have gladdened the heart of Martin Luther King, Jr., who did so much to bring it about.

The 1990 census showed that of 30 million black Americans, over 9 million lived in households with an annual income of $35,000 or more, the usual definition of middle class. Among black Americans in 1968, there were five times as many high school dropouts as college graduates. In 1998, among blacks age twenty-five to forty-four, the numbers were even. In 1970, only 15.3 percent of blacks age eighteen to thirty-five had any college education; by 1998, the figure was 48.3 percent (compared to 59.8 percent among whites). In suburb after suburb, from Carson, California, to Southfield, Michigan, to

America Reborn

Queens, New York, the median household income for blacks exceeded that of whites, as the new black middle class abandoned the inner city for safer streets and better schools, just as the whites did. Asian-Americans and Hispanics were doing even better, following in the classic footsteps of the Irish, Italian, and Jewish immigrants who found and forged such opportunity in America, and made so many compromises with its brutal rules.

There were shadows on the picture, of course—witness the way Florida and California and some other states spent more on prisons than on colleges. There was a curious thread of extremism running through the country, from the right-wing antigovernment militia zealots who blew up the federal office building in Oklahoma City in 1995 to the antiabortion fanatics who opened fire on abortion clinics and the doctors working in them. There was also a serious problem with American democracy, from a low turnout of barely 50 percent of eligible voters for the 1996 presidential election to a campaign finance system that was uncomfortably close to institutionalized corruption. In 1992 for the first time, the federal election cycle required politicians to raise over $1 billion, mostly for television advertising, which increasingly shifted political influence into the hands of those able to afford it.

Other shadows were looming for the future, most evidently across the Pacific, where the challenge of China's rapid economic growth and fast-modernizing military capability was creating a regional superpower that may prove as difficult to manage in the twenty-first century as the Soviet Union had been in the twentieth. The threat of terrorism, whether homegrown or international, and of nuclear proliferation in India and Pakistan, pointed to the ways that America's awesome military could be outflanked. Russia's bumpy progress toward a kind of democracy and a kind of free-market capitalism was far from secure, and in Asia there was outspoken resentment at America's economic and cultural influence.

There were also signs of unease at home, in the liberal wing of the Democratic party and in the labor unions, at the way in which the prosperity of the 1990s was being divided. The share of national wealth enjoyed by the richest 5 percent was by 1998 the largest it had been since the 1920s, while the share of the poorest 20 percent was the lowest. There were signs that the new American economy of the information age and global free trade could be re-creating an eerily Victorian social system. A small number of superrich and a large and affluent upper-middle class sat happily over a stubbornly depressed and often-criminal underclass, with a large class of respectable poor in the middle, just a paycheck or two away from financial disaster. The traditional American mechanism for social mobility to break out of this pattern, the public school system, was performing poorly by international standards. Such cautionary admonitions won little response from a Republican Congress that liked to repeat Clinton's celebrated phrase that "the era of big government is over" and preferred to leave education to the local school boards.

These tremors of unease perhaps explained why America at the end of the century was not enjoying quite that fulsome mood of self-congratulation that attended Reagan's proud announcement in 1984 that it was "Morning in America." Perhaps Clinton was a less persuasive actor. Perhaps the public doubts about Clinton's character and the Whitewater, fund-raising, and sexual scandals that continued to nag him accounted for this. It was a terrible blot on the Clinton record to be only the third president to face impeachment proceedings, only the second to be impeached, and the first to have confessed to lying under oath. And yet Clinton's popularity and economic record, and the changing cultural standards of the American electorate, gave him a crucial mandate in the 1998 midterm elections. The largest single generational cohort in the electorate were baby boomers, who had, like Clinton, lived through the sexual revolution and did not consider prevarication about sexual profligacy to warrant impeachment and removal from office. Indeed, there were times when the entire proceedings smacked more of the entertainment industry than of judicial process. The United States in the Clinton era seemed yet again to be following the example of ancient Rome, offering both bread and circuses.

But then one of the functions of the modern president is, if not to entertain, then to act as something more than the traditional father and leader of his people. The media revolution had widened the potential of the role. John Kennedy had been the country's young prince, even perhaps its lover, bringing a youthful virility and a barely disguised eroticism to the role. After Nixon became the national villain, Carter presented himself as the nation's pastor, and Reagan dominated the world stage and soothed the national insecurities as only a born actor could. The need for a presidency that reached beyond traditional symbols and beyond the usual solemnities of duty was the stronger in the 1990s.

The nature of the office, and the power it had wielded for sixty years, was changing subtly but decisively in response to a changing international environment. Clinton was to be the first president to grapple with the twilight of the "Imperial Presidency," Arthur Schlesinger, Jr.'s term for the period beginning in 1932. One of the most distinctive rhythms of American political history has been the tidal flow of power from White House to Congress and back again. If the usual business of government was shared in creative but often uneasy tension between the two, crisis always strengthened the presidential hand. From the presidencies of Jackson, Lincoln, Teddy Roosevelt, and Wilson, a clear pattern emerged of the military, economic, or political crisis becoming the occasion of a shift in the balance of power from the Capitol to the White House. But the power subsequently shifted back again.

The striking feature of American history since 1932 is that the crisis never stopped. For six decades, the tide of power did not again wash back up Pennsylvania Avenue to the Congress. The Great Depression led into World War II, which led in turn to the Cold War. These were three challenges, each threatening the very existence and character of the American state, which flowed almost seamlessly from one to the next. The clear and present danger to the American state embodied in each of these crises was in itself a justification of big and activist government, in which all of the resources of the nation-state had to be rallied, led, and directed by the president.

Until 1939, the members of the White House staff were little more than household servants, and the American head of state had to make do with a singularly truncated court. The president had authority to hire only four staff aides above the clerical rank. By 1945, Roosevelt had eleven administrative assistants. Truman had thirteen. Eisenhower had thirty-seven. By 1972, Nixon had forty-eight. The executive office staff, swollen to 1,175 during Eisenhower's first term, grew to 5,395 under Nixon. This mass of political courtiers was but the most intimate layer of a growing federal bureaucracy, the machinery of big government.

Truman's establishment in 1947 of the National Security Council and the Central Intelligence Agency brought two unprecedented new tools of executive authority under the president's own hand. Truman went further, creating the Council of Economic Advisers as an independent source of economic advice, and the Atomic Energy Commission, to keep the awesome new power of atomic energy under the president's direct control.

These new institutions stemmed not just from presidential ambition but from a series of fundamentally transformed situations that a president had to face. The most immediately dramatic was the development of the atomic bomb, imposing a new technological imperative upon the traditional responsibilities of the president, as commander in chief, and the Congress, as the body with the constitutional authority to declare war. After the sneak attack on Pearl Harbor, the prospect of a surprise nuclear strike on American targets was immeasurably more conceivable. Consequently, the decision-making process became more urgent. As the nuclear balance developed in the 1950s and thereafter, the president required the powers to wage instant, retaliatory war, without the time for the constitutional niceties.

All this could be justified in the name of national security. The threat was immediate, and so the president had to have the right to engage in instant controls over the economy, just as he required the power to embark on instant nuclear war. The threat was everywhere, so the president required the latitude to deploy troops to threatened areas abroad at his will, as Truman did to Korea. The threat was insidious, and so the president had to have the power to meet fire with fire, to meet subversion with covert operations, to overthrow hostile regimes with secret armies. Presidential policy had to be empowered to overthrow elected governments abroad, if they were deemed to challenge America's strategic interests. Only one nation in the West had the resources to sustain that struggle, and the only American institution that could provide that strategic will was the presidency, required to become imperial by the mortal danger of the threat. The Cold War defined the modern presidency, and recast the job into the role of commander in chief of the Free World. And the rest of the world, in consequence, was to be almost as fascinated by the dramas of presidential elections as the Americans themselves.

American citizens and America's allies and its former enemies alike grew so accustomed to this presidential greatness that its enfeeblement was not immediately apparent. But in the aftermath of the Cold War, it was clear that the existence of the United States was no longer threatened. In the 1990s, there was no Great Depression to require emergency powers. There was no world war, no Cold War substitute, and no nuclear missiles poised and targeted at American cities. And in the absence of mortal threat, there was less obvious need for big government, or for an imperial president to rule it.

The result of the Cold War was a victory more strategically sweeping than any since Trafalgar in 1805, which established the global dominance of the Royal Navy, and the triumph of Britain's then-revolutionary industrial and commercial system. American commerce, American culture, and American values now appear poised to dominate in their turn. This might have happened anyway, but as the man at the helm, who would have been held responsible for failure, Clinton may claim some credit for the way Americans have adjusted with remarkable speed from the Cold War strategy of leading a global military alliance to organizing the new free-trading and capital-mobile global economy. Clinton might have waxed too lyrical about the triumph of free markets and free institutions, and *democracy* may not quite be the word for the emergent structures of Russia and Mexico, let alone China, but his arguments retained their force even after the financial crisis that hit Asia and Russia in 1998.

The world was generally a more prosperous, more peaceful, and more hopeful place at the end of the twentieth century than it had been throughout it. It had even begun, if belatedly, at the international conference at Kyoto in 1997, to tackle the creeping environmental disaster that global industrialization had brought. The American Century, and the extraordinary people who steered it through shooting wars, depressions, the Cold War, and racial turmoil, had built not just a global economy but an emergent global sensibility, informed and created by a global media that America had pioneered.

That global sensibility cannot be defined with precision. Its essential components include a belief in the rule of law and the rejection of racism, in both the rights of private property and the obligations of public authority to educate its people, tend its sick and elderly, cleanse the environment, and respect the beliefs and rights of others. These emergent global codes owed much of their inspiration to the great religious works that had guided human societies for millennia, and some to the French belief in the rights of man and the British tradition of parliamentary democracy and common law. They had faced two mortal challenges in the twentieth century, from Nazism and from the distorted Soviet version of communism. America had been instrumental in the defeat of each, even as it was slowly, painfully, but with determination becoming a universal nation that contained and embraced every tribe of the human race and every form of its faiths and sought to make space and opportunity for them all. Flawed and unruly though it was, rapacious and bullying as it sometimes appeared, America at the end of the second millennium was a place the Founding Fathers might just have recognized, could frequently have deprecated, but most certainly would have enjoyed.

Acknowledgments

The concept and structure of this book owe a great deal to my agent, Derek Johns, and my editor, Jonathan Segal, whose help and friendship I deeply value. Jonathan and my friend Peter Tauber helped saved me from many a foreigner's solecisms, not least in the chapter on baseball. Interviews and conversations with George Bush and Bill Clinton, with James Baker, Warren Christopher and Madeleine Albright, with Brent Scowcroft, Bob Zoellick, and Tony Lake, gave me a palpable sense of the presidency and of American foreign policy. Conversations with the late William Colby and Richard Helms taught me about the CIA, and General William Odom and the privilege of lecturing at the National War College gave me some insights into the military as an institution.

Although private papers have been consulted in the various presidential archives and in the New York Public Library's collection of the Goldman papers, and I have had the pleasure of long acquaintance with John Steinbeck's widow, Elaine, a work of this scope necessarily depends on secondary research. Arthur Schlesinger, James McGregor Burns, Samuel Eliot Morison, and Denis and Hugh Brogan provided my introduction to American history, and I kept their works all close at hand. My friend Seymour Martin Lipsett taught me why America was different, while the books of J. F. K. Galbraith urged me to keep thinking about comparisons. My colleague of many a talk show, Michael Barone, was invaluable for his history of the years from Roosevelt to Reagan as much as his essential *Almanac of American Politics.* The pioneering works of Richard Barnett, David Calleo, and Diane Kunz on the American economy's surge toward globalization were constantly consulted.

Beyond these and other general works, and the memoirs and writings of the subjects of each chapter, I have leaned heavily on a number of specialized books.

As well as the voluminous writings of Theodore Roosevelt, I rely heavily on William Harbough's *Life and Times,* on Henry Pringle, Richard Hofstadter, and Edmund Morris's biography.

For Emma Goldman, Richard Drinnon's *Rebel in Paradise* was essential, backed up by Robert Le Murray's *Red Scare,* Max Lowenthal's *The Federal Bureau of Investigation,* and the reports to Congress of Attorney General Palmer.

Pershing's memoir, *My Experiences in the World War,* ghostwritten by the future general George Marshall, is a strikingly one-sided account that has to be read in con-

Acknowledgments

junction with the memoirs of France's Marshal Foch and the even more self-serving reminiscences of Britain's Sir Douglas Haig. Dennis Winter's *Haig's Command* was a useful corrective to them all, backed up by Gene A. Smith's biography of Pershing and Frank VanDiver's *Life and Times.*

Beyond Robert Lacey's excellent biography of Henry Ford, the broader analysis of the social role of American engineering and systems owes a great deal to Thomas Hughes's *American Genesis* and John Jordan's *Machine Age Ideology.*

For Woodrow Wilson, the essential guides were Arthur Stanley Link, August Hecksher and Thomas Bailey, in conjunction with the Wilson papers and Thomas J. Knock's *Quest for a New World Order.*

For Babe Ruth, along with advice from almost every American male of my acquaintance, Charles Alexander's *Our Game* and James Michener's *Sports in America* were particularly useful, reinforced by Harold Seymour's *The Golden Age.* The biographies of Ruth by Robert Creamer and Marshall Smelser were also helpful.

Despite a new biography by Sharlene P. and Ted W. Nelson, William Boeing is a curiously underchronicled figure. Wayne Biddle's excellent study of the early aviation pioneers *Barons of the Sky,* and *Superfortress* by General Curtis LeMay and Gil Yonne, helped extend the efforts of the Boeing corporation's own historical division.

Beyond Category by John Edward Hasse is a virtually definitive biography of Duke Ellington, but Daniel Kayman's *American Music,* Wilfred Mekers's *Music in a New Found Land,* and *The March of Jazz* by James Lincoln Collins were also helpful.

For Winston Churchill, the standard biographies by Martin Gilbert and William Manchester were essential. But for the wider issues of Anglo-American relations, see Sir Robin Renwick's *Fighting With Allies, Oceans Apart* by David Dimbleby and David Reynolds, *Anglo-American Defence Relations* by John Baylis, and the delightfully iconoclastic *Blood, Class and Nostalgia* by Christopher Hitchens.

Beyond visits to Fallingwater, the Guggenheim, the Johnson factory, Taliesin West, and other buildings by Frank Lloyd Wright, which are perhaps the best way to appreciate this remarkable genius, the most consulted works on Frank Lloyd Wright's architecture were written by Neil Levine, Edgar Kaufman, Henry J. Michel, and W. A. Shirer.

For Lucky Luciano, the Valachi papers and Nicholas Gage's *Mafia U.S.A.* were essential reading, but not half as useful as Robert Lacey's biography of Luciano's friend and partner Meyer Lansky.

FDR has inspired more books than any other single figure in this collection, but beyond the standard works by James McGregor Burns, Arthur Schlesinger, and Doris Kearns Goodwin, I found Rexford Tugwell, Dexter Perkins, and Basil Rauch to be particularly helpful guides.

Katharine Hepburn's *Me* is a deeply satisfying autobiography but needs amplification and context from the biographies by Charles Higham and Sheridan Morely and Ronald Bergen's *An Independent Woman.* Neil Gabler's *An Empire of Their Own* was helpful on the Hollywood studio system.

Walter Reuther's *Collected Papers,* edited by Henry Christman, and Irving Howe's *The UAW and Walter Reuther* are the essential starting point, along with John Barnard's biography and Nelson Lichtenstein's *The Most Dangerous Man in Detroit.* Thomas R. Brookes's wider history of the labor movement, *Toil and Trouble,* and Philip Taft's work on the AFL provided context.

John Steinbeck's biography by Jackson Benson is thoughtful and thorough, and

Acknowledgments

Catherine Reef's biography was also useful. I was also fortunate in having a father-in-law, Graham Watson, who was Steinbeck's literary agent and close friend.

Antony Heilbut's *Exiled in Paradise* is a remarkably wide and thoughtful account of the epic that brought so many of Europe's intellectuals to America in the 1930s. For Albert Einstein and the atomic bomb, the works of Richard Rhodes, *The Nuclear Barons* by Peter Pringle and James Spigelman, and Stephane Groueff's *The Manhattan Project* were all helpful.

General Marshall is the subject of readable biographies by Leonard Mosely, Ed Cray, and Mark Stoler, and more scholarly tomes by Forrest Pogue. But American perspectives are given balance by David Fraser's biography of Field Marshal Alanbrooke, and by Arthur Bryant's edition of Alanbrooke's war diaries, *The Turn of the Tide. Grand Strategy* by Sir Michael Howard, and the official U.S. history, *Strategic Planning and Coalition Warfare* by M. Matloff and E. M. Snell, were essential. Dean Acheson's *Present at the Creation* and C. L. Mee's *The Marshall Plan* were also useful.

William F. Buckley is his own best publicist, but his works require the balance of the excellent biography by John Judis. Godfrey Hodgson's *The World Turned Rightside Up* and David Frum's *What's Right?* provided a broader context for American conservatism, along with Pat Buchanan's *Right from the Beginning* and R. A. Goldberg's biography of Barry Goldwater.

Richard Bissell is a central figure in Evan Thomas's remarkably sympathetic and perceptive study of the early CIA, *The Very Best Men.* Ben Rich's *Skunk Works* is an inimitable account of the birth of the U2 and Blackbird spy planes, and Thomas Power's book on CIA Director Richard Helms, *The Man Who Kept the Secrets,* is a good guide to the embarrassments the CIA suffered in the 1960s and 1970s.

Billy Graham is the subject of several almost worthless hagiographies, which are more than compensated by the excellent *Prophet With Honor* by William Martin. A wider context is provided by Gary Wills's *Under God,* by Penny Leroux's *People of God,* and by the collected essays *Piety and Politics,* edited by R. J. Neuhaus and M. Cromartie.

One of the great pleasures of this book has been the duty to see again so many Disney films and cartoons, to revisit Disneyland and Disney World, and to come across Steven Watts's thorough and thoughtful biography. Christopher Finch's *Art of Disney* and Richard Schickel's *The Disney Version: The Life, Times, Art and Commerce of Walt Disney* were useful. Marc Eliot's *Hollywood's Dark Prince* provided an interesting, if overheated, critique.

Richard Nixon's own books, particularly *Six Crises* and *I Gave Them a Sword,* are extraordinarily revealing, buttressing the Kissinger memoirs, the Roger Morris biography, and *From the President,* Bruce Oudes's edition of Nixon's memoranda. Alan Drury's *Courage and Hesitation,* the Haldeman memoirs, and John Erlichman's *Witness to Power* were all useful. The significance of the new economic policy announced on August 15, 1971, has been stressed in David Calleo's *Beyond American Hegemony,* in a special twentieth anniversary editorial in the *Wall Street Journal* by its editor, Robert Bartley, and in my own *The Cold War: A History.*

Taylor Branch's momumental *Parting the Waters* and David Lewis's biography are essential to get beyond the hagiographies of Dr. Martin Luther King, Jr. For the background of the 1960s, there are few better places to start than Richard N. Goodwin's *Remembering America,* but Tom Wells's *The War Within* and Rhodri Jeffreys-Jones's *Peace Now* were important adjuncts.

Acknowledgments

Having had the pleasure of dining with Betty Friedan and enjoying her acute and restless intelligence, I found Daniel Horowitz's new assessment of her political roots particularly useful, along with Judith Hennessee's *Life.* The historical and political backgrounds stem from Carole Hymonwitz's and Michael Weissman's *History of Women in America,* Nancy Woloch's *Women and the American Experience,* and Susan Faludi's *Backlash.*

Alan Greenspan has not yet inspired a serous biography. D. M. Jones's *The Politics of Money* is a highly technical and inside account of the way the Federal Reserve Board reaches its decisions, but dates from 1991. William Greider's history of the Fed, *Secrets of the Temple,* is the essential background, but I also benefited from conversations with Laura D'Andrea Tyson and Professor Alan Blinder.

My own biography of Bill Clinton, *The President We Deserve,* was my starting point, along with a long personal acquaintance, a number of interviews, including one long conversation aboard Air Force One, and the day-to-day experience of covering him and his administration. Bob Woodward's *The Agenda,* Elizabeth Drew's *On the Edge,* the works of David Maraniss, and Warren Christopher's *In the Stream of History* were also useful.

My wife, Julia Watson, and our two daughters shared the most recent nine years of the American experience, and all came to share my own deep affection for the country and its people, which helped extend their extraordinary patience as this book was being researched and written. They have my deepest devotion and gratitude.

Index

Index

Index

Index

Index

Index

Index

Index

Index

Index

Index

Index

Index

Index

Index

United Airlines, 100, 101
United Artists, 181
United Auto Workers, 316, 325
United Mine Workers, 199, 200
United Nations, 125–6, 175, 252, 358
United States: Anglo-American alliance,
    61–2, 119–27, 128, 130, 173, 234,
    237, 307; architecture in, 134–46;
    balance of payments, 299–302, 350;
    central bank of, 341–52; compe-
    tition in, 211; conservatism in,
    246–56; crime in, 147–59; economy
    of, *see* economy; expansionism in,
    3–6, 7–8, 14–15; global role of, 128,
    131–3, 175, 245, 304, 341, 345–6,
    351, 352, 353–9, 367–8; literature of,
    202–16; median income in, 199–200,
    360, 364; New America, 353–68;
    race relations in, *see* civil rights;
    refugees to, 217–27; religion in,
    269–82, 288; suburban development
    in, 135–6; unions in, *see* labor
    unions; war and, *see* Cold War;
    specific wars
United Technologies, 101
Universal Studios, 181, 226
Urey, Harold, 223
U.S. Steel, 3, 12–13, 162, 198

Valachi, Joe, 148, 149, 157
Valenti, Jack, 214
Vandenberg, Arthur, 250, 356
Vanderbilt, Consuelo, 120
Van Devanter, Willis, 172
van t' Hoff, Robert, 141
Vasquez, Marino, 31
Veblen, Thorstein, 10
Vidal, Gore, 203, 211, 256
Vietnam war, 245, 310; antiwar protests
    of, 25, 32, 255, 267, 282, 303–4, 308,
    326, 359, 360; costs of, 131, 268, 299,
    301–2, 309, 311, 350, 359; Europe
    and, 302, 304; fall of Saigon in,
    298–9, 304, 305; writers and,
    213–14, 215
Villa, Pancho, 34–5, 39
Vinson, Carl, 103
Volcker, Paul, 350

Wagner, Honus, 81
Wagner Act (1935), 171, 190–1, 192, 193
Walker, Jimmy, 153
Wallace, George, 254–5
Wallace, Henry, 196, 334
Walter, Bruno, 220
Walz, Skip, 260
war: aviation and, 42–3, 91–105, 128,
    197, 234, 284–5; business
    possibilities of, 92; central bank
    and, 344; defense budgets and, 104,
    105, 131–2, 245, 348–50, 358–9;
    nuclear, *see* nuclear weapons;
    presidential powers in, 39, 229, 343,
    366–7; social mobility in, 249;
    technology and, 15, 40, 41, 233; T.
    Roosevelt as voice for, 4–6, 7–9,
    15–16, 36, 37, 72; Wilson and, 9, 46,
    59–63, 70–1; *see also specific wars*
Warner Bros., 181, 224
Washington, Booker T., 11
Washington, George, 5, 23, 45
Watergate, 247, 299, 303, 305, 309–11
Watts, Steven, 294
Wayne, John, 179, 271
Weaver, Randy, 274–5
Weaver, Vicki, 275
Webster, Daniel, 344
Weinberg, Bo, 154
Welch, Jack, 343
West, Mae, 178
West, Rebecca, 31
West, Selden, 186
Westervelt, Conrad, 92, 93
West Side Story (Bernstein), 116
Whistler, James McNeill, 126
Whiteman, Paul, 111
Whyte, William H., 331
Wigner, Eugene, 222
Wilder, Billy, 187, 225–6
Wilder, Thornton, 129
Wilkins, Roy, 320, 327
Will, George F., 85, 254
Williams, Rev. A. D., 320
Williams, Robert, 323
Wills, Garry, 254
Wilson, Charles E., 198
Wilson, Edmund, 163

Index

Photographic Credits

TITAN

The Life of John D. Rockefeller, Sr.

by Ron Chernow

In the course of his 98 years, John D. Rockefeller, Sr., was both a rapacious robber baron, whose Standard Oil Company rode roughshod over an industry, and a philanthropist who donated lavishly to universities and medical centers. Drawing on unprecedented access to Rockefeller's private papers, National Book Award–winning biographer Ron Chernow reconstructs his subject's single-minded pursuit of wealth, his profound devotion to his family, and the wry humor that made him the country's most colorful codger.

Biography/0-679-75703-1

THE CATCHER WAS A SPY

The Mysterious Life of Moe Berg

by Nicholas Dawidoff

Moe Berg is the only major-league baseball player whose baseball card is on display at the headquarters of the CIA. For Berg was not only a third-string catcher from 1923 to 1939—he was also a spy for the OSS during World War II. As Nicholas Dawidoff follows Berg through his glamorous (though equivocal) careers in sports and espionage and into the long, nomadic years of living on the hospitality of such acquaintances as Joe DiMaggio and Albert Einstein, he succeeds in establishing who Berg was beneath his carefully constructed cover.

Biography/0-679-76289-2

WINCHELL

Gossip, Power, and the Culture of Celebrity

by Neal Gabler

Neal Gabler's biography of Walter Winchell, the fast-talking gossip columnist and radio broadcaster, has a significance that transcends its subject. For in telling Winchell's story, Gabler also uncovers the roots of our current obsession with celebrity. By the time he was in his thirties, Winchell had propelled himself from Dickensian poverty to a life that was almost indistinguishable from those of the celebrities he covered. Ultimately, in Winchell's hands, celebrity became a commodity and gossip a weapon of social empowerment.

Biography/0-679-76439-9

GENIUS

The Life and Science of Richard Feynman

by James Gleick

To his colleagues, Richard Feynman was not so much a genius as he was a full-blown magician. The path Feynman cleared for twentieth-century physics led from the making of the atomic bomb to a Nobel Prize–winning theory of quantum electrodynamics to his devastating exposé of the *Challenger* space shuttle disaster. Now James Gleick unravels the dense skein of Feynman's thought as well as the paradoxes of his character in a biography of outstanding lucidity.

Biography/0-679-74704-4

ANNE SEXTON

A Biography

by Diane Middlebrook

Anne Sexton began writing poetry to keep from killing herself. She held on to language for dear life and somehow—in spite of alcoholism and mental illness—managed to create a body of work that won a Pulitzer Prize. Diane Middlebrook's insightful and compassionate biography reconciles the many Anne Sextons: the 1950s housewife; the abused child who became an abusive mother; the seductress; the suicidal woman who carried "kill-me pills" in her handbag; and the poet who transmuted confession into lasting art.

Biography/0-679-74182-8

CLINT EASTWOOD

A Biography

by Richard Schickel

From the first time audiences heard Dirty Harry Callahan growl, "Make my day," Clint Eastwood has been an icon of American manhood in all its coolness and ferocity. But that icon is also an actor of surprising subtlety, a filmmaker of vast intelligence and originality, and an intensely private man who eludes the stereotypes. Richard Schickel talks with Eastwood's family, friends, and colleagues—and, above all, with his notoriously reticent subject—to produce a candid and unerring close-up of one of America's brightest stars.

Biography/0-679-74991-8